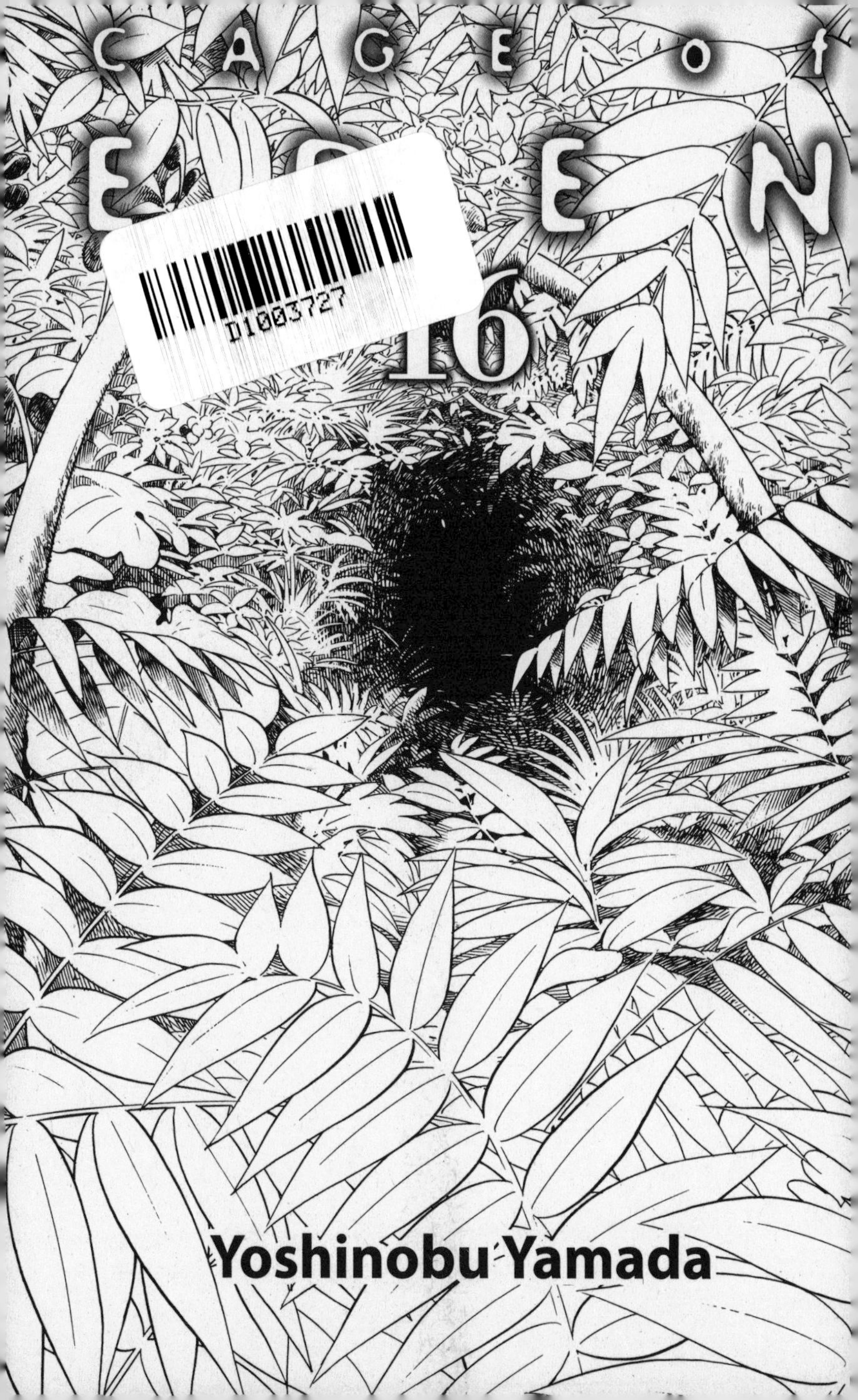
CAGE of
E E N
16
Yoshinobu Yamada

CAGE of EDEN

CONTENTS

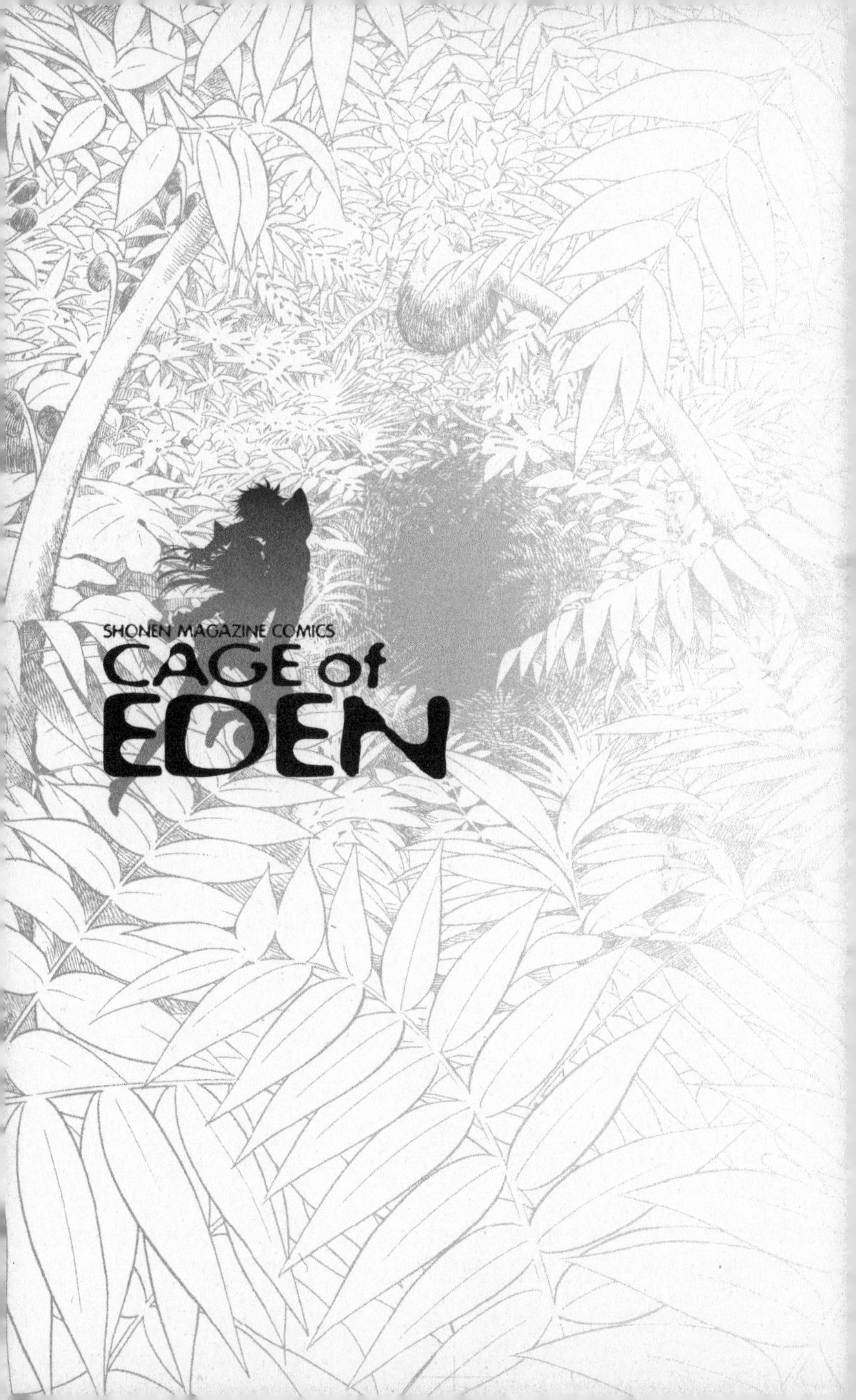
SHONEN MAGAZINE COMICS
CAGE of EDEN

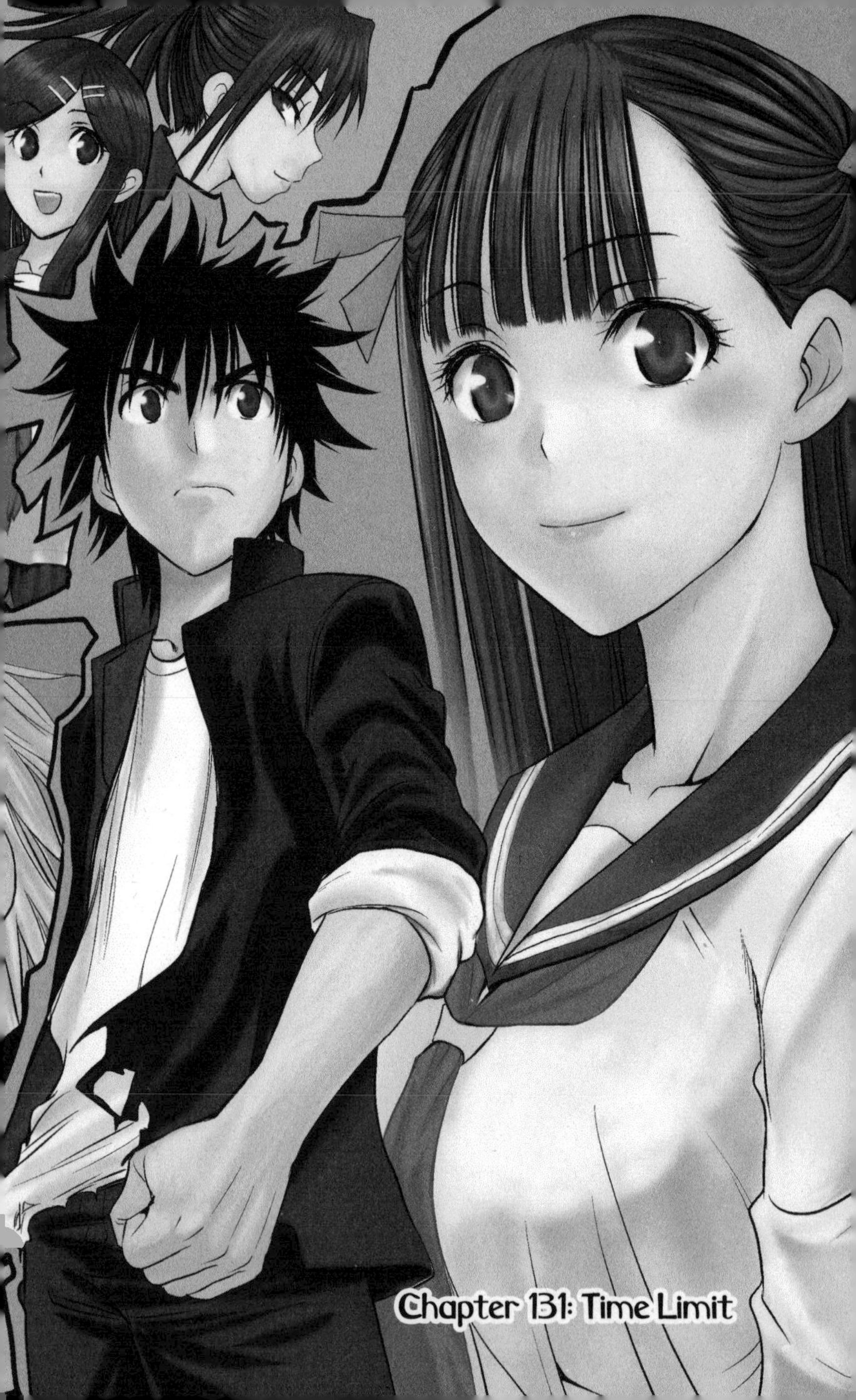
Chapter 131: Time Limit

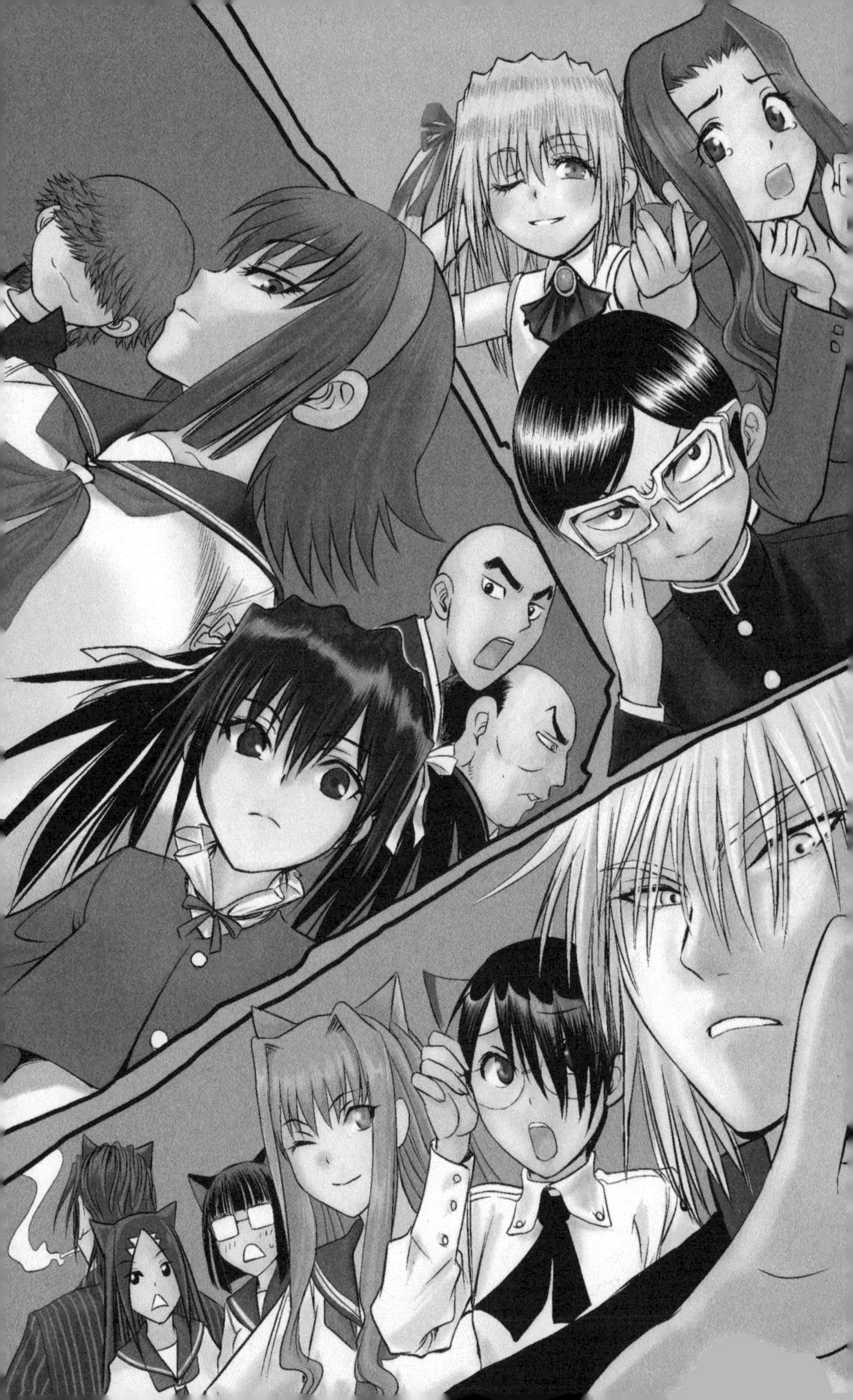

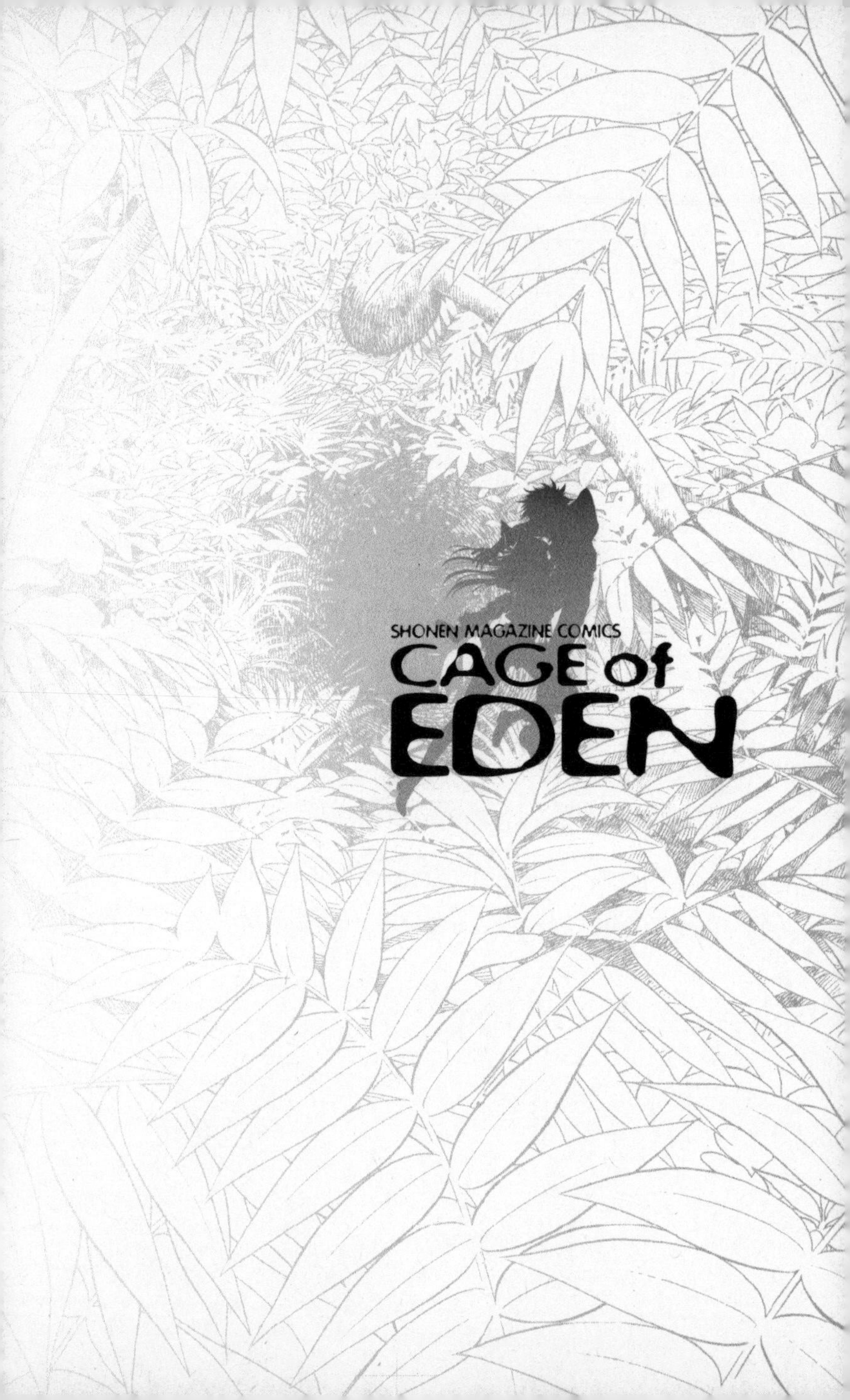
SHONEN MAGAZINE COMICS
CAGE of EDEN

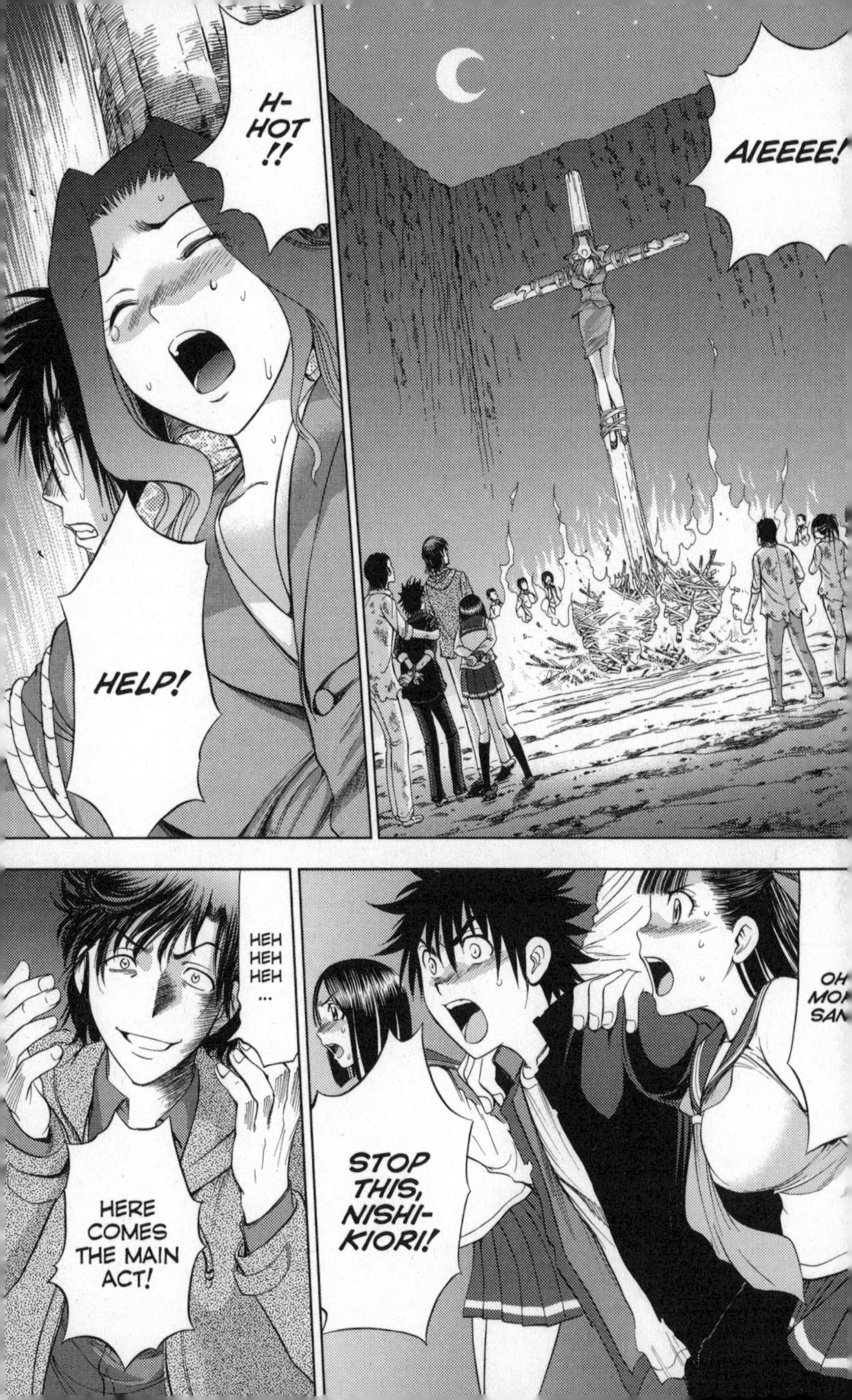
AIEEEE!
H-HOT!!
HELP!
STOP THIS, NISHIKIORI!
HEH HEH HEH ...
HERE COMES THE MAIN ACT!

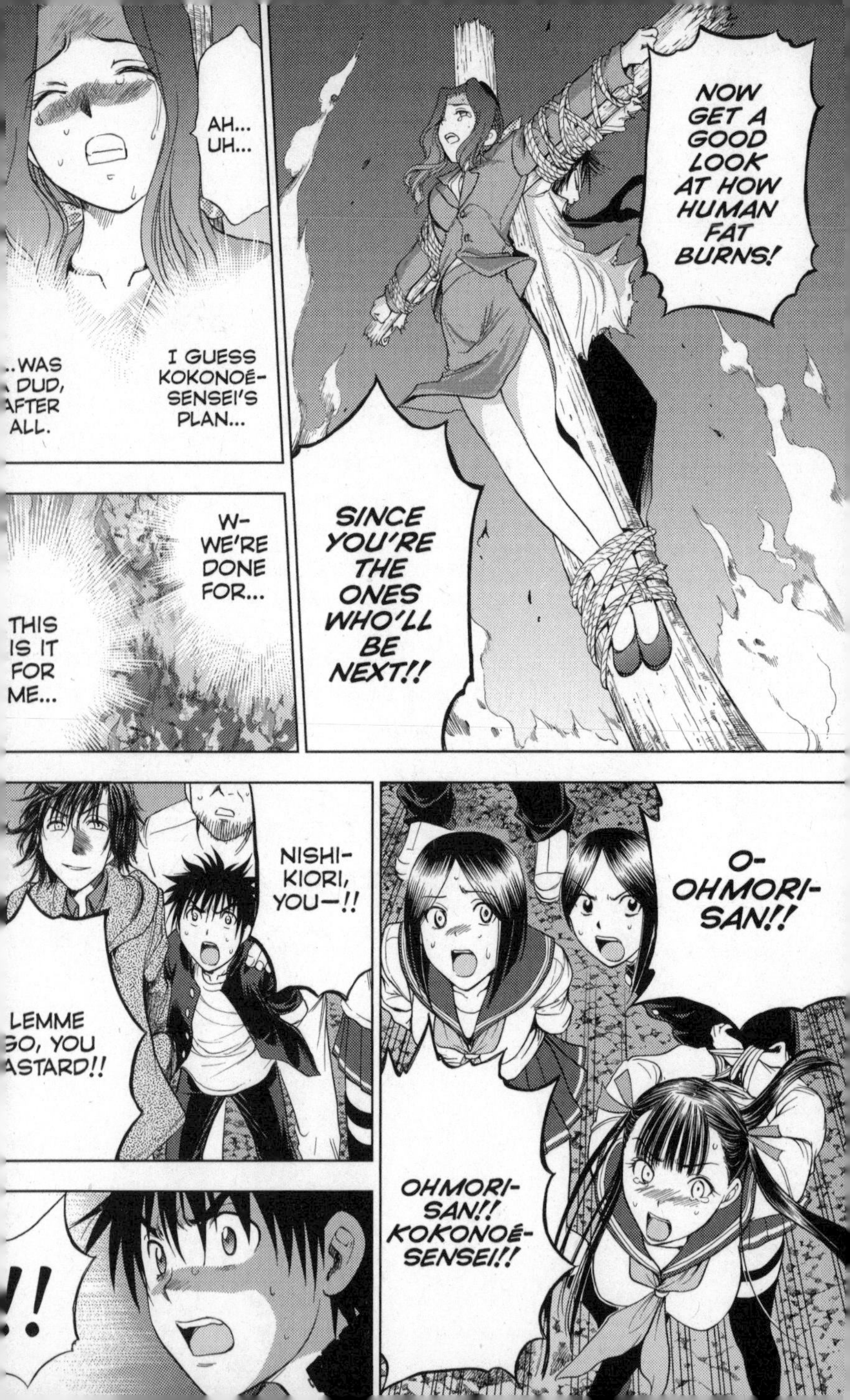
NOW GET A GOOD LOOK AT HOW HUMAN FAT BURNS!
SINCE YOU'RE THE ONES WHO'LL BE NEXT!!
AH... UH...
I GUESS KOKONOÉ-SENSEI'S PLAN...
..WAS A DUD, AFTER ALL.
W-WE'RE DONE FOR...
THIS IS IT FOR ME...
O-OHMORI-SAN!!
OHMORI-SAN!! KOKONOÉ-SENSEI!!
NISHI-KIORI, YOU—!!
LEMME GO, YOU ASTARD!!
!!

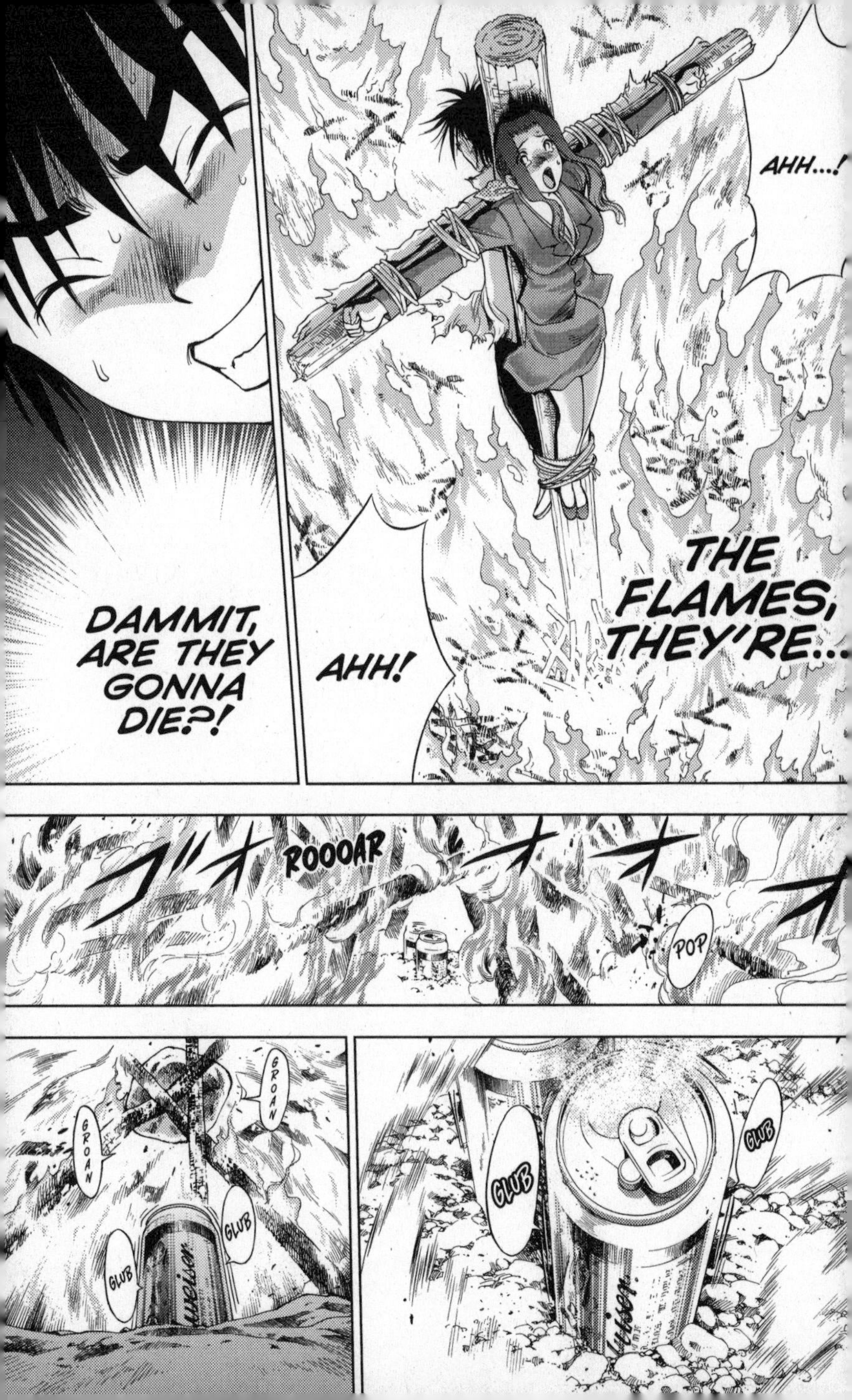
AHH...!
THE FLAMES, THEY'RE...
AHH!
DAMMIT, ARE THEY GONNA DIE?!
ROOOAR
POP
GLUB
GLUB
GROAN
GROAN
GLUB
GLUB

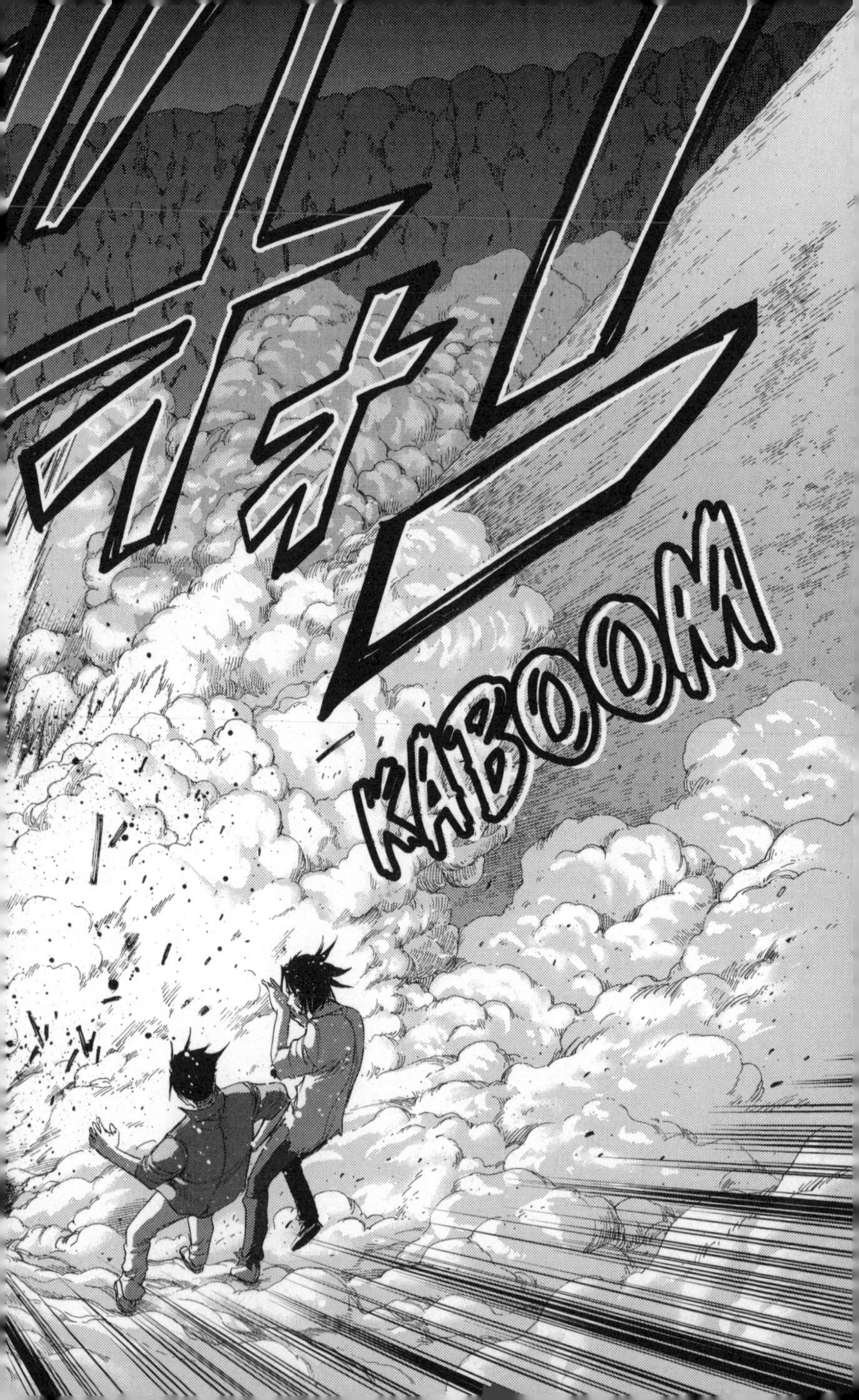
KABOOM

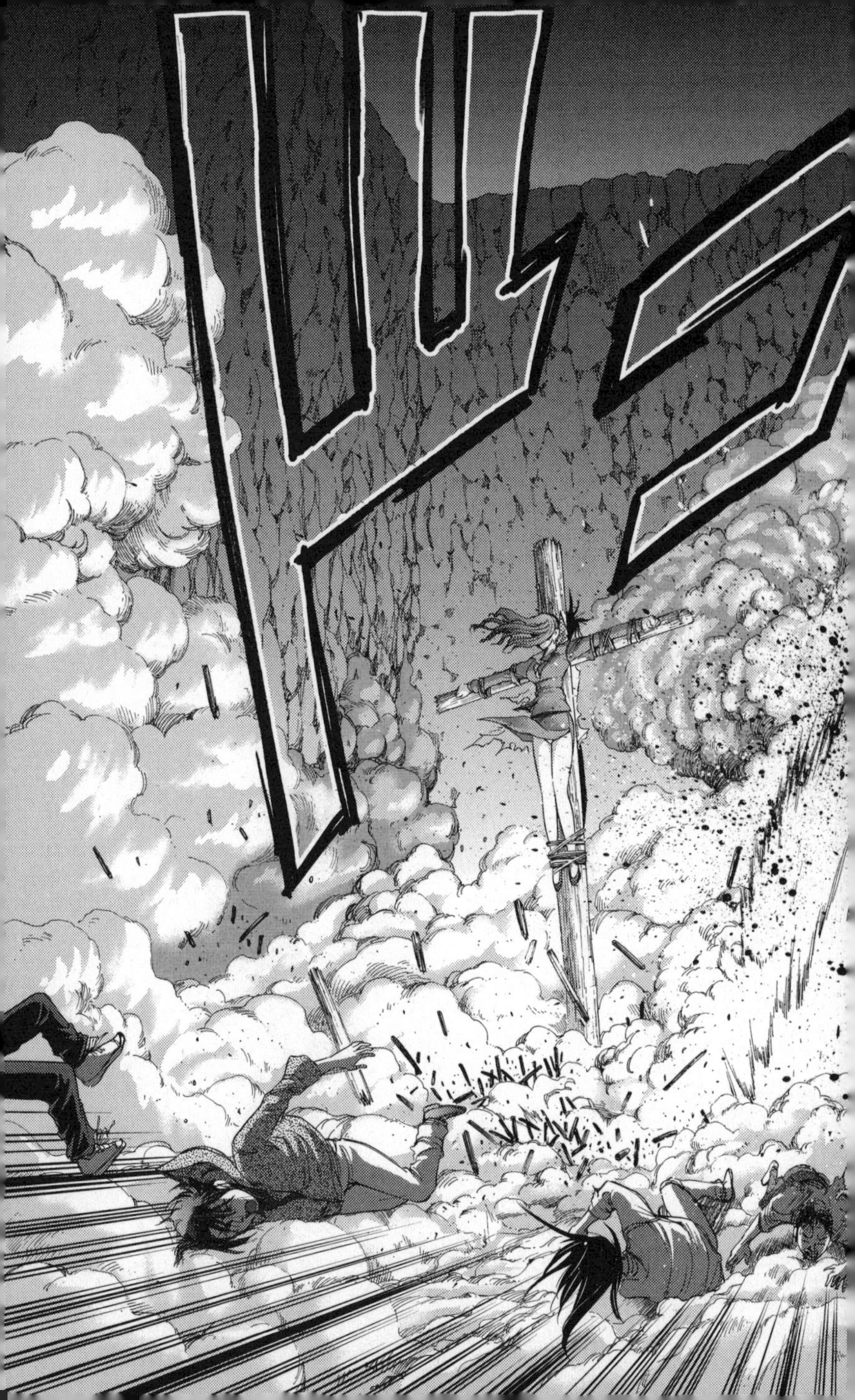

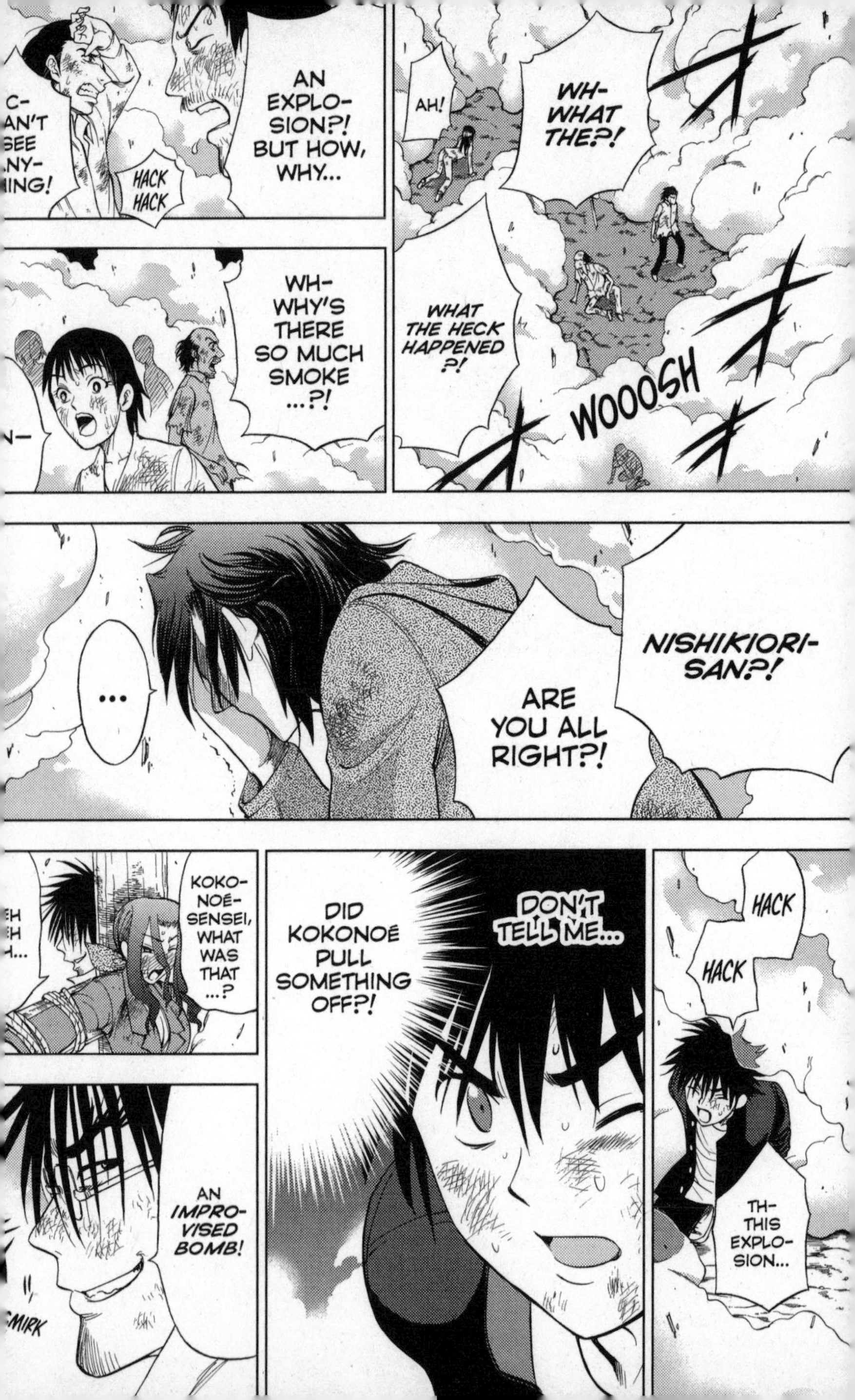
WH- WHAT THE?!
AH!
WHAT THE HECK HAPPENED ?!
WOOOSH
AN EXPLOSION?! BUT HOW, WHY...
HACK HACK
C- AN'T SEE
WH- WHY'S THERE SO MUCH SMOKE ...?!
NISHIKIORI-SAN?!
ARE YOU ALL RIGHT?!
...
HACK
HACK
TH- THIS EXPLOSION...
DON'T TELL ME...
DID KOKONOÉ PULL SOMETHING OFF?!
KOKONOÉ-SENSEI, WHAT WAS THAT ...?
AN IMPROVISED BOMB!
SMIRK

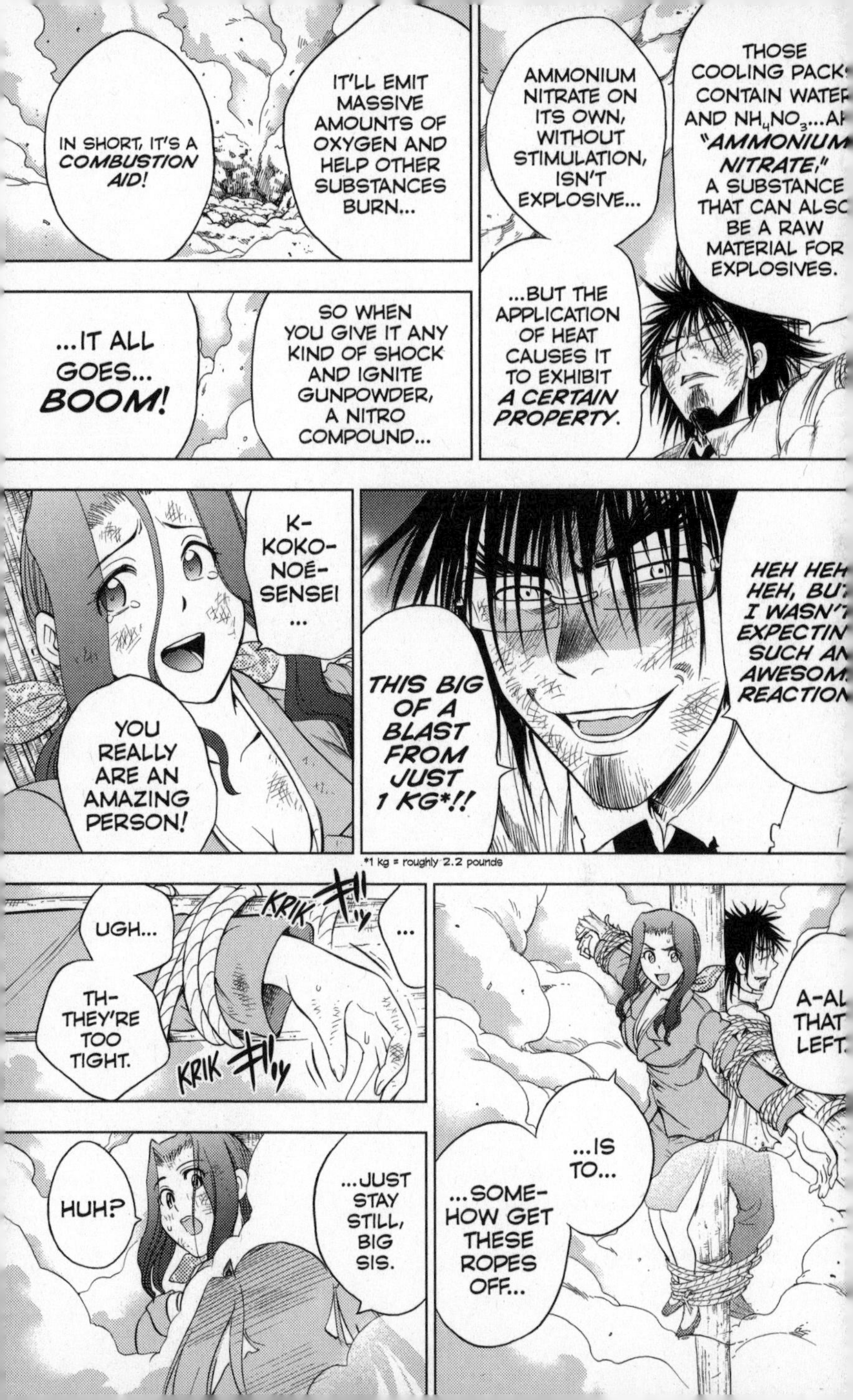
THOSE COOLING PACK CONTAIN WATE AND NH_4NO_3...A "AMMONIUM NITRATE," A SUBSTANCE THAT CAN ALS BE A RAW MATERIAL FOR EXPLOSIVES.
AMMONIUM NITRATE ON ITS OWN, WITHOUT STIMULATION, ISN'T EXPLOSIVE...
...BUT THE APPLICATION OF HEAT CAUSES IT TO EXHIBIT *A CERTAIN PROPERTY.*
IT'LL EMIT MASSIVE AMOUNTS OF OXYGEN AND HELP OTHER SUBSTANCES BURN...
IN SHORT, IT'S A *COMBUSTION AID!*
SO WHEN YOU GIVE IT ANY KIND OF SHOCK AND IGNITE GUNPOWDER, A NITRO COMPOUND...
...IT ALL GOES... ***BOOM!***
HEH HEH HEH, BU I WASN' EXPECTIN SUCH A AWESOM REACTIO
THIS BIG OF A BLAST FROM JUST 1 KG!!*
K-KOKONOÉ-SENSEI...
YOU REALLY ARE AN AMAZING PERSON!
A-AL THAT LEFT.
...IS TO...
...SOMEHOW GET THESE ROPES OFF...
...
KRIK
UGH...
TH-THEY'RE TOO TIGHT.
KRIK
...JUST STAY STILL, BIG SIS.
HUH?

*1 kg = roughly 2.2 pounds

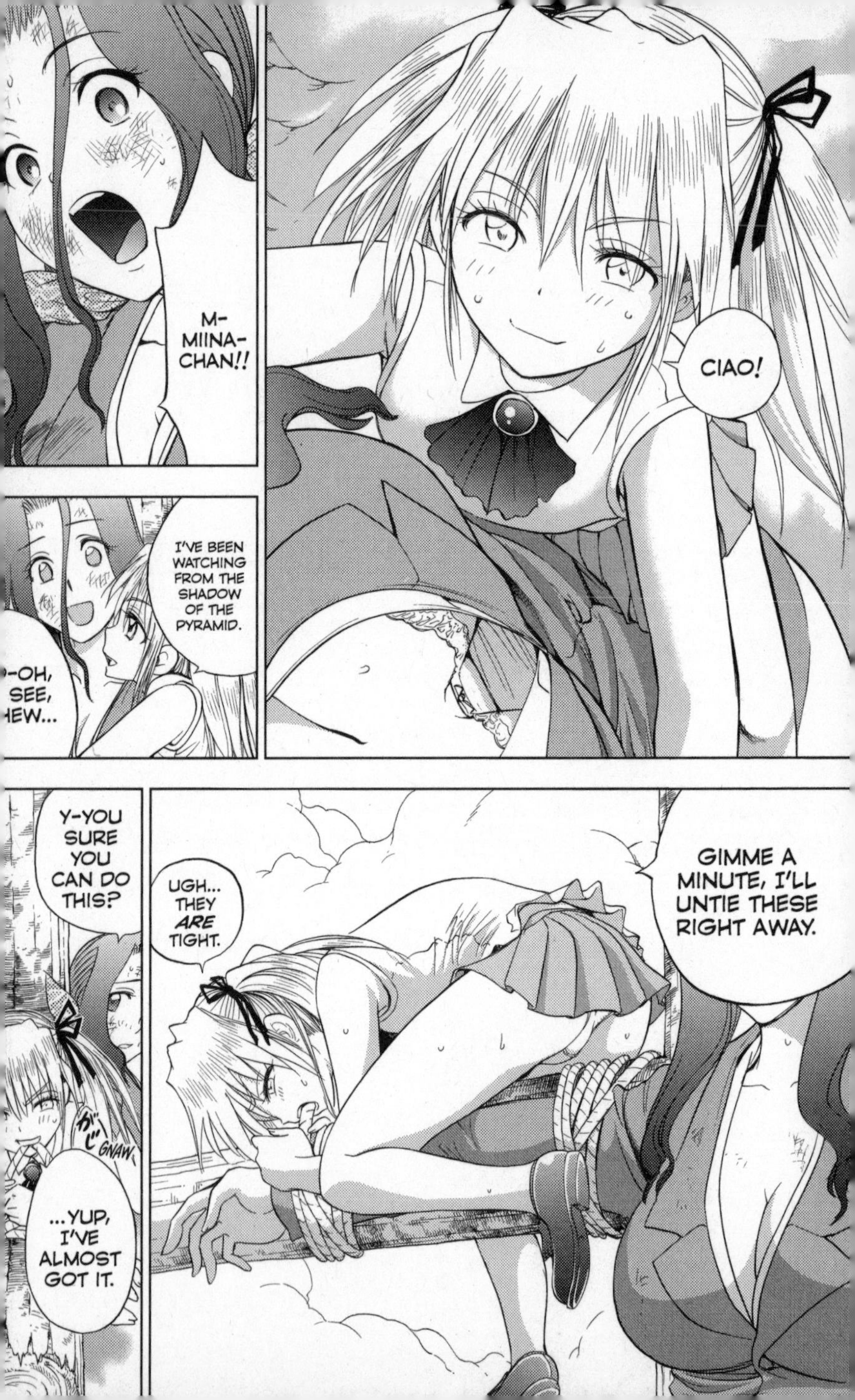

CIAO!
M-MIINA-CHAN!!
I'VE BEEN WATCHING FROM THE SHADOW OF THE PYRAMID.
-OH, SEE, HEW...
GIMME A MINUTE, I'LL UNTIE THESE RIGHT AWAY.
UGH... THEY *ARE* TIGHT.
Y-YOU SURE YOU CAN DO THIS?
がじ GNAW
...YUP, I'VE ALMOST GOT IT.

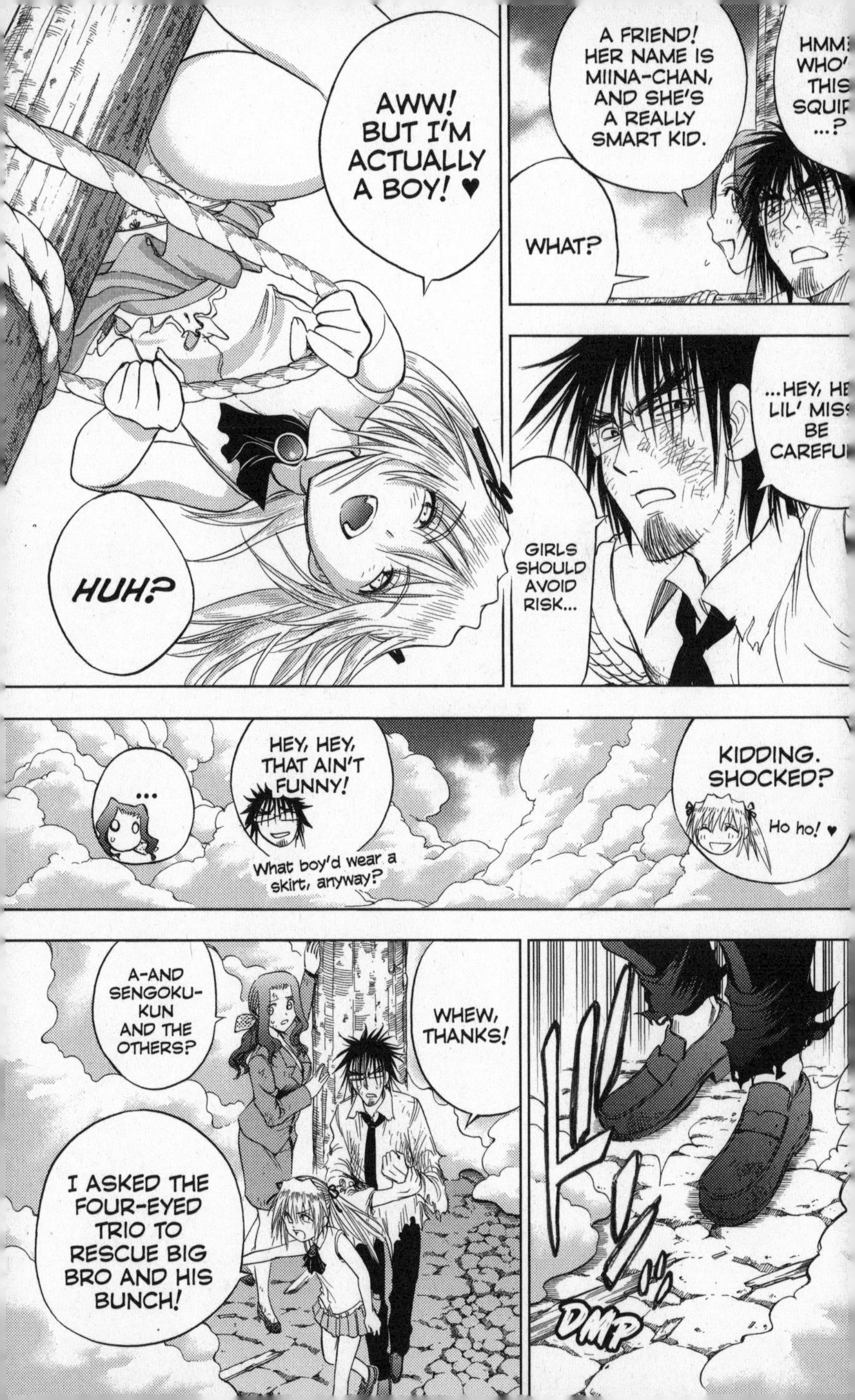
HMM WHO' THIS SQUIR ...?
A FRIEND! HER NAME IS MIINA-CHAN, AND SHE'S A REALLY SMART KID.
WHAT?
...HEY, HE LIL' MISS BE CAREFU
GIRLS SHOULD AVOID RISK...
AWW! BUT I'M ACTUALLY A BOY! ♥
HUH?
KIDDING. SHOCKED?
Ho ho! ♥
HEY, HEY, THAT AIN'T FUNNY!
What boy'd wear a skirt, anyway?
...
DMP
WHEW, THANKS!
A-AND SENGOKU-KUN AND THE OTHERS?
I ASKED THE FOUR-EYED TRIO TO RESCUE BIG BRO AND HIS BUNCH!

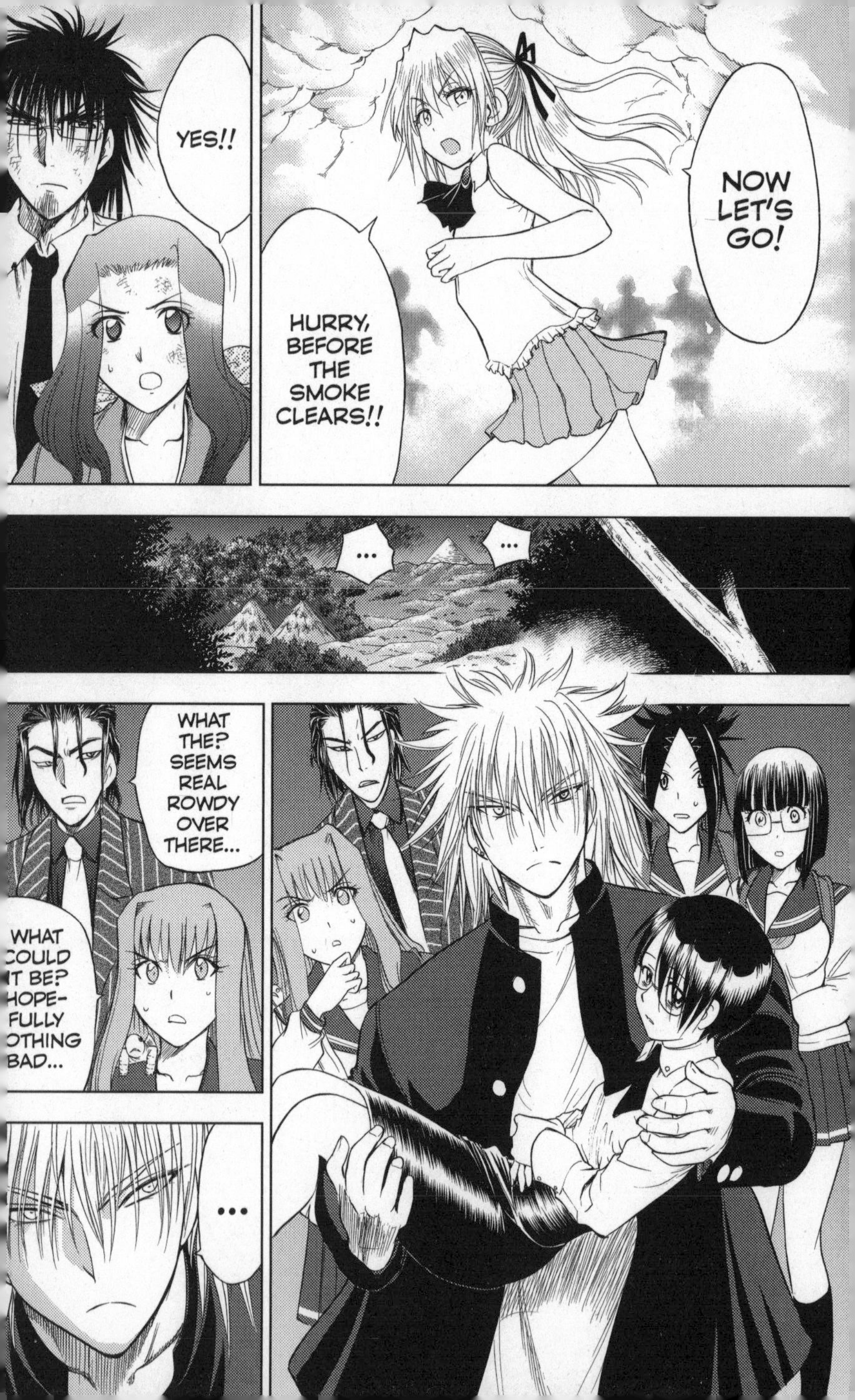
NOW LET'S GO!
HURRY, BEFORE THE SMOKE CLEARS!!
YES!!
...
...
WHAT THE? SEEMS REAL ROWDY OVER THERE...
WHAT COULD IT BE? HOPE-FULLY NOTHING BAD...
...

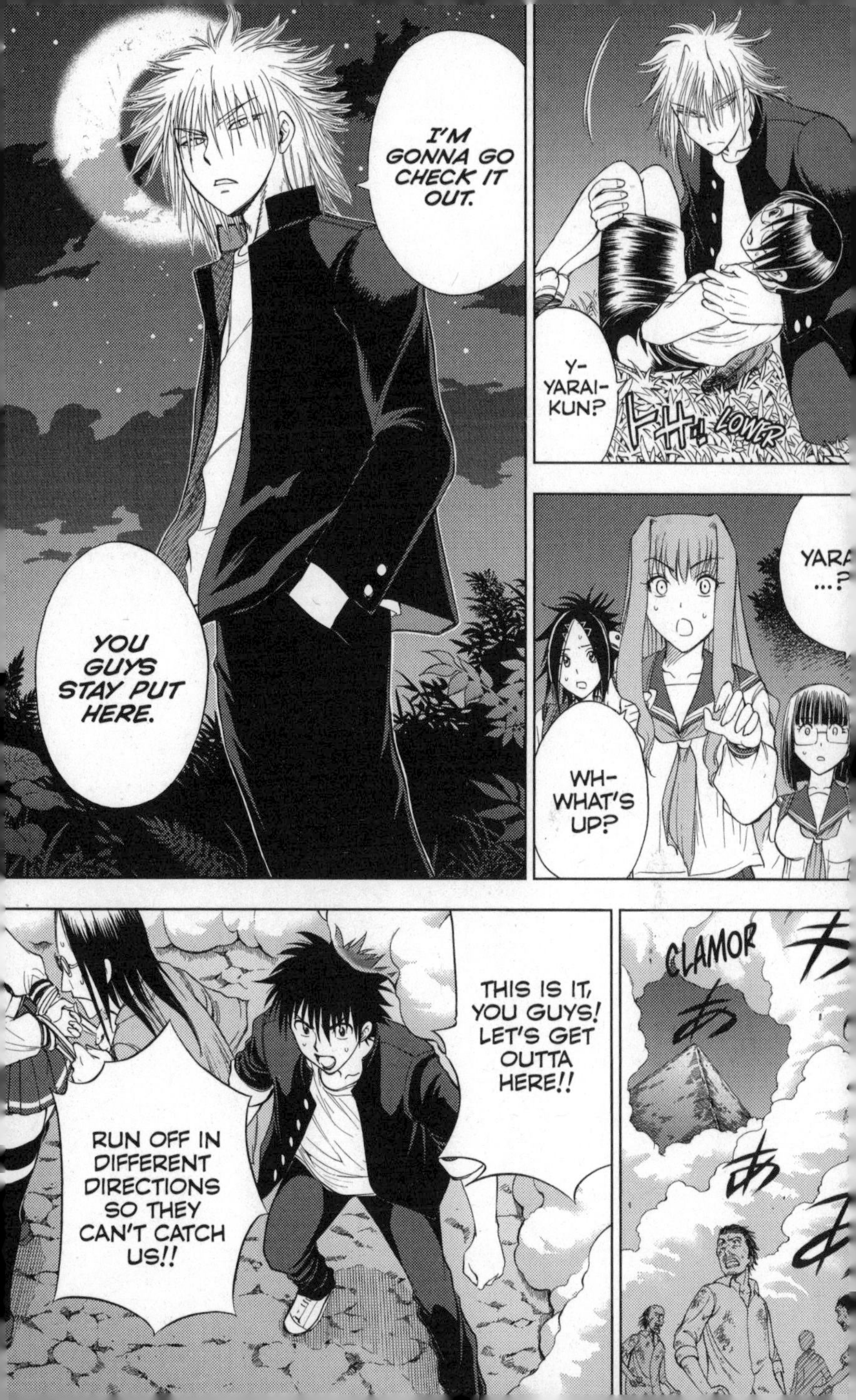
Y-YARAI-KUN?
LOWER
YARA ...?
WH-WHAT'S UP?
I'M GONNA GO CHECK IT OUT.
YOU GUYS STAY PUT HERE.
CLAMOR
THIS IS IT, YOU GUYS! LET'S GET OUTTA HERE!!
RUN OFF IN DIFFERENT DIRECTIONS SO THEY CAN'T CATCH US!!

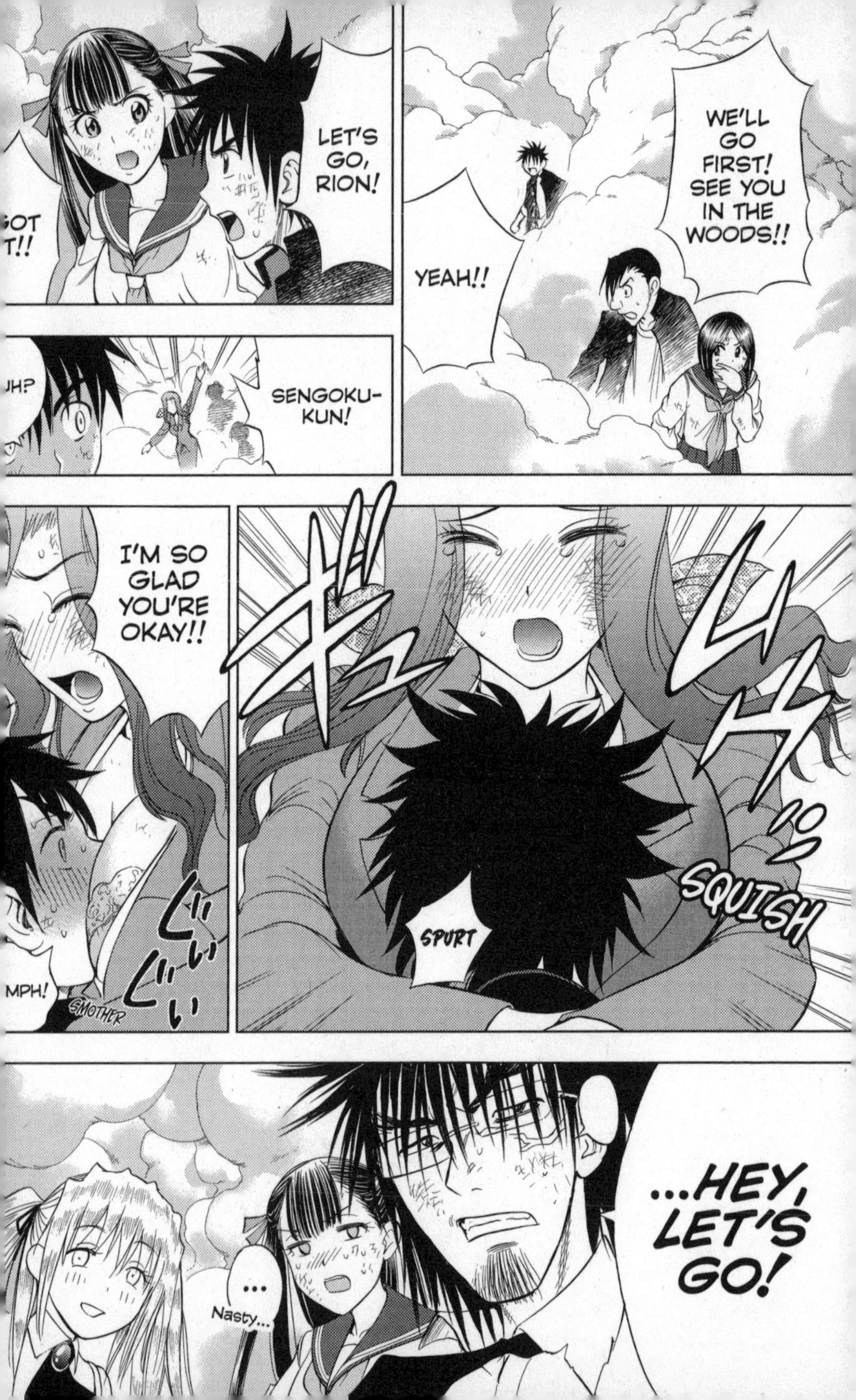

WE'LL GO FIRST! SEE YOU IN THE WOODS!!
YEAH!!
LET'S GO, RION!
GOT T!!
SENGOKU-KUN!
UH?
SQUISH
SPURT
I'M SO GLAD YOU'RE OKAY!!
SMOTHER
MPH!
...HEY, LET'S GO!
...
Nasty...

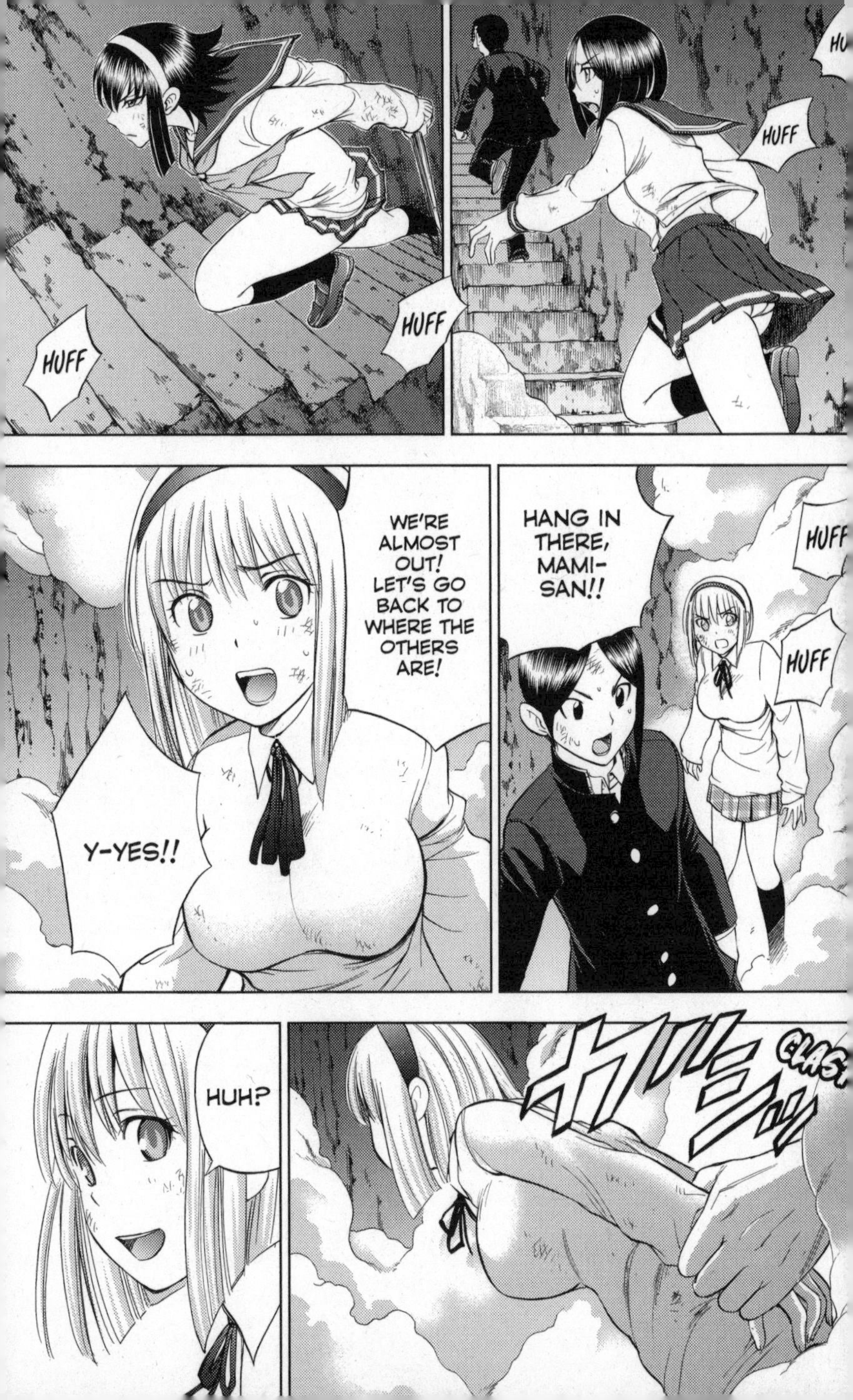
HUFF
HUFF
HUFF
HANG IN THERE, MAMI-SAN!!
HUFF
HUFF
WE'RE ALMOST OUT! LET'S GO BACK TO WHERE THE OTHERS ARE!
Y-YES!!
HUH?

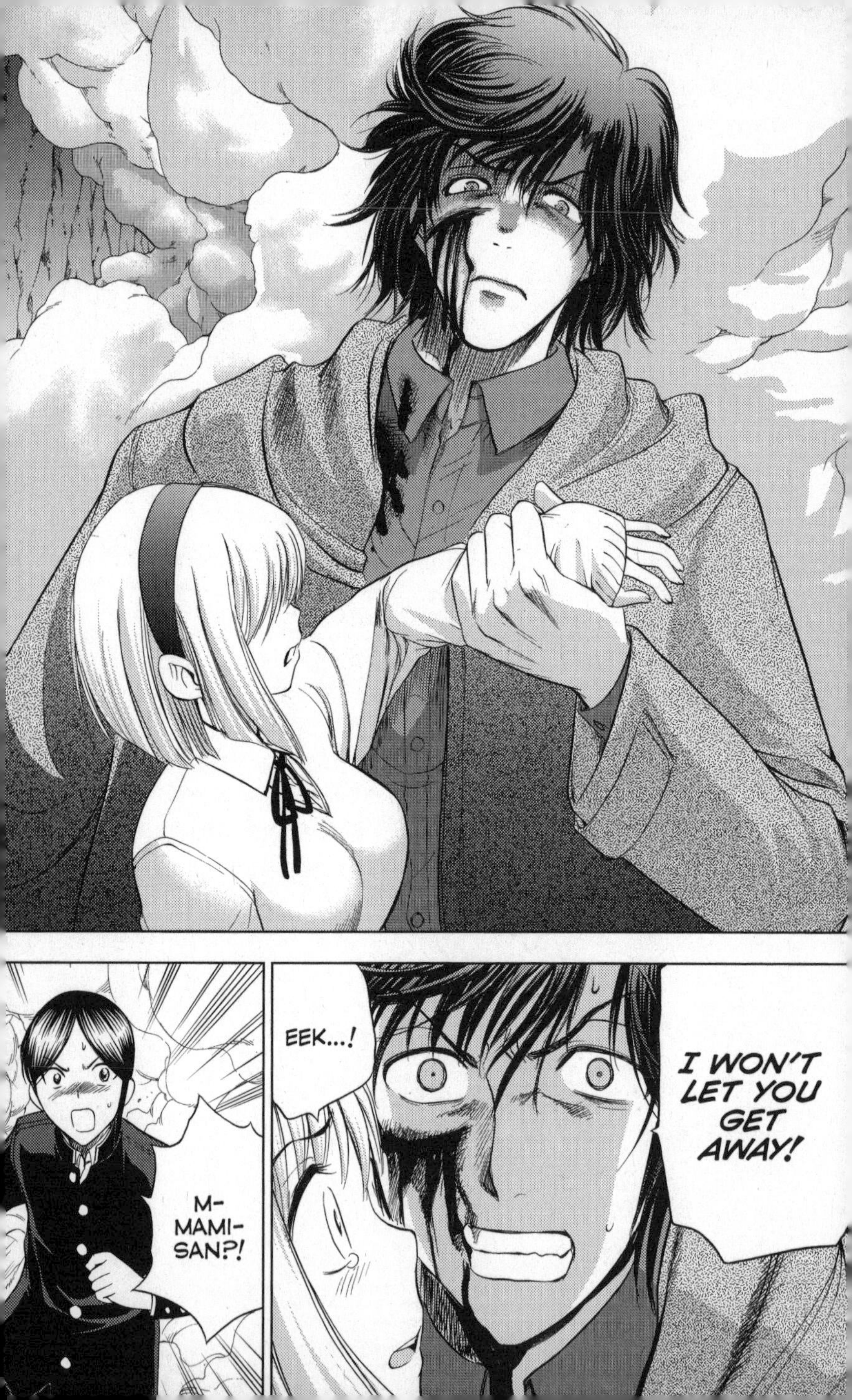
I WON'T LET YOU GET AWAY!
EEK...!
M-MAMI-SAN?!

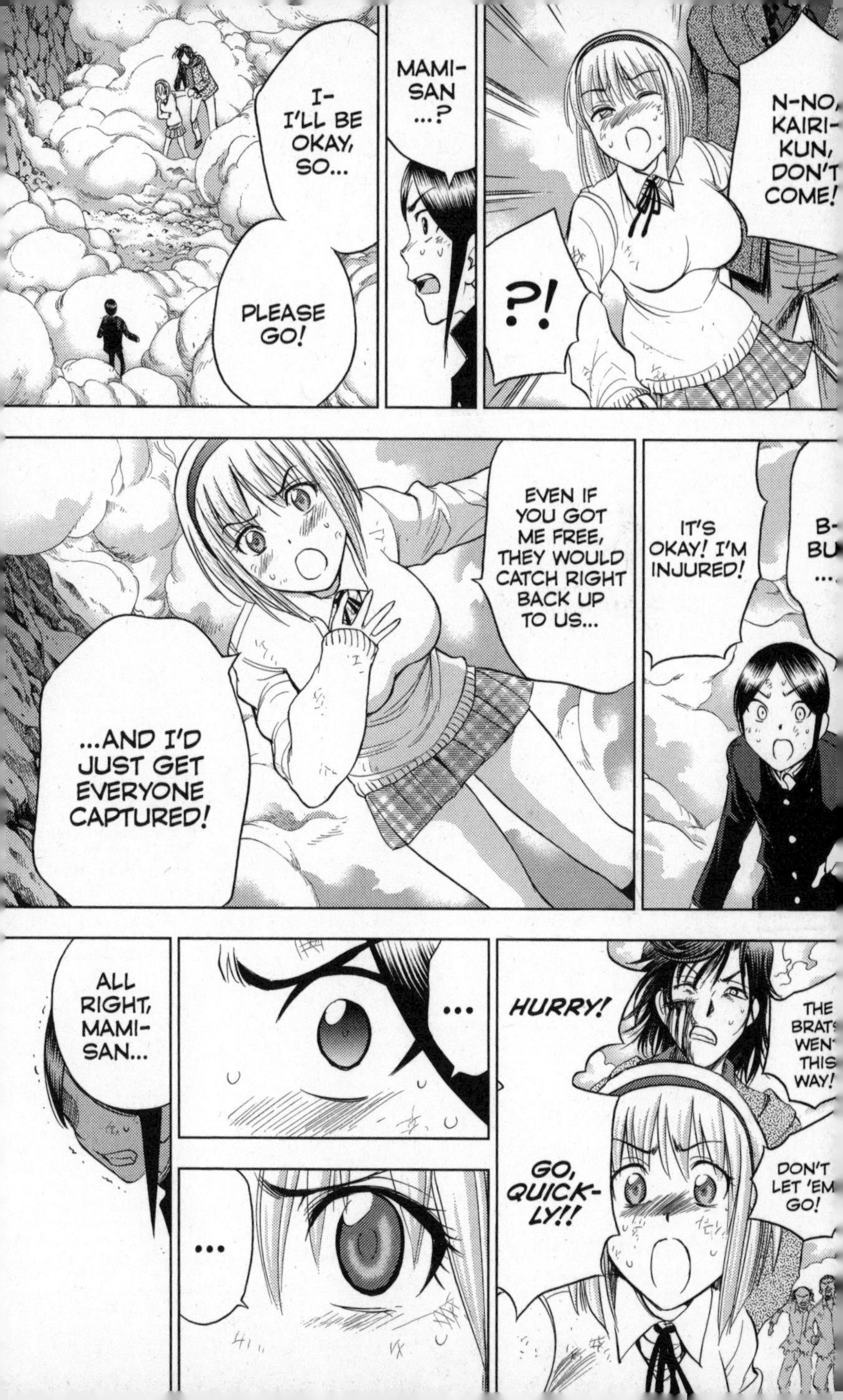
N-NO, KAIRI-KUN, DON'T COME!
?!
MAMI-SAN ...?
I- I'LL BE OKAY, SO...
PLEASE GO!
B-BU...
IT'S OKAY! I'M INJURED!
EVEN IF YOU GOT ME FREE, THEY WOULD CATCH RIGHT BACK UP TO US...
...AND I'D JUST GET EVERYONE CAPTURED!
THE BRATS WENT THIS WAY!
HURRY!
DON'T LET 'EM GO!
GO, QUICKLY!!
...
...
ALL RIGHT, MAMI-SAN...

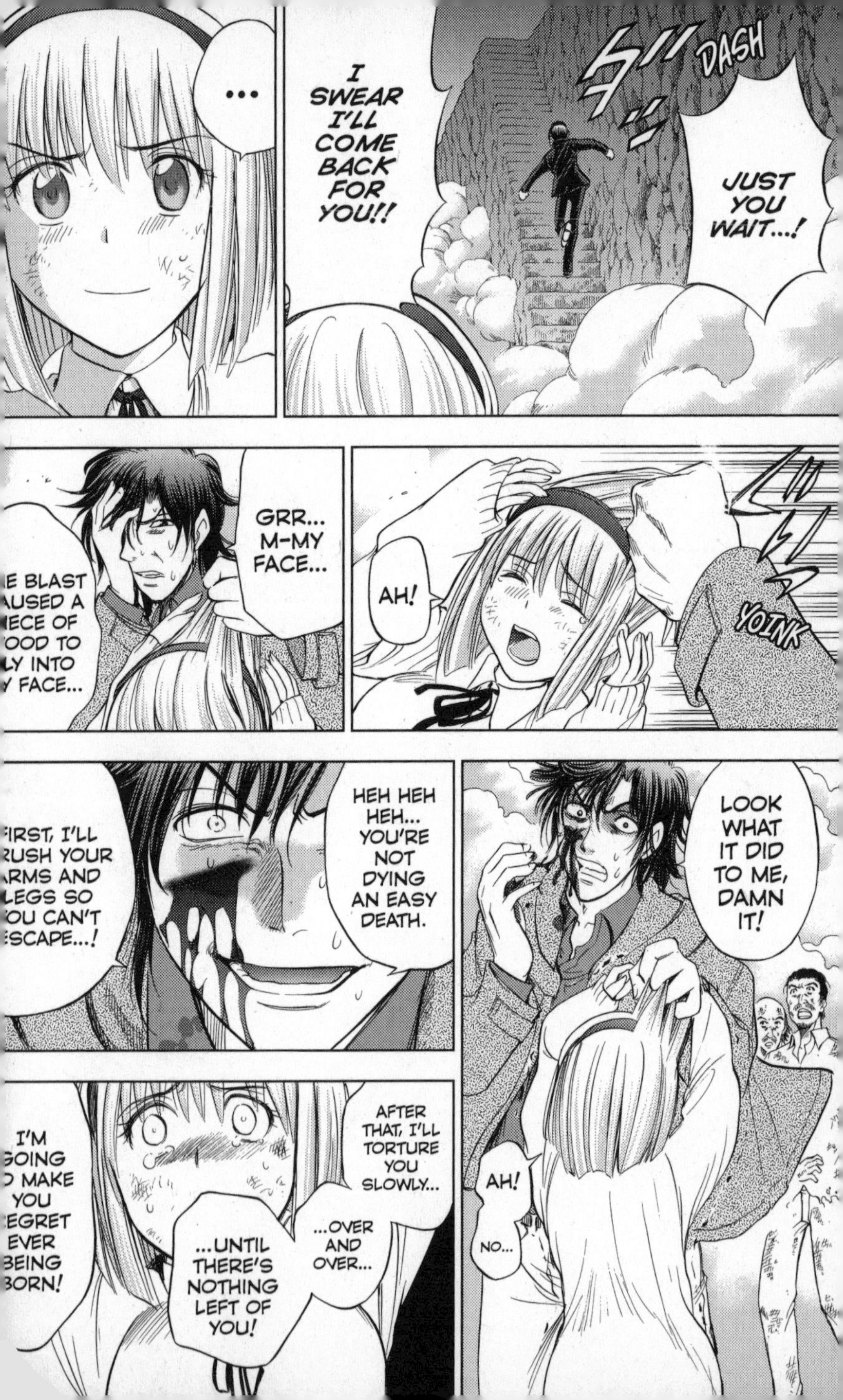
DASH
JUST YOU WAIT...!
I SWEAR I'LL COME BACK FOR YOU!!
...
YOINK
AH!
GRR... M-MY FACE...
E BLAST AUSED A IECE OF OOD TO LY INTO Y FACE...
LOOK WHAT IT DID TO ME, DAMN IT!
AH!
NO...
HEH HEH HEH... YOU'RE NOT DYING AN EASY DEATH.
FIRST, I'LL RUSH YOUR RMS AND LEGS SO OU CAN'T SCAPE...!
AFTER THAT, I'LL TORTURE YOU SLOWLY...
...OVER AND OVER...
...UNTIL THERE'S NOTHING LEFT OF YOU!
I'M GOING O MAKE YOU EGRET EVER BEING BORN!

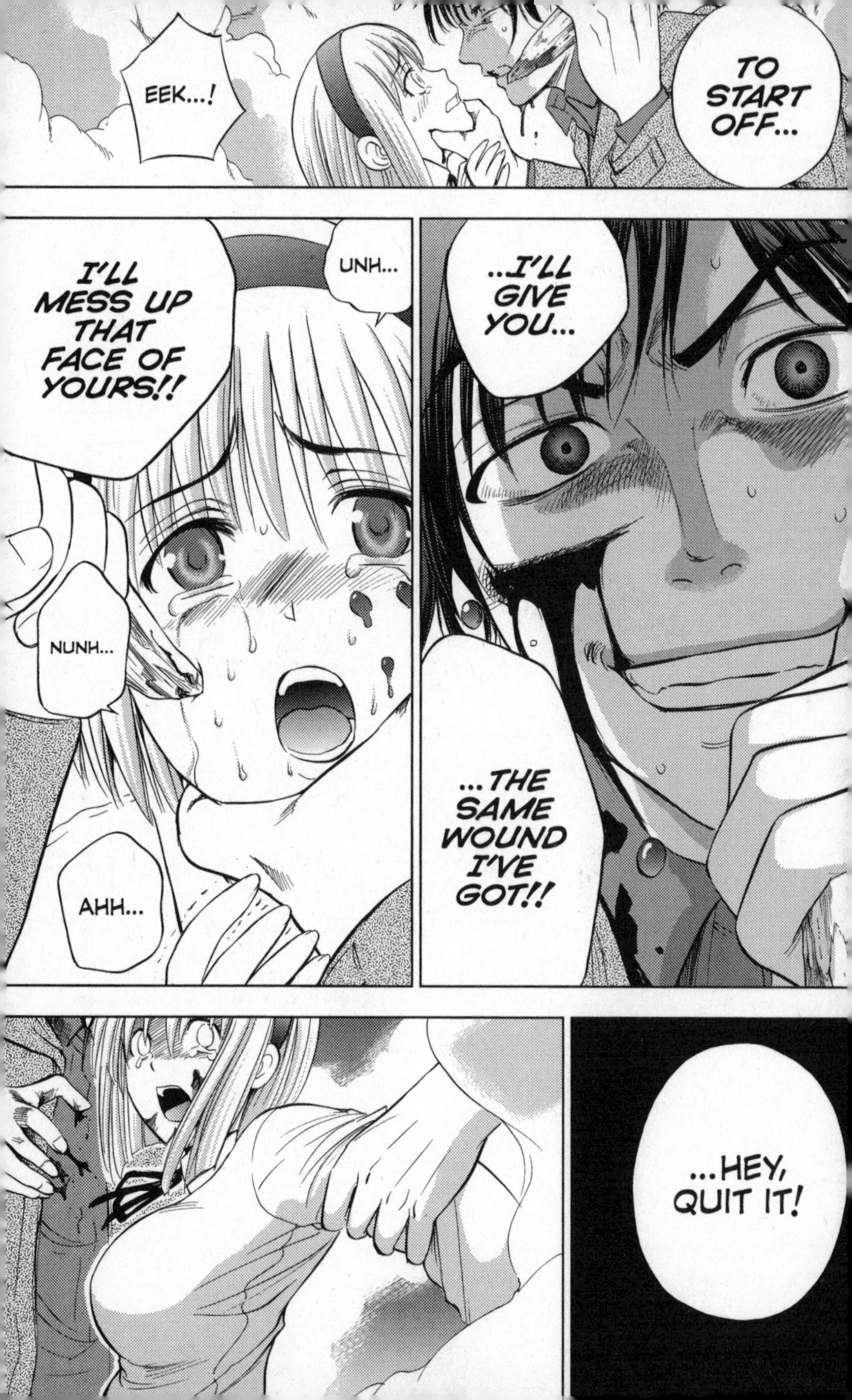
TO START OFF...
EEK...!
...I'LL GIVE YOU...
...THE SAME WOUND I'VE GOT!!
UNH...
I'LL MESS UP THAT FACE OF YOURS!!
NUNH...
AHH...
...HEY, QUIT IT!

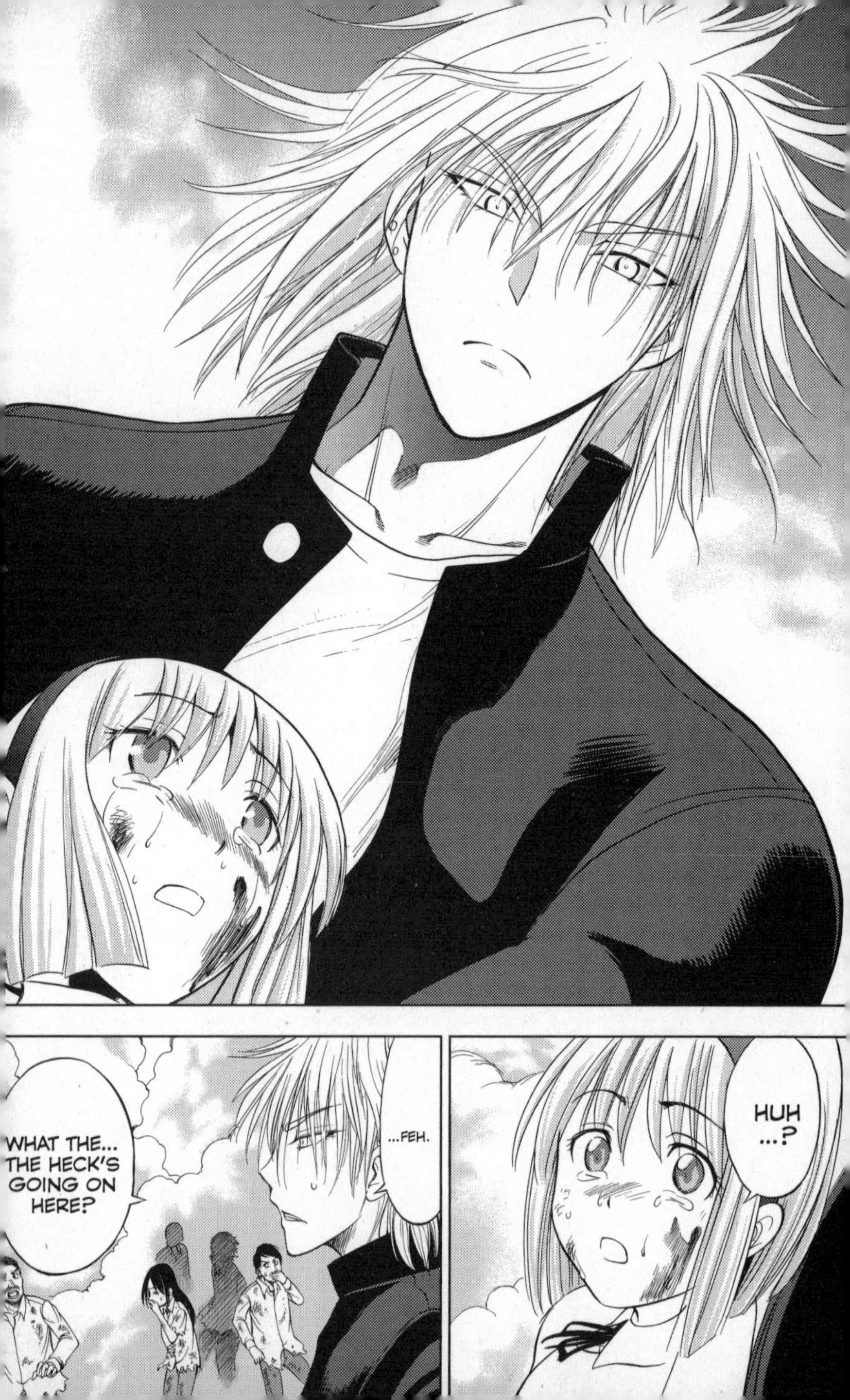
HUH ...?
...FEH.
WHAT THE... THE HECK'S GOING ON HERE?

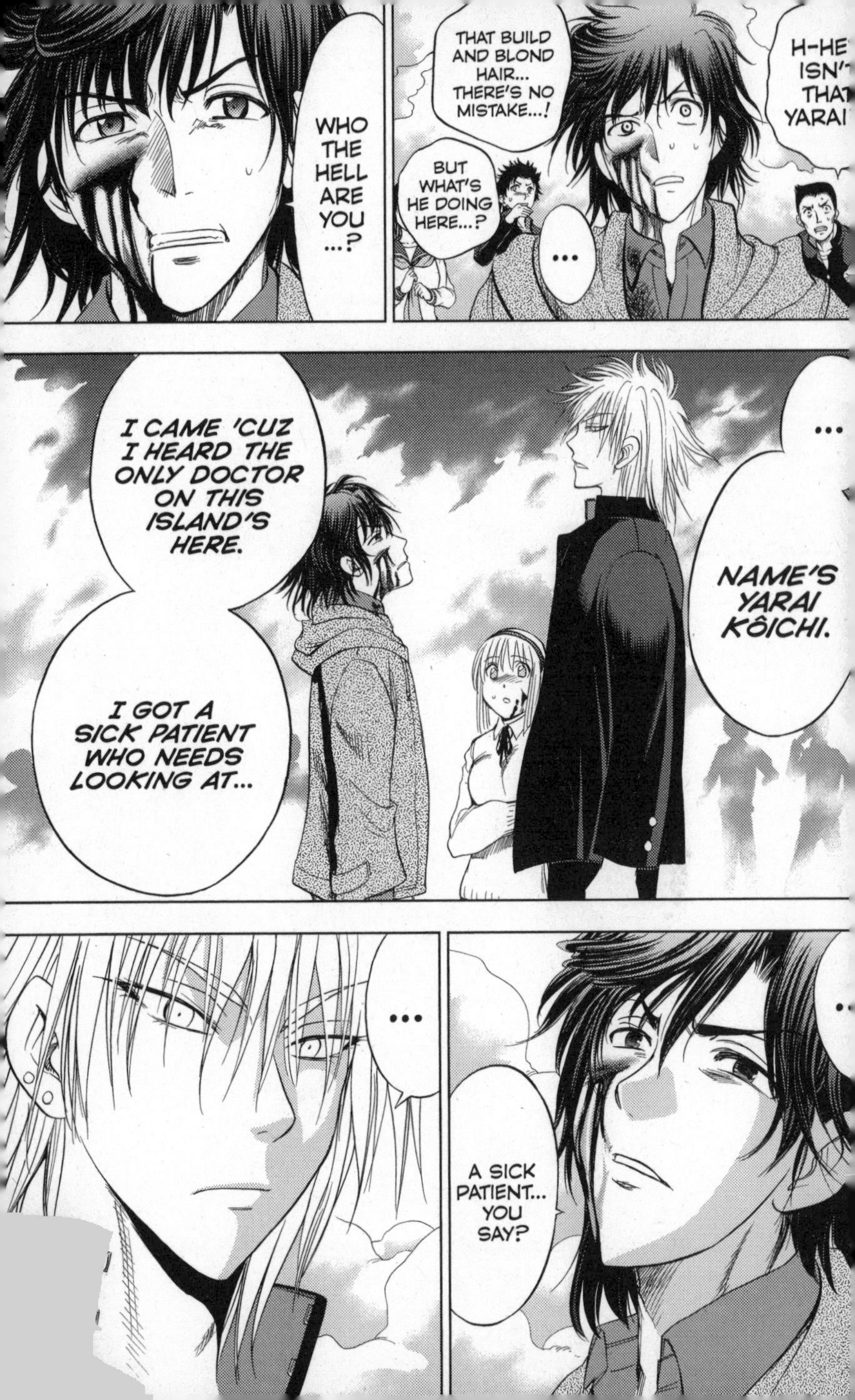
H-HE ISN'T THAT YARAI
THAT BUILD AND BLOND HAIR... THERE'S NO MISTAKE...!
BUT WHAT'S HE DOING HERE...?
...
WHO THE HELL ARE YOU...?
...
NAME'S YARAI KÔICHI.
I CAME 'CUZ I HEARD THE ONLY DOCTOR ON THIS ISLAND'S HERE.
I GOT A SICK PATIENT WHO NEEDS LOOKING AT...
...
A SICK PATIENT... YOU SAY?
...

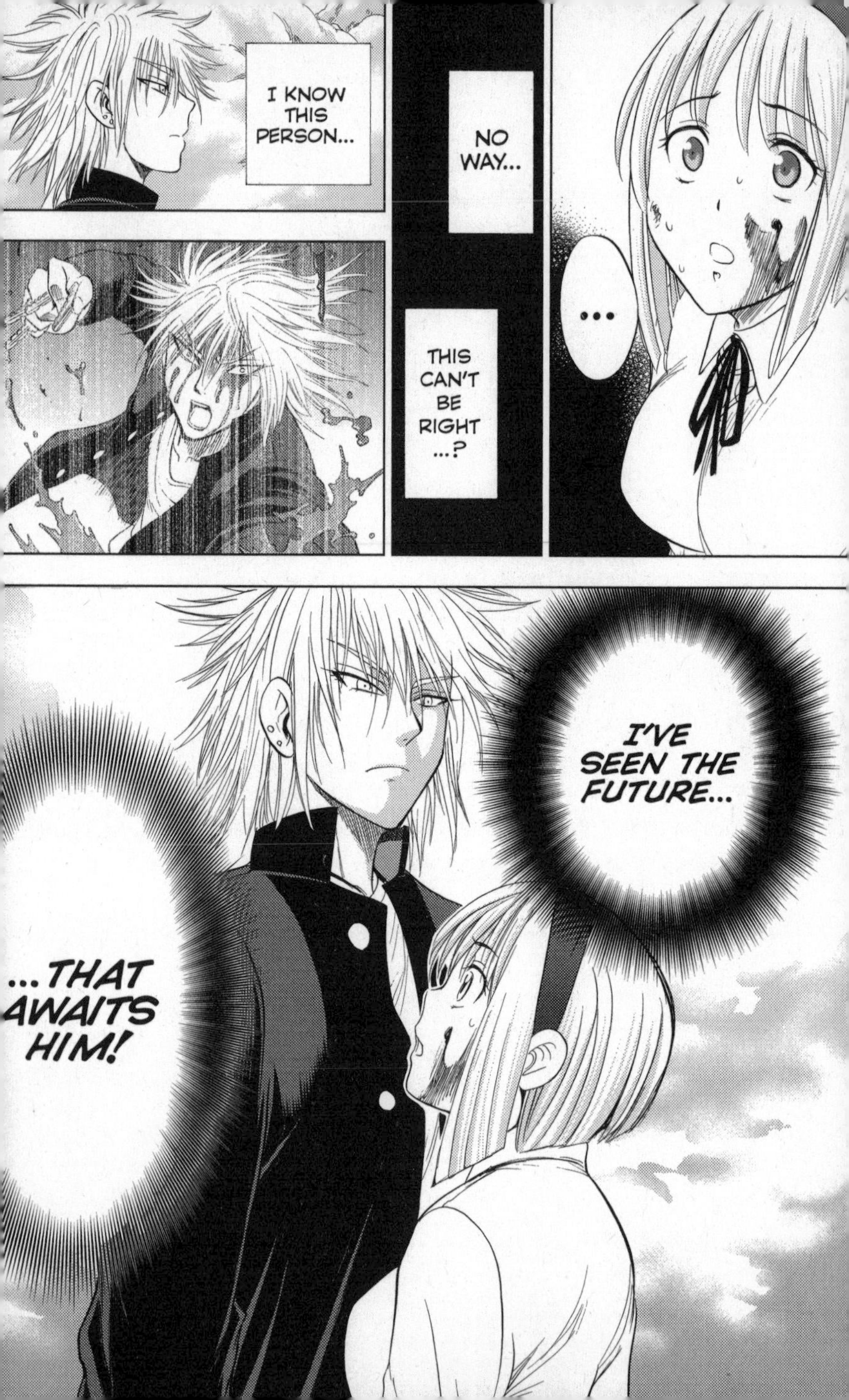
...
NO WAY...
THIS CAN'T BE RIGHT ...?
I KNOW THIS PERSON...
I'VE SEEN THE FUTURE...
...THAT AWAITS HIM!

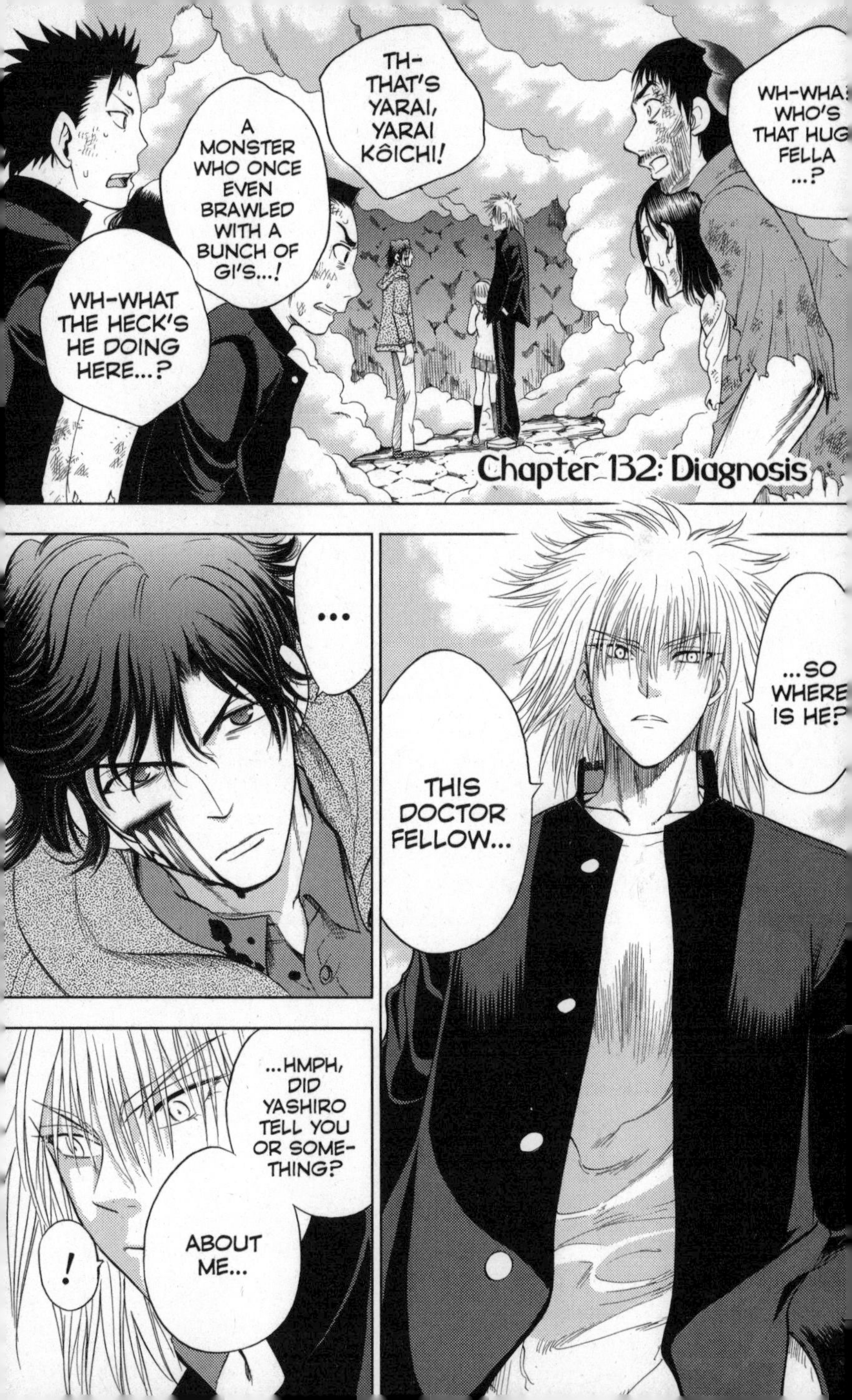
WH-WHA:
WHO'S THAT HUG FELLA ...?
TH- THAT'S YARAI, YARAI KÔICHI!
A MONSTER WHO ONCE EVEN BRAWLED WITH A BUNCH OF GI'S...!
WH-WHAT THE HECK'S HE DOING HERE...?
Chapter 132: Diagnosis
...SO WHERE IS HE?
THIS DOCTOR FELLOW...
...
...HMPH, DID YASHIRO TELL YOU OR SOMETHING?
ABOUT ME...
!

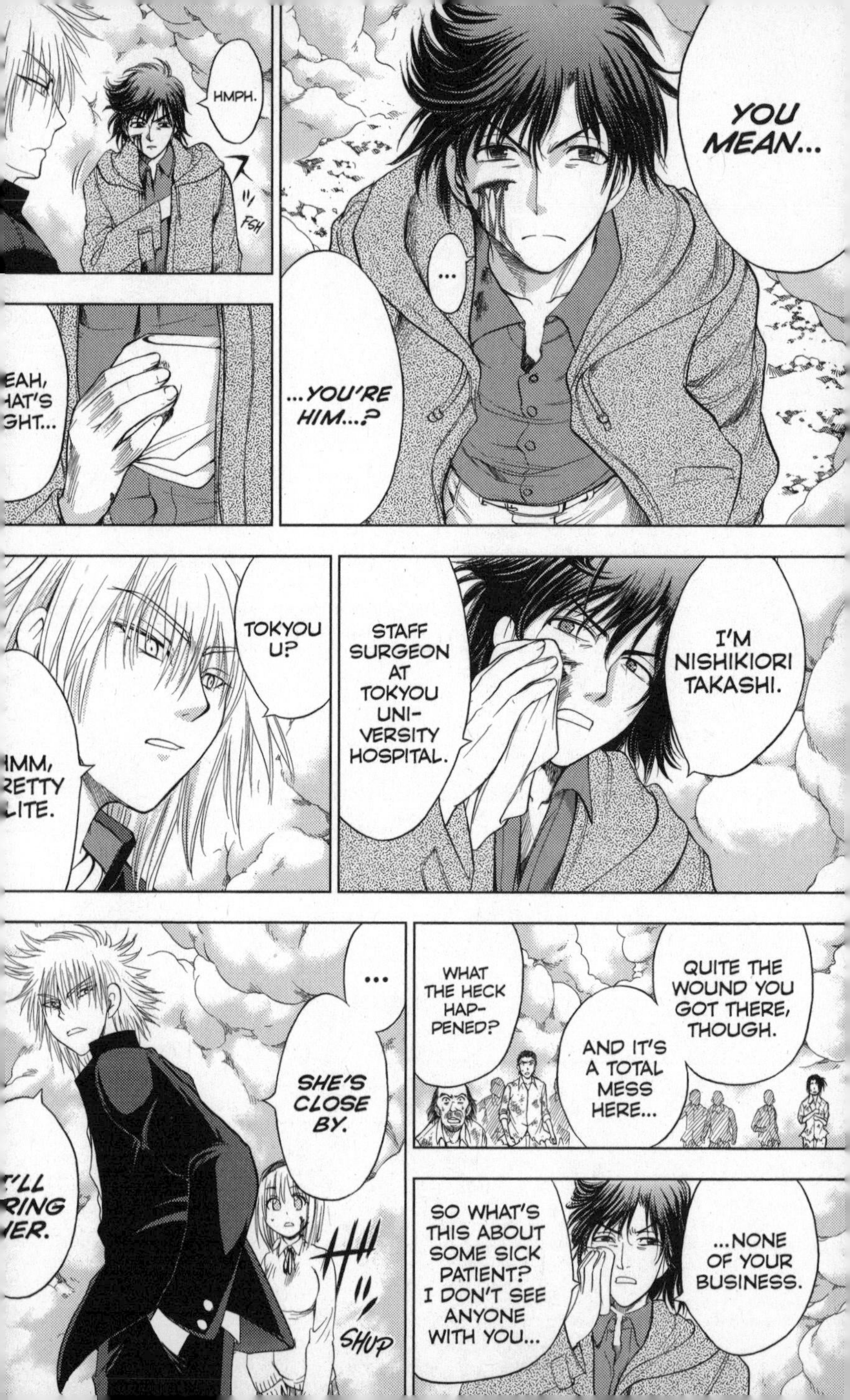
YOU MEAN...
...
...YOU'RE HIM...?
HMPH.
FSH
EAH, HAT'S GHT...
I'M NISHIKIORI TAKASHI.
STAFF SURGEON AT TOKYOU UNI-VERSITY HOSPITAL.
TOKYOU U?
HMM, RETTY LITE.
QUITE THE WOUND YOU GOT THERE, THOUGH.
AND IT'S A TOTAL MESS HERE...
WHAT THE HECK HAP-PENED?
...NONE OF YOUR BUSINESS.
SO WHAT'S THIS ABOUT SOME SICK PATIENT? I DON'T SEE ANYONE WITH YOU...
...
SHE'S CLOSE BY.
SHUP
'LL RING ER.

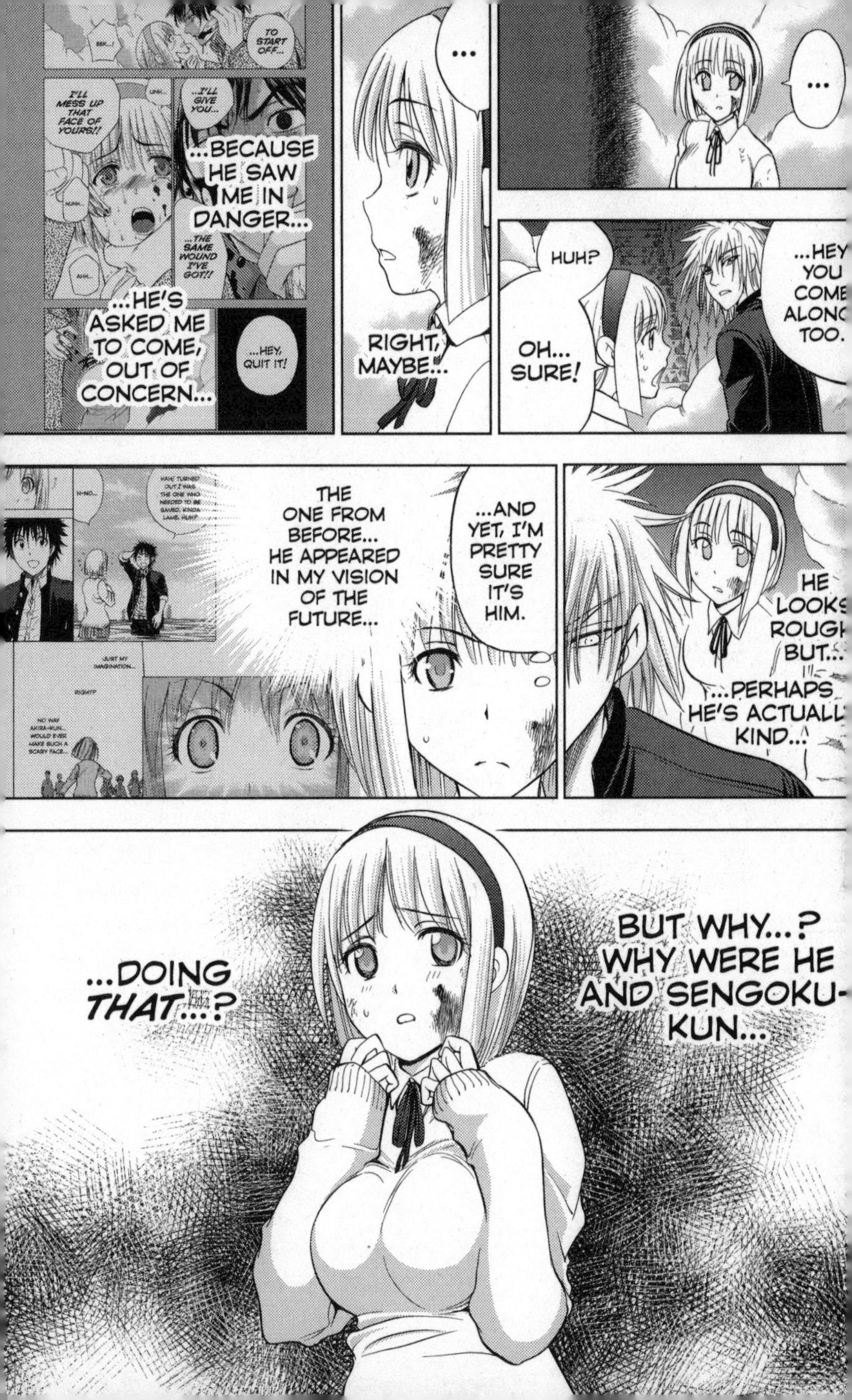

...
...HEY YOU COME ALONG TOO.
HUH?
OH... SURE!
...
RIGHT, MAYBE...
TO START OFF...
EEK...!
...I'LL GIVE YOU...
...BECAUSE HE SAW ME IN DANGER...
...THE SAME WOUND I'VE GOT!!
UNH...
I'LL MESS UP THAT FACE OF YOURS!!
...HEY, QUIT IT!
...HE'S ASKED ME TO COME, OUT OF CONCERN...
HE LOOKS ROUGH BUT...
...PERHAPS HE'S ACTUALLY KIND...
...AND YET, I'M PRETTY SURE IT'S HIM.
THE ONE FROM BEFORE... HE APPEARED IN MY VISION OF THE FUTURE...
HAH! TURNED OUT I WAS THE ONE WHO NEEDED TO BE SAVED. KINDA LAME, HUH?
N-NO...
JUST MY IMAGINATION...
RIGHT?
NO WAY AKIRA-KUN... WOULD EVER MAKE SUCH A SCARY FACE...
BUT WHY...? WHY WERE HE AND SENGOKU-KUN...
...DOING *THAT*...?

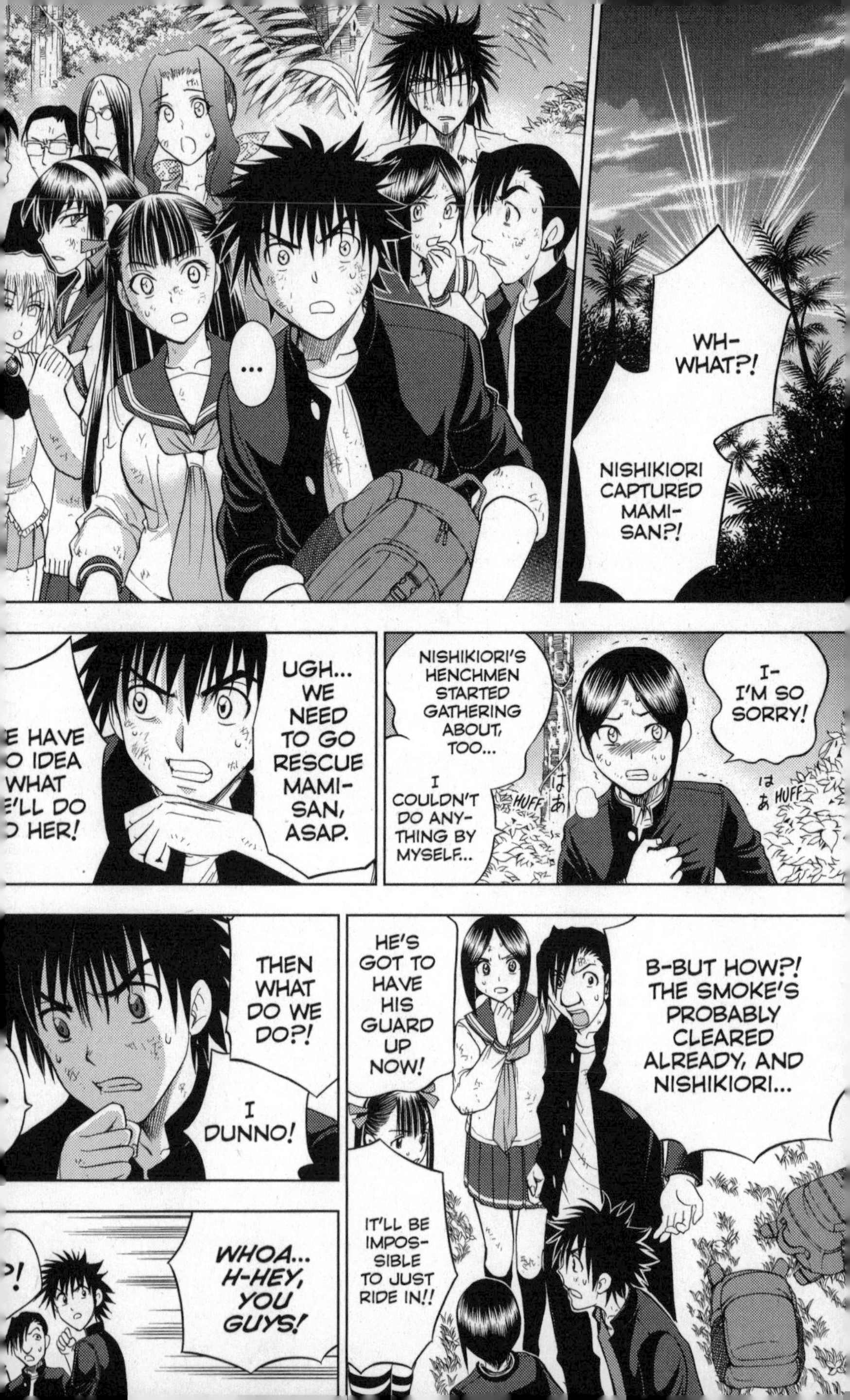
WH- WHAT?!
NISHIKIORI CAPTURED MAMI-SAN?!
...
I- I'M SO SORRY!
HUFF
はあ
NISHIKIORI'S HENCHMEN STARTED GATHERING ABOUT, TOO...
I COULDN'T DO ANYTHING BY MYSELF...
HUFF
はあ
UGH... WE NEED TO GO RESCUE MAMI-SAN, ASAP.
E HAVE O IDEA WHAT E'LL DO O HER!
B-BUT HOW?! THE SMOKE'S PROBABLY CLEARED ALREADY, AND NISHIKIORI...
HE'S GOT TO HAVE HIS GUARD UP NOW!
IT'LL BE IMPOSSIBLE TO JUST RIDE IN!!
THEN WHAT DO WE DO?!
I DUNNO!
WHOA... H-HEY, YOU GUYS!
?!

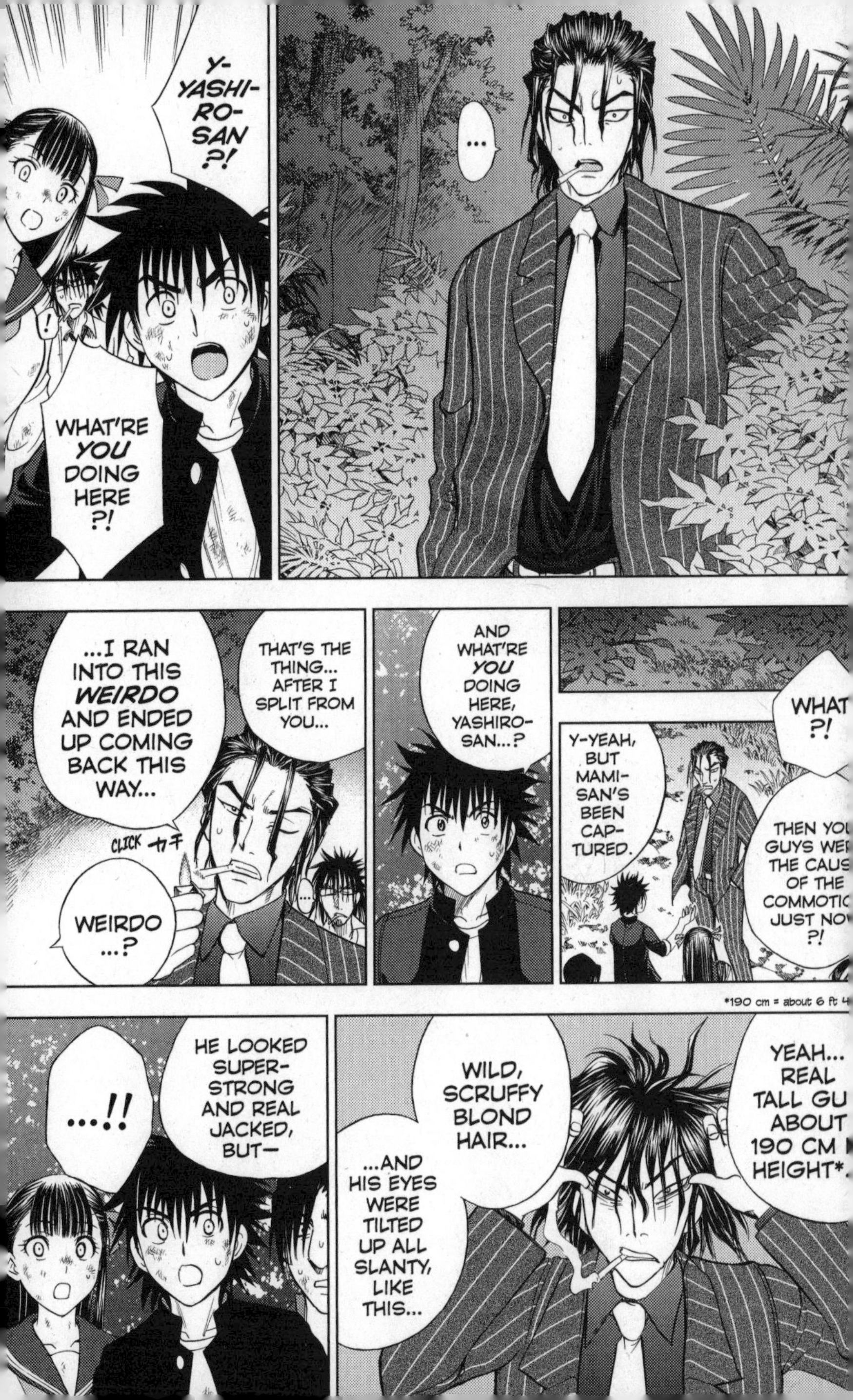
...
Y-YASHIRO-SAN?!
!
WHAT'RE *YOU* DOING HERE?!
WHAT?!
THEN YOU GUYS WER THE CAUS OF THE COMMOTIC JUST NO ?!
Y-YEAH, BUT MAMI-SAN'S BEEN CAPTURED.
AND WHAT'RE *YOU* DOING HERE, YASHIRO-SAN...?
THAT'S THE THING... AFTER I SPLIT FROM YOU...
...I RAN INTO THIS *WEIRDO* AND ENDED UP COMING BACK THIS WAY...
CLICK カチ
...
WEIRDO...?
*190 cm = about 6 ft 4
YEAH... REAL TALL GU ABOUT 190 CM HEIGHT*.
WILD, SCRUFFY BLOND HAIR...
...AND HIS EYES WERE TILTED UP ALL SLANTY, LIKE THIS...
HE LOOKED SUPER-STRONG AND REAL JACKED, BUT—
...!!

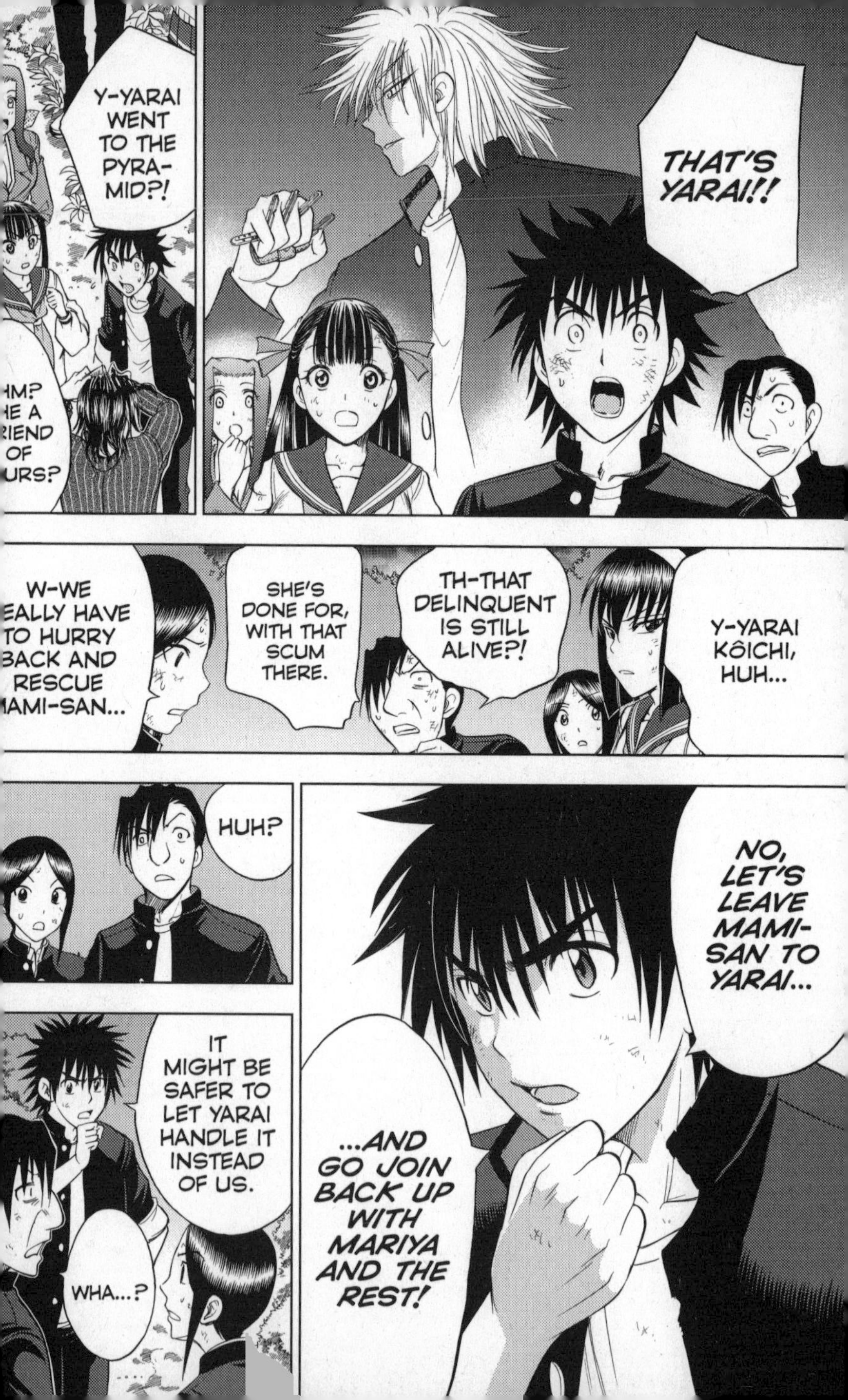
THAT'S YARAI!!
Y-YARAI WENT TO THE PYRA-MID?!
HM? HE A RIEND OF URS?
Y-YARAI KÔICHI, HUH...
TH-THAT DELINQUENT IS STILL ALIVE?!
SHE'S DONE FOR, WITH THAT SCUM THERE.
W-WE EALLY HAVE TO HURRY BACK AND RESCUE AMI-SAN...
NO, LET'S LEAVE MAMI-SAN TO YARAI...
...AND GO JOIN BACK UP WITH MARIYA AND THE REST!
HUH?
IT MIGHT BE SAFER TO LET YARAI HANDLE IT INSTEAD OF US.
WHA...?

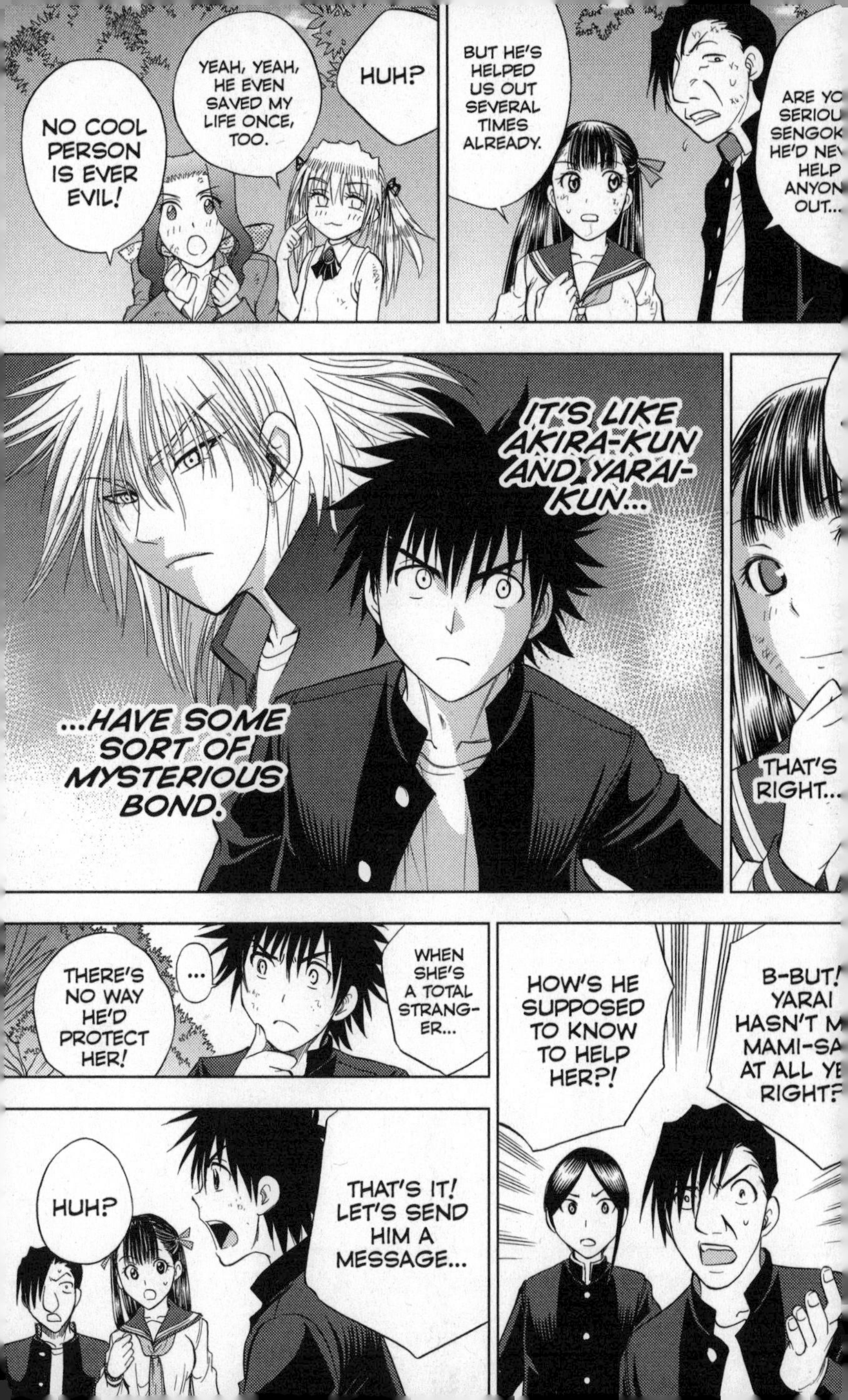
ARE YO SERIOU SENGOK HE'D NEV HELP ANYON OUT...
BUT HE'S HELPED US OUT SEVERAL TIMES ALREADY.
HUH?
YEAH, YEAH, HE EVEN SAVED MY LIFE ONCE, TOO.
NO COOL PERSON IS EVER EVIL!
THAT'S RIGHT...
IT'S LIKE AKIRA-KUN AND YARAI-KUN...
...HAVE SOME SORT OF MYSTERIOUS BOND.
B-BUT! YARAI HASN'T M MAMI-SA AT ALL YE RIGHT?
HOW'S HE SUPPOSED TO KNOW TO HELP HER?!
WHEN SHE'S A TOTAL STRANGER...
...
THERE'S NO WAY HE'D PROTECT HER!
THAT'S IT! LET'S SEND HIM A MESSAGE...
HUH?

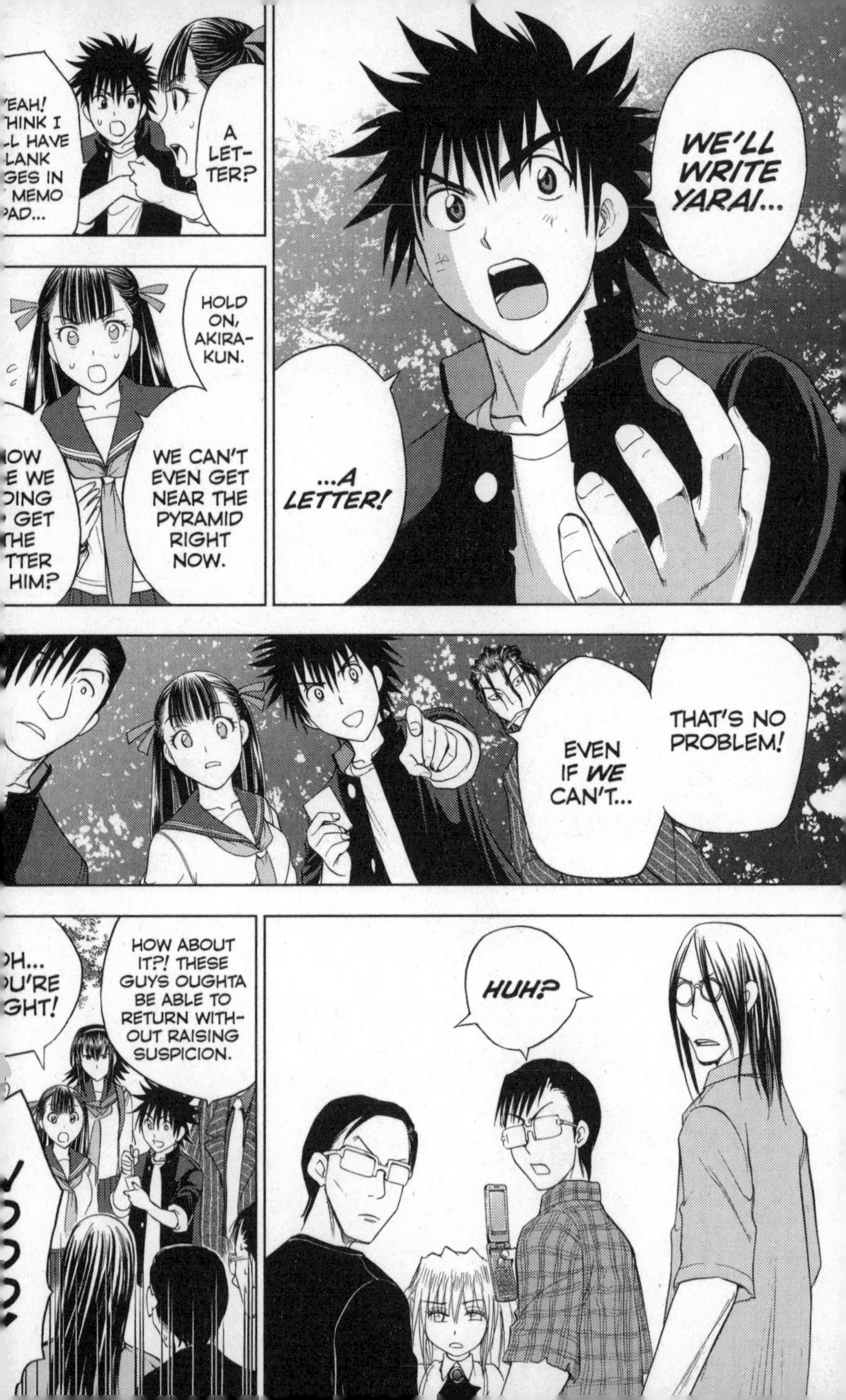
WE'LL WRITE YARAI...
...A LETTER!
A LETTER?
'EAH! THINK I 'LL HAVE LANK GES IN MEMO PAD...
HOLD ON, AKIRA-KUN.
WE CAN'T EVEN GET NEAR THE PYRAMID RIGHT NOW.
OW E WE OING GET THE TTER HIM?
THAT'S NO PROBLEM!
EVEN IF WE CAN'T...
HUH?
HOW ABOUT IT?! THESE GUYS OUGHTA BE ABLE TO RETURN WITHOUT RAISING SUSPICION.
H... U'RE GHT!

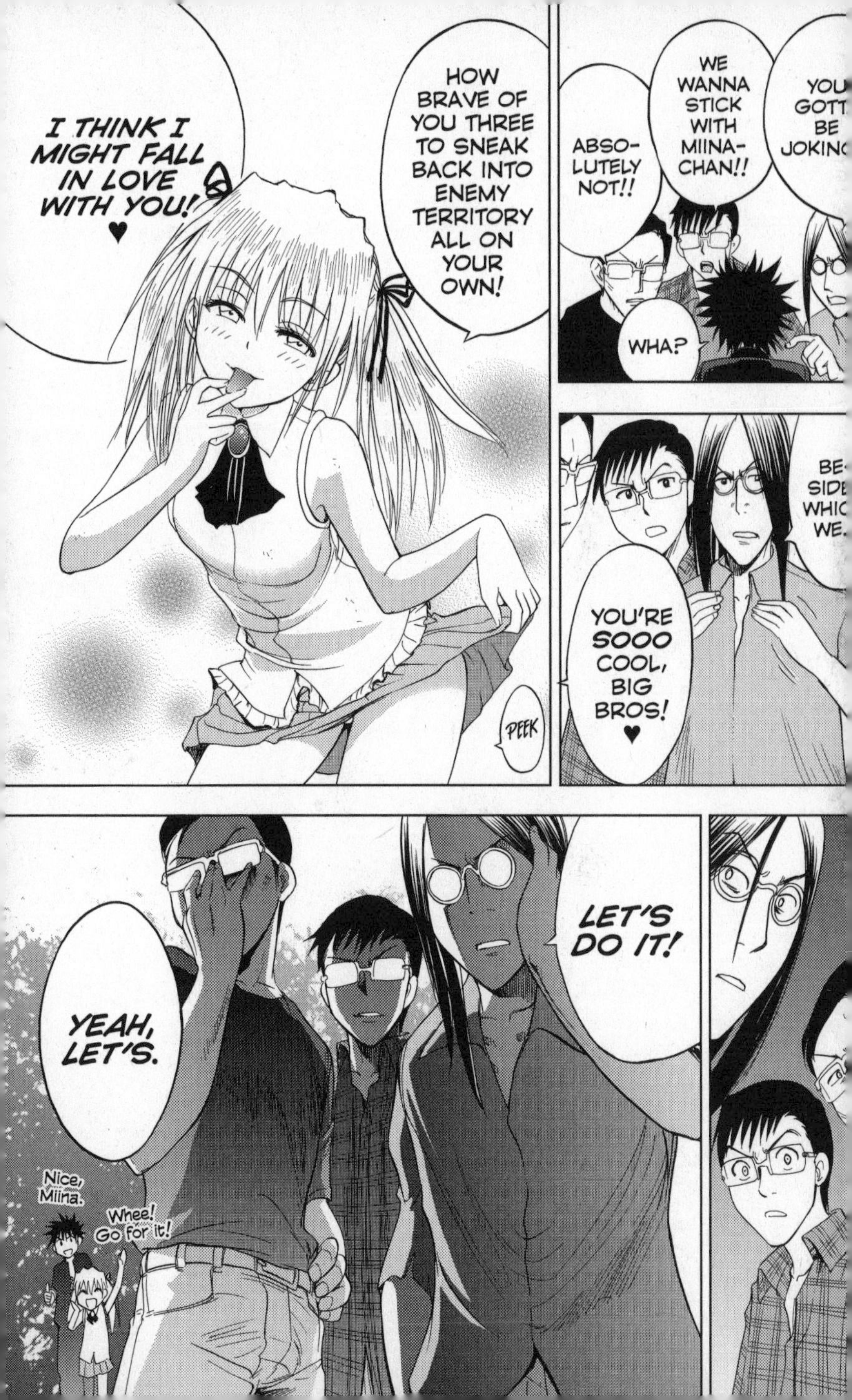
YOU GOTT BE JOKIN
WE WANNA STICK WITH MIINA-CHAN!!
ABSO-LUTELY NOT!!
WHA?
BE-SIDE WHIC WE
YOU'RE SOOO COOL, BIG BROS! ♥
HOW BRAVE OF YOU THREE TO SNEAK BACK INTO ENEMY TERRITORY ALL ON YOUR OWN!
I THINK I MIGHT FALL IN LOVE WITH YOU! ♥
PEEK
LET'S DO IT!
YEAH, LET'S.
Whee! Go for it!
Nice, Miina.

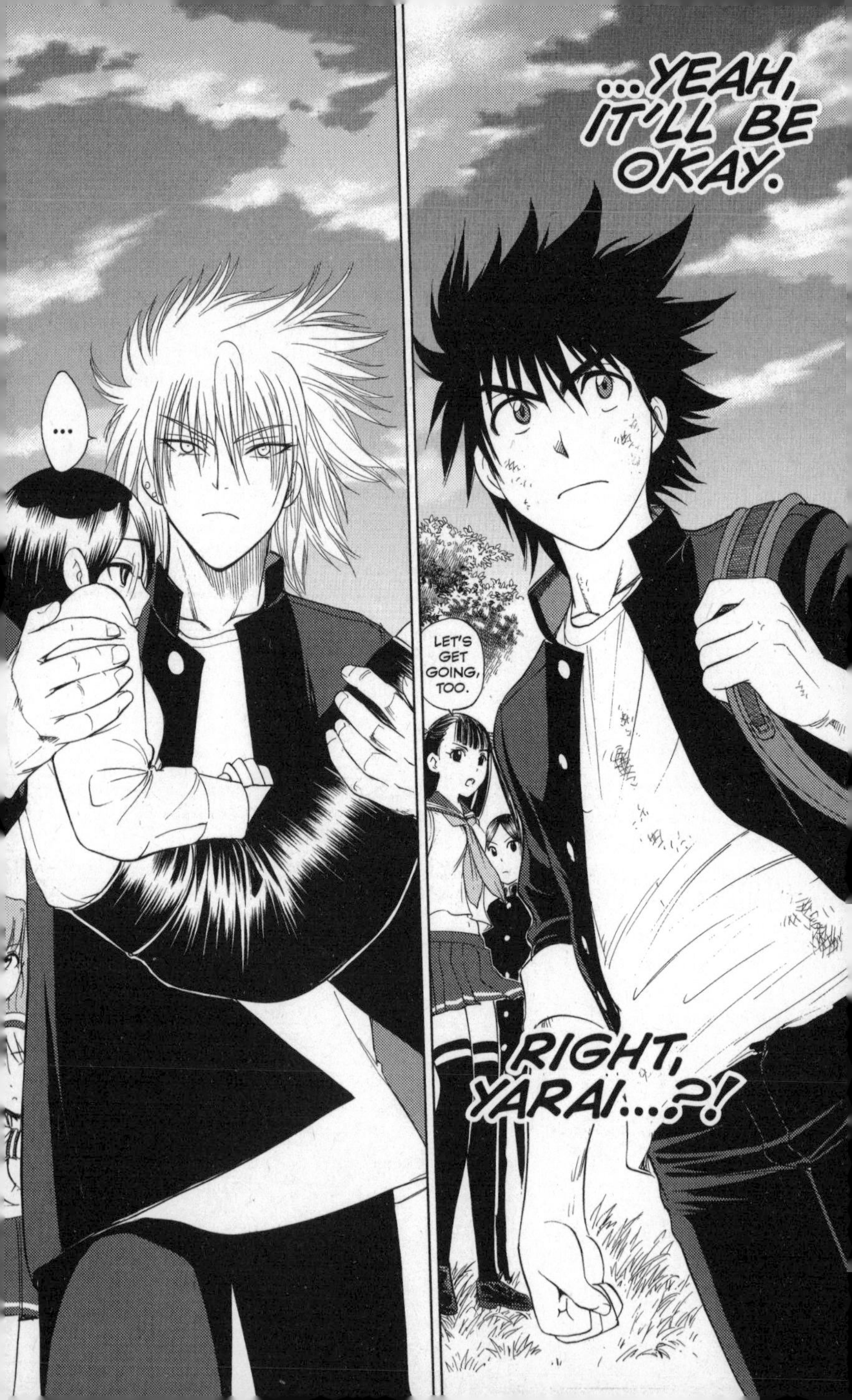
...YEAH, IT'LL BE OKAY.
LET'S GET GOING, TOO.
RIGHT, YARAI...?!
...

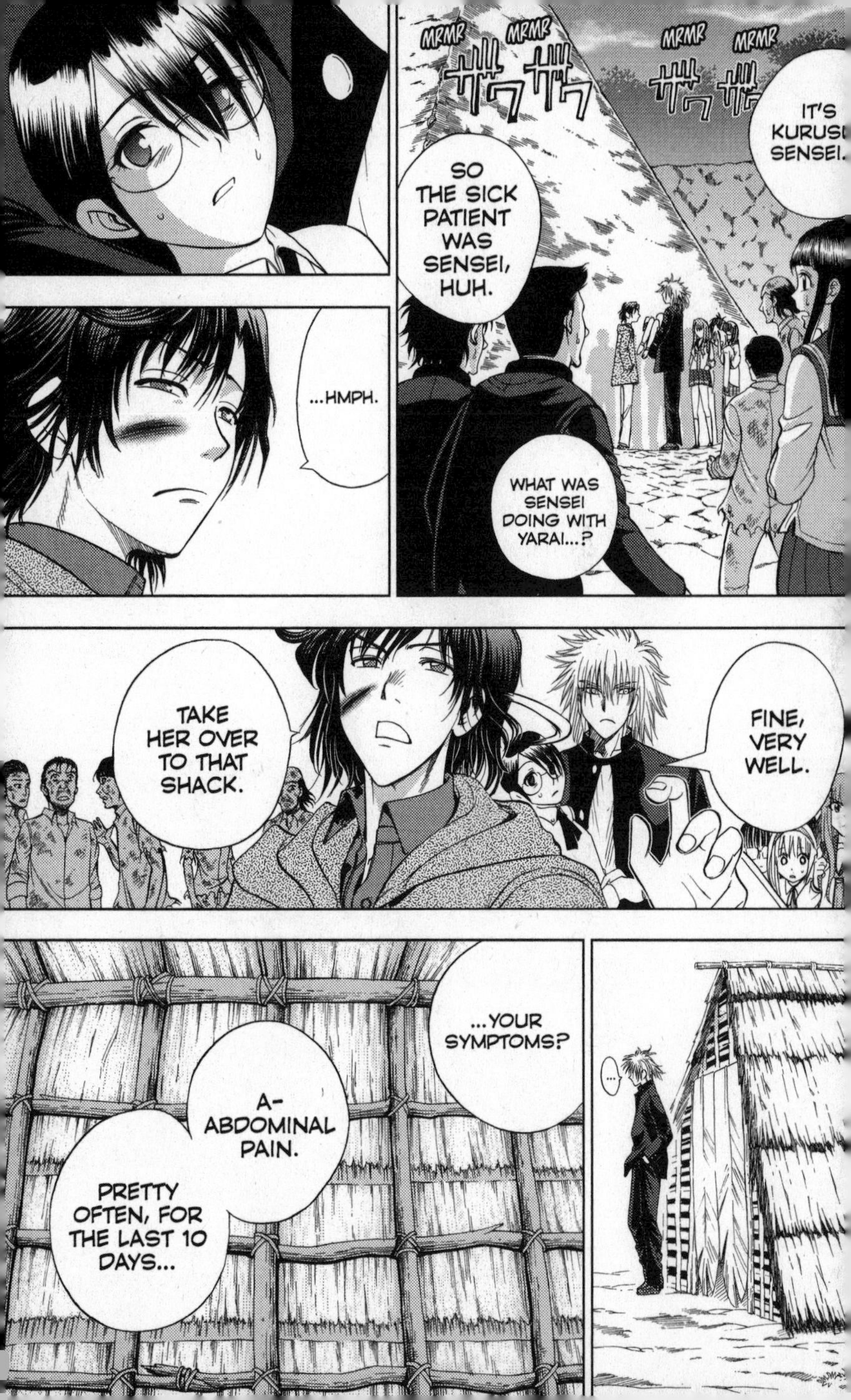
MRMR MRMR MRMR MRMR
ザワ ザワ ザワ ザワ
IT'S KURUS SENSEI.
SO THE SICK PATIENT WAS SENSEI, HUH.
WHAT WAS SENSEI DOING WITH YARAI...?
...HMPH.
FINE, VERY WELL.
TAKE HER OVER TO THAT SHACK.
...
...YOUR SYMPTOMS?
A- ABDOMINAL PAIN.
PRETTY OFTEN, FOR THE LAST 10 DAYS...

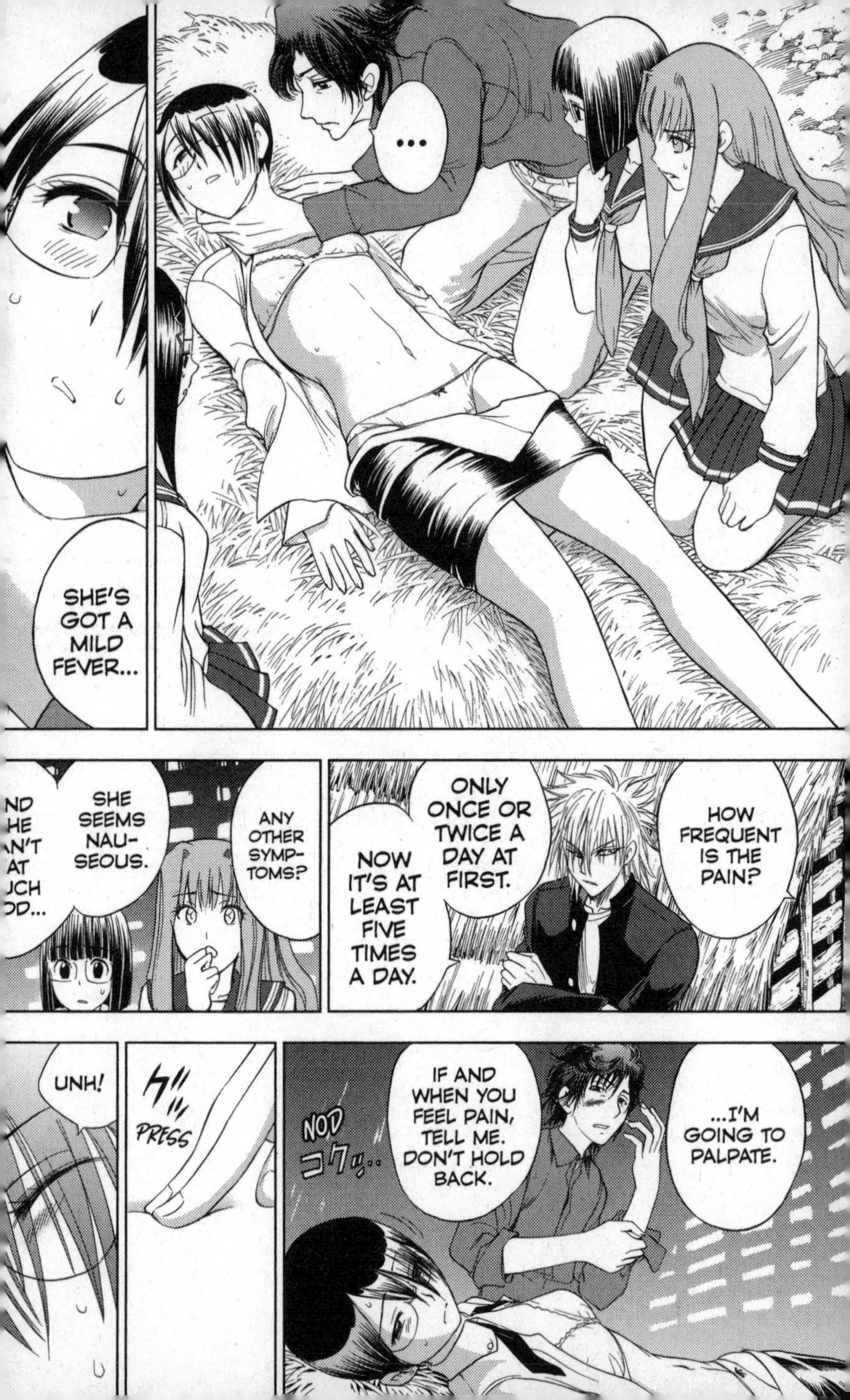
...
SHE'S GOT A MILD FEVER...
HOW FREQUENT IS THE PAIN?
ONLY ONCE OR TWICE A DAY AT FIRST.
NOW IT'S AT LEAST FIVE TIMES A DAY.
ANY OTHER SYMPTOMS?
SHE SEEMS NAU-SEOUS.
...I'M GOING TO PALPATE.
IF AND WHEN YOU FEEL PAIN, TELL ME. DON'T HOLD BACK.
NOD
PRESS
UNH!

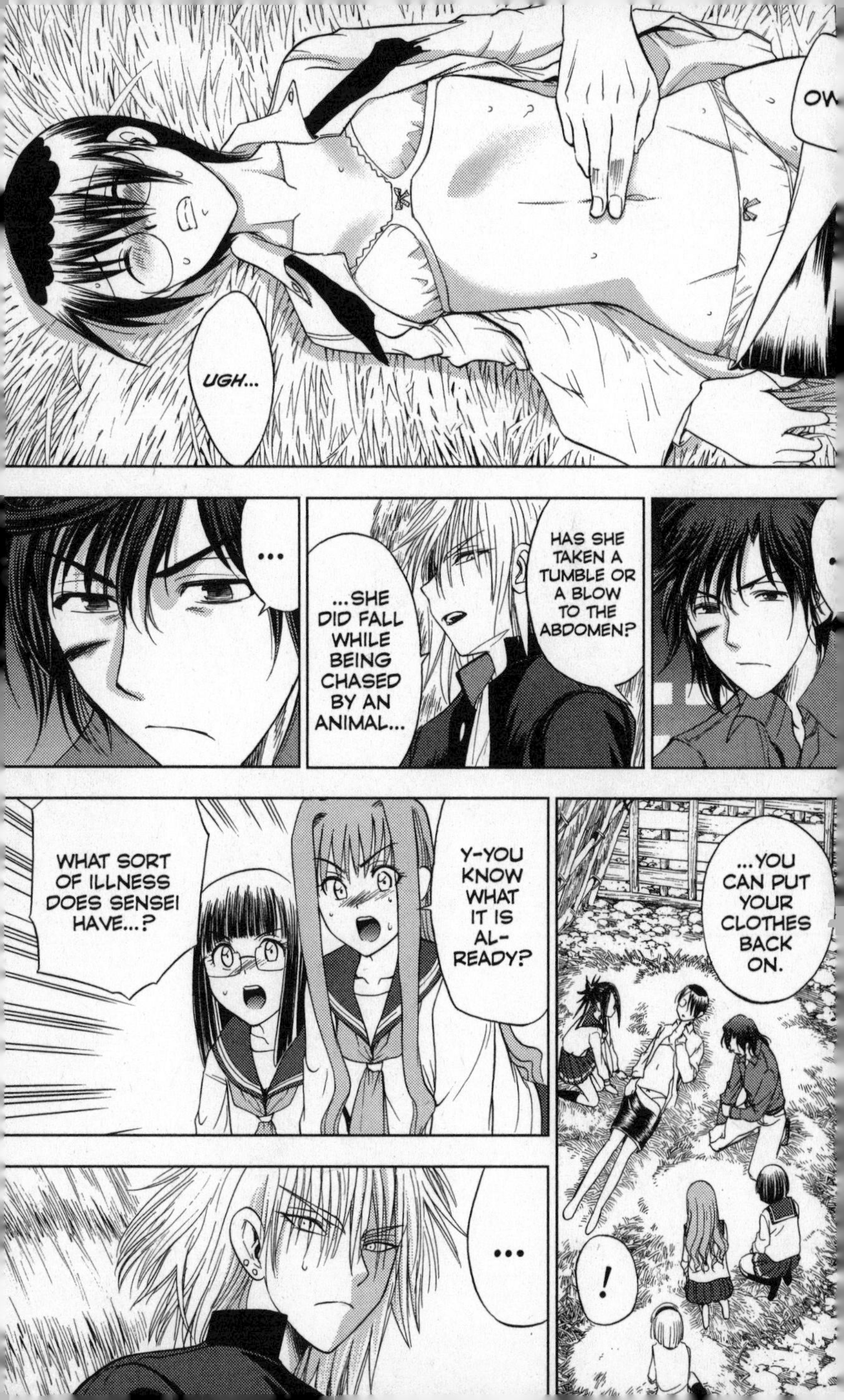

OW
UGH...
HAS SHE TAKEN A TUMBLE OR A BLOW TO THE ABDOMEN?
...SHE DID FALL WHILE BEING CHASED BY AN ANIMAL...
...
...YOU CAN PUT YOUR CLOTHES BACK ON.
!
Y-YOU KNOW WHAT IT IS AL-READY?
WHAT SORT OF ILLNESS DOES SENSEI HAVE...?
...

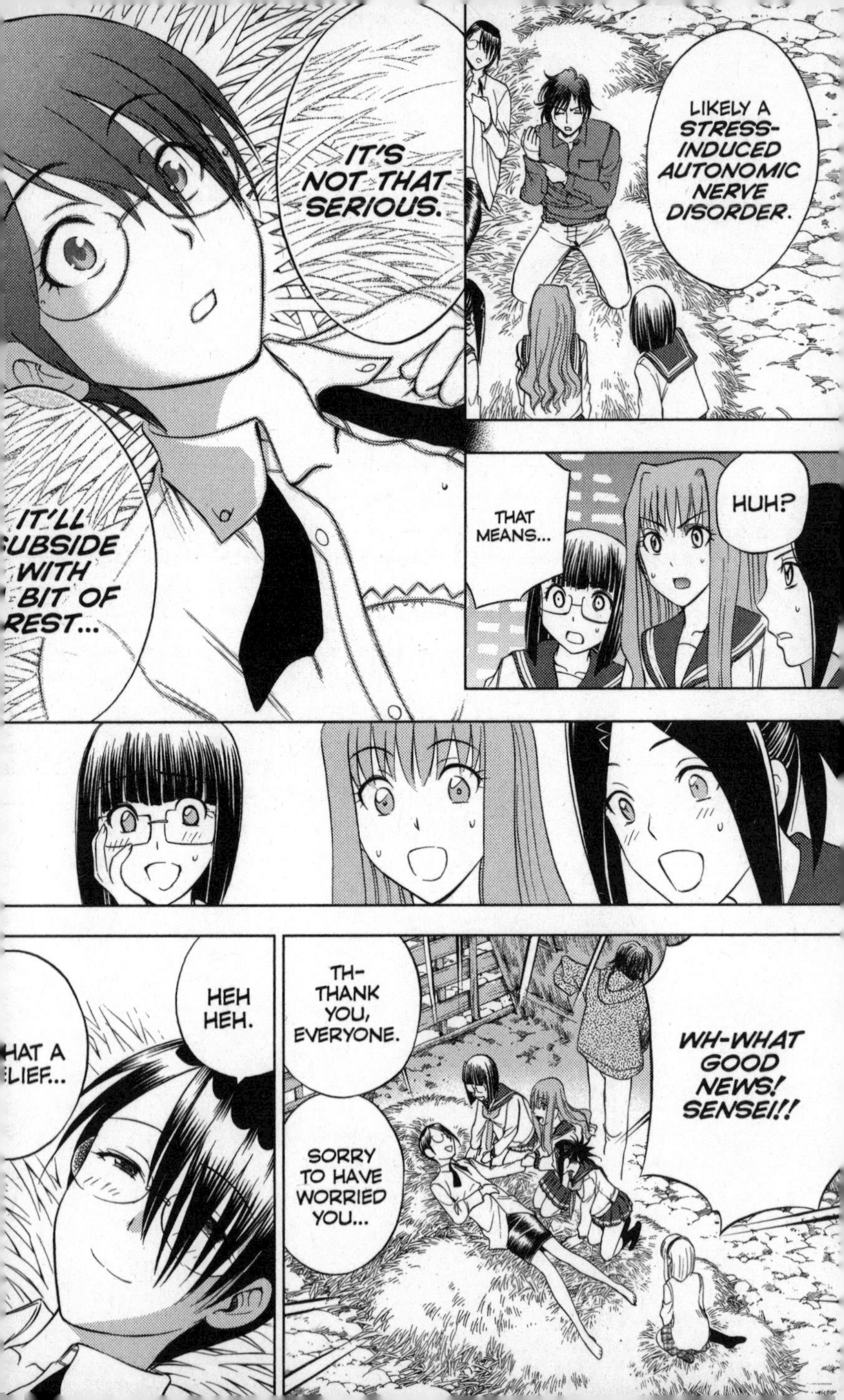
LIKELY A STRESS-INDUCED AUTONOMIC NERVE DISORDER.
HUH?
THAT MEANS...
IT'S NOT THAT SERIOUS.
IT'LL UBSIDE WITH BIT OF REST...
WH-WHAT GOOD NEWS! SENSEI!!
TH-THANK YOU, EVERYONE.
SORRY TO HAVE WORRIED YOU...
HEH HEH.
HAT A ELIEF...

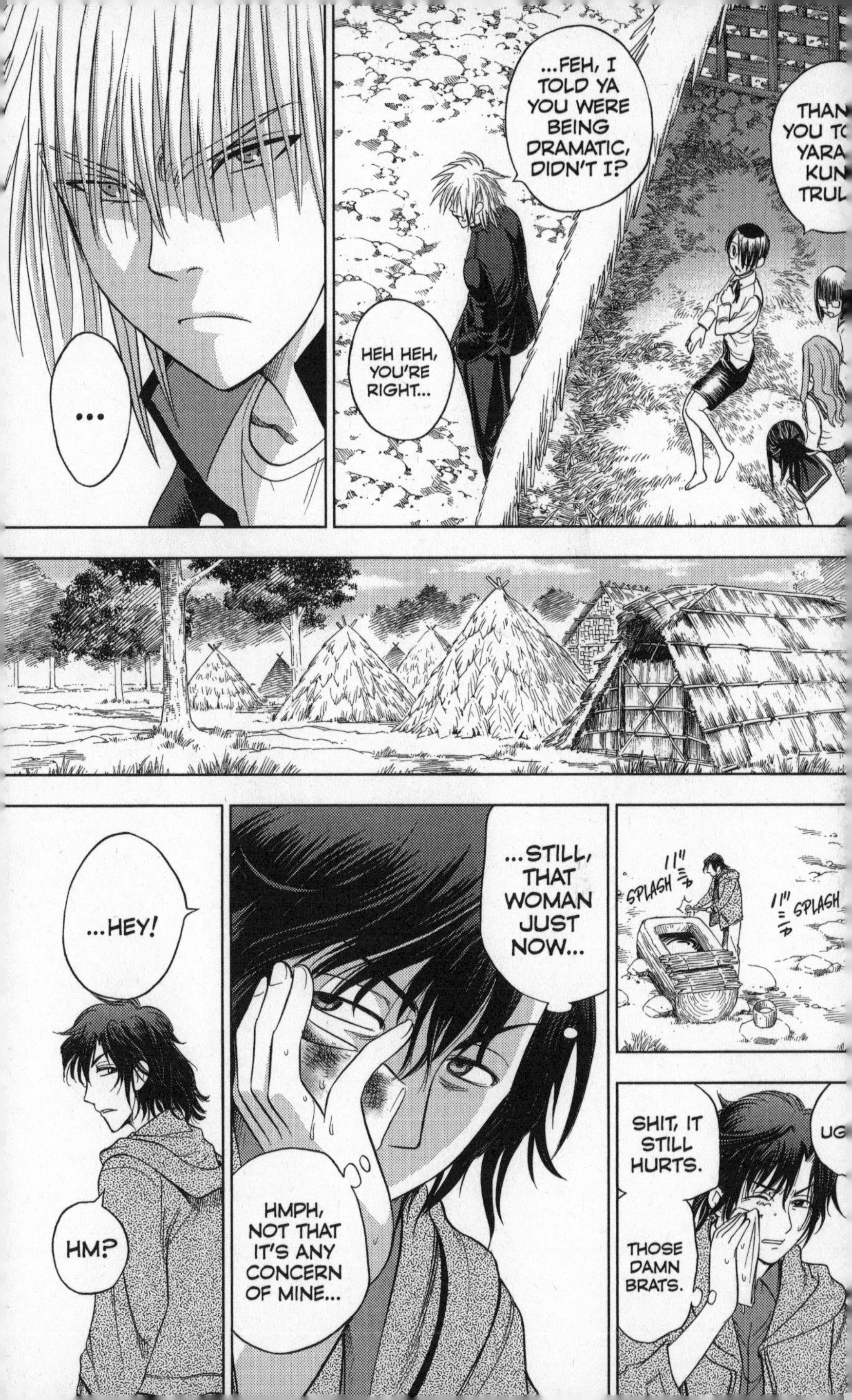
THAN YOU TO YARA KUN TRUL
...FEH, I TOLD YA YOU WERE BEING DRAMATIC, DIDN'T I?
HEH HEH, YOU'RE RIGHT...
...
SPLASH
SPLASH
UG
SHIT, IT STILL HURTS.
THOSE DAMN BRATS.
...STILL, THAT WOMAN JUST NOW...
HMPH, NOT THAT IT'S ANY CONCERN OF MINE...
...HEY!
HM?

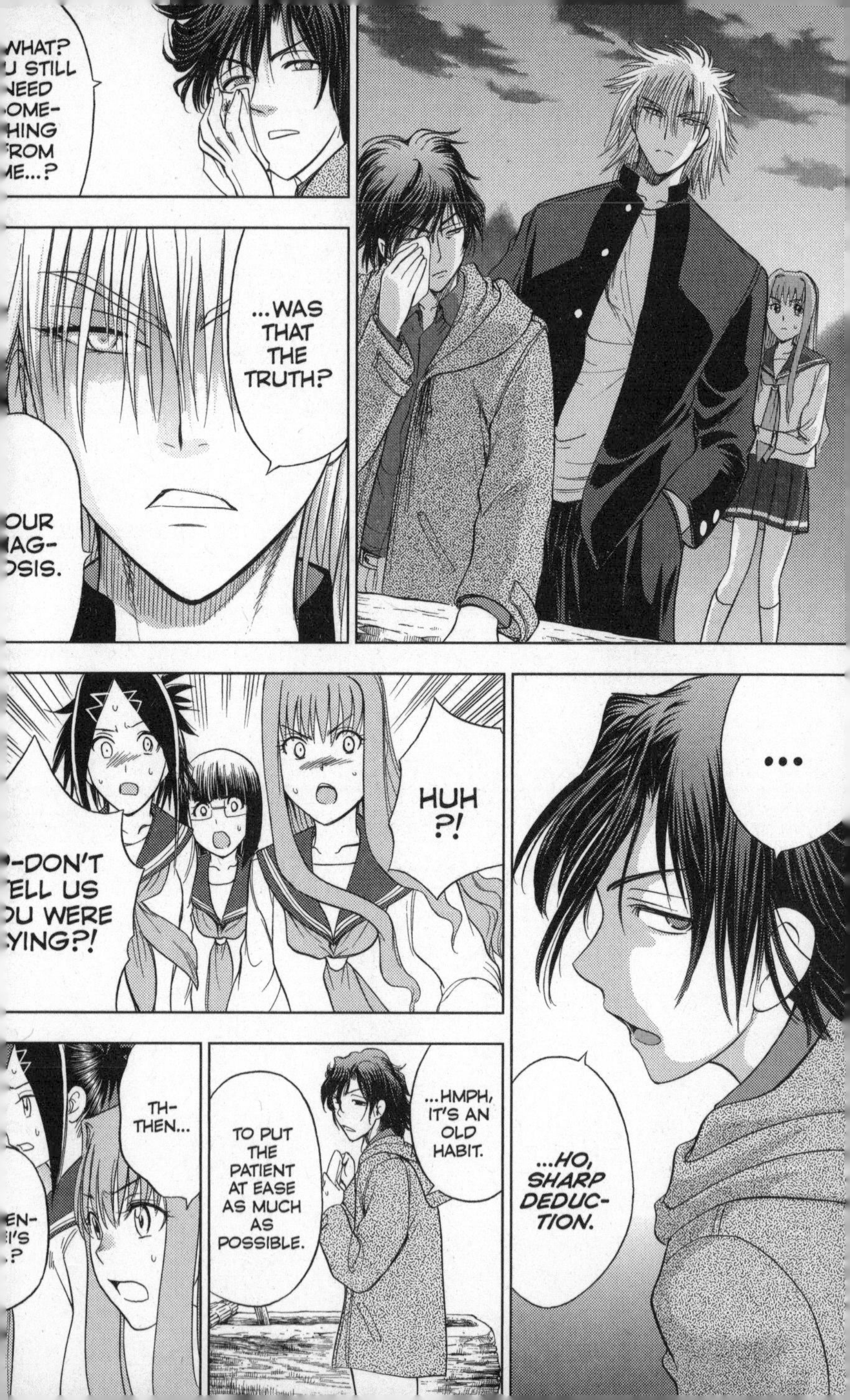
WHAT? U STILL NEED OME-HING FROM ME...?
...WAS THAT THE TRUTH?
OUR IAG-OSIS.
...
...HO, SHARP DEDUC-TION.
HUH?!
-DON'T ELL US OU WERE YING?!
...HMPH, IT'S AN OLD HABIT.
TO PUT THE PATIENT AT EASE AS MUCH AS POSSIBLE.
TH-THEN...
EN-EI'S ?

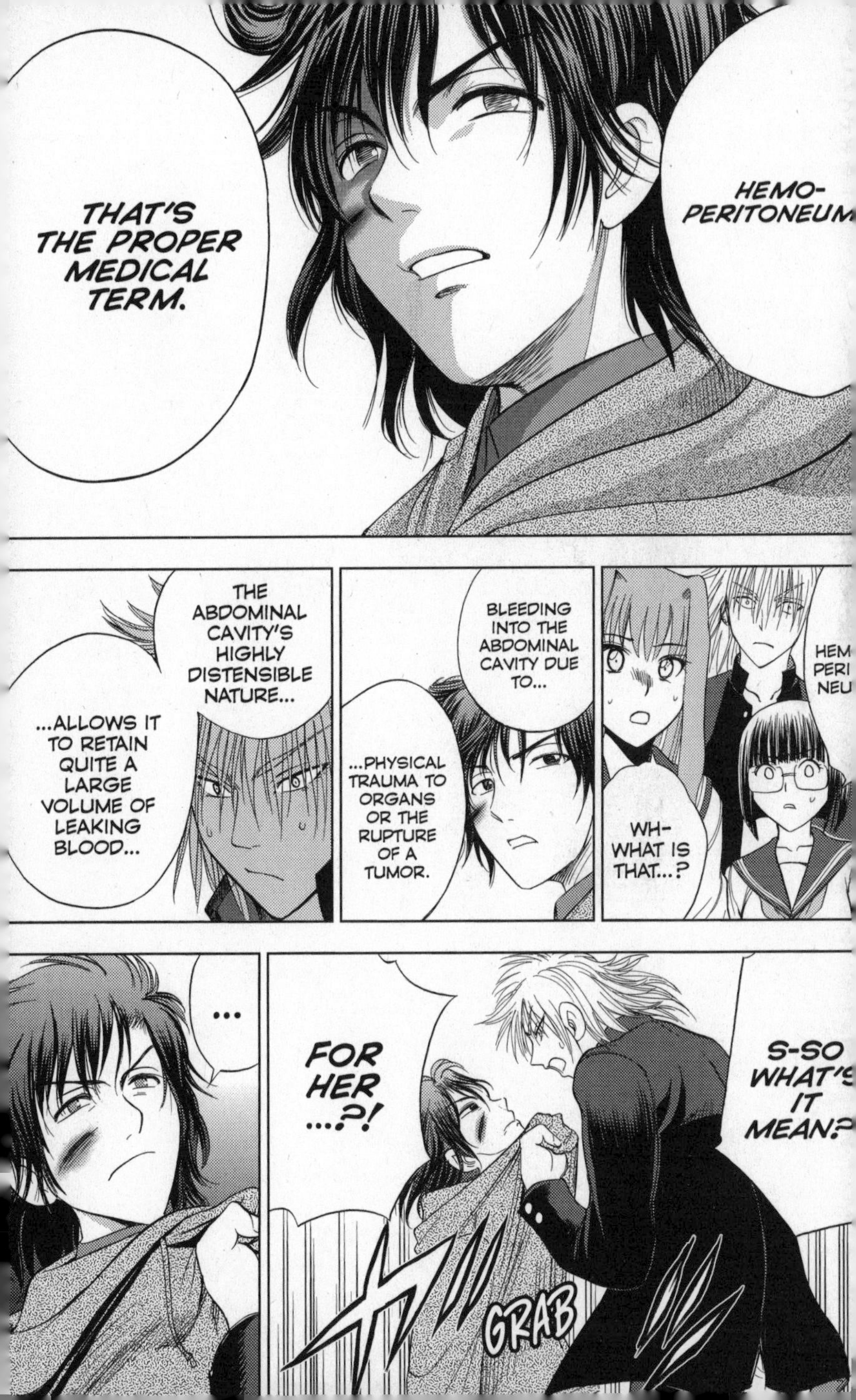

HEMO-PERITONEUM
THAT'S THE PROPER MEDICAL TERM.
HEM PERI NEU
WH- WHAT IS THAT...?
BLEEDING INTO THE ABDOMINAL CAVITY DUE TO...
...PHYSICAL TRAUMA TO ORGANS OR THE RUPTURE OF A TUMOR.
THE ABDOMINAL CAVITY'S HIGHLY DISTENSIBLE NATURE...
...ALLOWS IT TO RETAIN QUITE A LARGE VOLUME OF LEAKING BLOOD...
S-SO WHAT'S IT MEAN?
FOR HER ...?!
GRAB
...

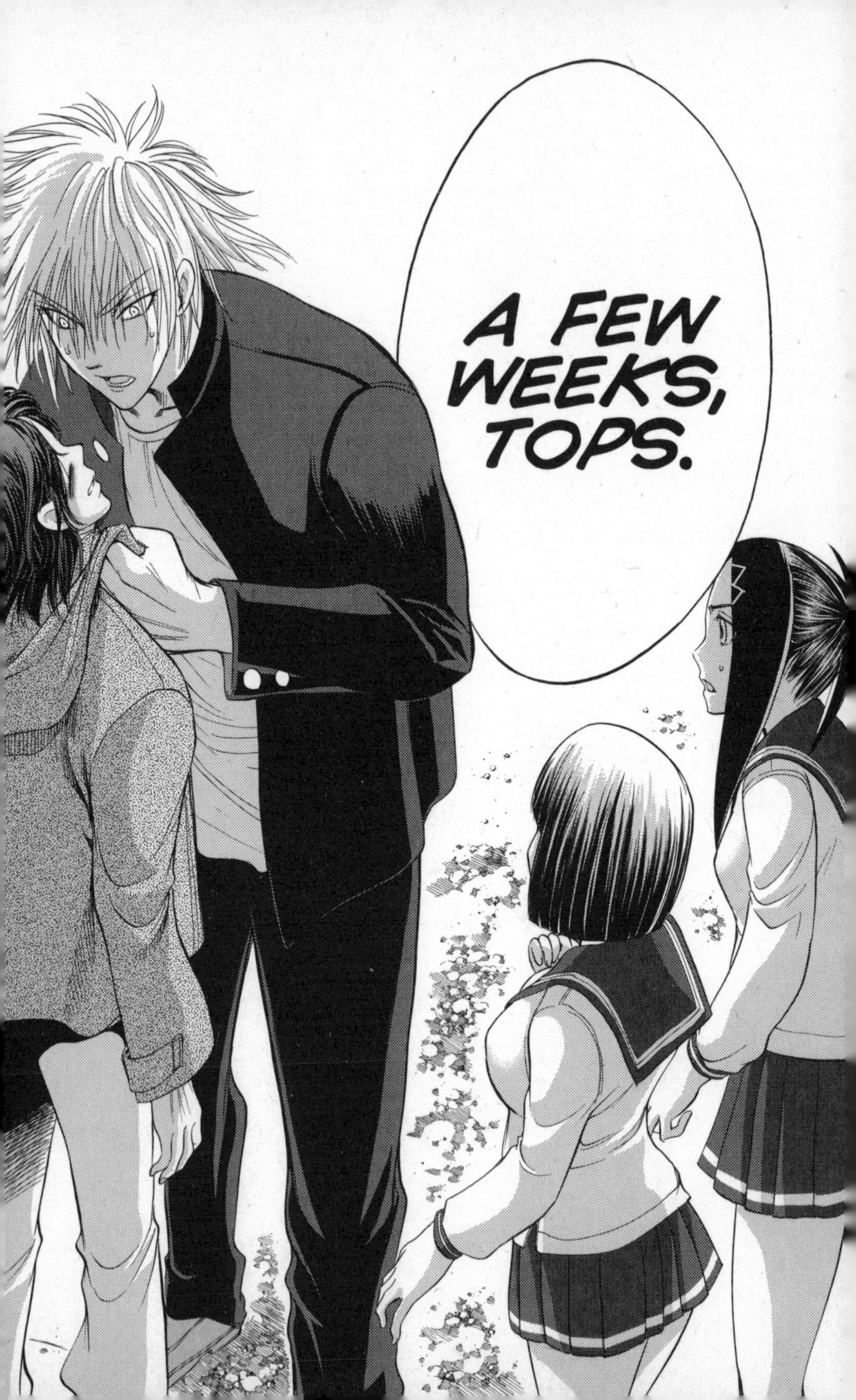
A FEW WEEKS, TOPS.

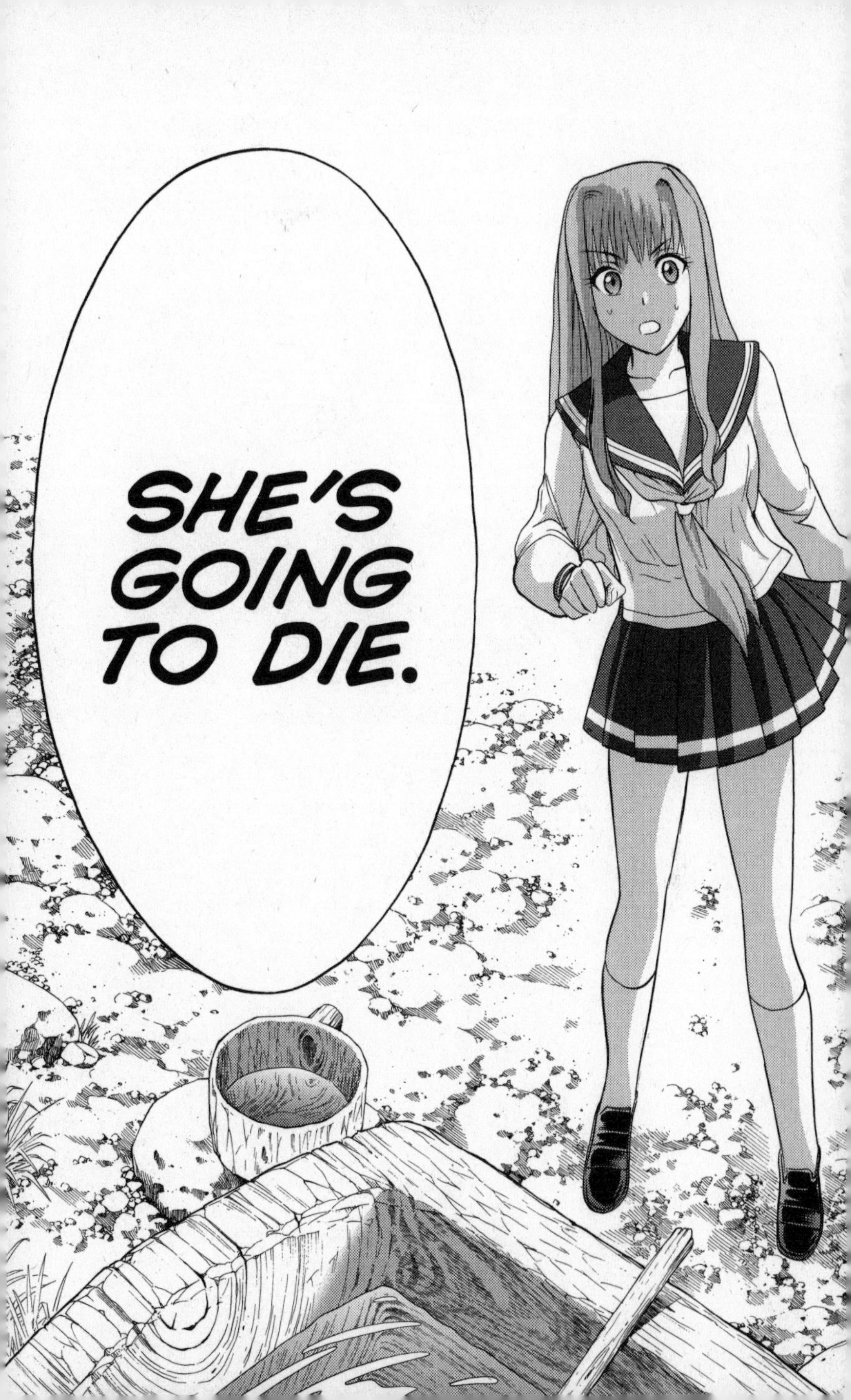
SHE'S GOING TO DIE.

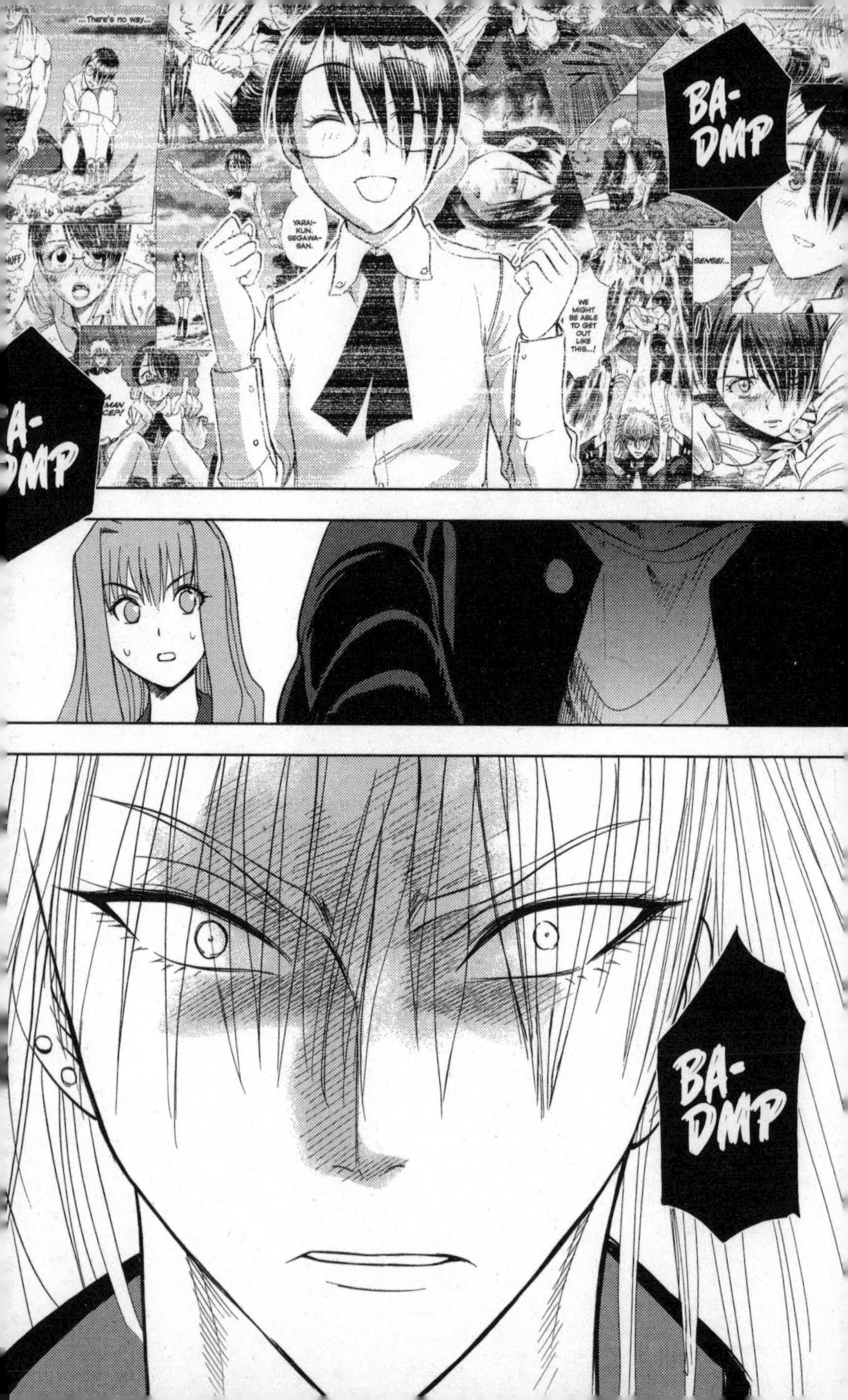
BA-DMP
SENSEI...
WE MIGHT BE ABLE TO GET OUT LIKE THIS...!
YARAI-KUN. SEGAWA-SAN.
...There's no way...
A-DMP
BA-DMP

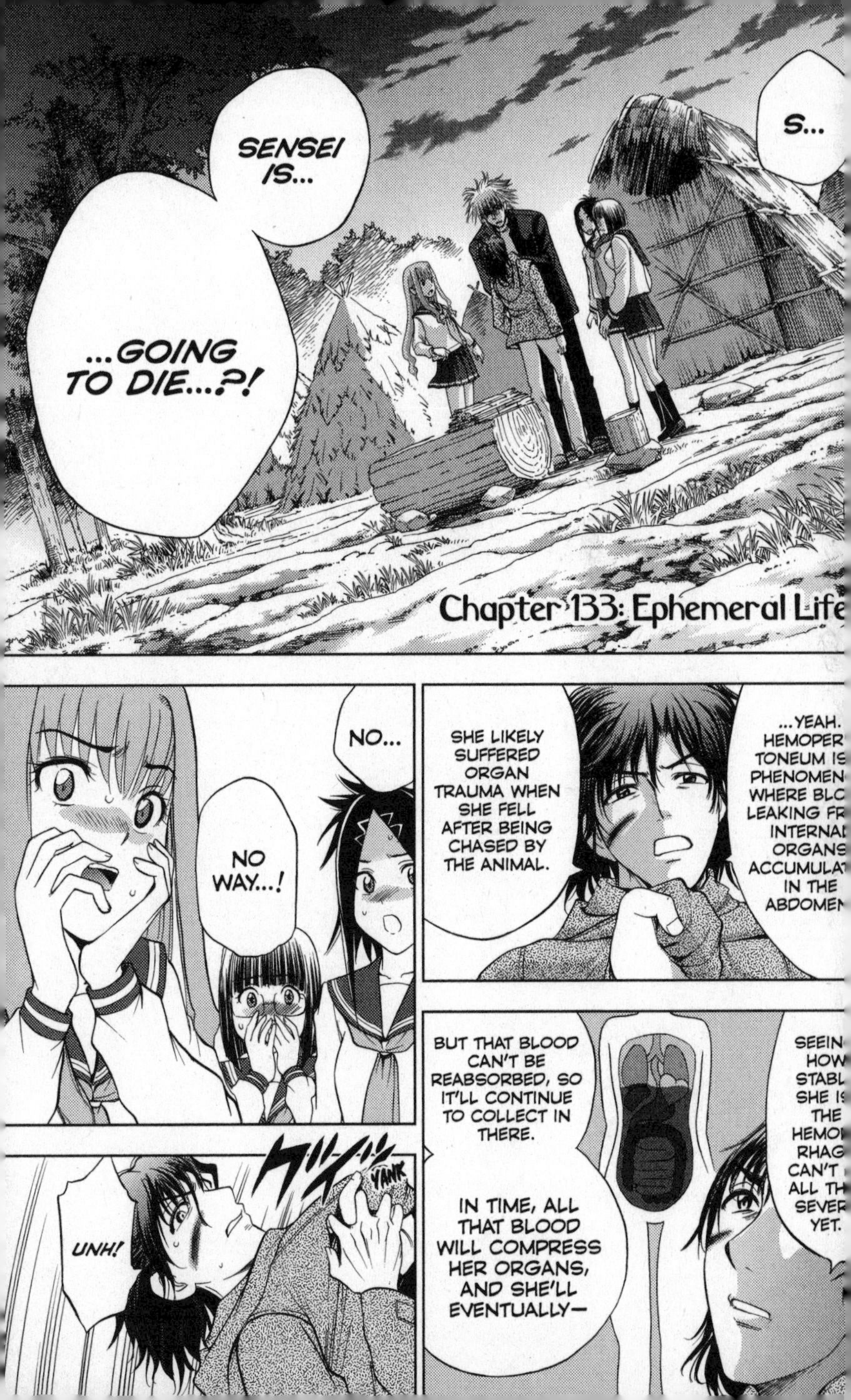
S...
SENSEI IS...
...GOING TO DIE...?!
Chapter 133: Ephemeral Life
...YEAH. HEMOPER TONEUM IS PHENOMEN WHERE BLO LEAKING FR INTERNAL ORGANS ACCUMULAT IN THE ABDOMEN
SHE LIKELY SUFFERED ORGAN TRAUMA WHEN SHE FELL AFTER BEING CHASED BY THE ANIMAL.
NO...
NO WAY...!
SEEIN HOW STABL SHE IS THE HEMOR RHAG CAN'T ALL TH SEVER YET.
BUT THAT BLOOD CAN'T BE REABSORBED, SO IT'LL CONTINUE TO COLLECT IN THERE.
IN TIME, ALL THAT BLOOD WILL COMPRESS HER ORGANS, AND SHE'LL EVENTUALLY—
YANK
UNH!

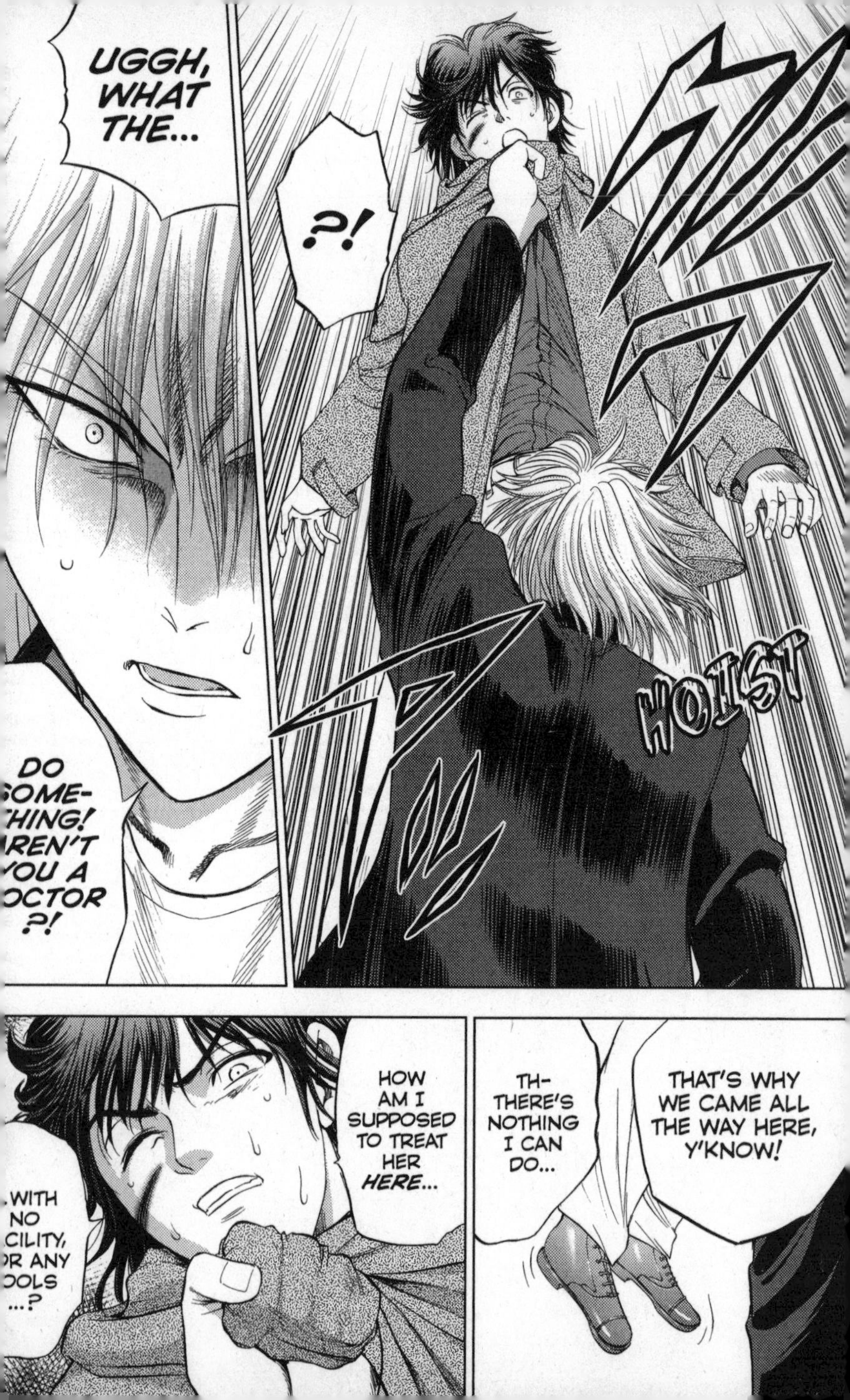
?!
HOIST
UGGH, WHAT THE...
DO SOME- HING! REN'T OU A OCTOR ?!
THAT'S WHY WE CAME ALL THE WAY HERE, Y'KNOW!
TH- THERE'S NOTHING I CAN DO...
HOW AM I SUPPOSED TO TREAT HER *HERE*...
WITH NO CILITY, R ANY OOLS ...?

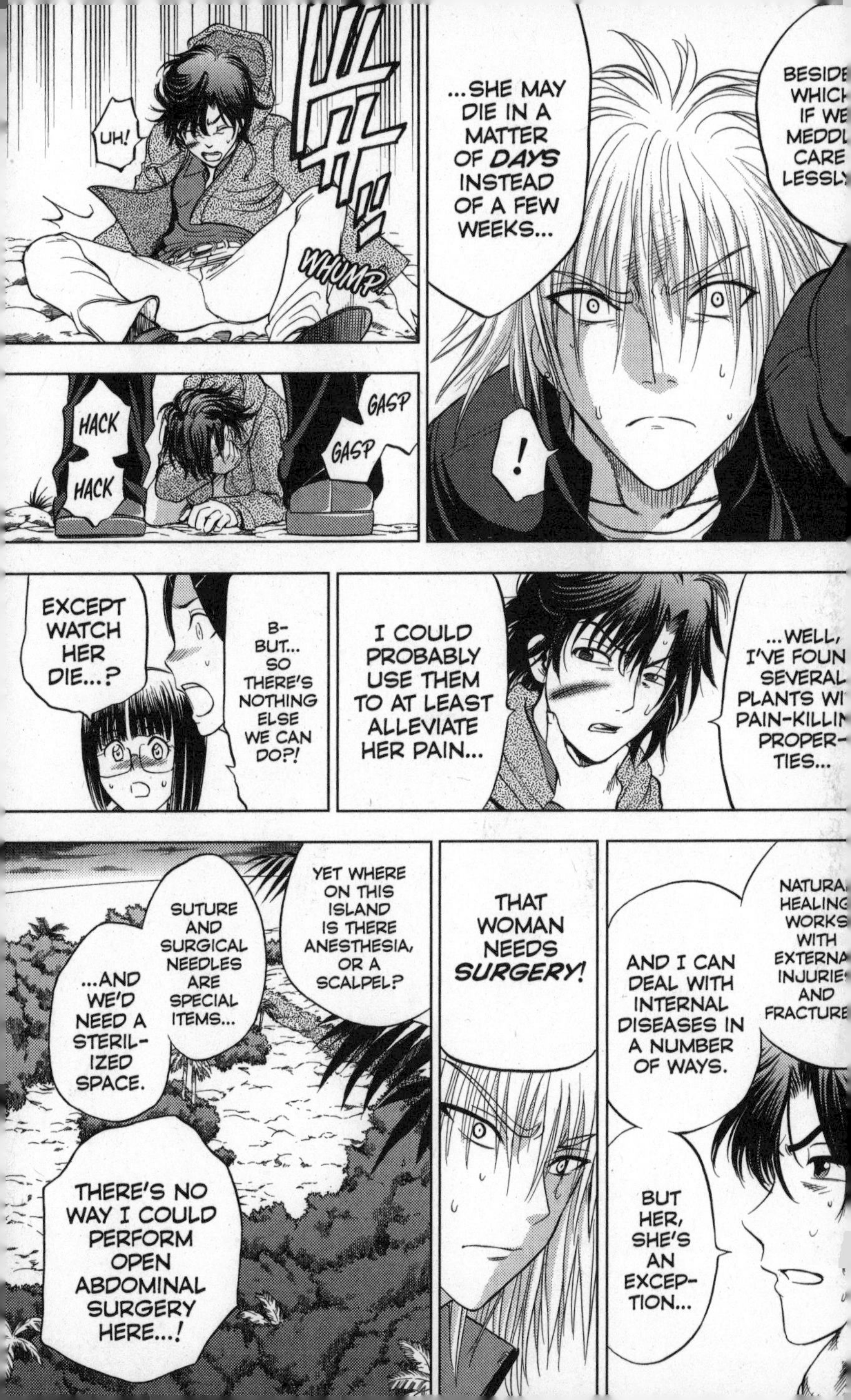
BESIDE WHICH IF WE MEDDL CARE LESSLY
...SHE MAY DIE IN A MATTER OF *DAYS* INSTEAD OF A FEW WEEKS...
!
UH!
WHUMP
HACK HACK
GASP GASP
...WELL, I'VE FOUN SEVERAL PLANTS WI PAIN-KILLIN PROPER-TIES...
I COULD PROBABLY USE THEM TO AT LEAST ALLEVIATE HER PAIN...
B-BUT... SO THERE'S NOTHING ELSE WE CAN DO?!
EXCEPT WATCH HER DIE...?
NATURA HEALING WORKS WITH EXTERNA INJURIE AND FRACTURE
AND I CAN DEAL WITH INTERNAL DISEASES IN A NUMBER OF WAYS.
BUT HER, SHE'S AN EXCEP-TION...
THAT WOMAN NEEDS *SURGERY*!
YET WHERE ON THIS ISLAND IS THERE ANESTHESIA, OR A SCALPEL?
SUTURE AND SURGICAL NEEDLES ARE SPECIAL ITEMS...
...AND WE'D NEED A STERIL-IZED SPACE.
THERE'S NO WAY I COULD PERFORM OPEN ABDOMINAL SURGERY HERE...!

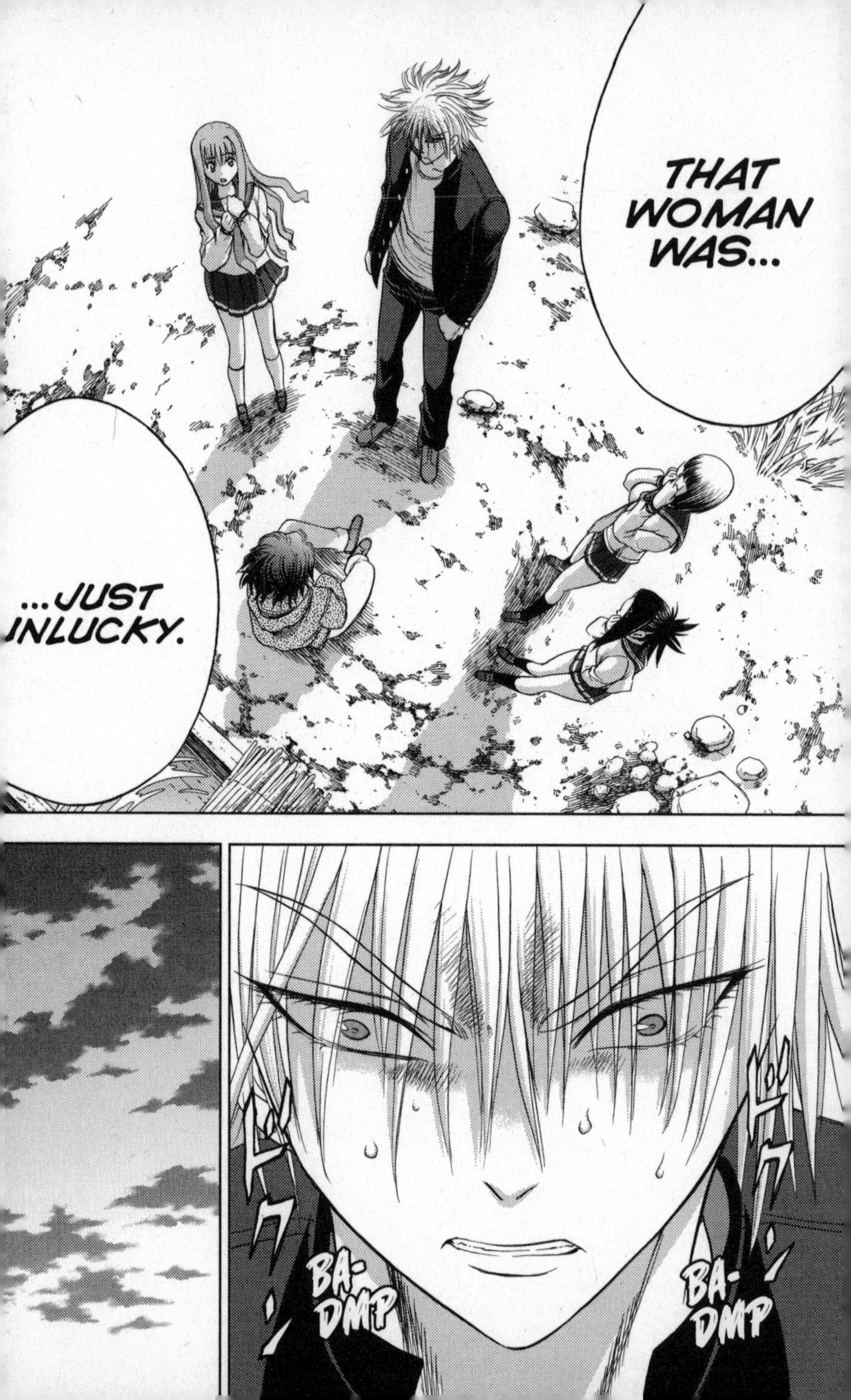
THAT WOMAN WAS...
...JUST UNLUCKY.
BA-DMP
BA-DMP

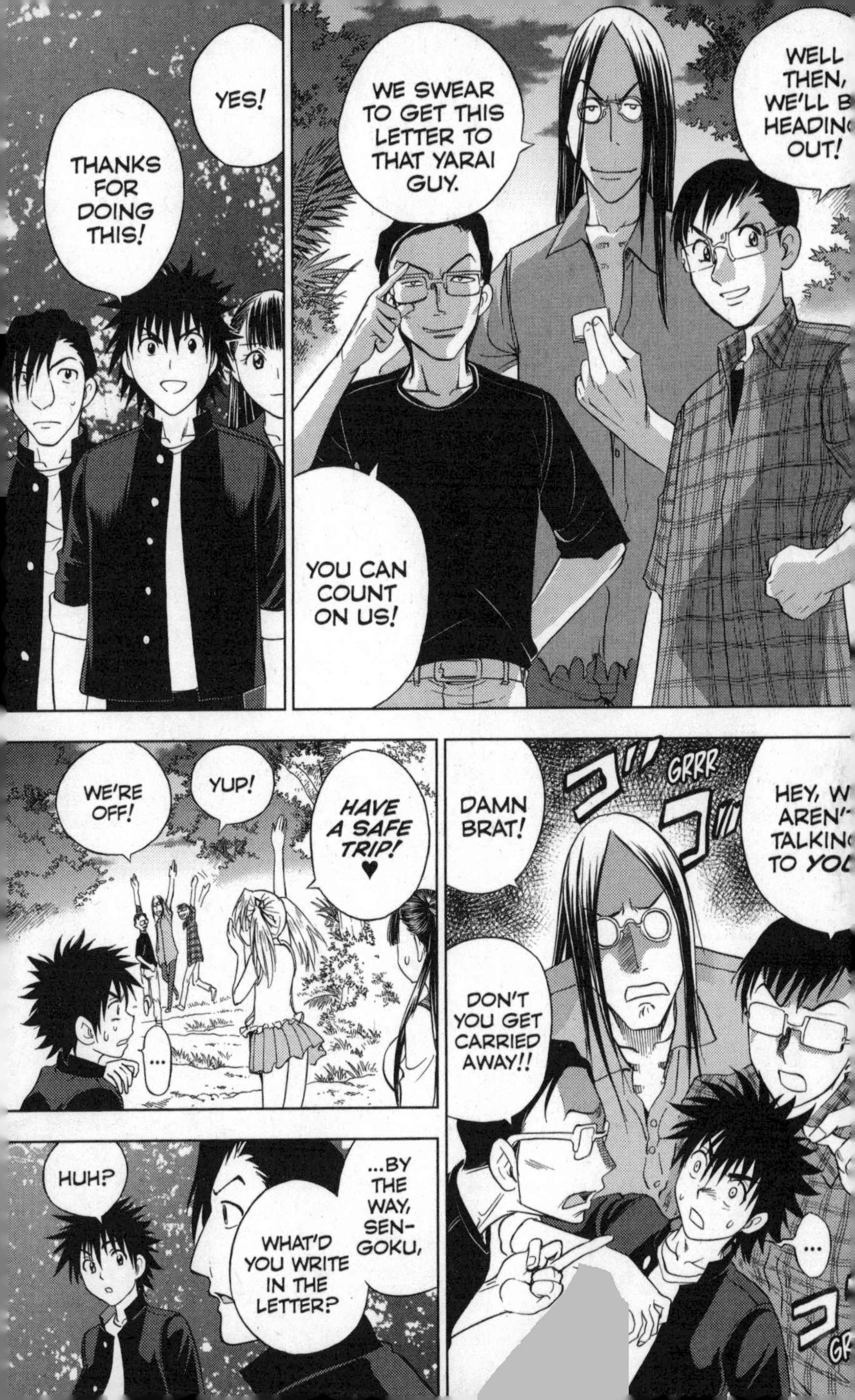
WELL THEN, WE'LL B HEADIN OUT!
WE SWEAR TO GET THIS LETTER TO THAT YARAI GUY.
YOU CAN COUNT ON US!
YES!
THANKS FOR DOING THIS!
HEY, W AREN' TALKIN TO YO
GRRR
DAMN BRAT!
DON'T YOU GET CARRIED AWAY!!
...
HAVE A SAFE TRIP! ♥
YUP!
WE'RE OFF!
...
...BY THE WAY, SEN-GOKU,
WHAT'D YOU WRITE IN THE LETTER?
HUH?

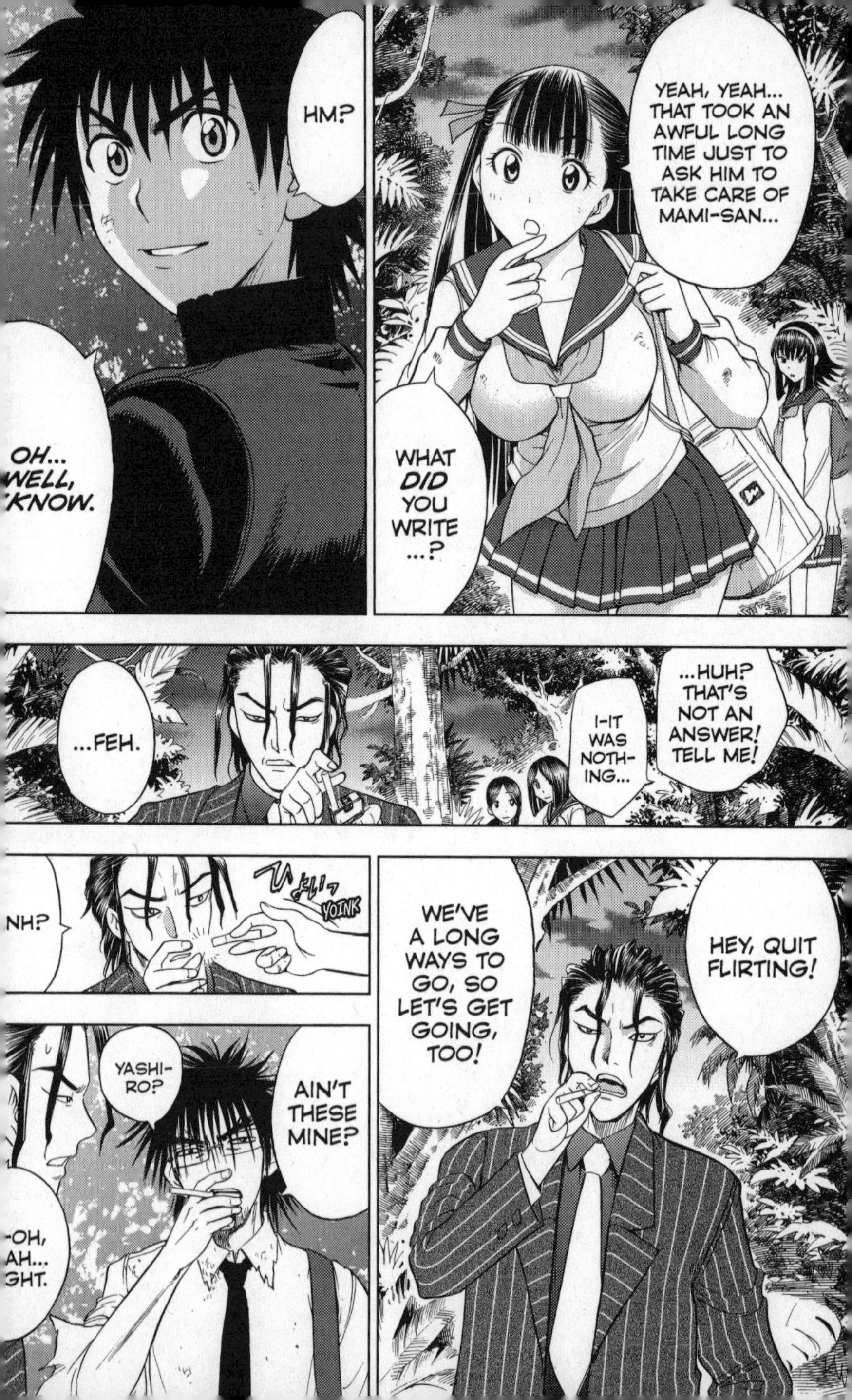
YEAH, YEAH... THAT TOOK AN AWFUL LONG TIME JUST TO ASK HIM TO TAKE CARE OF MAMI-SAN...
WHAT *DID* YOU WRITE ...?
HM?
OH... WELL, KNOW.
...HUH? THAT'S NOT AN ANSWER! TELL ME!
I-IT WAS NOTH-ING...
...FEH.
HEY, QUIT FLIRTING!
WE'VE A LONG WAYS TO GO, SO LET'S GET GOING, TOO!
NH?
YOINK
AIN'T THESE MINE?
YASHI-RO?
-OH, AH... GHT.

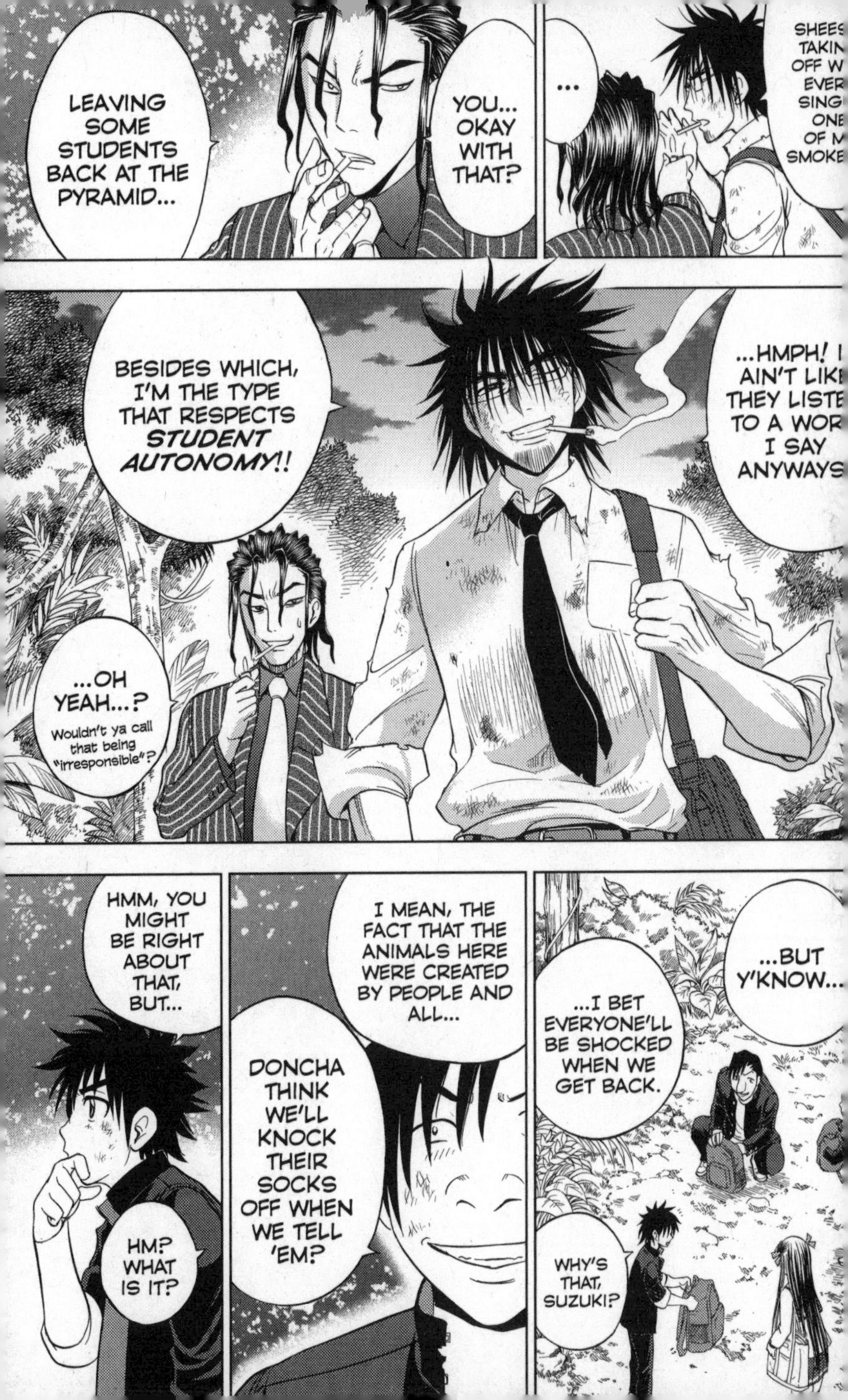
SHEES TAKIN OFF W EVER SING ONE OF M SMOKE
...
YOU... OKAY WITH THAT?
LEAVING SOME STUDENTS BACK AT THE PYRAMID...
...HMPH! I AIN'T LIKE THEY LISTE TO A WOR I SAY ANYWAYS
BESIDES WHICH, I'M THE TYPE THAT RESPECTS *STUDENT AUTONOMY*!!
...OH YEAH...?
Wouldn't ya call that being "irresponsible"?
...BUT Y'KNOW...
...I BET EVERYONE'LL BE SHOCKED WHEN WE GET BACK.
WHY'S THAT, SUZUKI!?
I MEAN, THE FACT THAT THE ANIMALS HERE WERE CREATED BY PEOPLE AND ALL...
DONCHA THINK WE'LL KNOCK THEIR SOCKS OFF WHEN WE TELL 'EM?
HMM, YOU MIGHT BE RIGHT ABOUT THAT, BUT...
HM? WHAT IS IT?

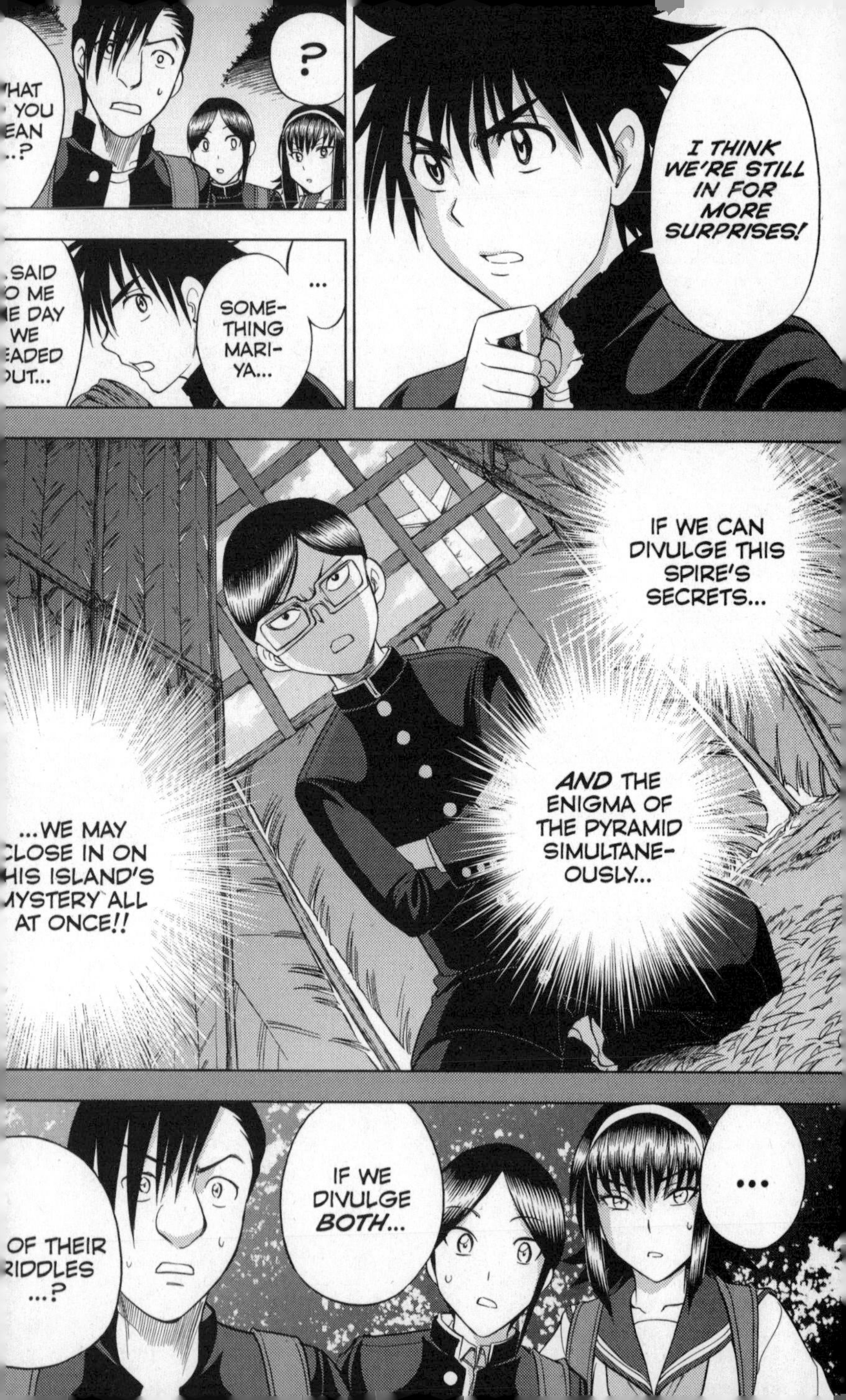

I THINK WE'RE STILL IN FOR MORE SURPRISES!
?
HAT YOU EAN ..?
...
SOME-THING MARI-YA...
SAID O ME E DAY WE EADED UT...
IF WE CAN DIVULGE THIS SPIRE'S SECRETS...
AND THE ENIGMA OF THE PYRAMID SIMULTANE-OUSLY...
...WE MAY LOSE IN ON HIS ISLAND'S MYSTERY ALL AT ONCE!!
...
IF WE DIVULGE BOTH...
OF THEIR IDDLES ...?

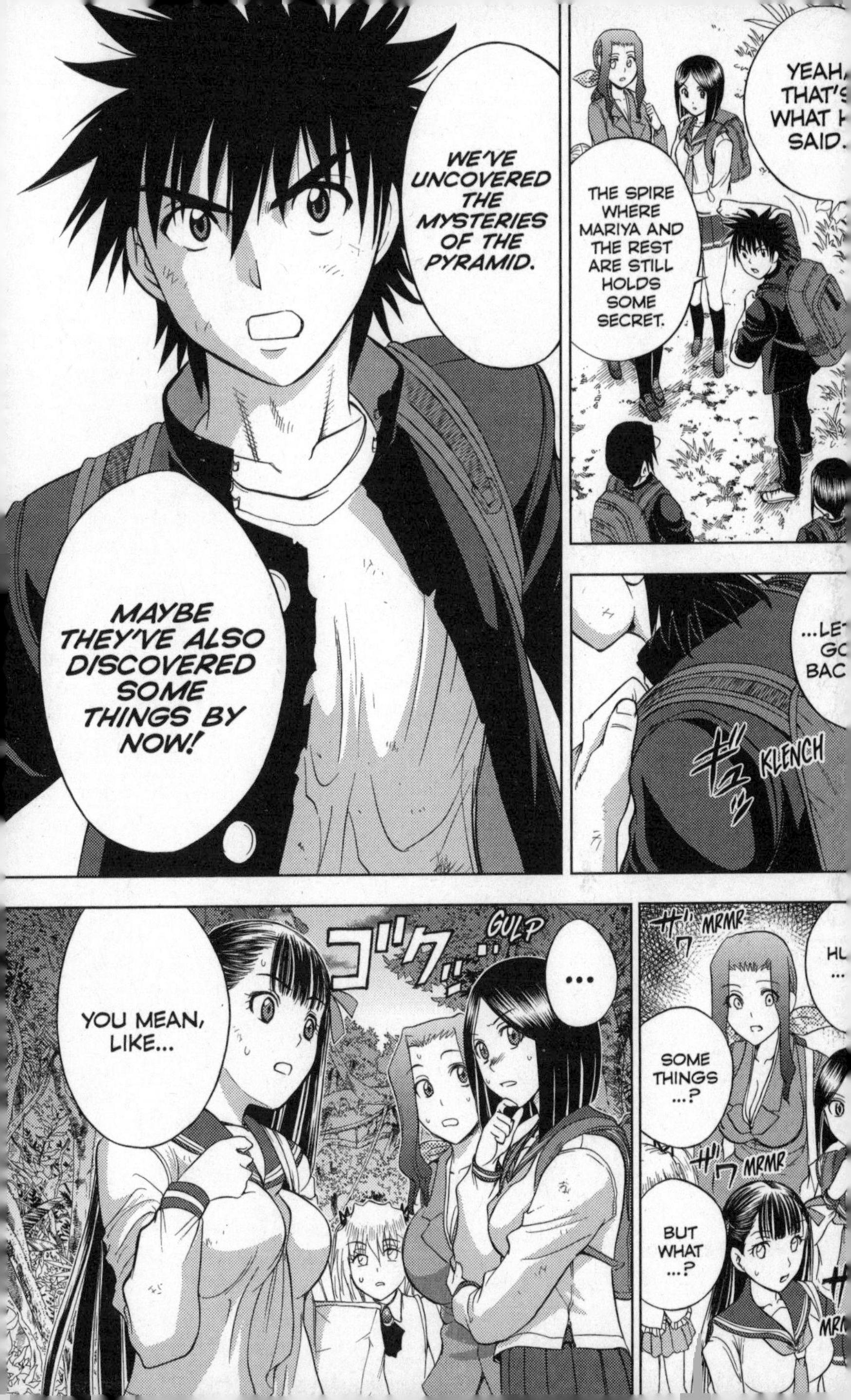
YEAH, THAT'S WHAT H SAID.
THE SPIRE WHERE MARIYA AND THE REST ARE STILL HOLDS SOME SECRET.
...LET GO BAC
KLENCH
WE'VE UNCOVERED THE MYSTERIES OF THE PYRAMID.
MAYBE THEY'VE ALSO DISCOVERED SOME THINGS BY NOW!
MRMR
HU ...
SOME THINGS ...?
MRMR
BUT WHAT ...?
MRM
GULP
...
YOU MEAN, LIKE...

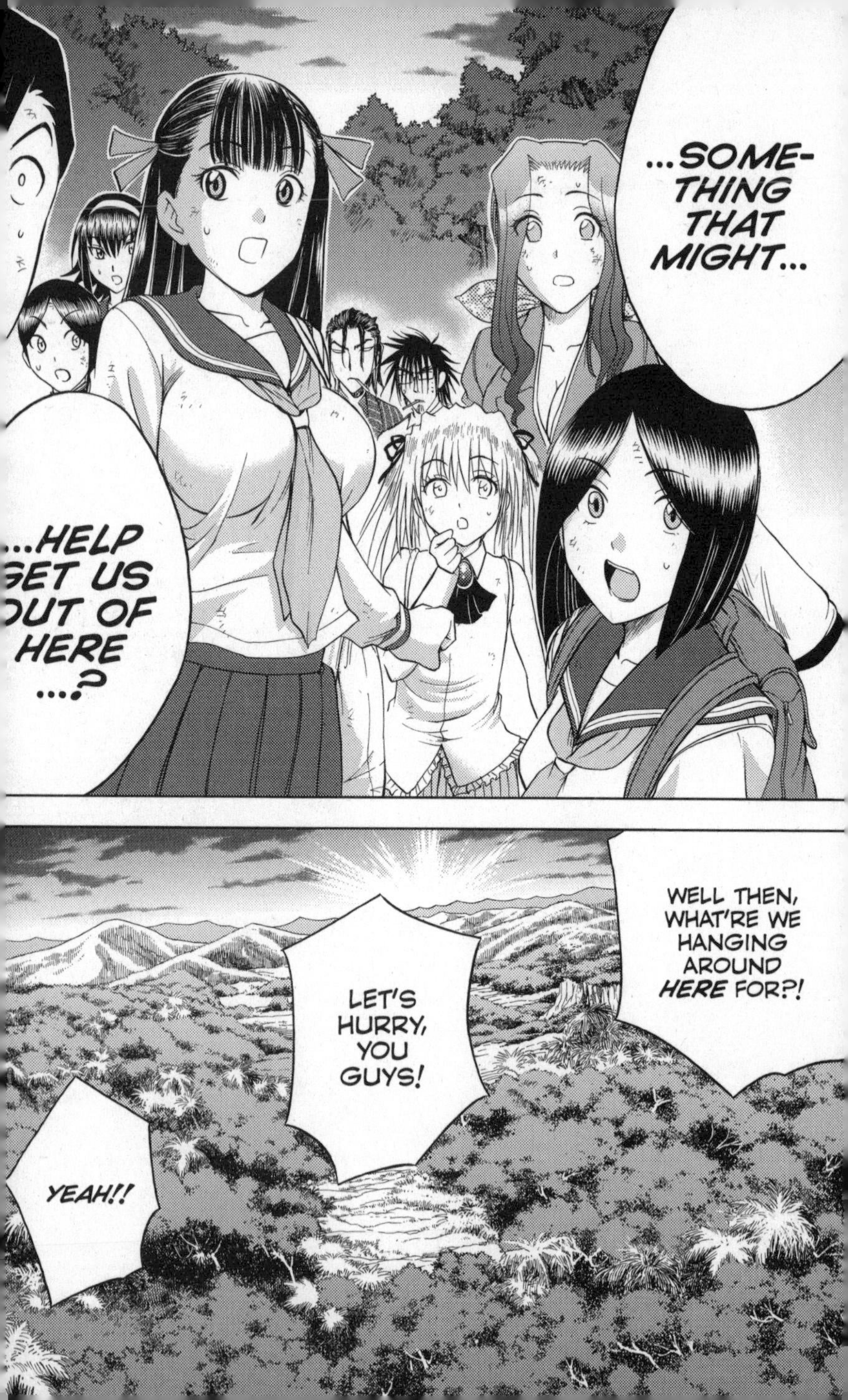
...SOME-THING THAT MIGHT...
...HELP GET US OUT OF HERE ...?
WELL THEN, WHAT'RE WE HANGING AROUND *HERE* FOR?!
LET'S HURRY, YOU GUYS!
YEAH!!

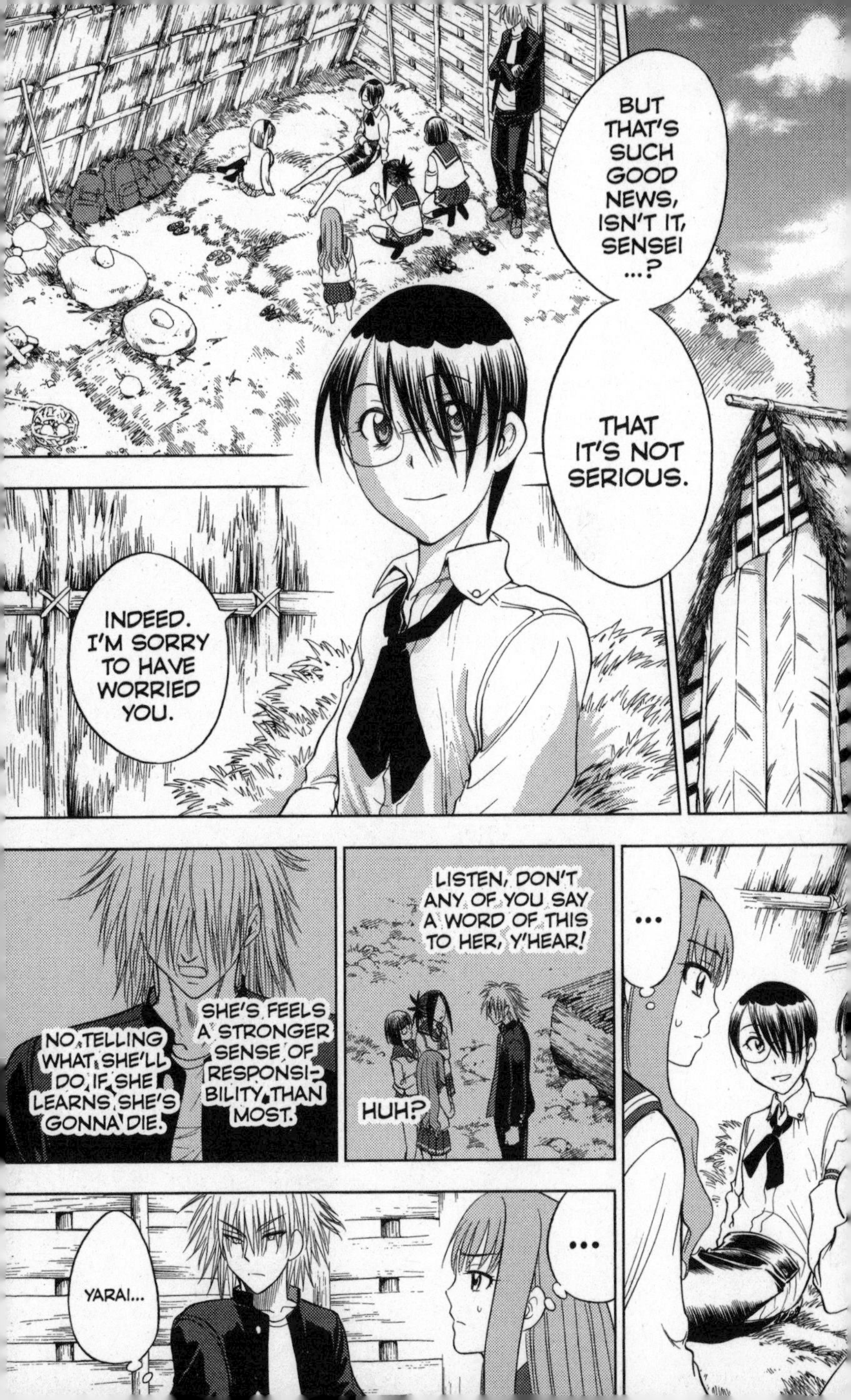

BUT THAT'S SUCH GOOD NEWS, ISN'T IT, SENSEI ...?
THAT IT'S NOT SERIOUS.
INDEED. I'M SORRY TO HAVE WORRIED YOU.
...
LISTEN, DON'T ANY OF YOU SAY A WORD OF THIS TO HER, Y'HEAR!
HUH?
SHE'S FEELS A STRONGER SENSE OF RESPONSI-BILITY THAN MOST.
NO TELLING WHAT SHE'LL DO IF SHE LEARNS SHE'S GONNA DIE.
...
YARAI...

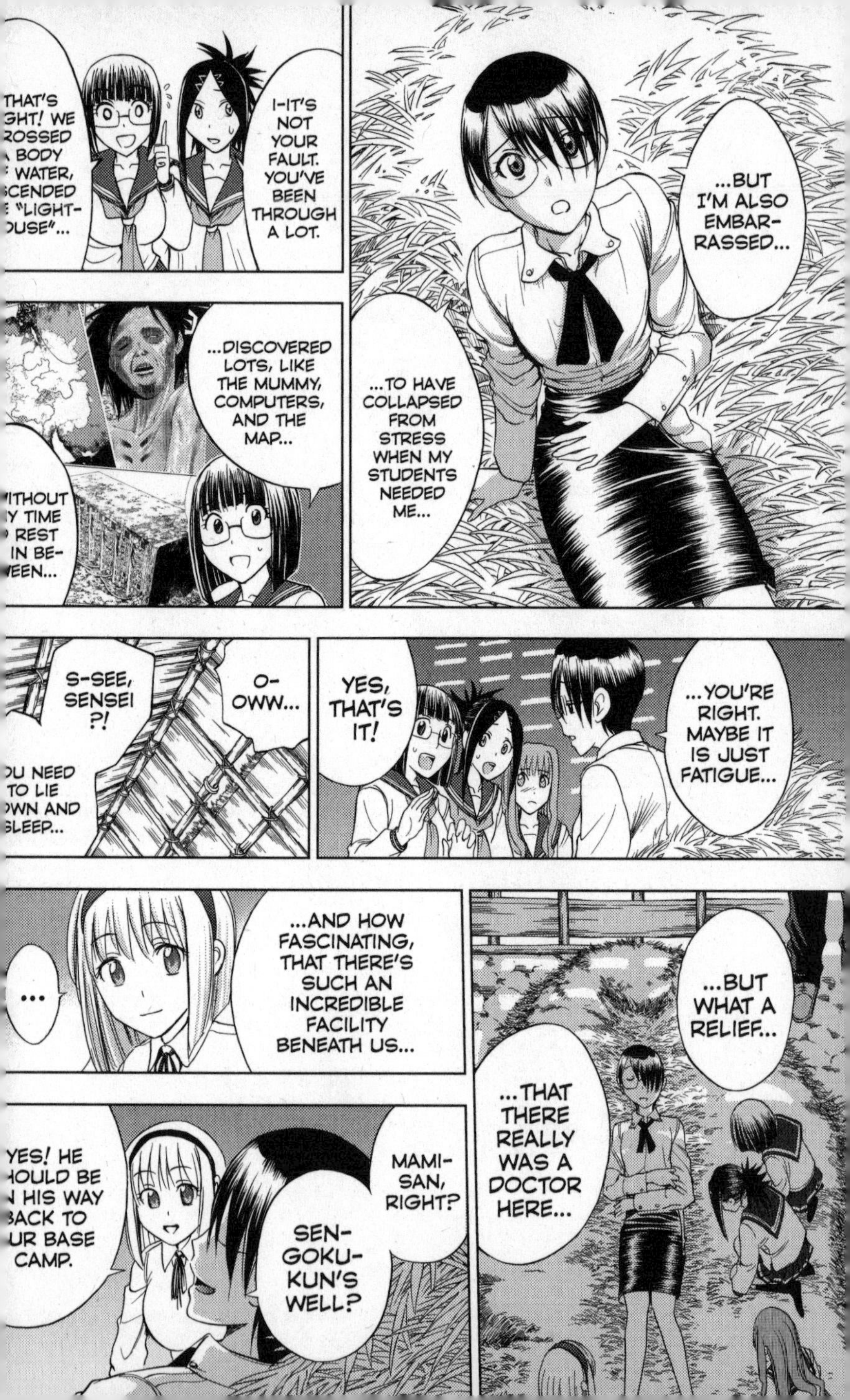
...BUT I'M ALSO EMBARRASSED...
...TO HAVE COLLAPSED FROM STRESS WHEN MY STUDENTS NEEDED ME...
I-IT'S NOT YOUR FAULT. YOU'VE BEEN THROUGH A LOT.
THAT'S GHT! WE ROSSED A BODY WATER, SCENDED "LIGHT- OUSE"...
...DISCOVERED LOTS, LIKE THE MUMMY, COMPUTERS, AND THE MAP...
ITHOUT Y TIME REST IN BE- EEN...
...YOU'RE RIGHT. MAYBE IT IS JUST FATIGUE...
YES, THAT'S IT!
O-OWW...
S-SEE, SENSEI ?!
OU NEED TO LIE OWN AND LEEP...
...BUT WHAT A RELIEF...
...THAT THERE REALLY WAS A DOCTOR HERE...
...AND HOW FASCINATING, THAT THERE'S SUCH AN INCREDIBLE FACILITY BENEATH US...
...
MAMI-SAN, RIGHT?
SEN-GOKU-KUN'S WELL?
YES! HE HOULD BE N HIS WAY BACK TO UR BASE CAMP.

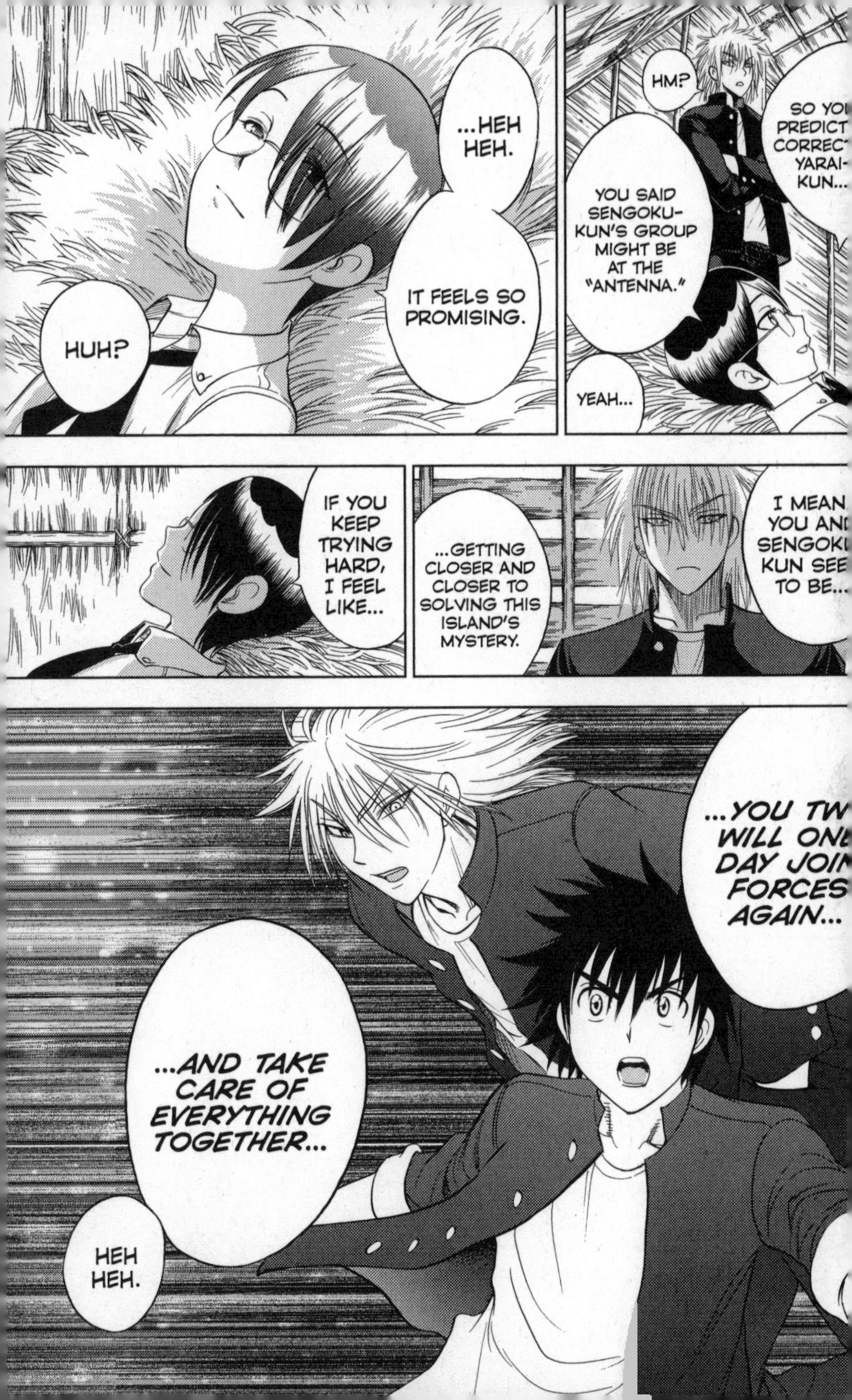
SO YO PREDICT CORRECT YARAI-KUN...
HM?
YOU SAID SENGOKU-KUN'S GROUP MIGHT BE AT THE "ANTENNA."
YEAH...
...HEH HEH.
IT FEELS SO PROMISING.
HUH?
I MEAN, YOU AN SENGOK KUN SEE TO BE...
...GETTING CLOSER AND CLOSER TO SOLVING THIS ISLAND'S MYSTERY.
IF YOU KEEP TRYING HARD, I FEEL LIKE...
...YOU TW WILL ON DAY JOI FORCES AGAIN...
...AND TAKE CARE OF EVERYTHING TOGETHER...
HEH HEH.

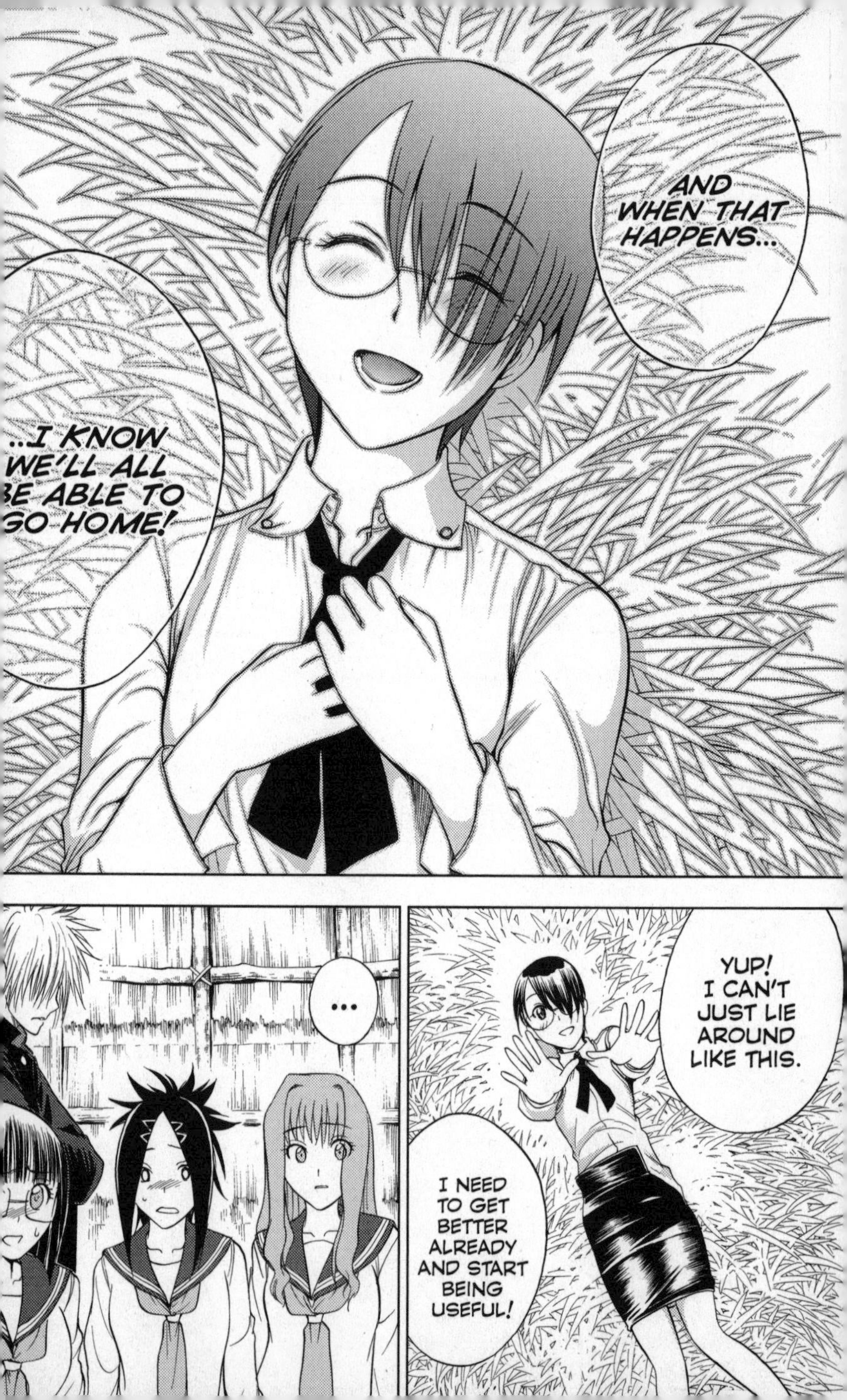
AND WHEN THAT HAPPENS...
..I KNOW WE'LL ALL BE ABLE TO GO HOME!
YUP! I CAN'T JUST LIE AROUND LIKE THIS.
I NEED TO GET BETTER ALREADY AND START BEING USEFUL!
...

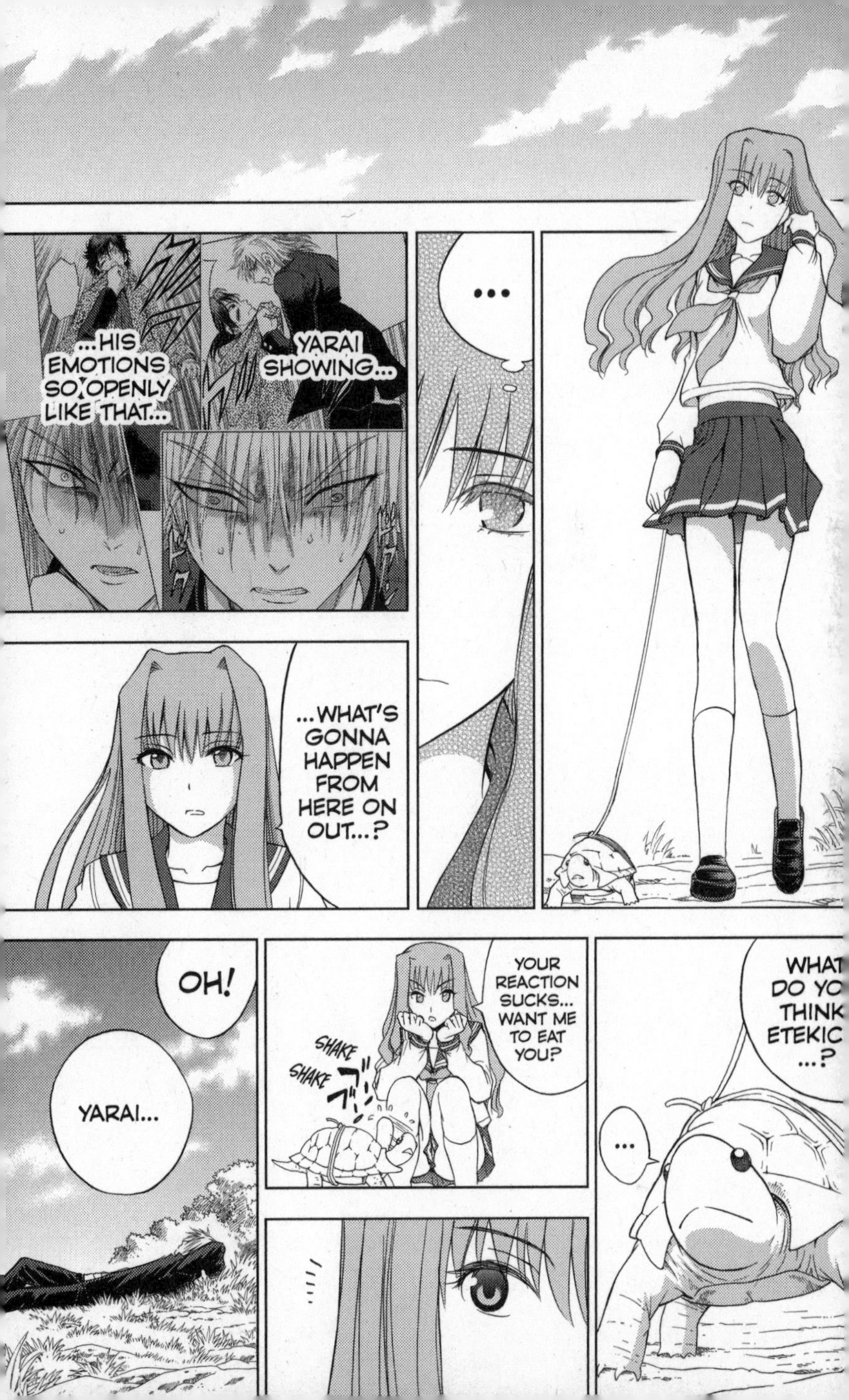
...
YARAI SHOWING...
...HIS EMOTIONS SO OPENLY LIKE THAT...
...WHAT'S GONNA HAPPEN FROM HERE ON OUT...?
WHAT DO YO THINK ETEKIC ...?
...
YOUR REACTION SUCKS... WANT ME TO EAT YOU?
SHAKE
SHAKE
OH!
YARAI...

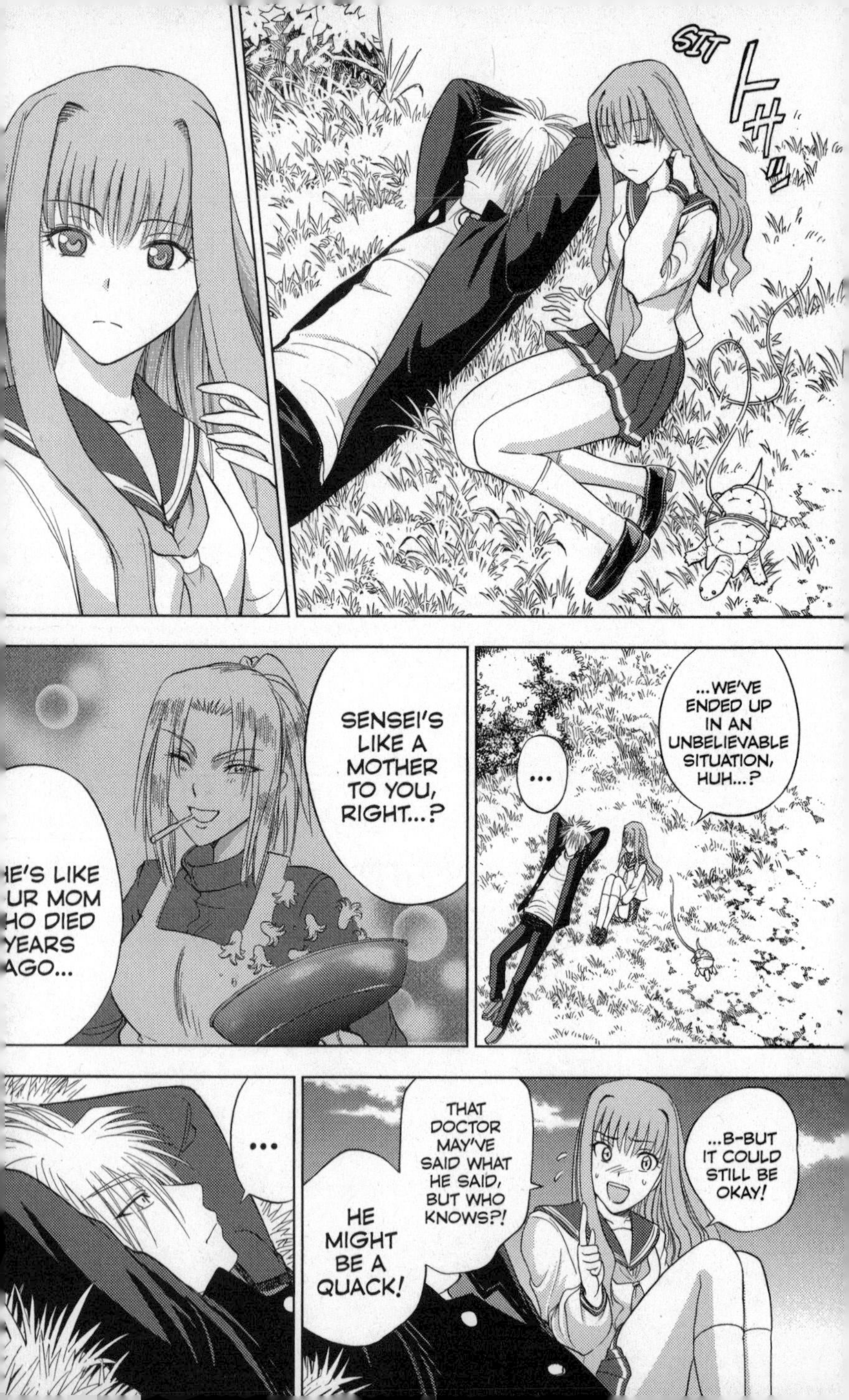
SIT
トサッ
...WE'VE ENDED UP IN AN UNBELIEVABLE SITUATION, HUH...?
...
SENSEI'S LIKE A MOTHER TO YOU, RIGHT...?
E'S LIKE UR MOM HO DIED YEARS AGO...
...B-BUT IT COULD STILL BE OKAY!
THAT DOCTOR MAY'VE SAID WHAT HE SAID, BUT WHO KNOWS?!
HE MIGHT BE A QUACK!
...

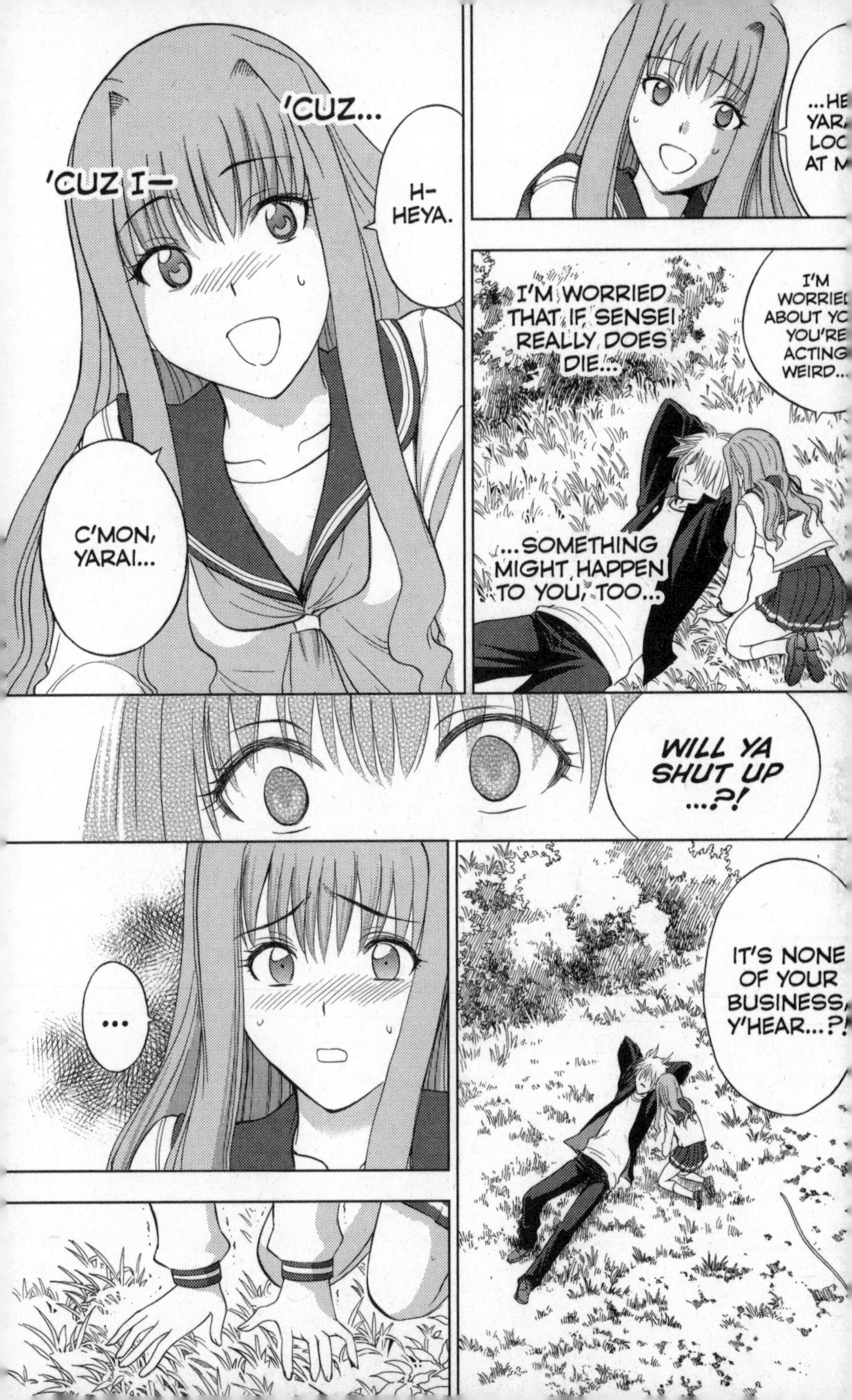
...HE YARA LOO AT M
I'M WORRIED ABOUT YO YOU'RE ACTING WEIRD...
I'M WORRIED THAT IF SENSEI REALLY DOES DIE...
...SOMETHING MIGHT HAPPEN TO YOU, TOO...
H- HEYA.
'CUZ...
'CUZ I—
C'MON, YARAI...
WILL YA SHUT UP ...?!
IT'S NONE OF YOUR BUSINESS, Y'HEAR...?!
...

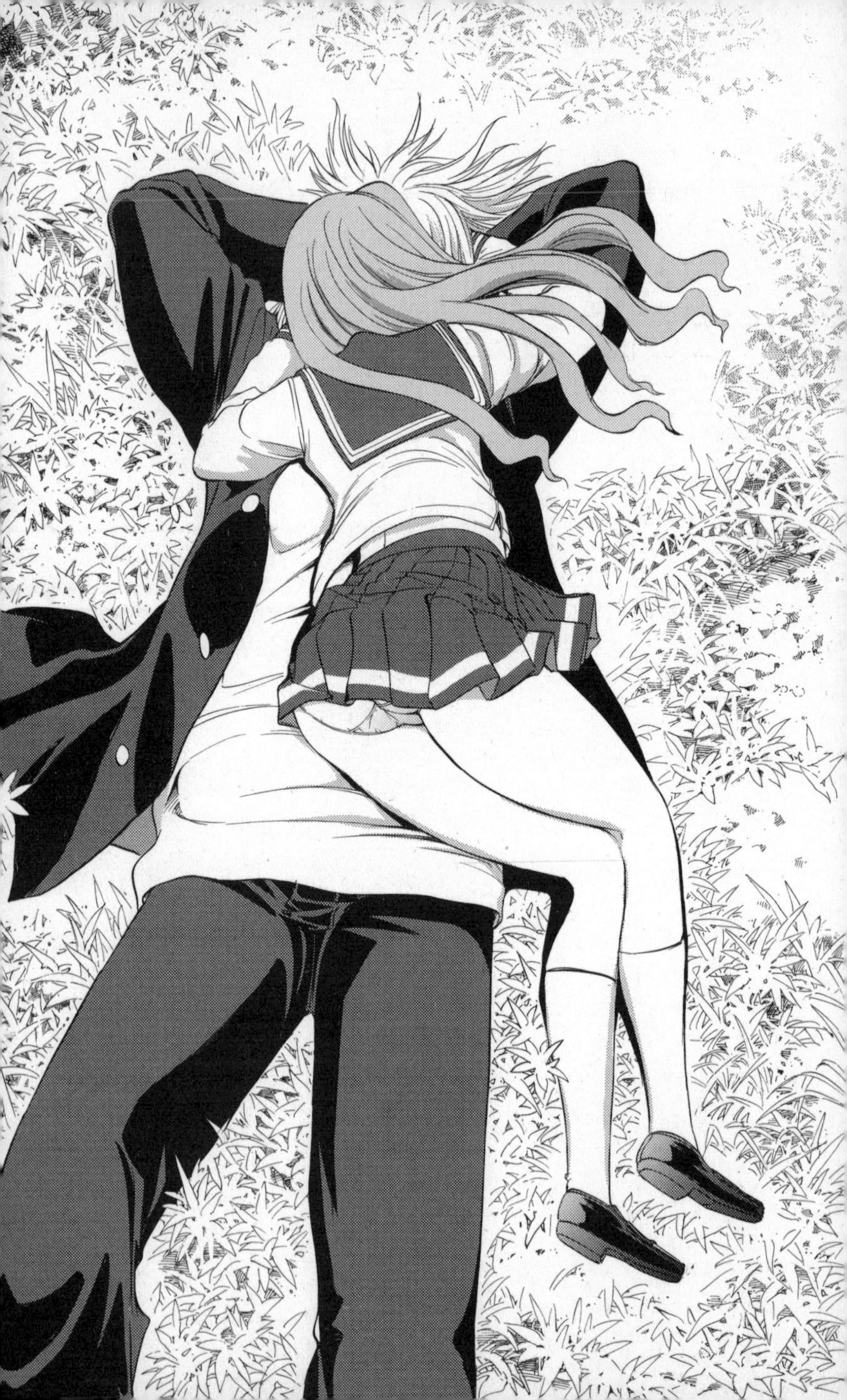

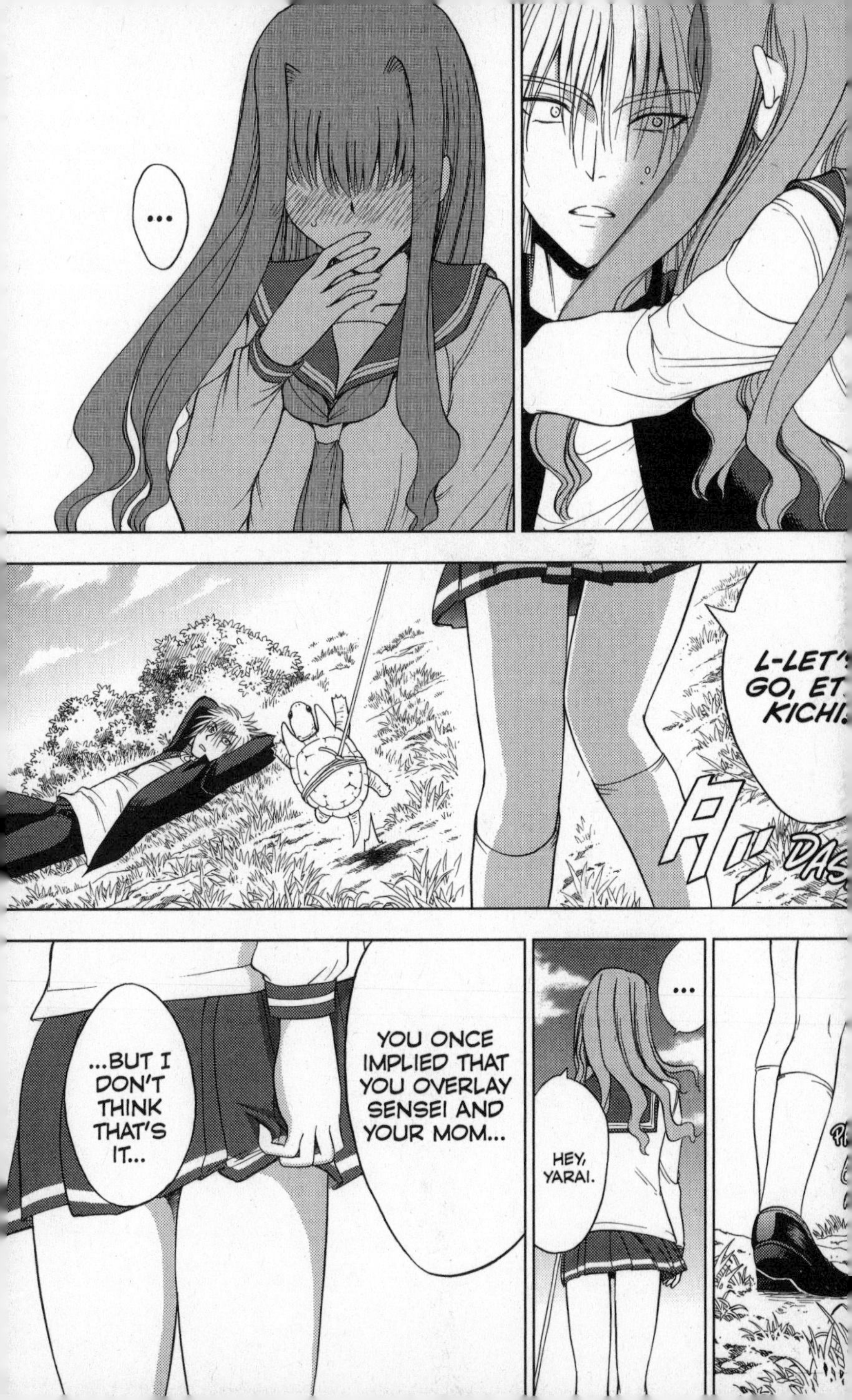

...
L-LET' GO, ET KICHI.
DAS
...
HEY, YARAI.
YOU ONCE IMPLIED THAT YOU OVERLAY SENSEI AND YOUR MOM...
...BUT I DON'T THINK THAT'S IT...

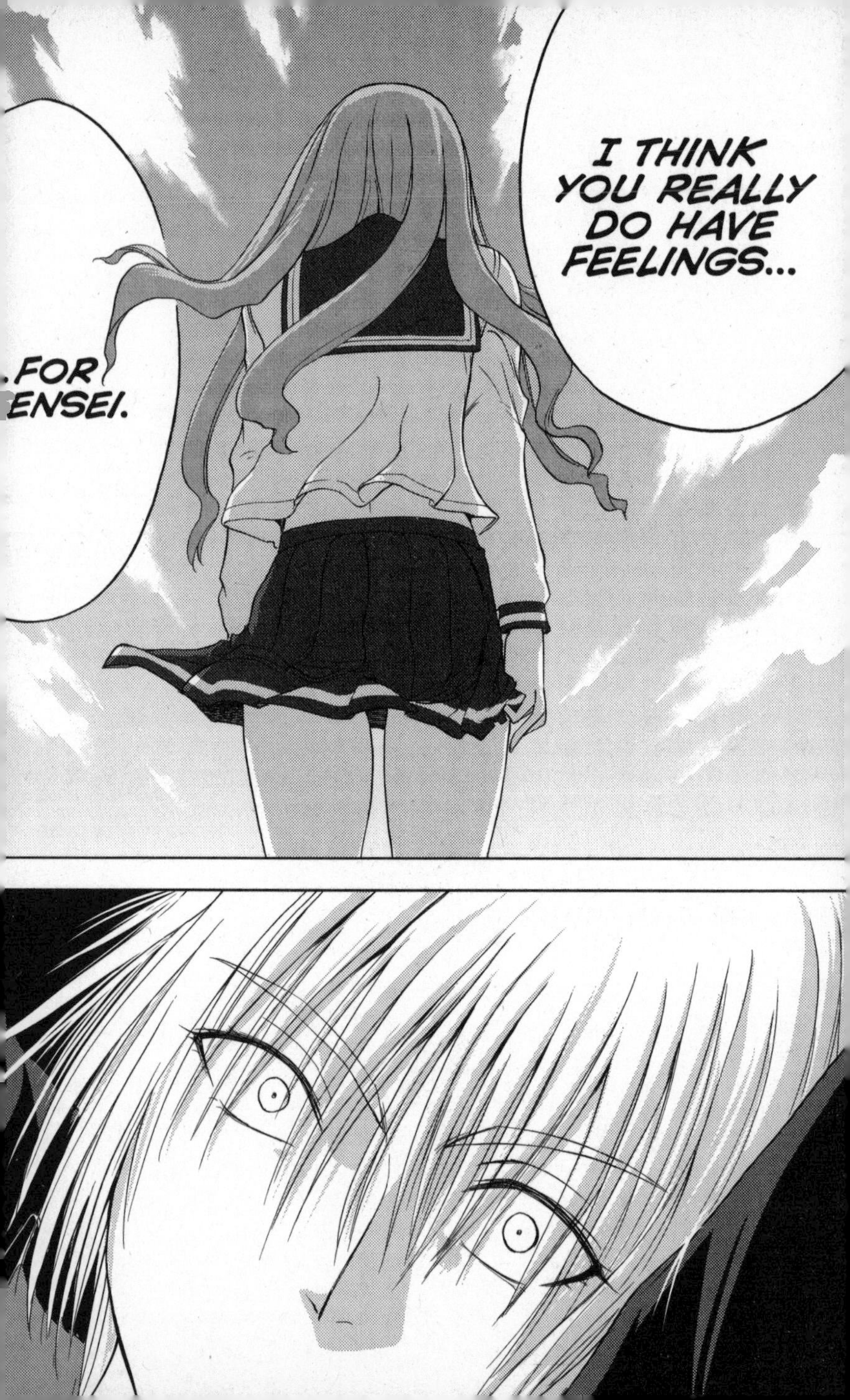
I THINK YOU REALLY DO HAVE FEELINGS...
.FOR ENSEI.

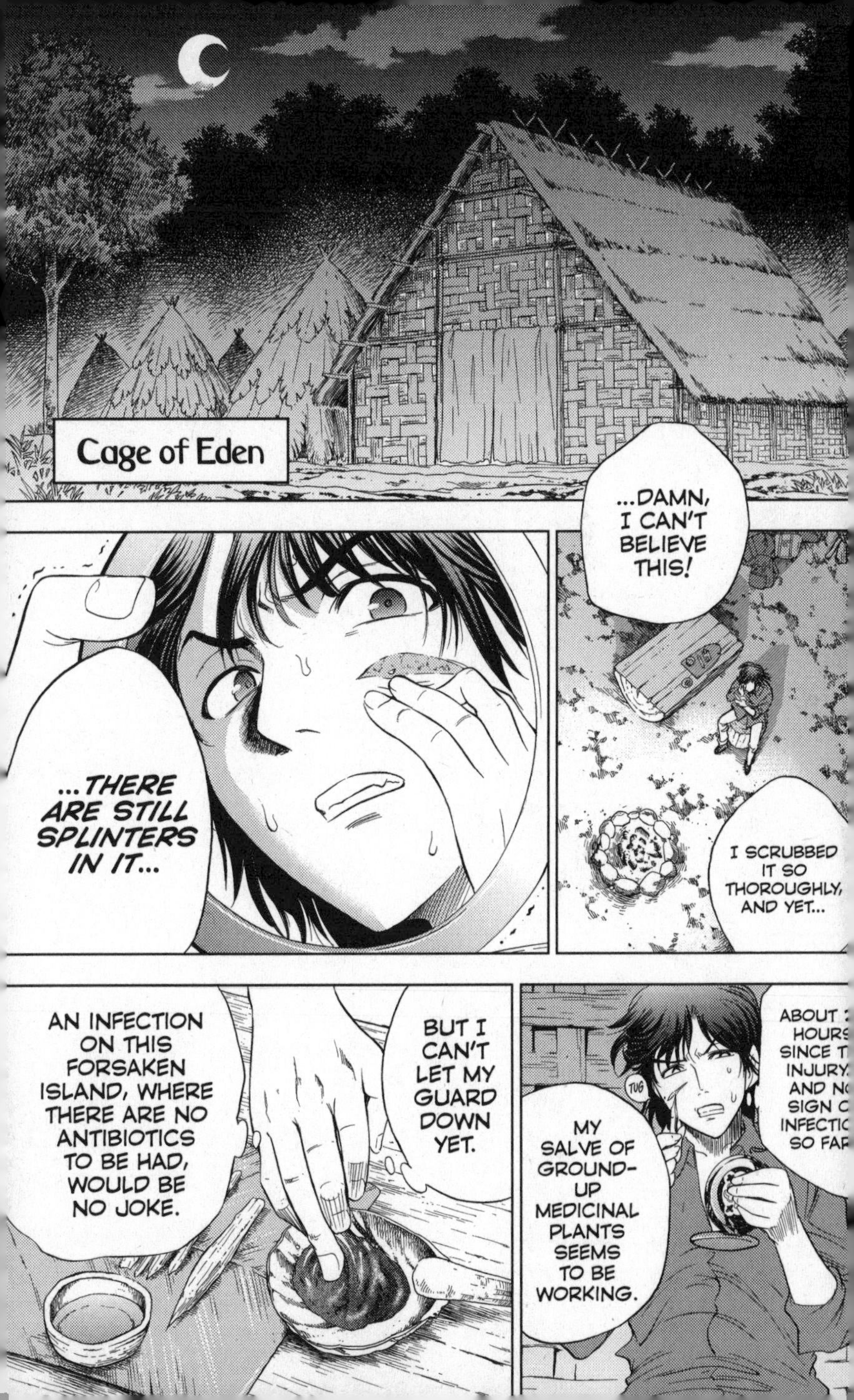
Cage of Eden
...DAMN, I CAN'T BELIEVE THIS!
I SCRUBBED IT SO THOROUGHLY, AND YET...
...THERE ARE STILL SPLINTERS IN IT...
ABOUT HOURS SINCE T INJURY AND N SIGN C INFECTIC SO FAR
TUG
MY SALVE OF GROUND-UP MEDICINAL PLANTS SEEMS TO BE WORKING.
BUT I CAN'T LET MY GUARD DOWN YET.
AN INFECTION ON THIS FORSAKEN ISLAND, WHERE THERE ARE NO ANTIBIOTICS TO BE HAD, WOULD BE NO JOKE.

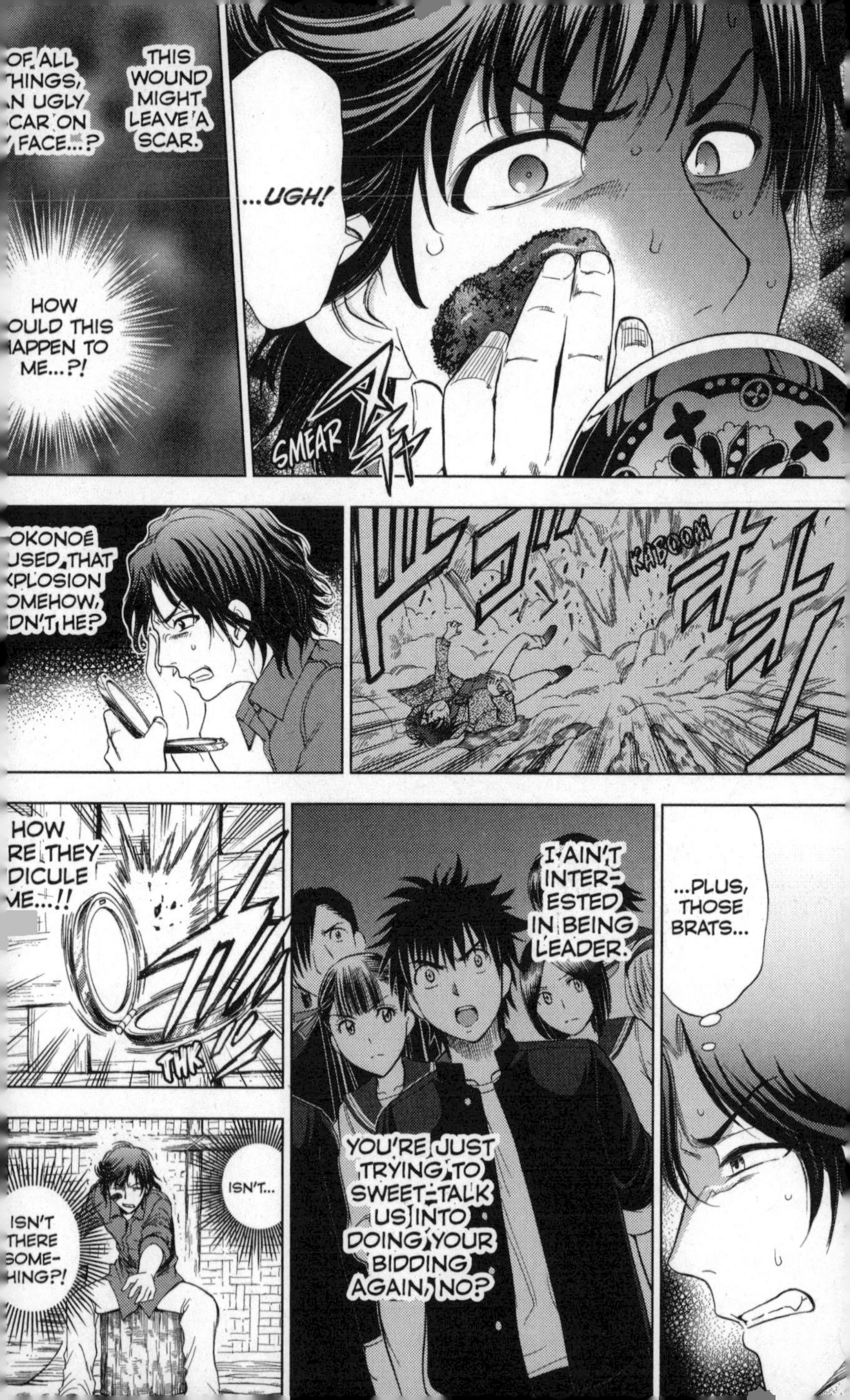
...UGH!
SMEAR
THIS WOUND MIGHT LEAVE A SCAR.
OF ALL THINGS, N UGLY CAR ON FACE...?
HOW OULD THIS APPEN TO ME...?!
KABOOM
OKONOE USED THAT XPLOSION OMEHOW, DN'T HE?
...PLUS, THOSE BRATS...
I AIN'T INTER-ESTED IN BEING LEADER.
YOU'RE JUST TRYING TO SWEET-TALK US INTO DOING YOUR BIDDING AGAIN, NO?
HOW RE THEY DICULE ME...!!
THK
ISN'T...
ISN'T THERE OME-HING?!

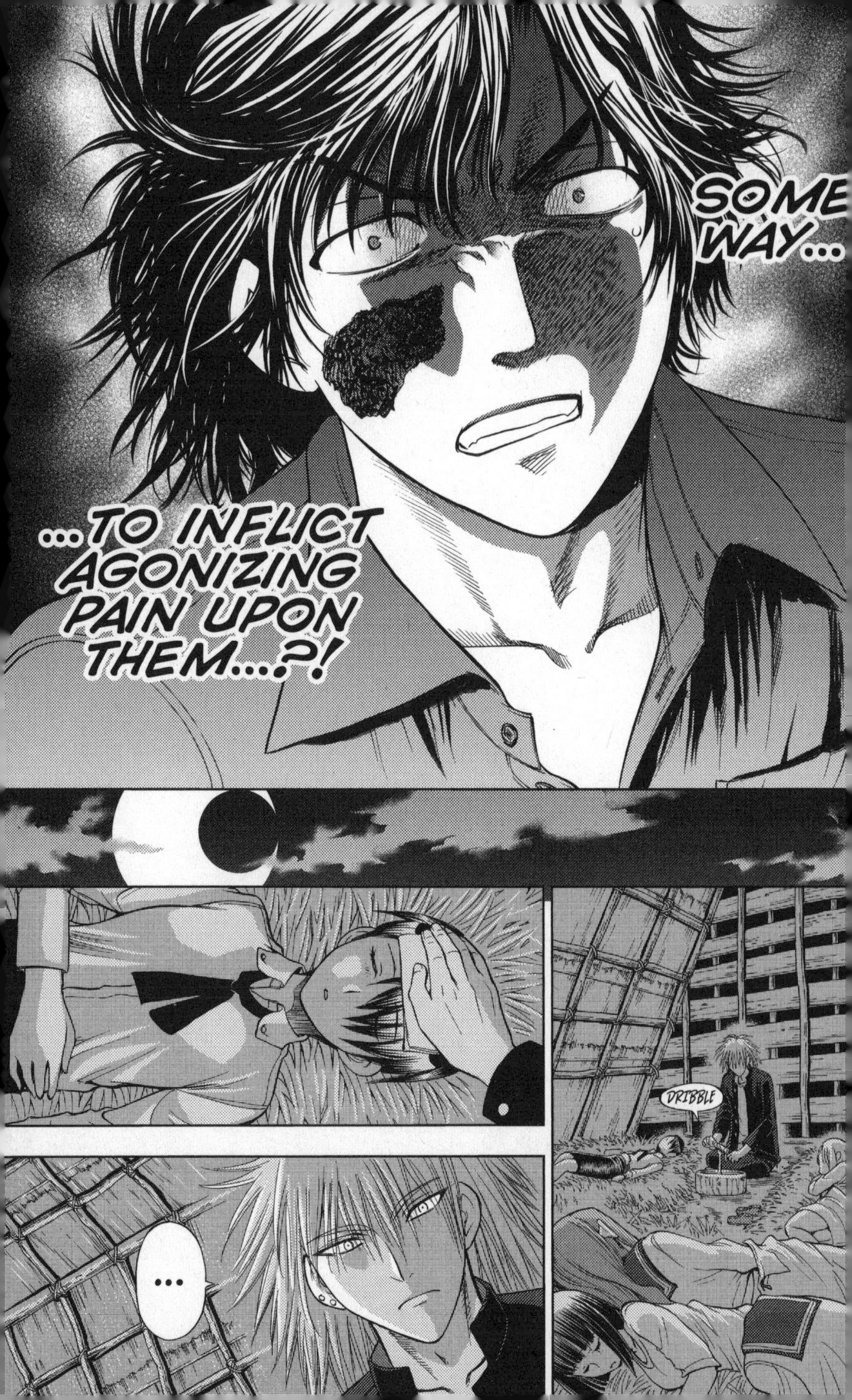
SOME WAY...
...TO INFLICT AGONIZING PAIN UPON THEM...?!
DRIBBLE
...

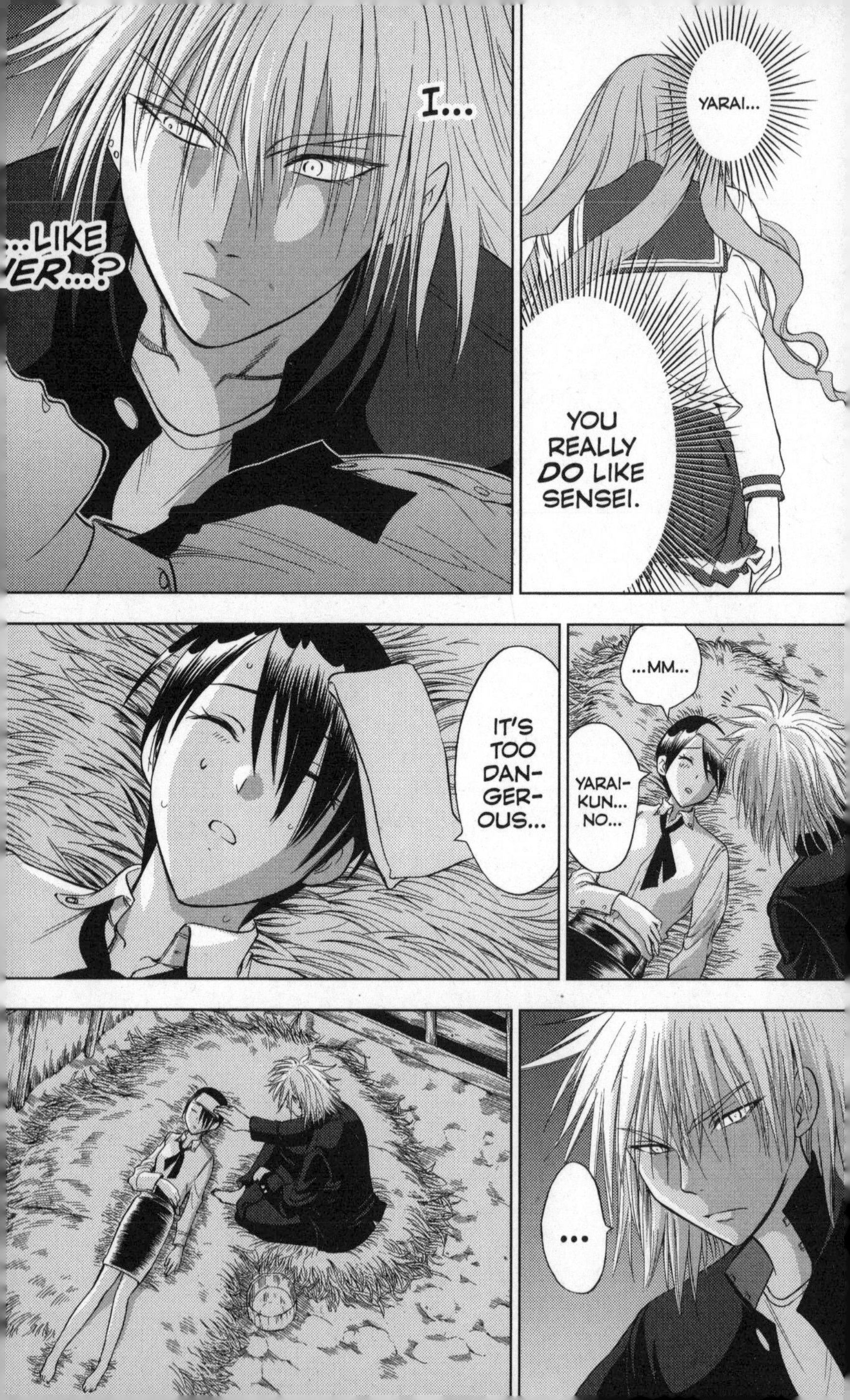
YARAI...
YOU REALLY *DO* LIKE SENSEI.
I...
...LIKE ER...?
...MM...
YARAI-KUN... NO...
IT'S TOO DAN-GER-OUS...
...

Chapter 134: Mami's Vision

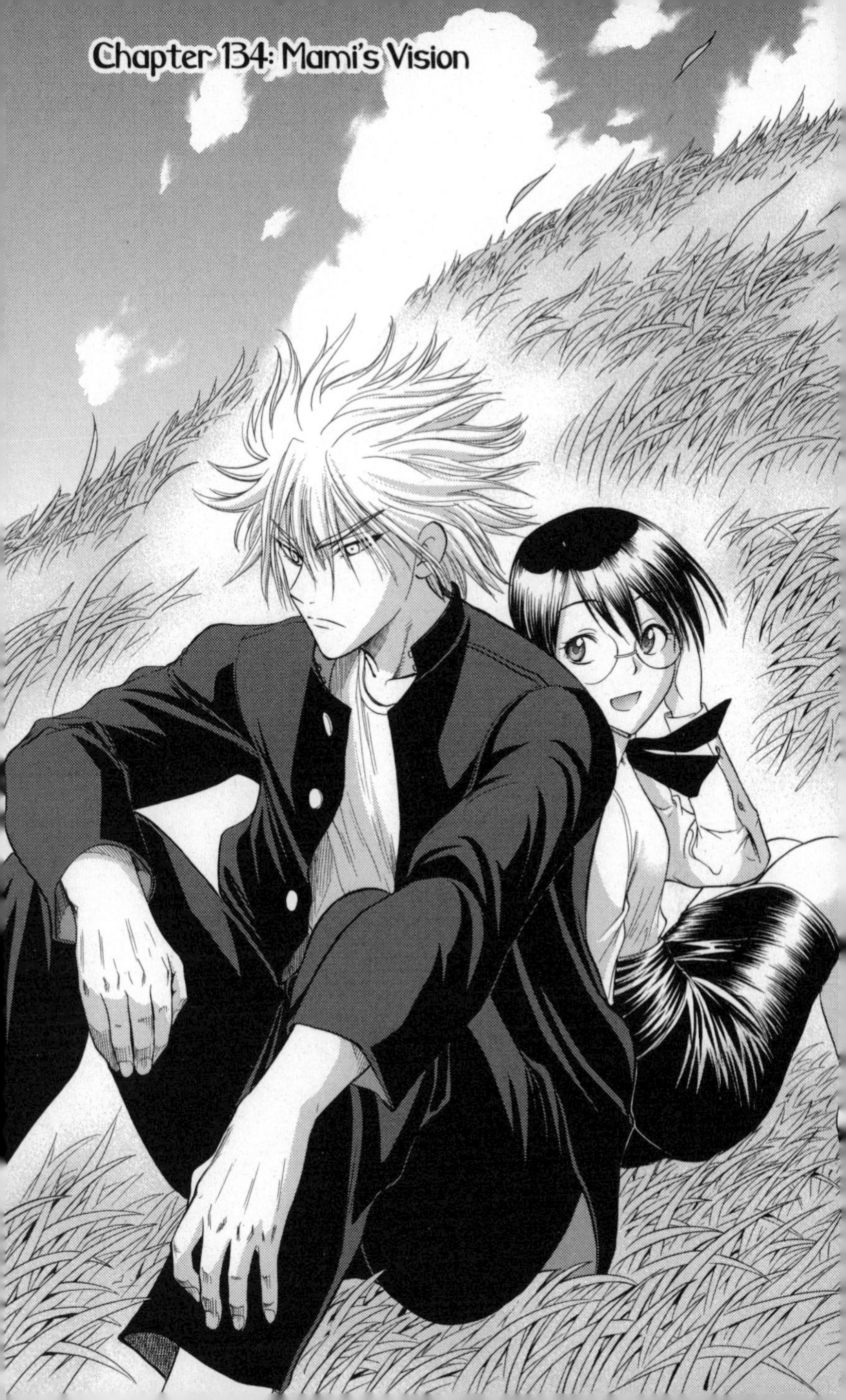

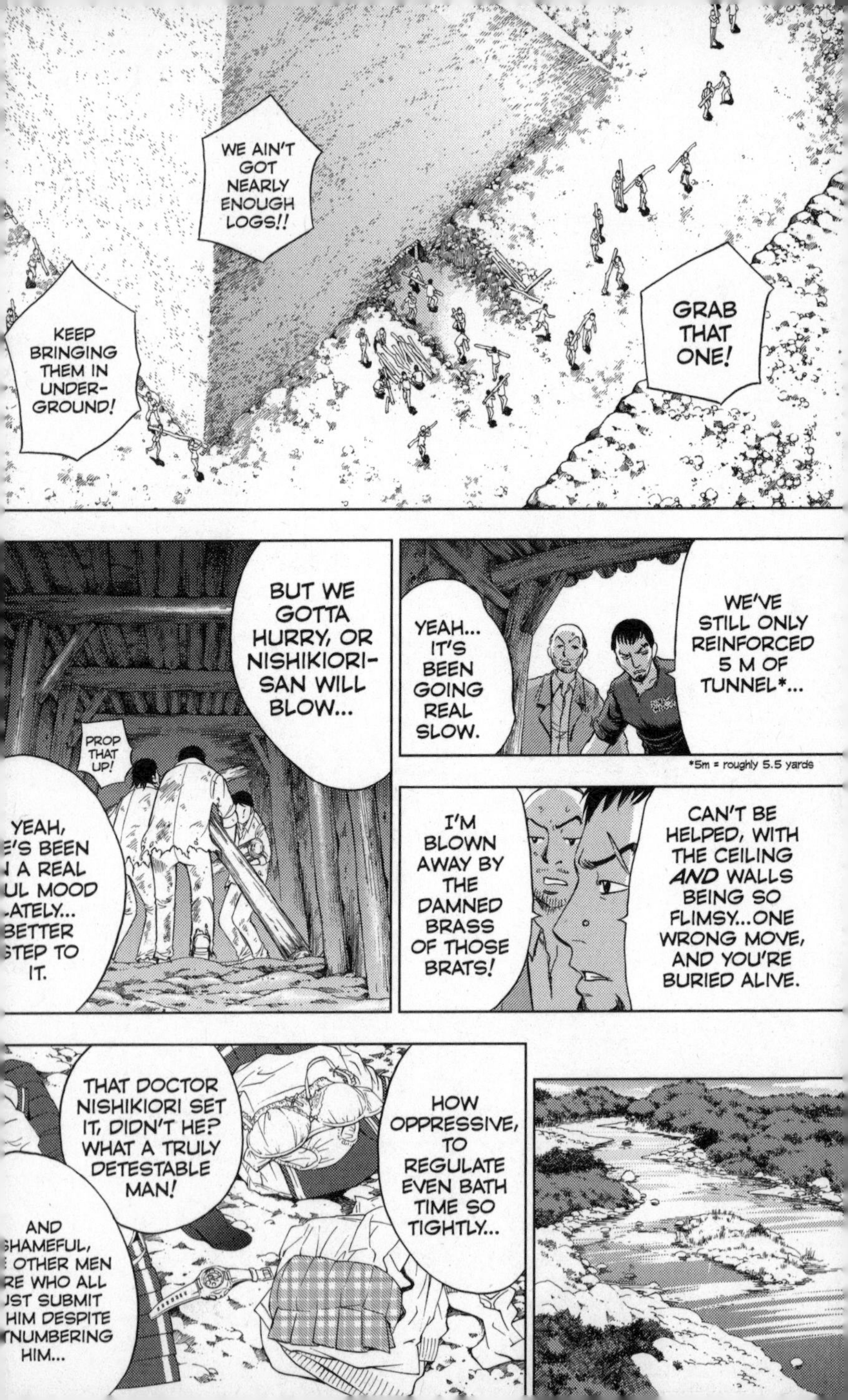
GRAB THAT ONE!
WE AIN'T GOT NEARLY ENOUGH LOGS!!
KEEP BRINGING THEM IN UNDER-GROUND!
WE'VE STILL ONLY REINFORCED 5 M OF TUNNEL*...
YEAH... IT'S BEEN GOING REAL SLOW.
*5m = roughly 5.5 yards
CAN'T BE HELPED, WITH THE CEILING *AND* WALLS BEING SO FLIMSY...ONE WRONG MOVE, AND YOU'RE BURIED ALIVE.
I'M BLOWN AWAY BY THE DAMNED BRASS OF THOSE BRATS!
BUT WE GOTTA HURRY, OR NISHIKIORI-SAN WILL BLOW...
PROP THAT UP!
YEAH, E'S BEEN N A REAL UL MOOD LATELY... BETTER STEP TO IT.
HOW OPPRESSIVE, TO REGULATE EVEN BATH TIME SO TIGHTLY...
THAT DOCTOR NISHIKIORI SET IT, DIDN'T HE? WHAT A TRULY DETESTABLE MAN!
AND SHAMEFUL, OTHER MEN RE WHO ALL UST SUBMIT HIM DESPITE TNUMBERING HIM...

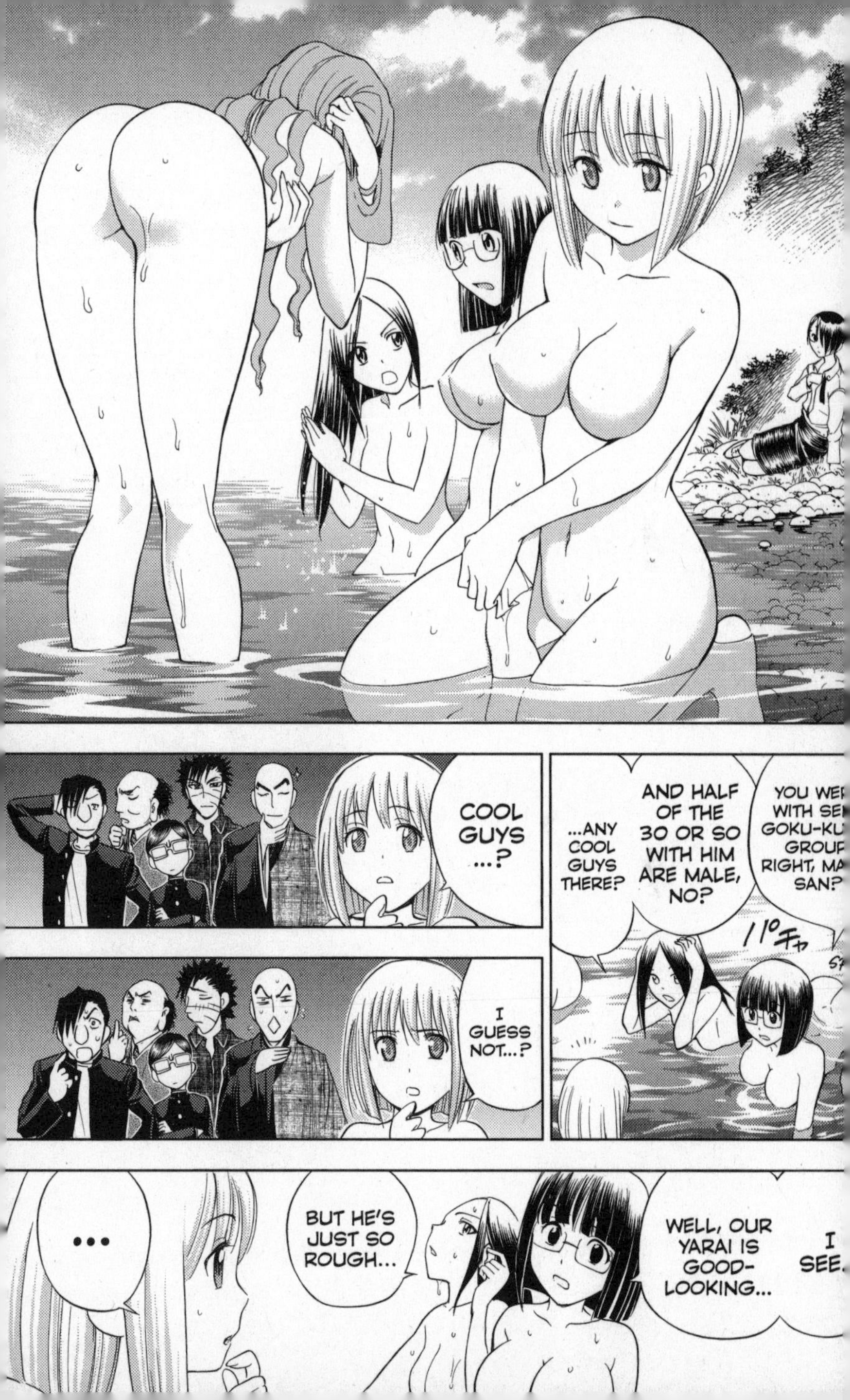
YOU WE WITH SE GOKU-KU GROUP RIGHT, MA SAN?
AND HALF OF THE 30 OR SO WITH HIM ARE MALE, NO?
...ANY COOL GUYS THERE?
パチャ
COOL GUYS ...?
I GUESS NOT...?
I SEE.
WELL, OUR YARAI IS GOOD-LOOKING...
BUT HE'S JUST SO ROUGH...
...

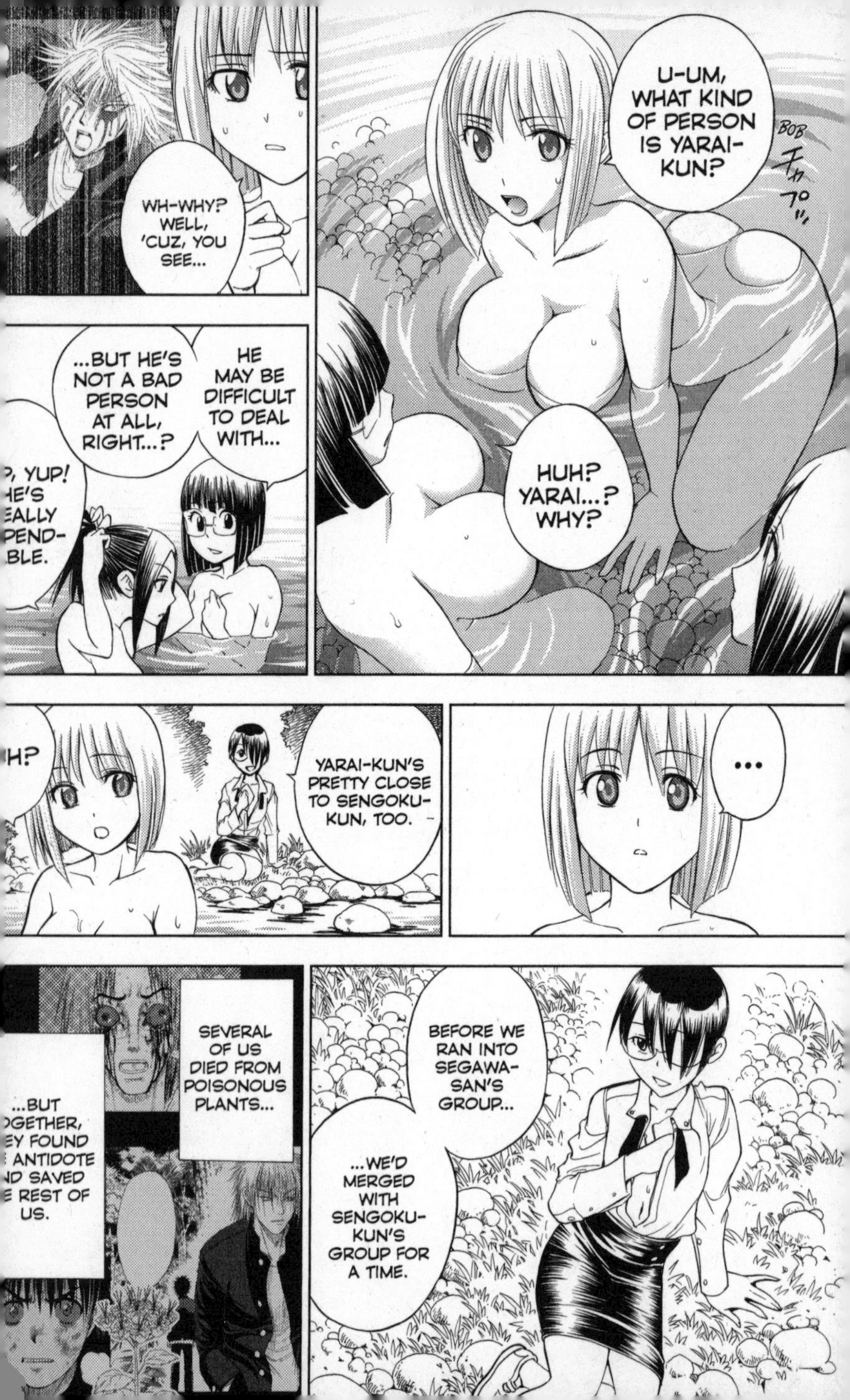
U-UM, WHAT KIND OF PERSON IS YARAI-KUN?
BOB
HUH? YARAI...? WHY?
WH-WHY? WELL, 'CUZ, YOU SEE...
HE MAY BE DIFFICULT TO DEAL WITH...
...BUT HE'S NOT A BAD PERSON AT ALL, RIGHT...?
P, YUP! HE'S EALLY PENDABLE.
...
YARAI-KUN'S PRETTY CLOSE TO SENGOKU-KUN, TOO.
H?
BEFORE WE RAN INTO SEGAWA-SAN'S GROUP...
...WE'D MERGED WITH SENGOKU-KUN'S GROUP FOR A TIME.
SEVERAL OF US DIED FROM POISONOUS PLANTS...
...BUT OGETHER, EY FOUND E ANTIDOTE ND SAVED E REST OF US.

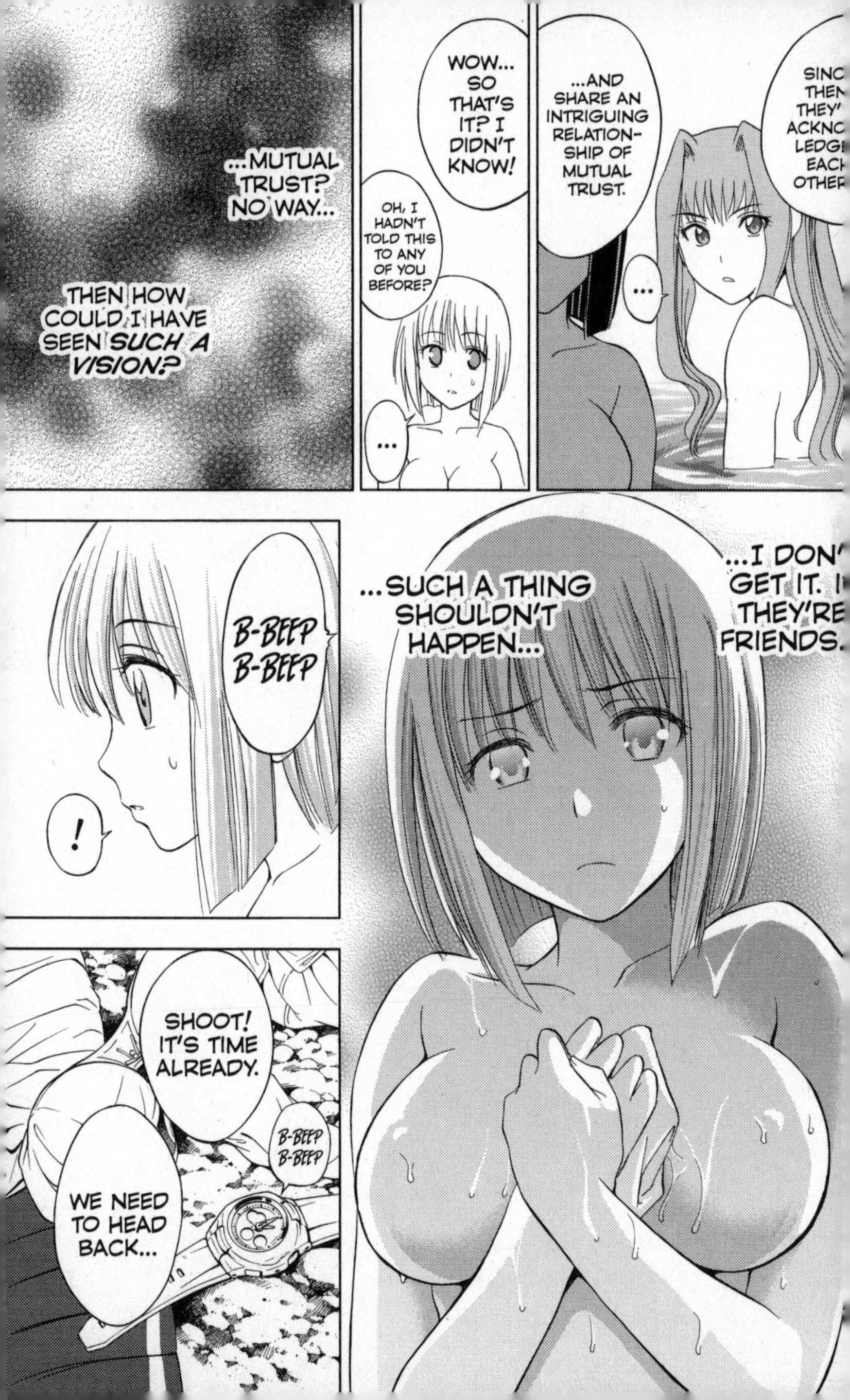
SINC THEN THEY' ACKNO LEDGE EACH OTHER
...AND SHARE AN INTRIGUING RELATION-SHIP OF MUTUAL TRUST.
...
WOW... SO THAT'S IT? I DIDN'T KNOW!
OH, I HADN'T TOLD THIS TO ANY OF YOU BEFORE?
...
...MUTUAL TRUST? NO WAY...
THEN HOW COULD I HAVE SEEN *SUCH A VISION?*
...I DON' GET IT. I THEY'RE FRIENDS.
...SUCH A THING SHOULDN'T HAPPEN...
B-BEEP B-BEEP
!
SHOOT! IT'S TIME ALREADY.
B-BEEP B-BEEP
WE NEED TO HEAD BACK...

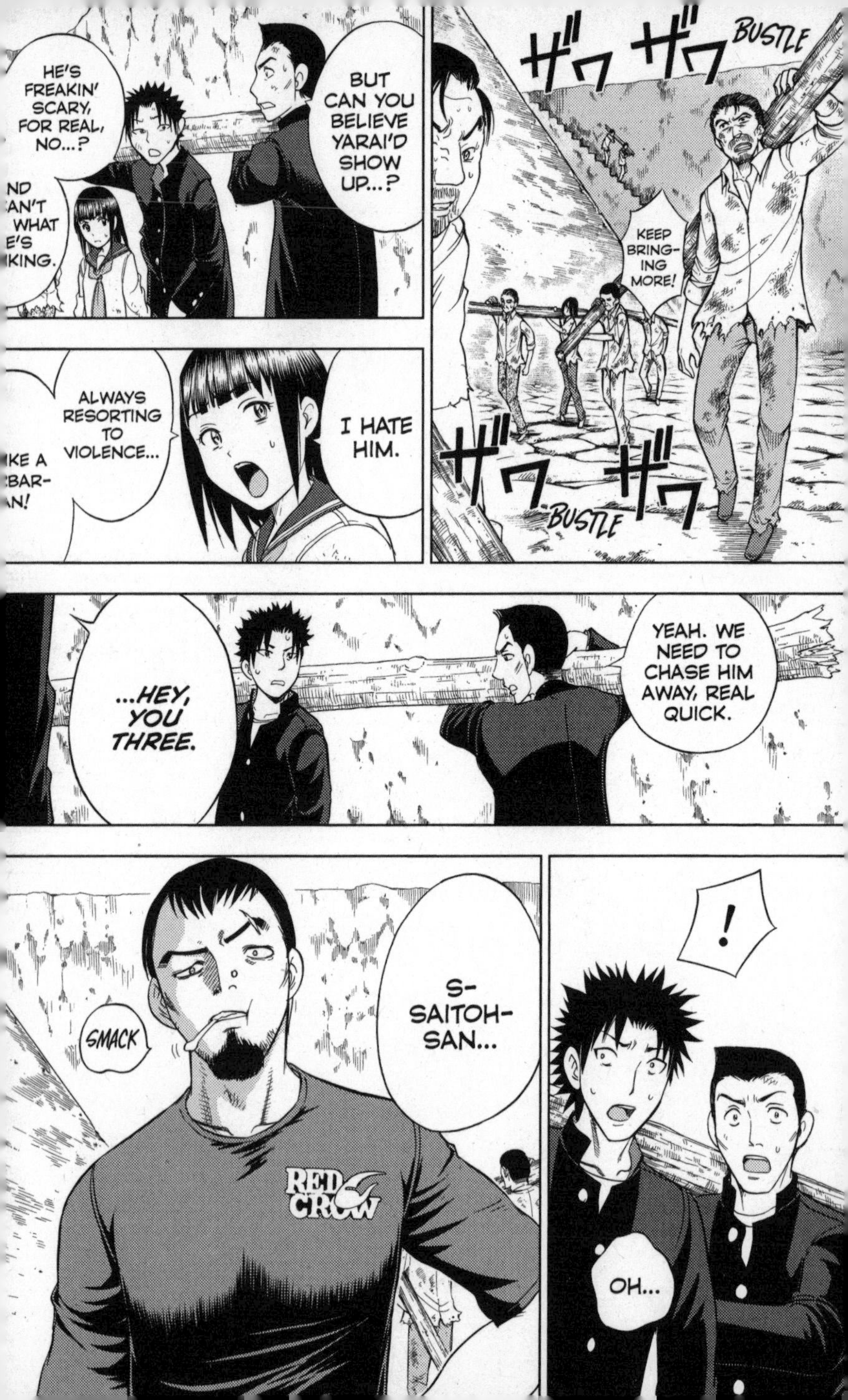
ザワ ザワ
BUSTLE
KEEP BRINGING MORE!
ザワ ザワ
BUSTLE
BUT CAN YOU BELIEVE YARAI'D SHOW UP...?
HE'S FREAKIN' SCARY, FOR REAL, NO...?
I HATE HIM.
ALWAYS RESORTING TO VIOLENCE...
YEAH. WE NEED TO CHASE HIM AWAY, REAL QUICK.
...HEY, YOU THREE.
!
S-SAITOH-SAN...
OH...
SMACK
RED CROW

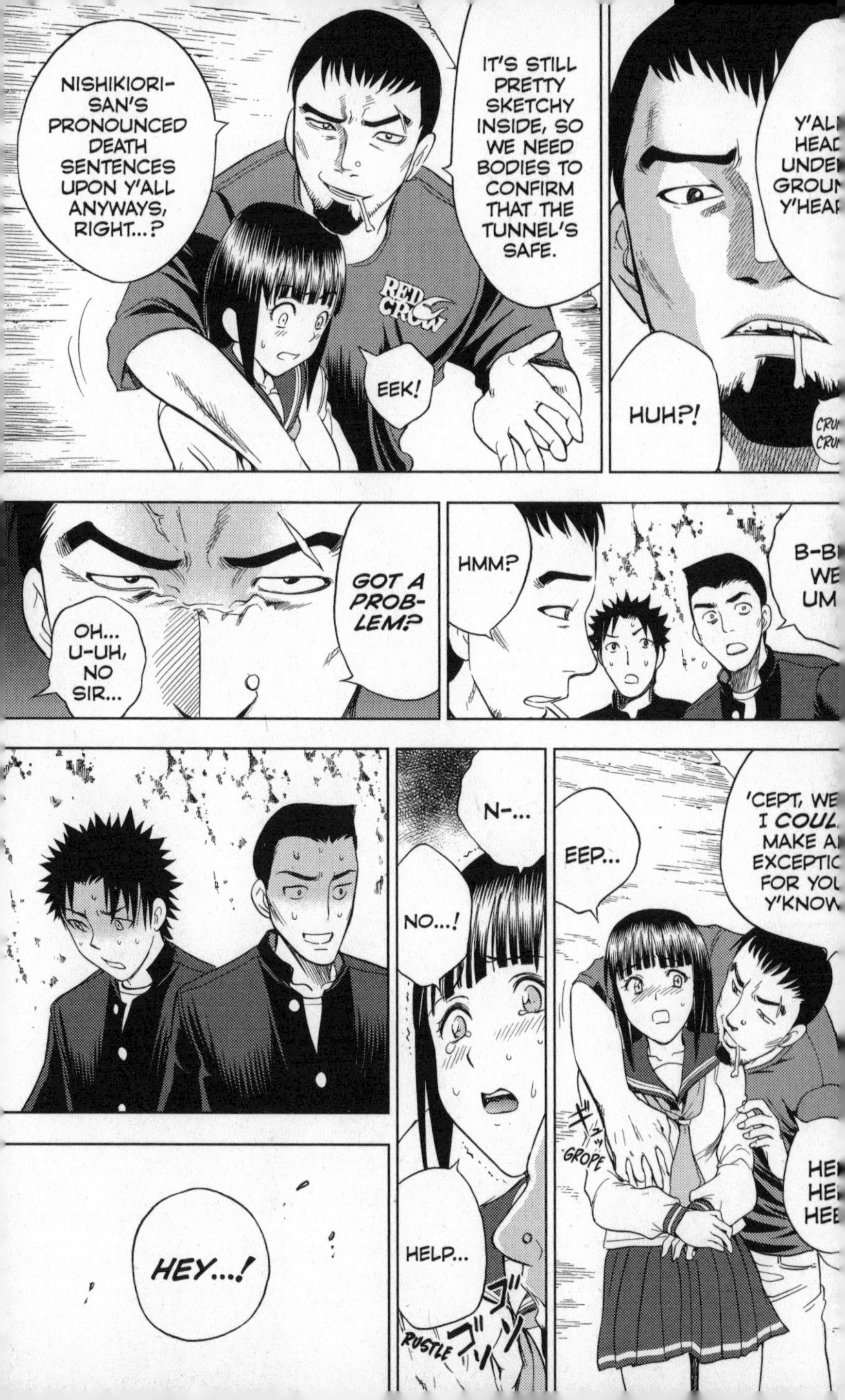
Y'AL HEAD UNDE GROUN Y'HEA
HUH?!
IT'S STILL PRETTY SKETCHY INSIDE, SO WE NEED BODIES TO CONFIRM THAT THE TUNNEL'S SAFE.
NISHIKIORI-SAN'S PRONOUNCED DEATH SENTENCES UPON Y'ALL ANYWAYS, RIGHT...?
EEK!
B-B WE UM
HMM?
GOT A PROB-LEM?
OH... U-UH, NO SIR...
'CEPT, WE I COUL MAKE A EXCEPTIC FOR YOU Y'KNOW
EEP...
GROPE
HE HE HEE
N-...
NO...!
HELP...
RUSTLE
HEY...!

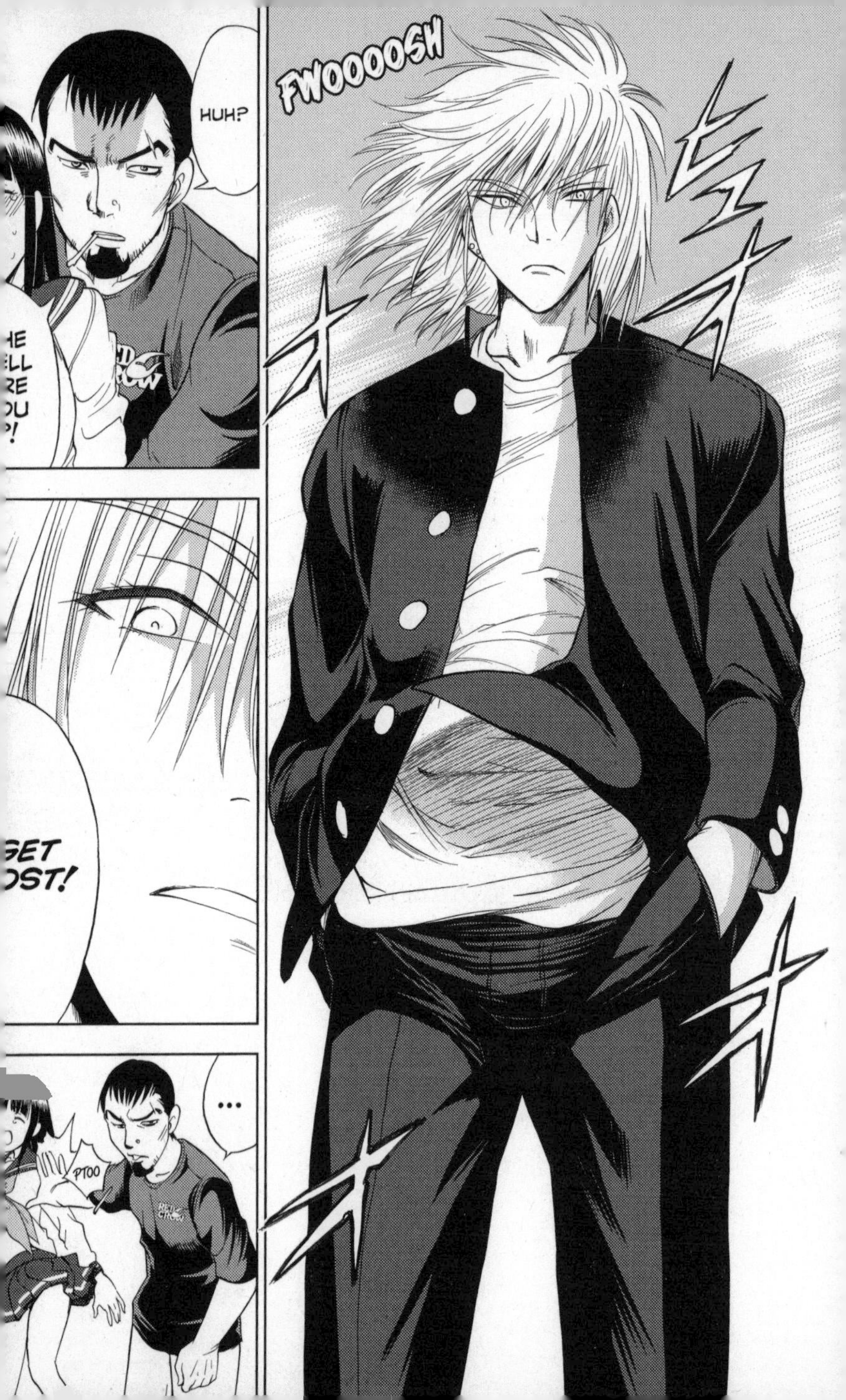
FWOOOOSH
HUH?
HE ELL RE OU P!
GET OST!
...
PTOO

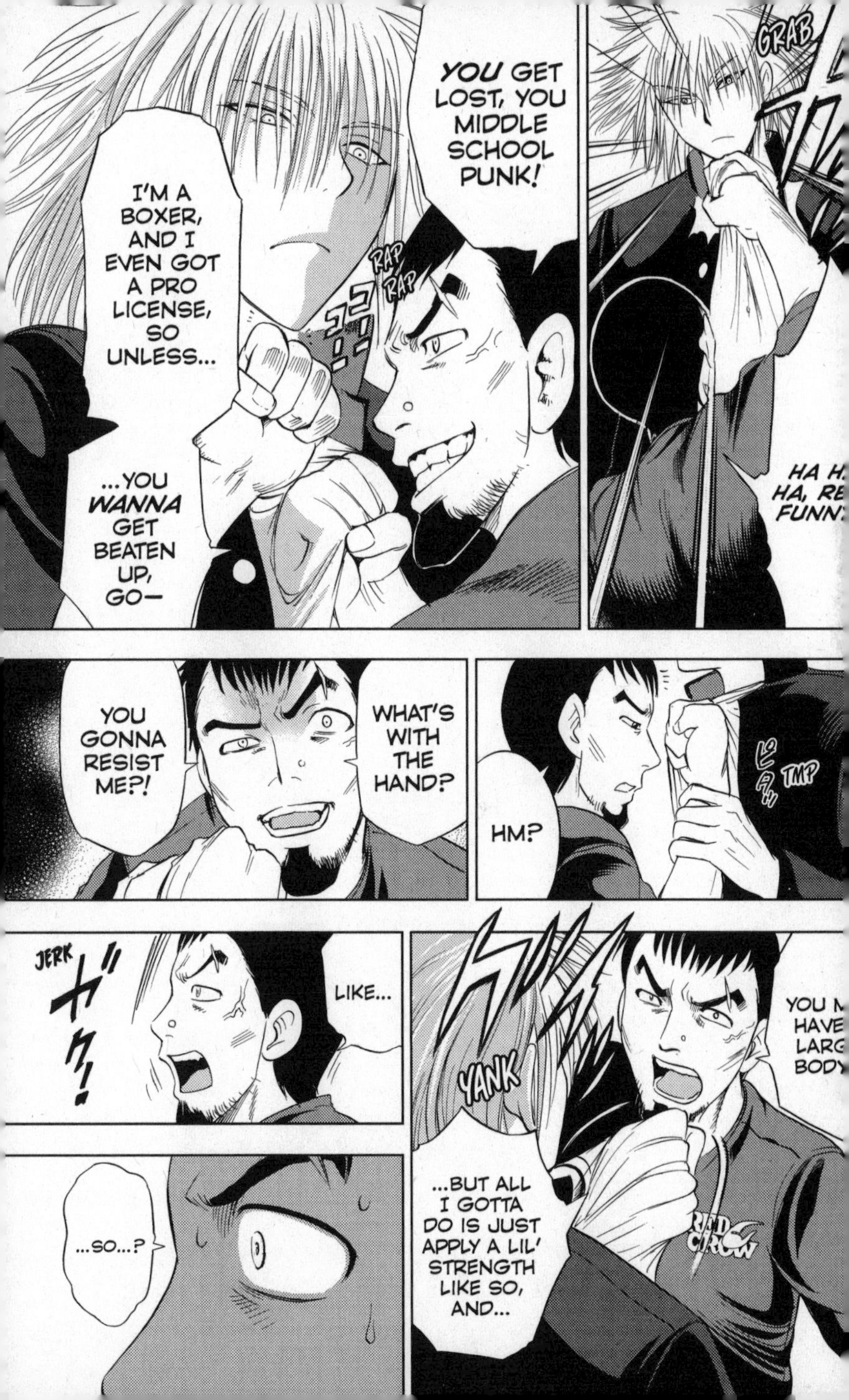
GRAB
HA H
HA, RE
FUNN
YOU GET LOST, YOU MIDDLE SCHOOL PUNK!
RAP RAP
I'M A BOXER, AND I EVEN GOT A PRO LICENSE, SO UNLESS...
...YOU WANNA GET BEATEN UP, GO—
TMP
HM?
WHAT'S WITH THE HAND?
YOU GONNA RESIST ME?!
YOU M
HAVE
LARG
BODY
YANK
...BUT ALL I GOTTA DO IS JUST APPLY A LIL' STRENGTH LIKE SO, AND...
RED CROW
JERK
LIKE...
...SO...?

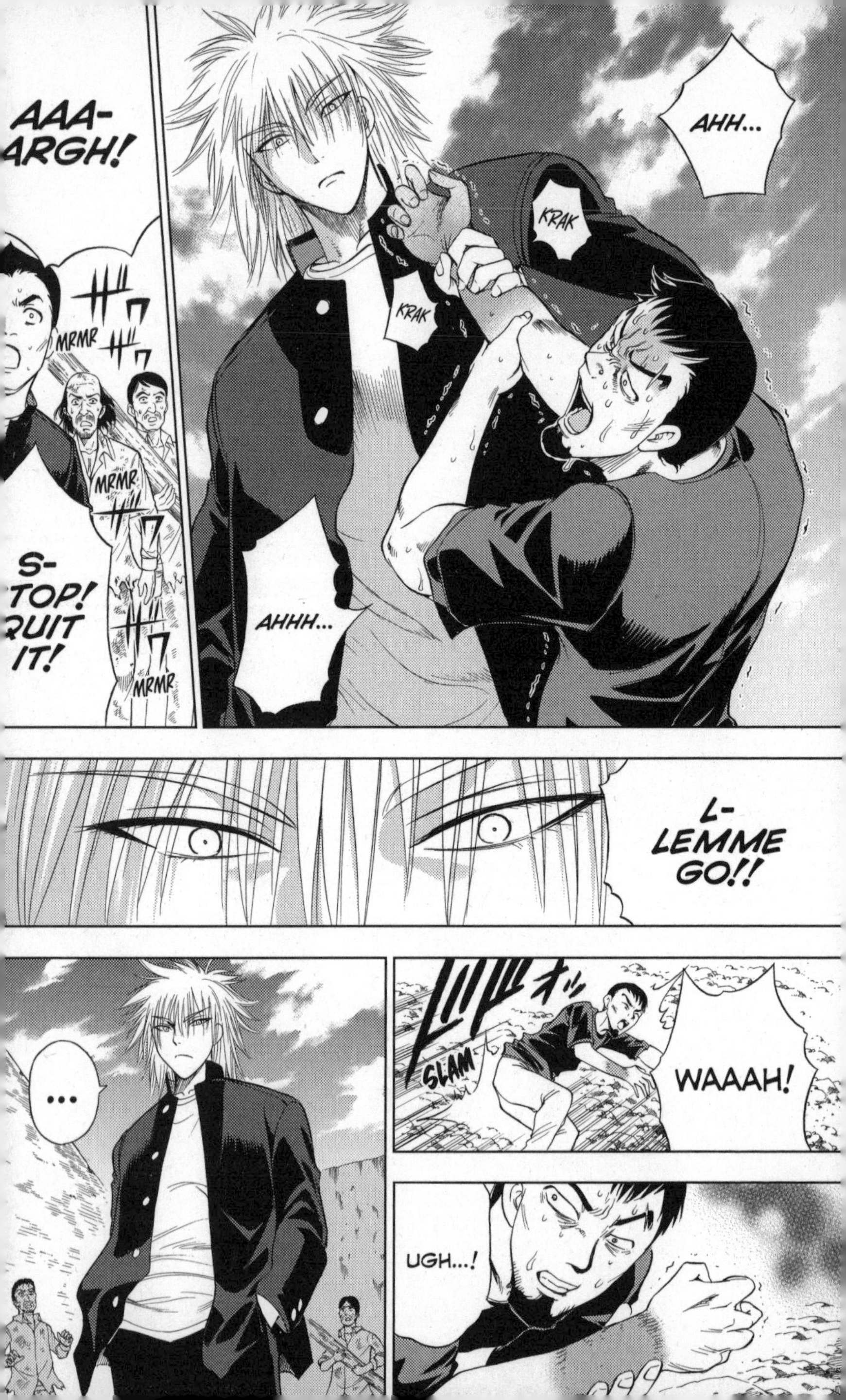
AHH...
KRAK
KRAK
AHHH...
AAA-ARGH!
ザワ
MRMR
ザワ
MRMR
ザワ
S-TOP! QUIT IT!
ザワ
MRMR
L-LEMME GO!!
WAAAH!
SLAM
UGH...!
...

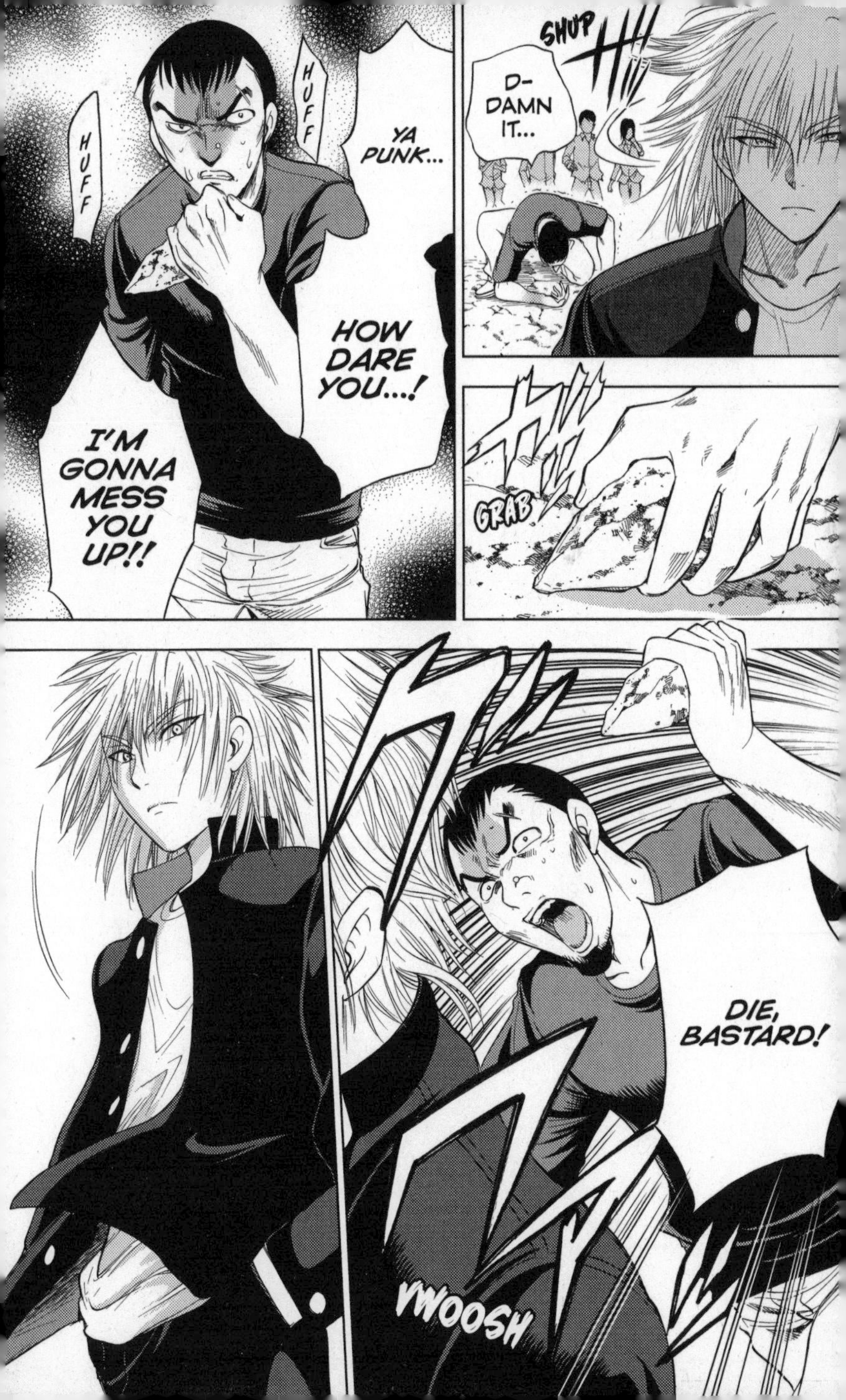
SHUP
D-DAMN IT...
GRAB
HUFF HUFF
HUFF HUFF
YA PUNK...
HOW DARE YOU...!
I'M GONNA MESS YOU UP!!
DIE, BASTARD!
VWOOSH

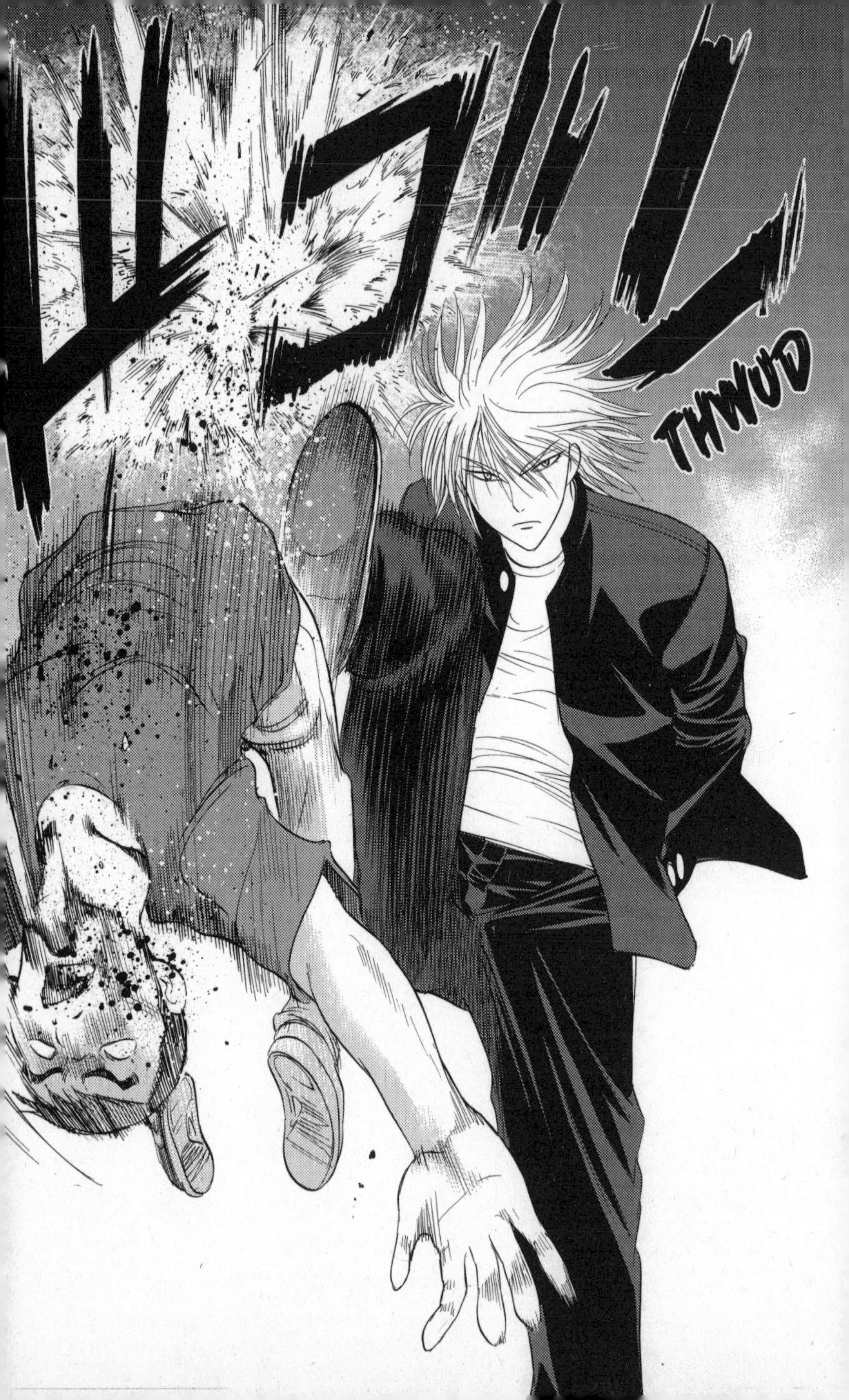
THWUD

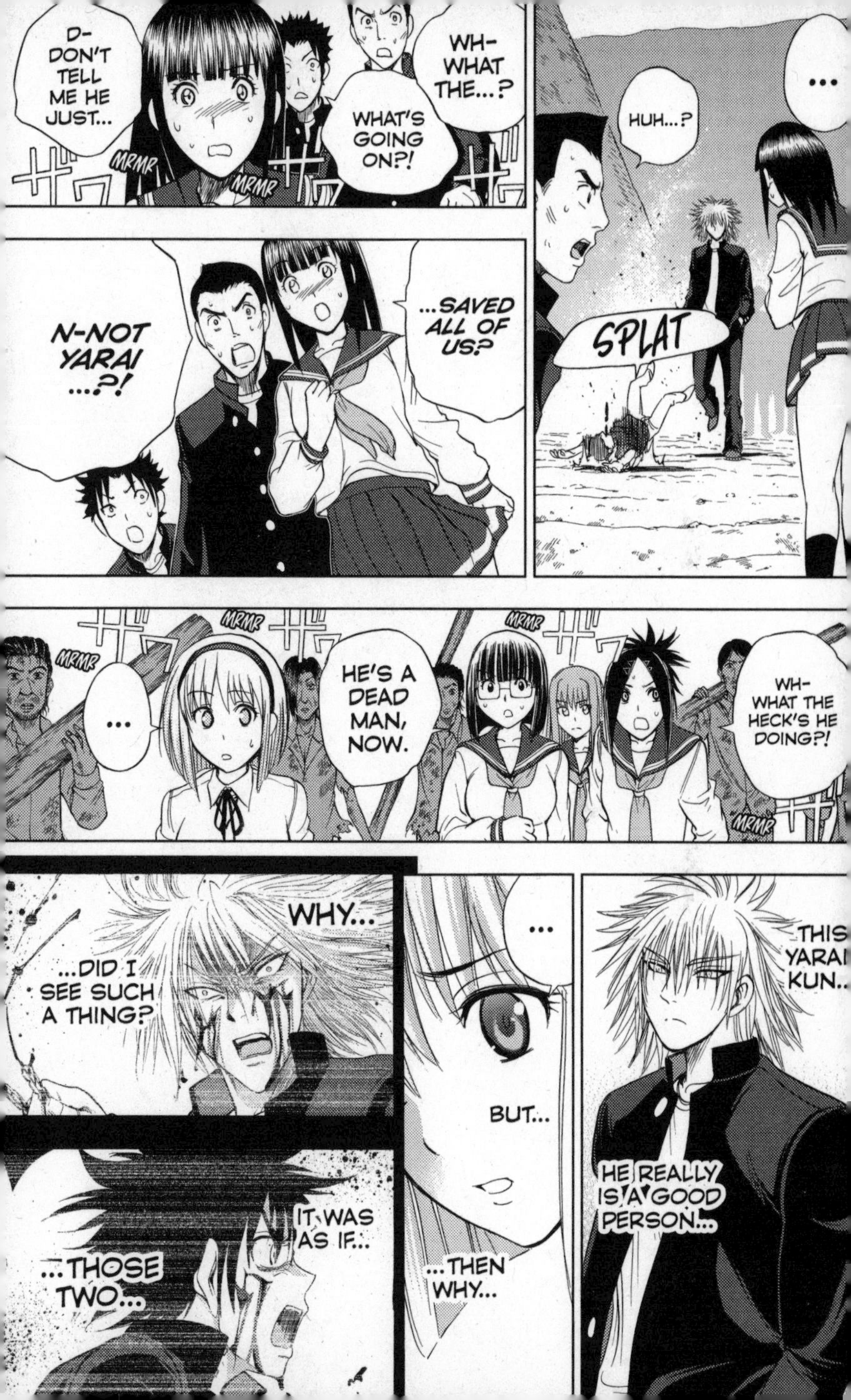
...
HUH...?
SPLAT
WH- WHAT THE...?
WHAT'S GOING ON?!
D- DON'T TELL ME HE JUST...
MRMR
MRMR
...SAVED ALL OF US?
N-NOT YARAI ...?!
MRMR
WH- WHAT THE HECK'S HE DOING?!
MRMR
HE'S A DEAD MAN, NOW.
MRMR
...
THIS YARAI KUN...
HE REALLY IS A GOOD PERSON...
...
BUT...
...THEN WHY...
WHY...
...DID I SEE SUCH A THING?
IT WAS AS IF...
...THOSE TWO...

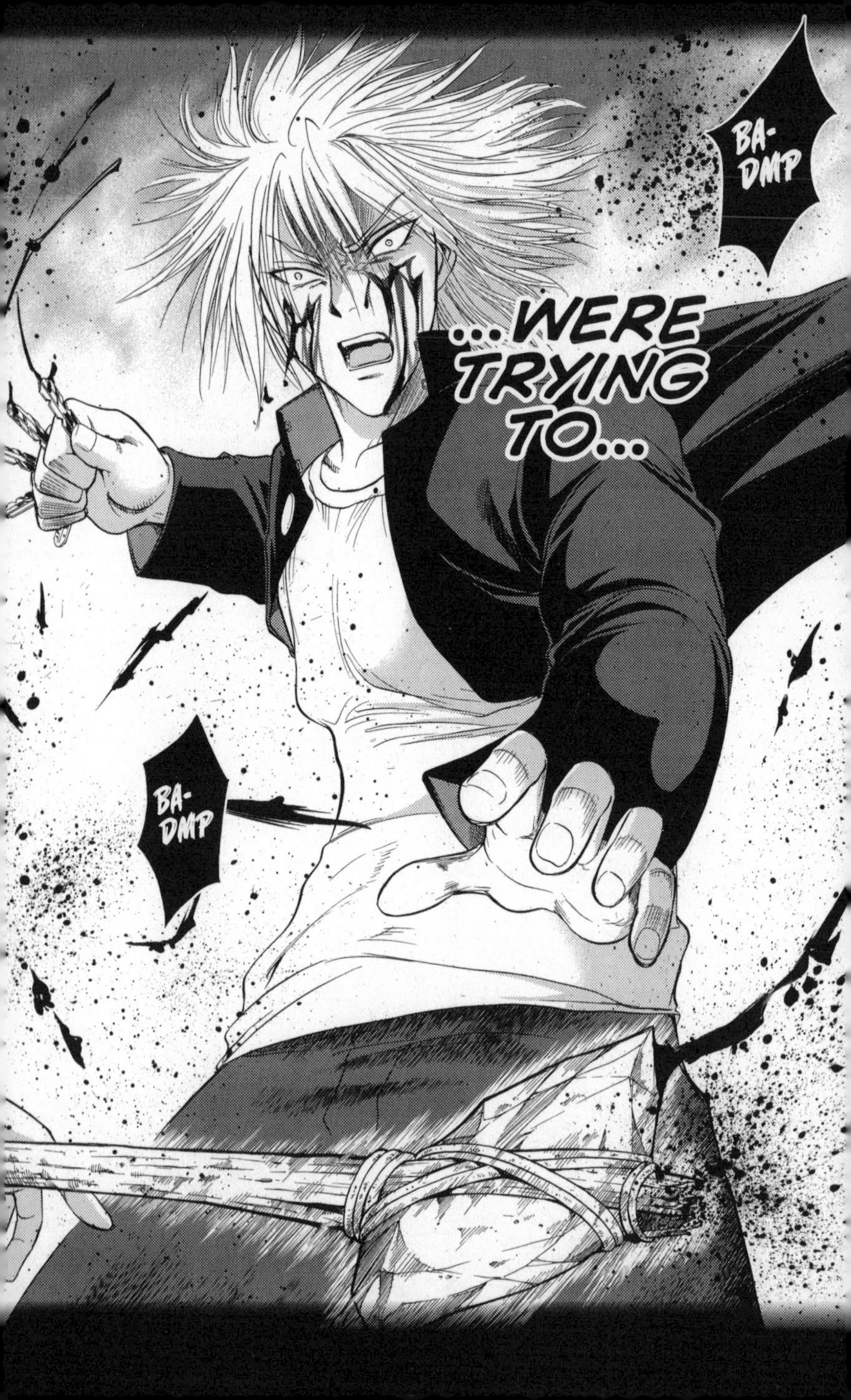
BA-
DMP
...WERE
TRYING
TO...
BA-
DMP

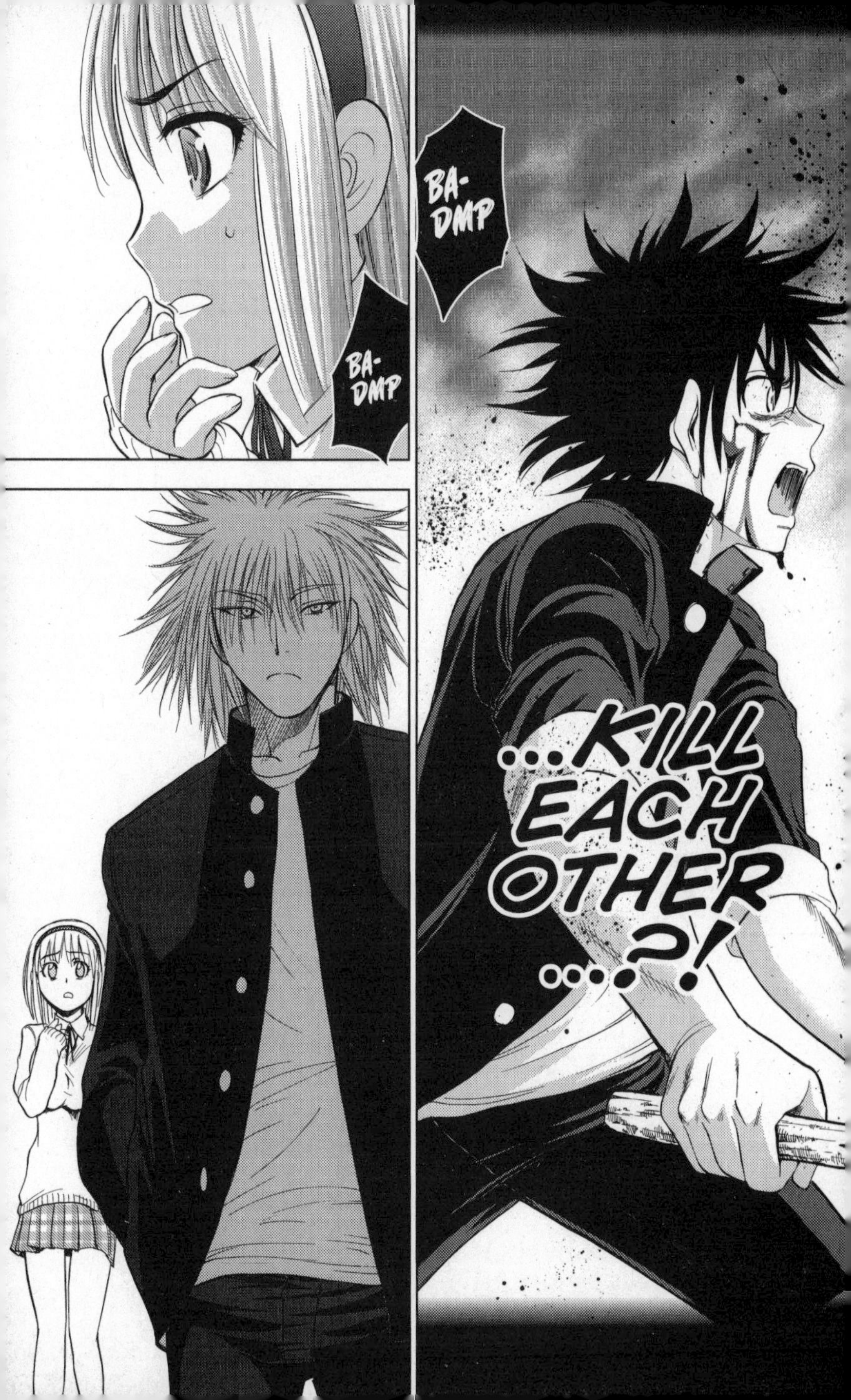
BA-DMP
...KILL EACH OTHER ...?!
BA-DMP

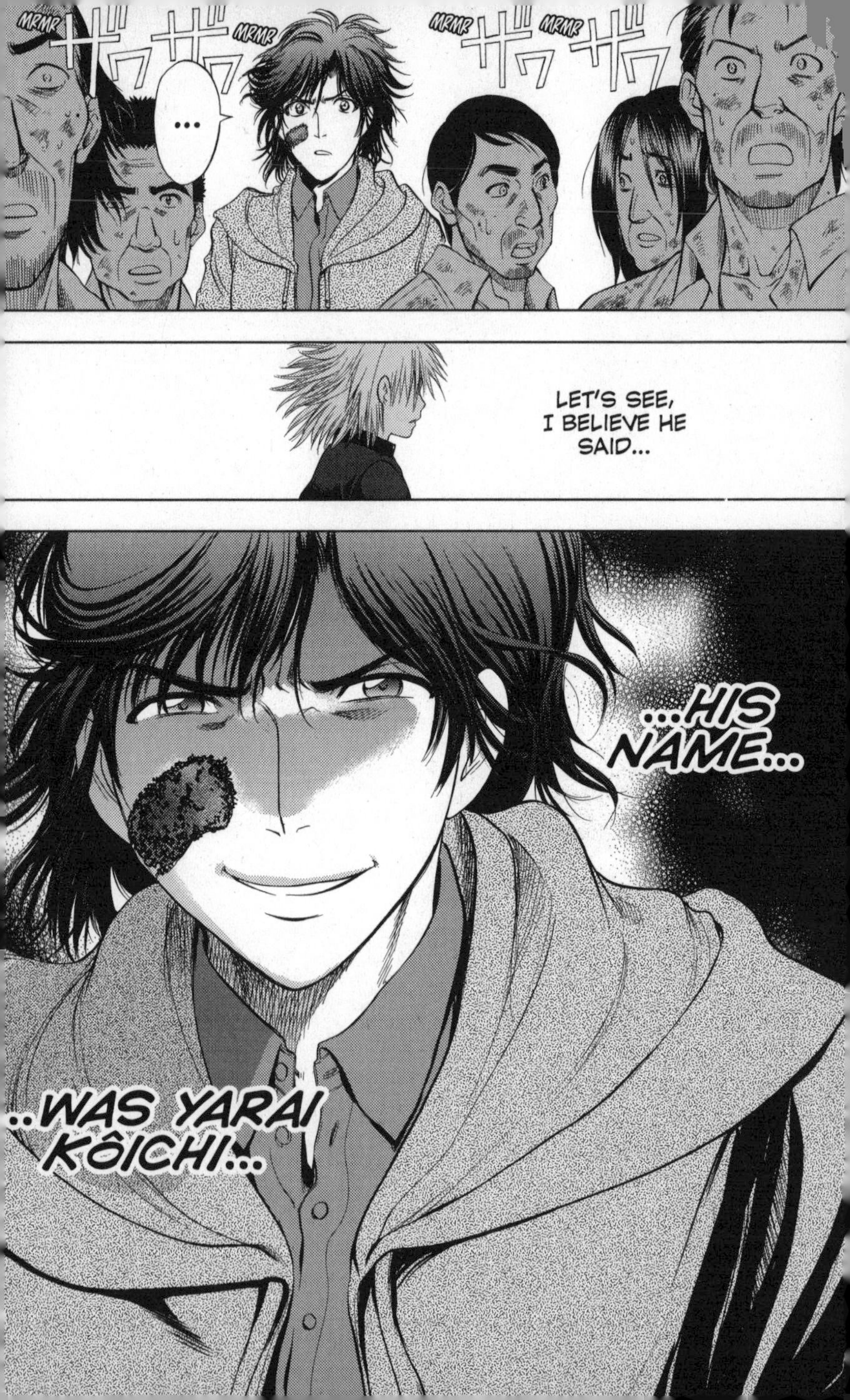
MRMR
ザワザワ
MRMR
MRMR
ザワザワ
MRMR
...
LET'S SEE, I BELIEVE HE SAID...
...HIS NAME...
...WAS YARAI KÔICHI...

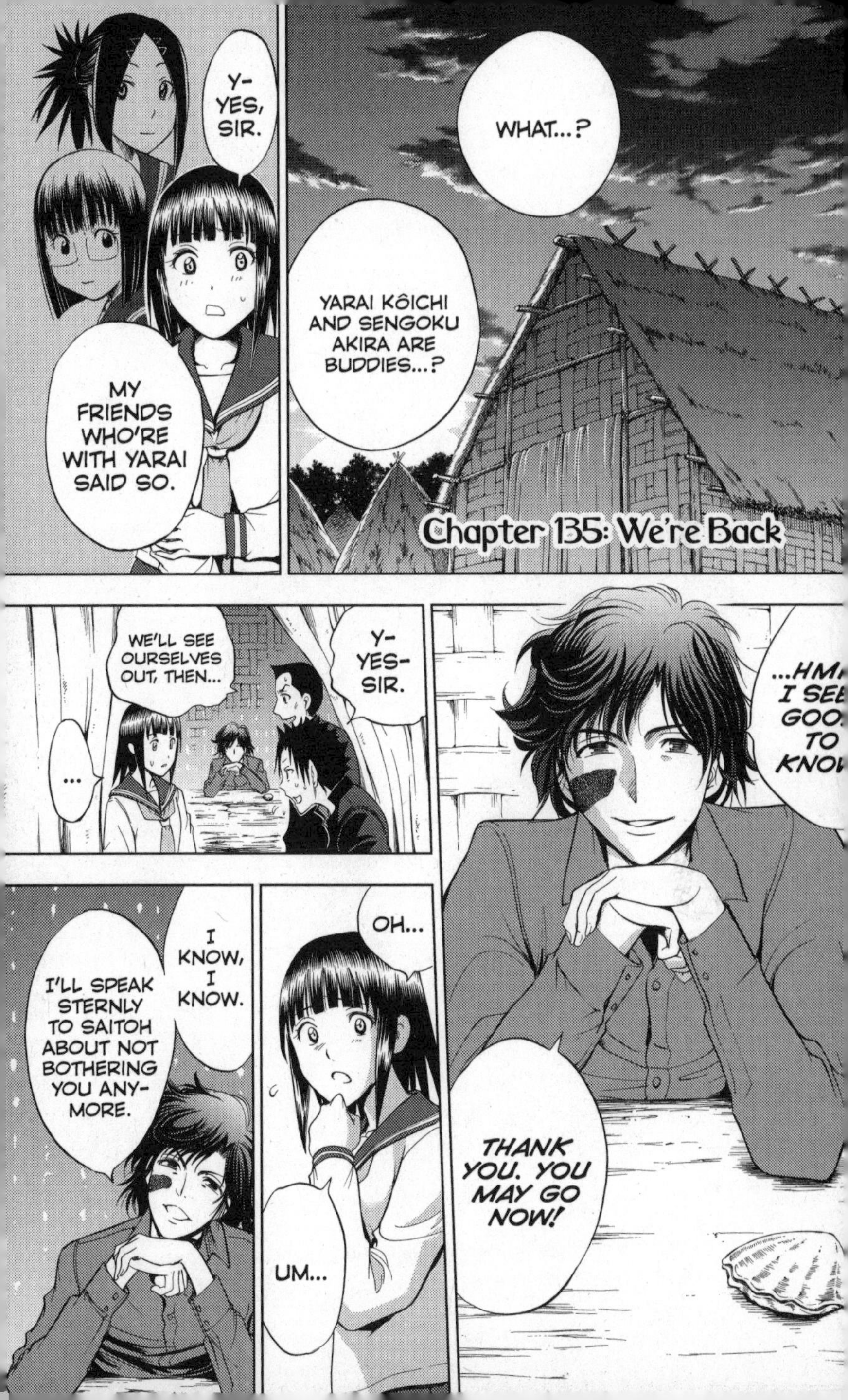
WHAT...?
YARAI KÔICHI AND SENGOKU AKIRA ARE BUDDIES...?
Chapter 135: We're Back
Y-YES, SIR.
MY FRIENDS WHO'RE WITH YARAI SAID SO.
...HM I SEE GOO TO KNOW
THANK YOU. YOU MAY GO NOW!
Y-YES-SIR.
WE'LL SEE OURSELVES OUT, THEN...
...
OH...
UM...
I KNOW, I KNOW.
I'LL SPEAK STERNLY TO SAITOH ABOUT NOT BOTHERING YOU ANYMORE.

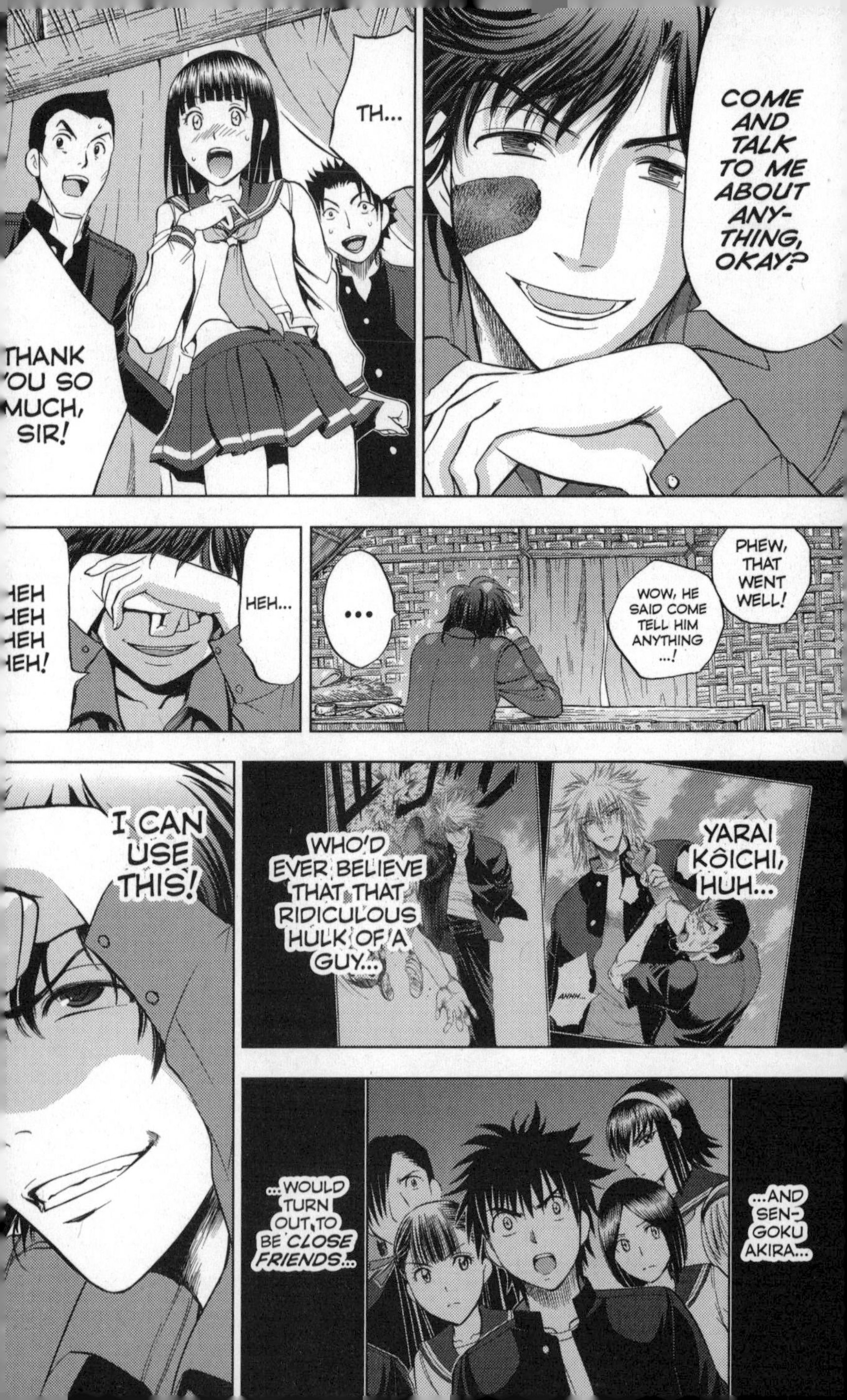
COME AND TALK TO ME ABOUT ANY-THING, OKAY?
TH...
THANK YOU SO MUCH, SIR!
PHEW, THAT WENT WELL!
WOW, HE SAID COME TELL HIM ANYTHING ...!
...
HEH...
HEH HEH HEH HEH!
YARAI KÔICHI, HUH...
ANNH...
WHO'D EVER BELIEVE THAT THAT RIDICULOUS HULK OF A GUY...
...AND SEN-GOKU AKIRA...
...WOULD TURN OUT TO BE *CLOSE FRIENDS*...
I CAN USE THIS!

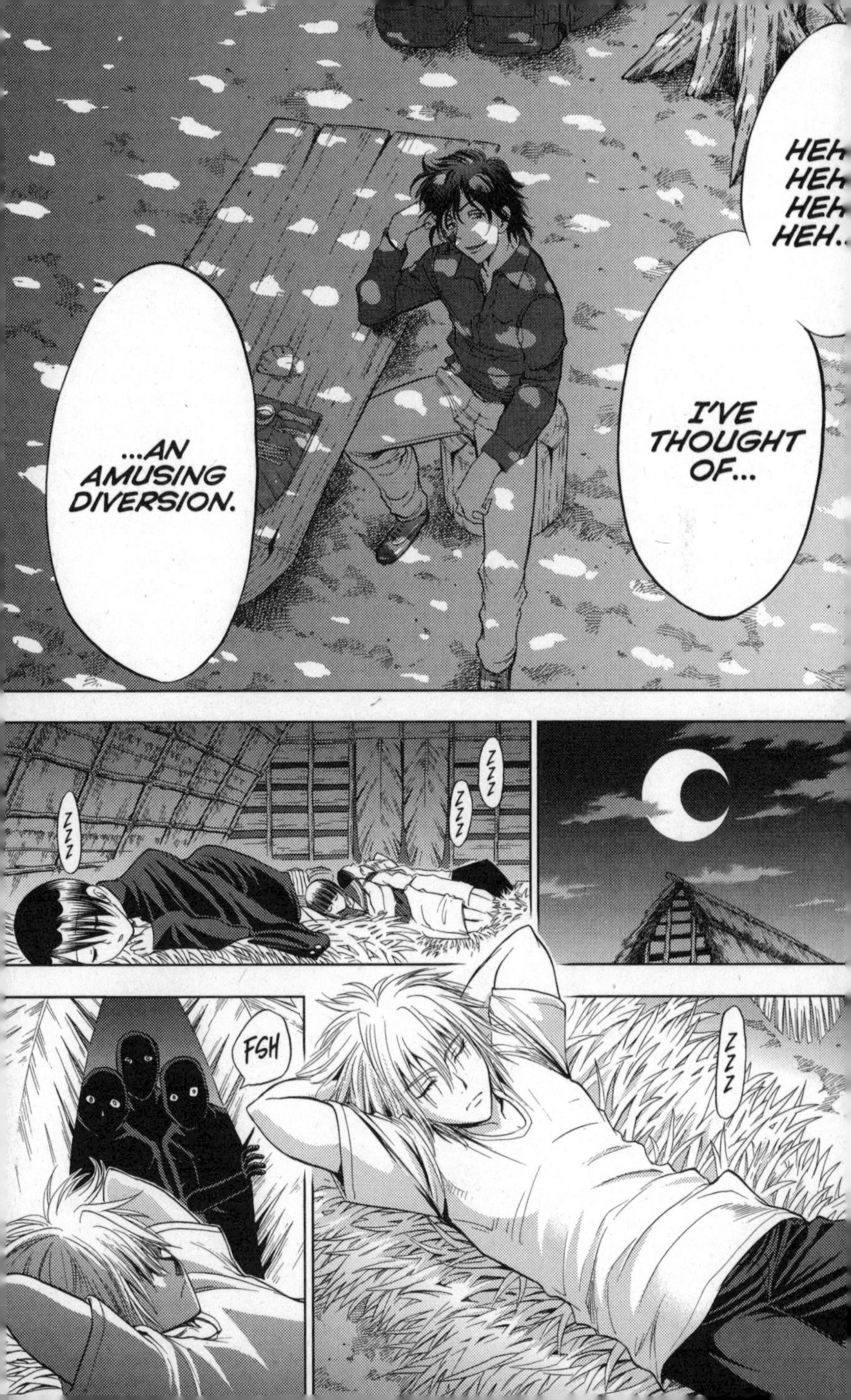
HEH HEH HEH HEH...
I'VE THOUGHT OF...
...AN AMUSING DIVERSION.
ZZZ
ZZZ
ZZZ
ZZZ
FSH

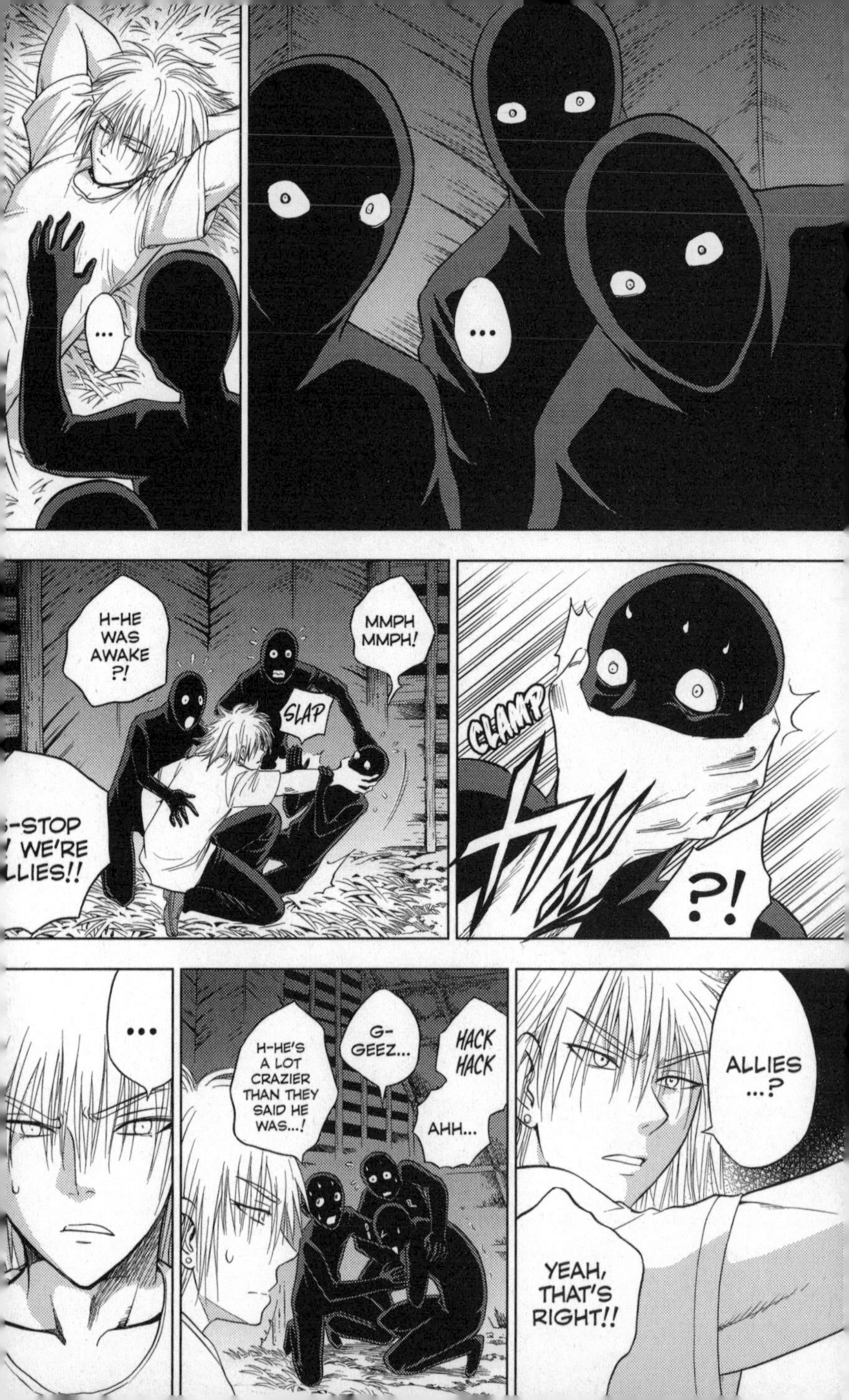
...
...
CLAMP
?!
MMPH MMPH!
H-HE WAS AWAKE ?!
SLAP
-STOP WE'RE LLIES!!
ALLIES ...?
YEAH, THAT'S RIGHT!!
HACK HACK
G-GEEZ...
H-HE'S A LOT CRAZIER THAN THEY SAID HE WAS...!
AHH...
...

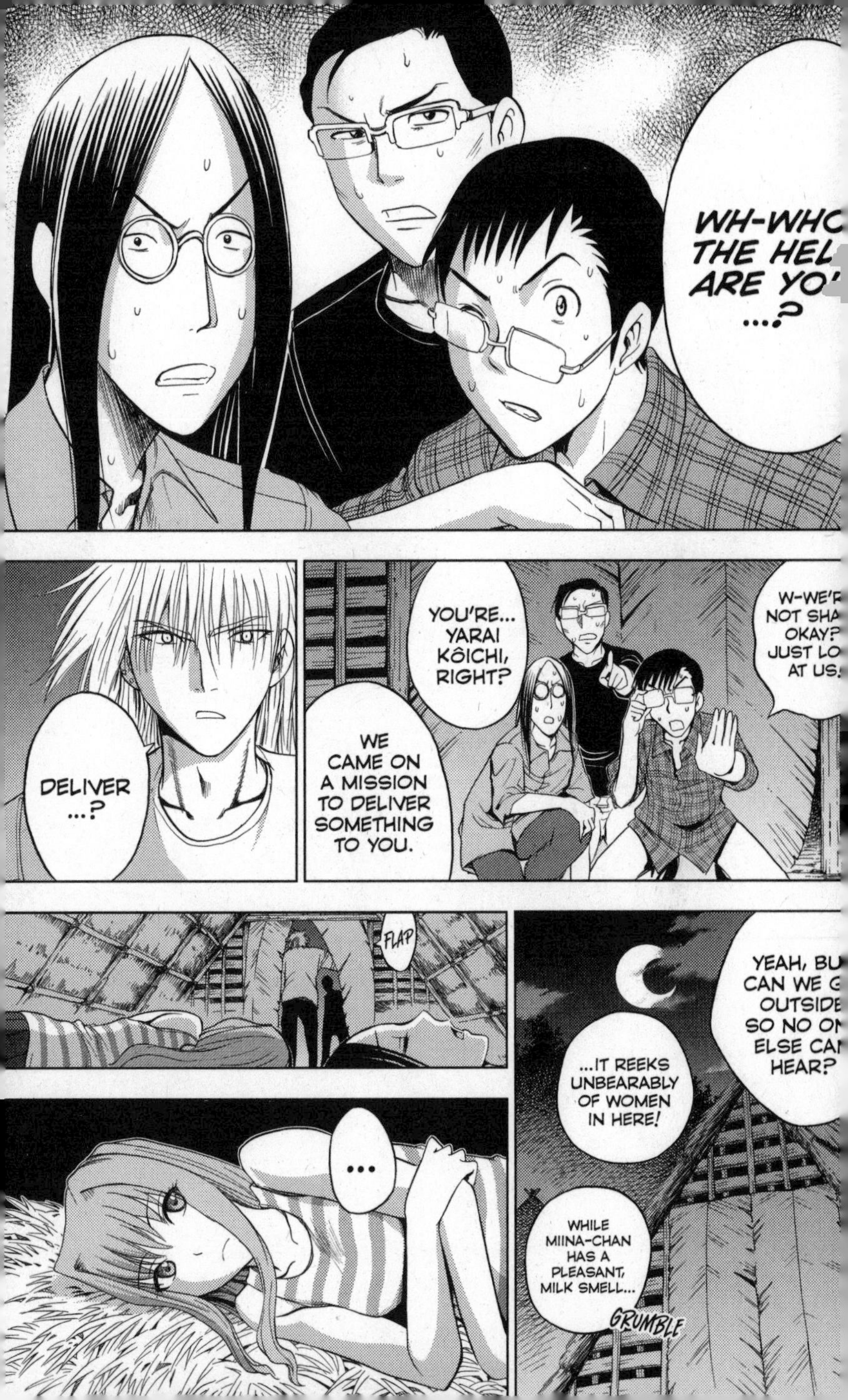
WH-WHO THE HEL ARE YO ...?
W-WE'R NOT SHA OKAY? JUST LO AT US!
YOU'RE... YARAI KÔICHI, RIGHT?
WE CAME ON A MISSION TO DELIVER SOMETHING TO YOU.
DELIVER ...?
YEAH, BU CAN WE G OUTSIDE SO NO ON ELSE CA HEAR?
...IT REEKS UNBEARABLY OF WOMEN IN HERE!
WHILE MIINA-CHAN HAS A PLEASANT, MILK SMELL...
GRUMBLE
FLAP
...

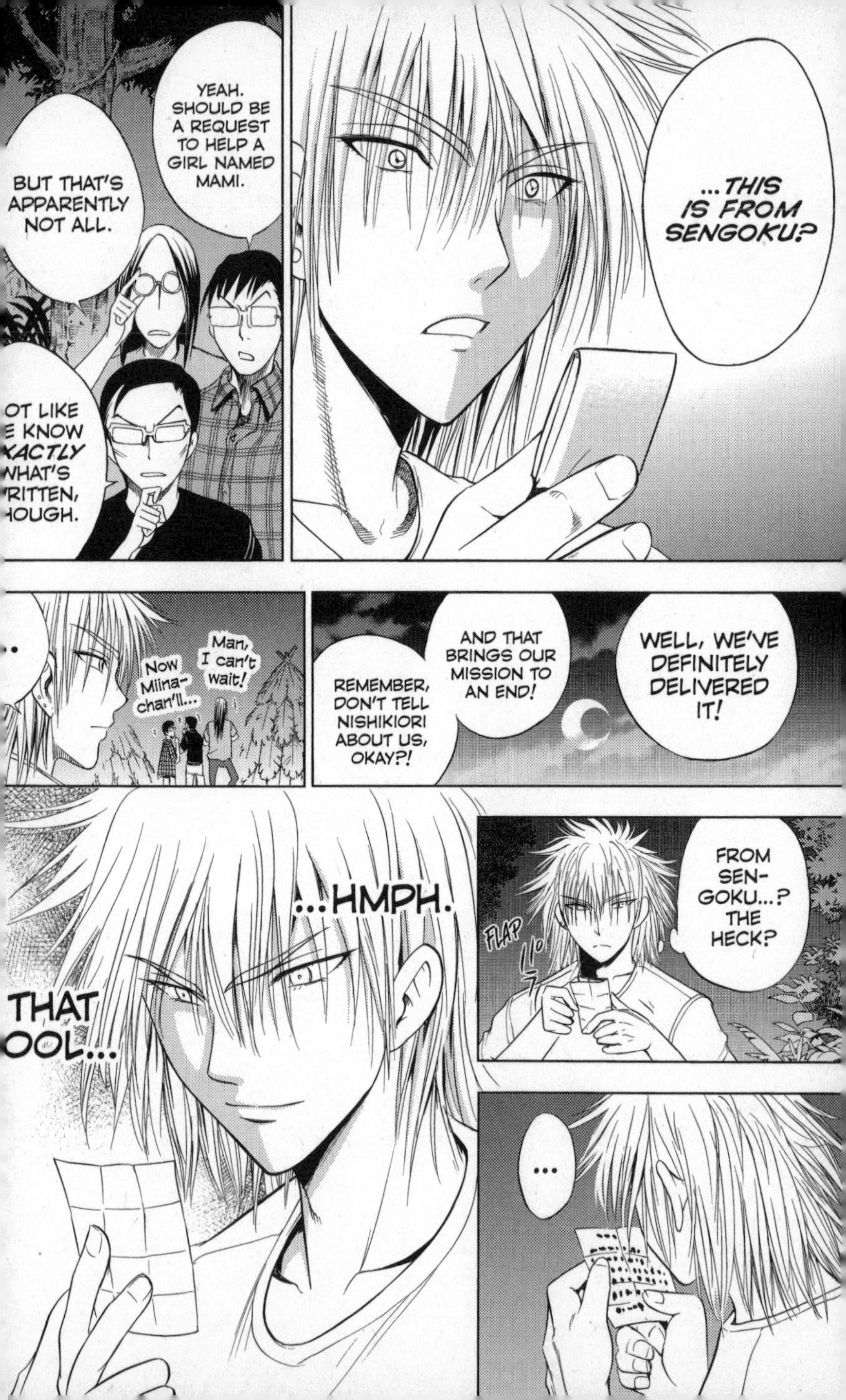
...THIS IS FROM SENGOKU?
YEAH. SHOULD BE A REQUEST TO HELP A GIRL NAMED MAMI.
BUT THAT'S APPARENTLY NOT ALL.
OT LIKE E KNOW XACTLY WHAT'S RITTEN, HOUGH.
WELL, WE'VE DEFINITELY DELIVERED IT!
AND THAT BRINGS OUR MISSION TO AN END!
REMEMBER, DON'T TELL NISHIKIORI ABOUT US, OKAY?!
..
Man, I can't wait!
Now Miina-chan'll...
FROM SEN-GOKU...? THE HECK?
FLAP
...
...HMPH.
THAT OOL...

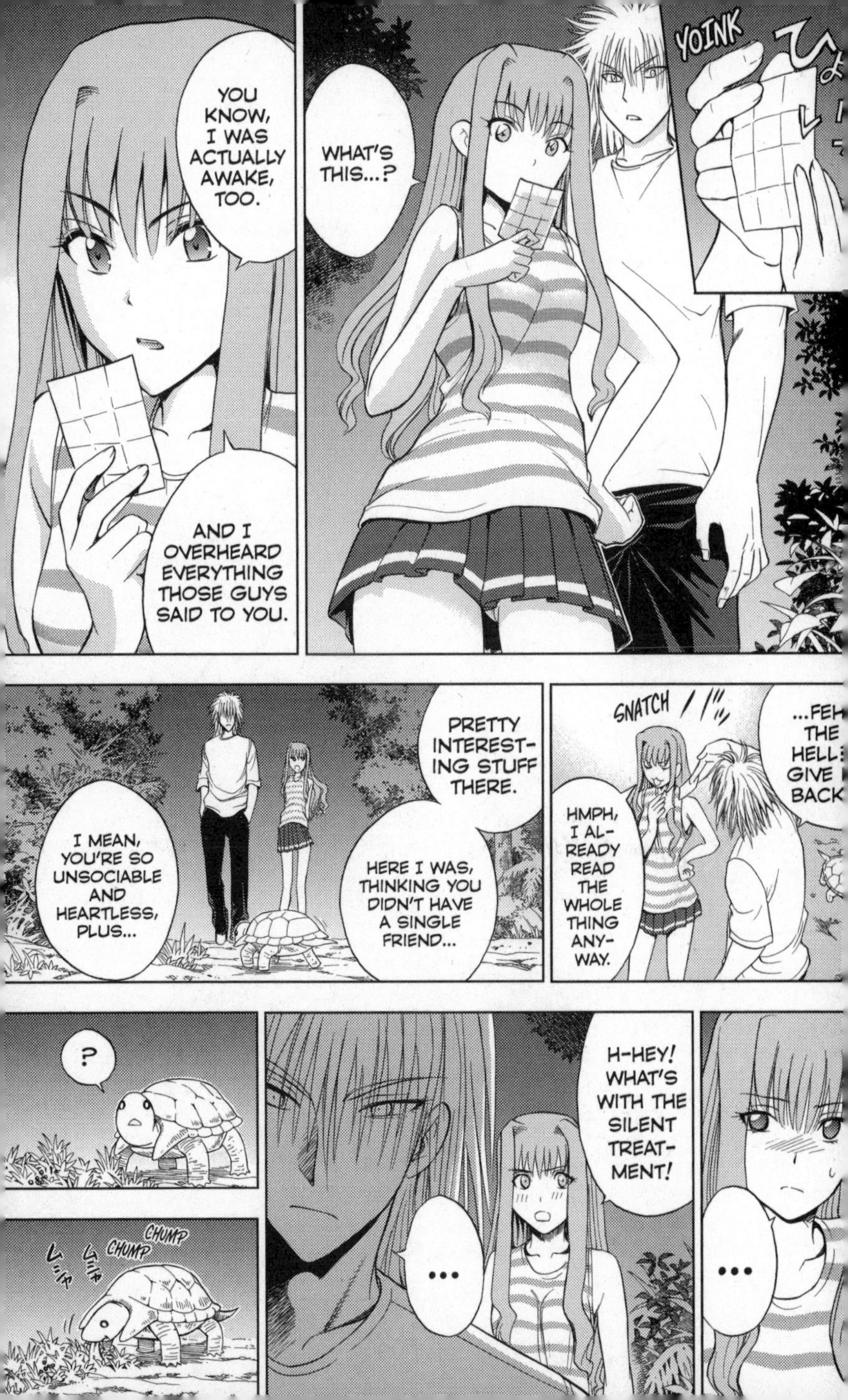
YOINK
WHAT'S THIS...?
YOU KNOW, I WAS ACTUALLY AWAKE, TOO.
AND I OVERHEARD EVERYTHING THOSE GUYS SAID TO YOU.
...FEH
THE HELL
GIVE
BACK
SNATCH
HMPH, I ALREADY READ THE WHOLE THING ANYWAY.
PRETTY INTERESTING STUFF THERE.
HERE I WAS, THINKING YOU DIDN'T HAVE A SINGLE FRIEND...
I MEAN, YOU'RE SO UNSOCIABLE AND HEARTLESS, PLUS...
...
H-HEY! WHAT'S WITH THE SILENT TREATMENT!
...
?
CHUMP
CHUMP

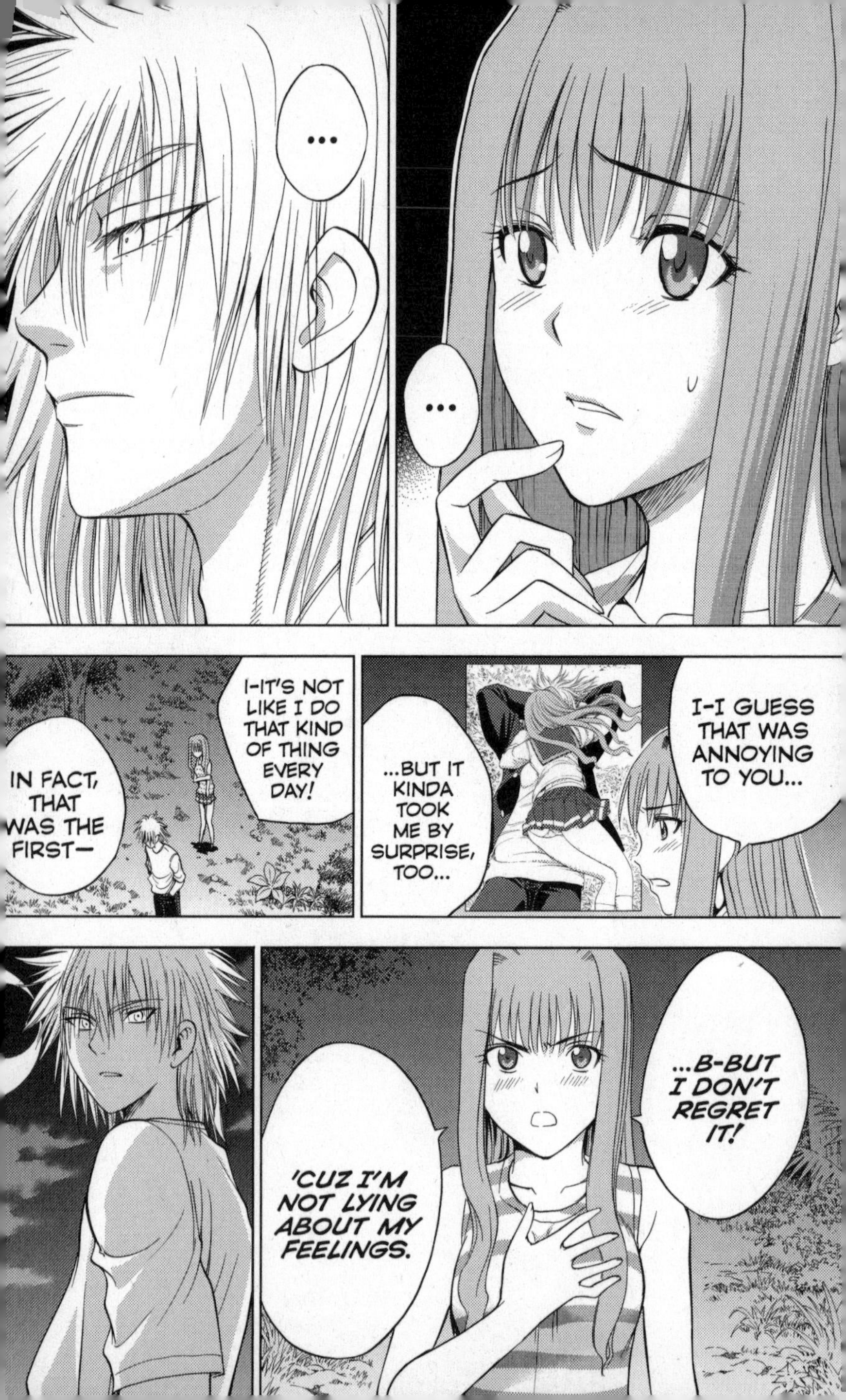
...
...
I-I GUESS THAT WAS ANNOYING TO YOU...
...BUT IT KINDA TOOK ME BY SURPRISE, TOO...
I-IT'S NOT LIKE I DO THAT KIND OF THING EVERY DAY!
IN FACT, THAT WAS THE FIRST—
...B-BUT I DON'T REGRET IT!
'CUZ I'M NOT LYING ABOUT MY FEELINGS.

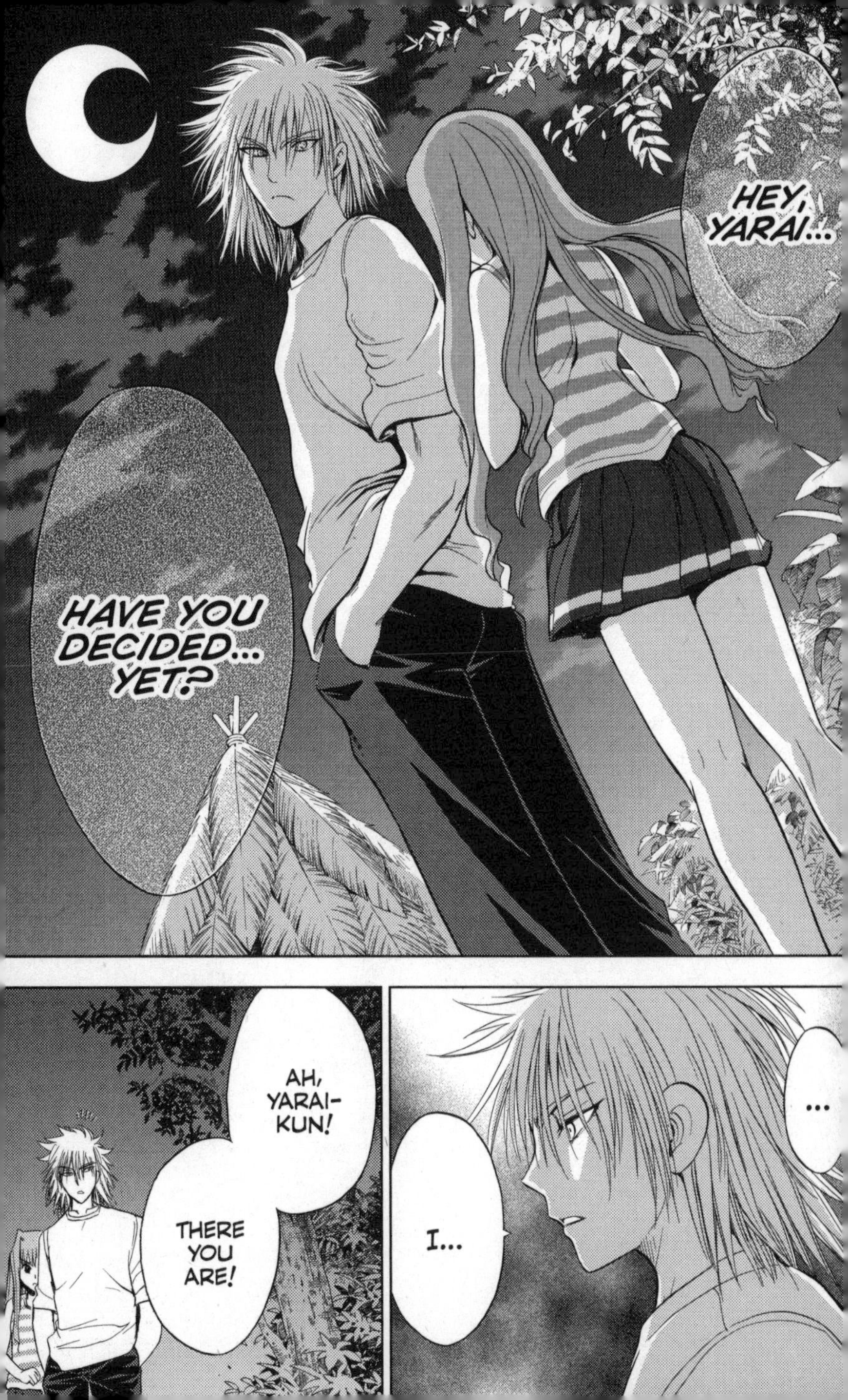
HEY, YARAI...
HAVE YOU DECIDED... YET?
...
I...
AH, YARAI-KUN!
THERE YOU ARE!

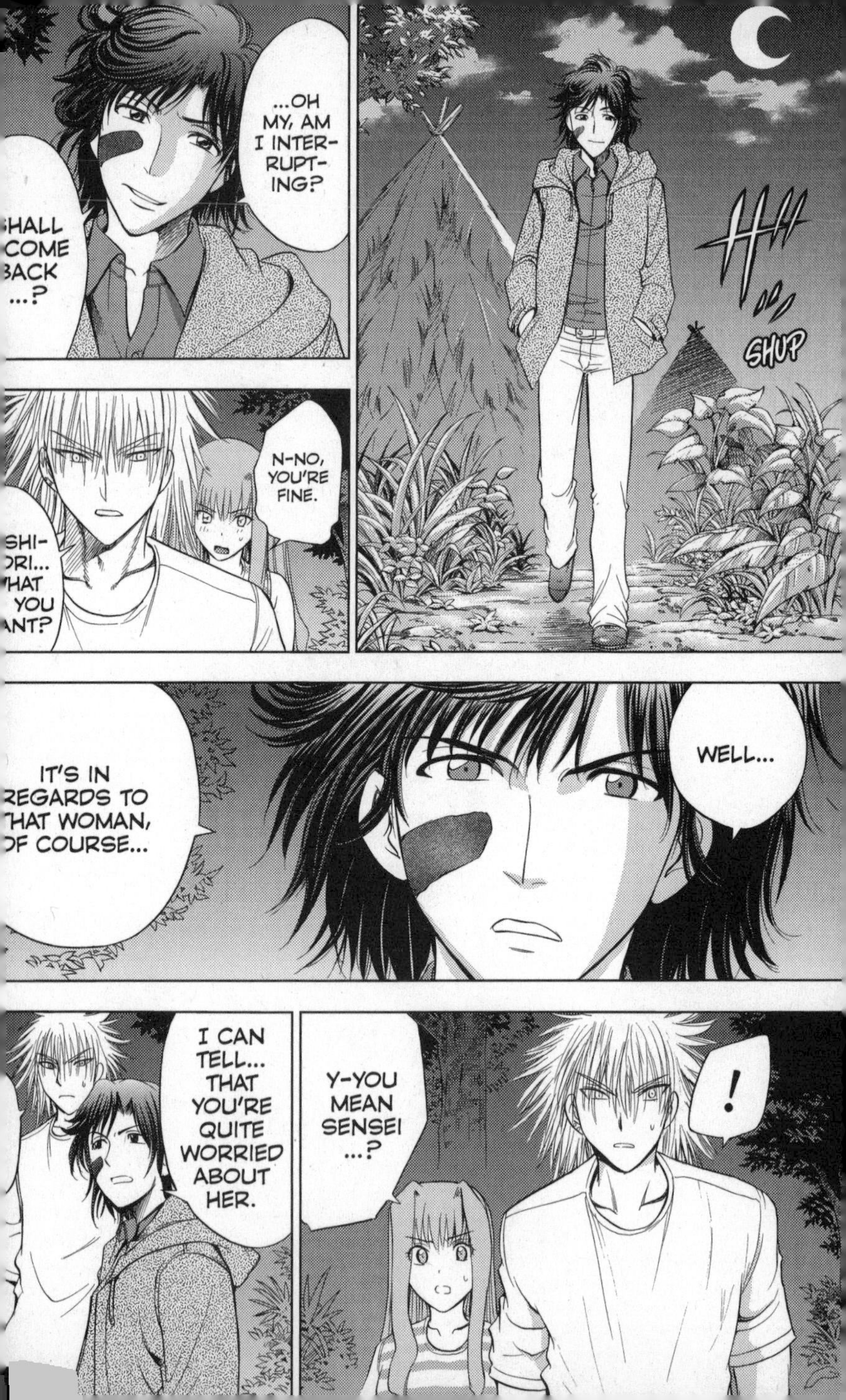
SHUP
...OH MY, AM I INTERRUPTING?
HALL COME BACK ...?
N-NO, YOU'RE FINE.
SHIORI... HAT YOU ANT?
WELL...
IT'S IN EGARDS TO HAT WOMAN, F COURSE...
!
Y-YOU MEAN SENSEI ...?
I CAN TELL... THAT YOU'RE QUITE WORRIED ABOUT HER.

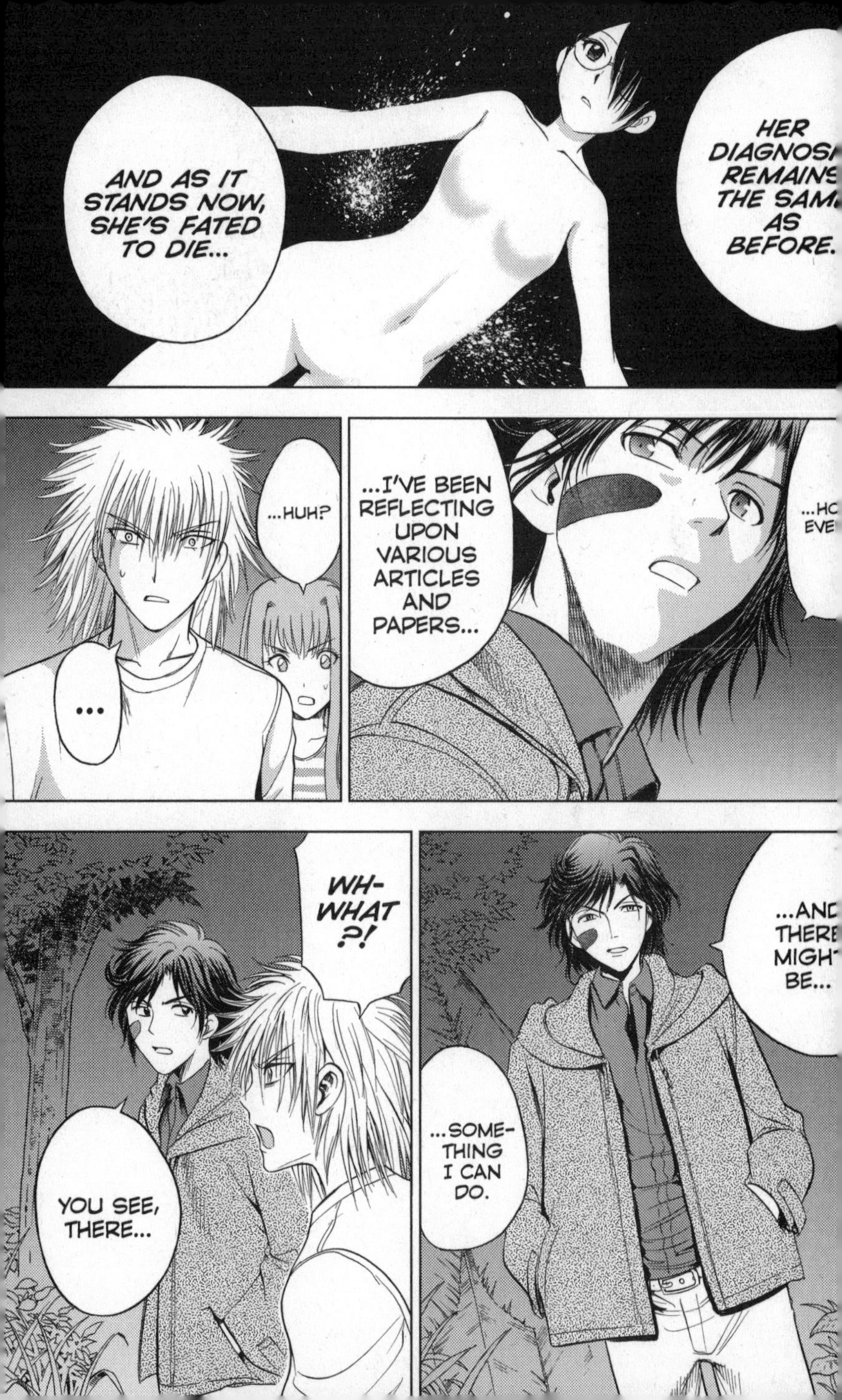
HER DIAGNOSI REMAINS THE SAM AS BEFORE.
AND AS IT STANDS NOW, SHE'S FATED TO DIE...
...HO EVE
...I'VE BEEN REFLECTING UPON VARIOUS ARTICLES AND PAPERS...
...HUH?
...
...AND THERE MIGHT BE...
...SOME-THING I CAN DO.
WH-WHAT?!
YOU SEE, THERE...

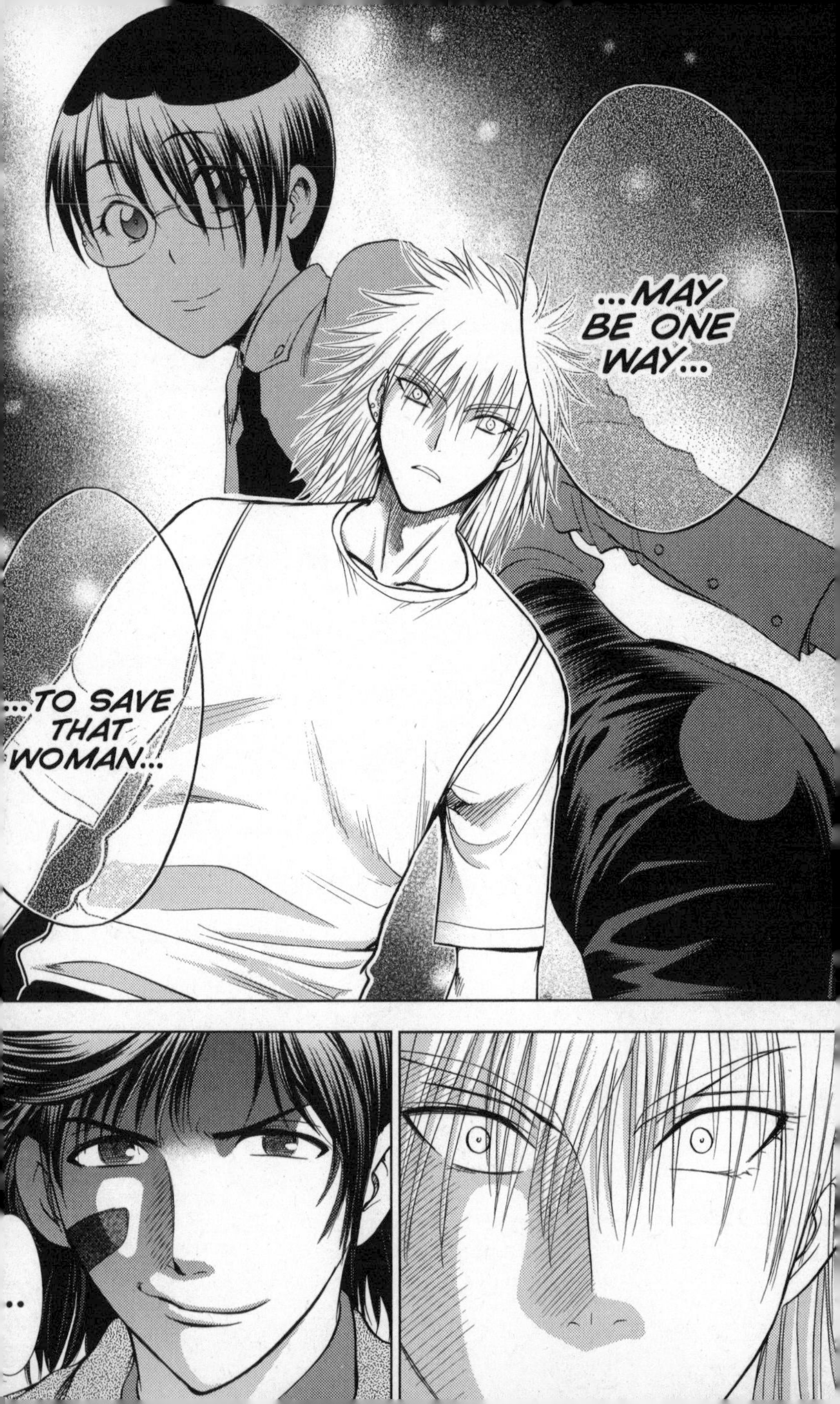
...MAY BE ONE WAY...
...TO SAVE THAT WOMAN...

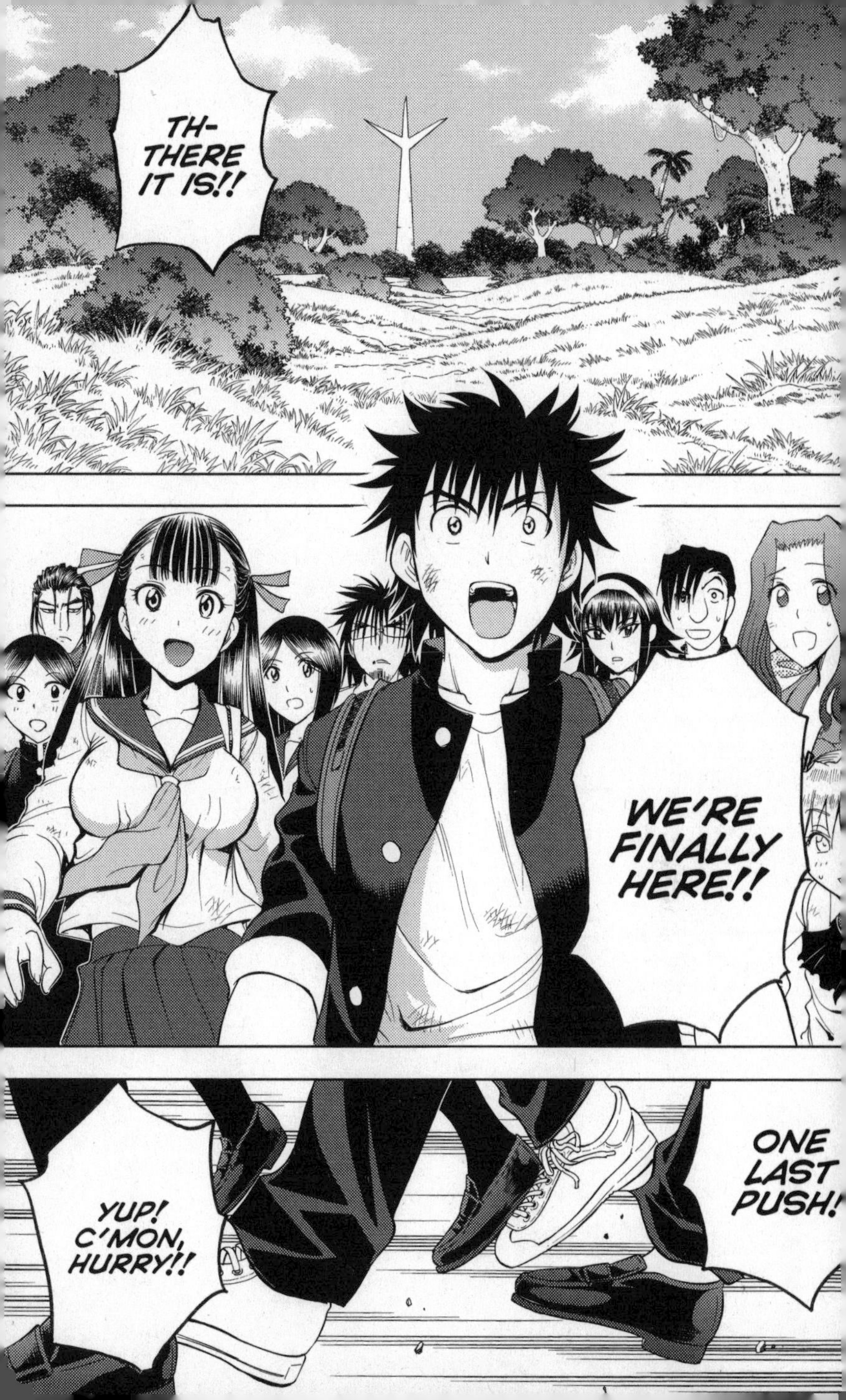
TH- THERE IT IS!!
WE'RE FINALLY HERE!!
ONE LAST PUSH!
YUP! C'MON, HURRY!!

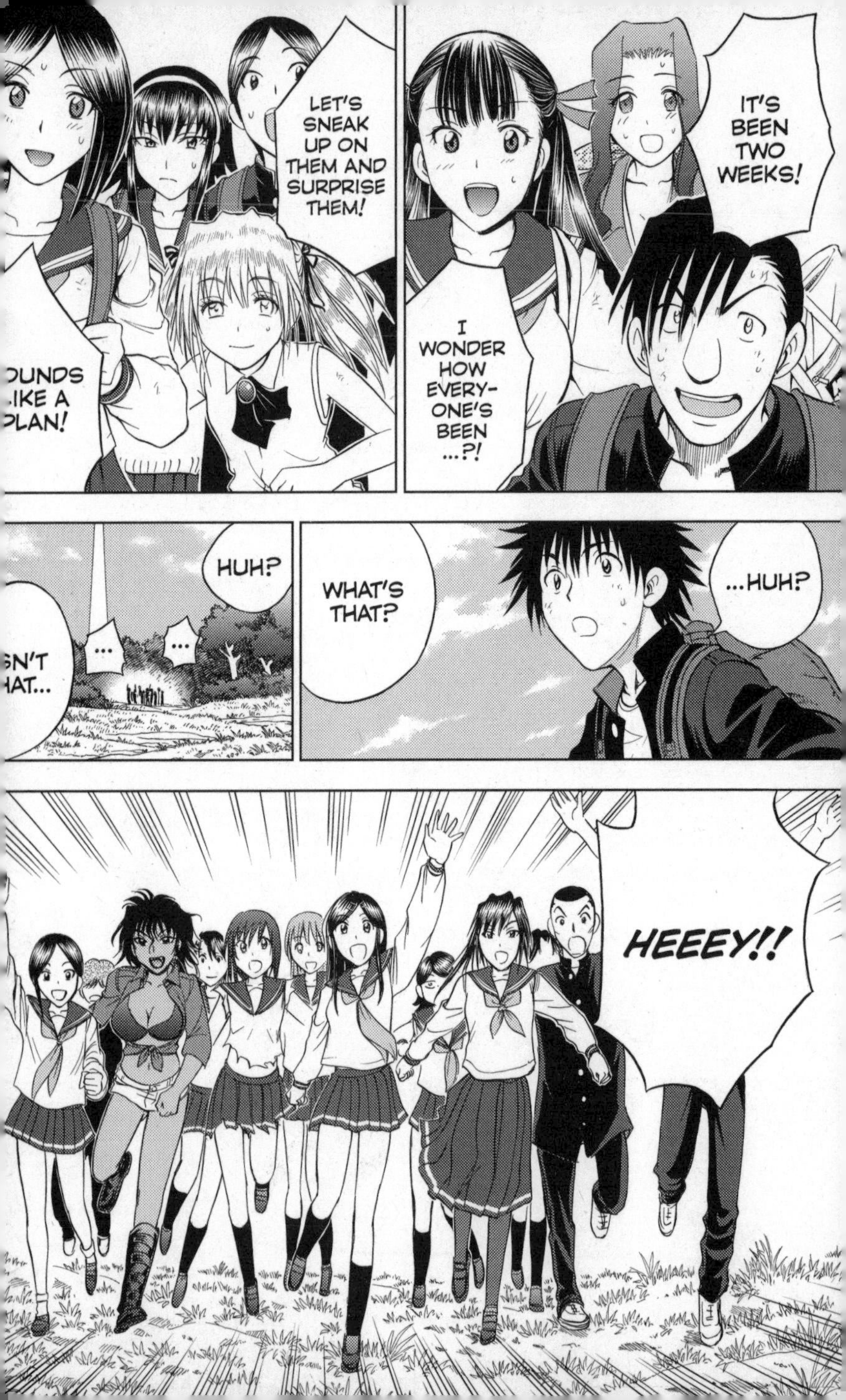
IT'S BEEN TWO WEEKS!
I WONDER HOW EVERY-ONE'S BEEN ...?!
LET'S SNEAK UP ON THEM AND SURPRISE THEM!
OUNDS IKE A PLAN!
...HUH?
WHAT'S THAT?
HUH?
...
...
SN'T HAT...
HEEEY!!

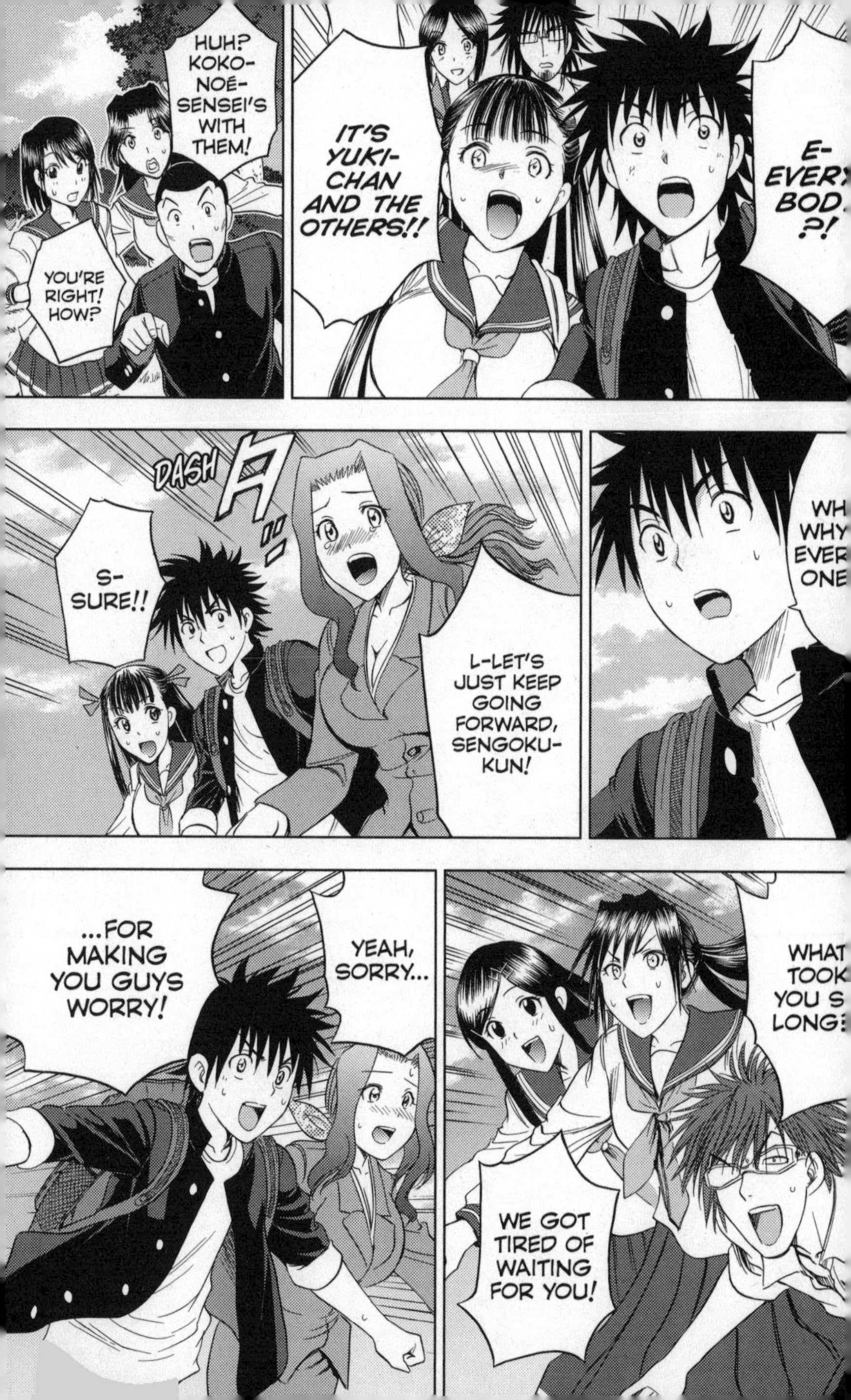
E-EVERY BOD ?!
IT'S YUKI-CHAN AND THE OTHERS!!
HUH? KOKONOE-SENSEI'S WITH THEM!
YOU'RE RIGHT! HOW?
WH WHY EVER ONE
L-LET'S JUST KEEP GOING FORWARD, SENGOKU-KUN!
DASH
S-SURE!!
WHAT TOOK YOU S LONG
WE GOT TIRED OF WAITING FOR YOU!
YEAH, SORRY...
...FOR MAKING YOU GUYS WORRY!

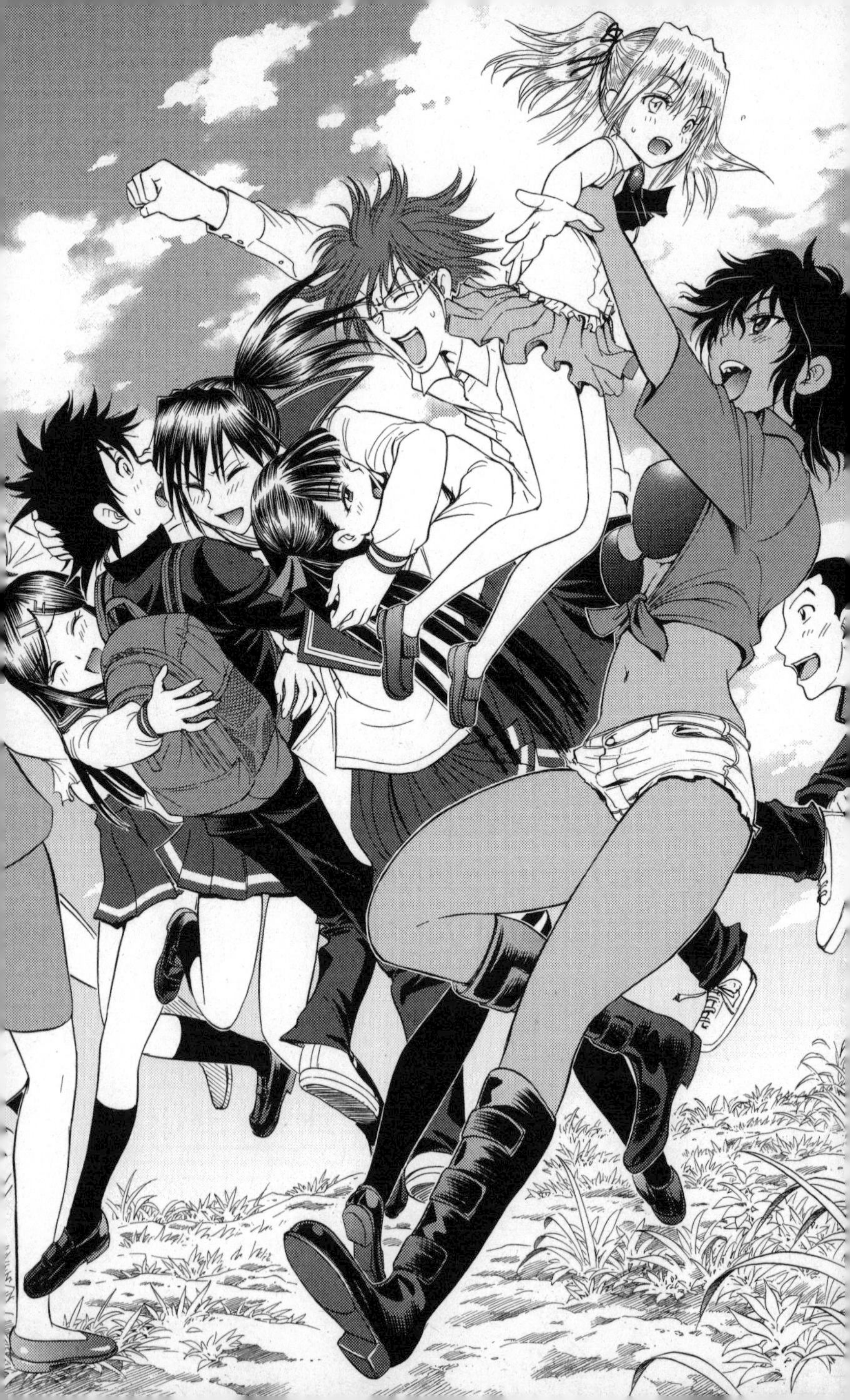

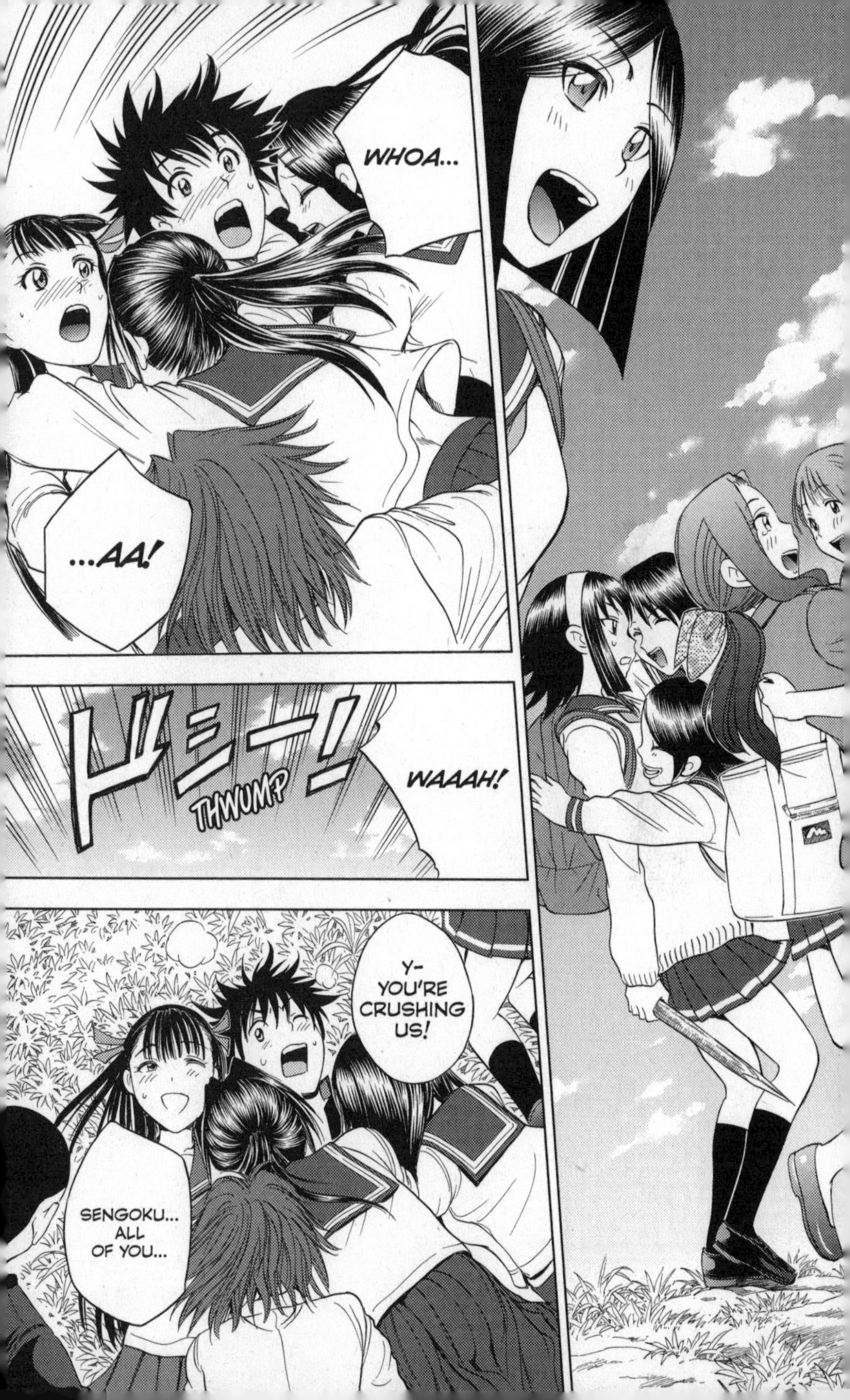
WHOA...
...AA!
WAAAH!
ドシーー!
THWUMP
Y-YOU'RE CRUSHING US!
SENGOKU... ALL OF YOU...

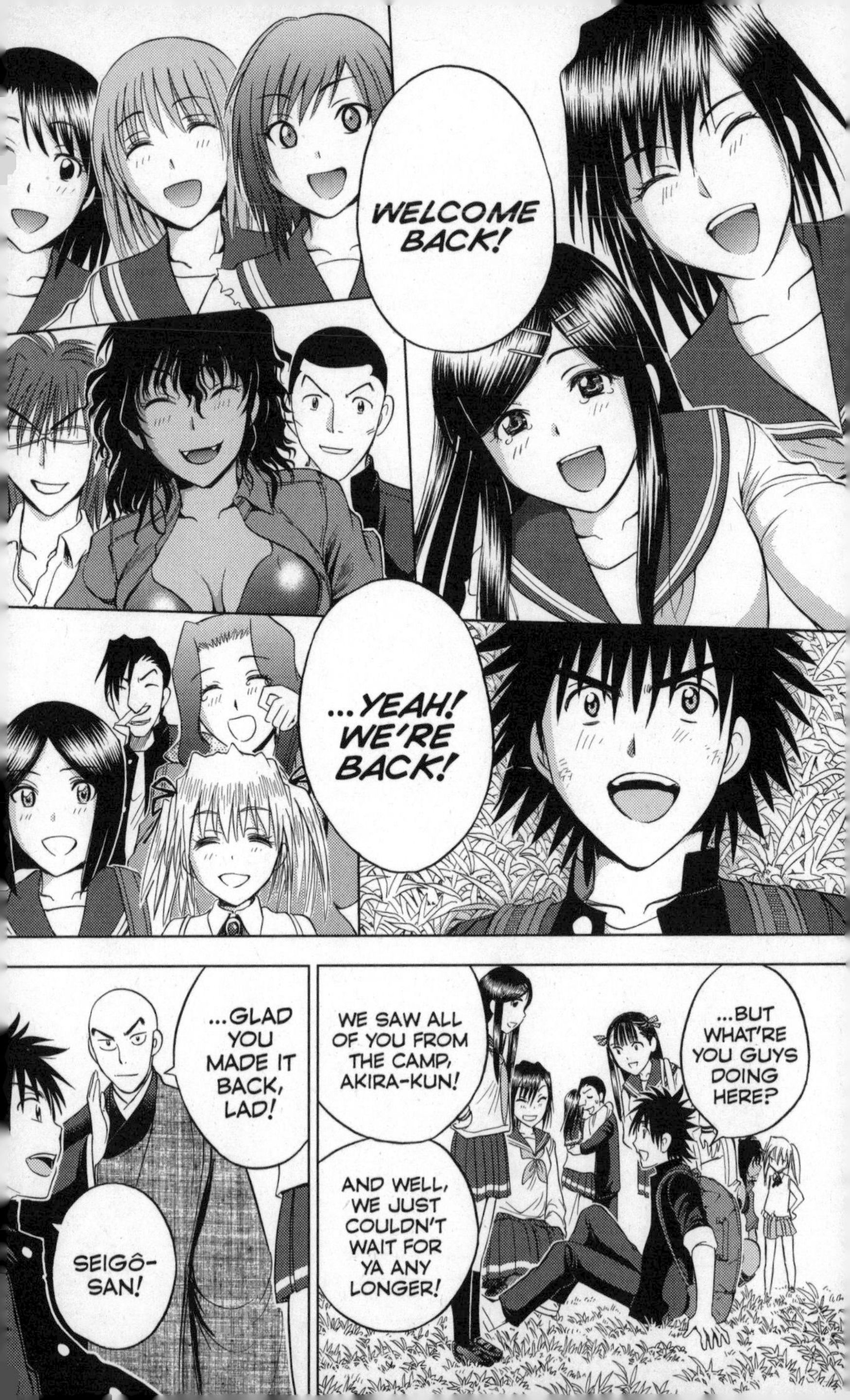
WELCOME BACK!
...YEAH! WE'RE BACK!
...BUT WHAT'RE YOU GUYS DOING HERE?
WE SAW ALL OF YOU FROM THE CAMP, AKIRA-KUN!
AND WELL, WE JUST COULDN'T WAIT FOR YA ANY LONGER!
...GLAD YOU MADE IT BACK, LAD!
SEIGÔ-SAN!

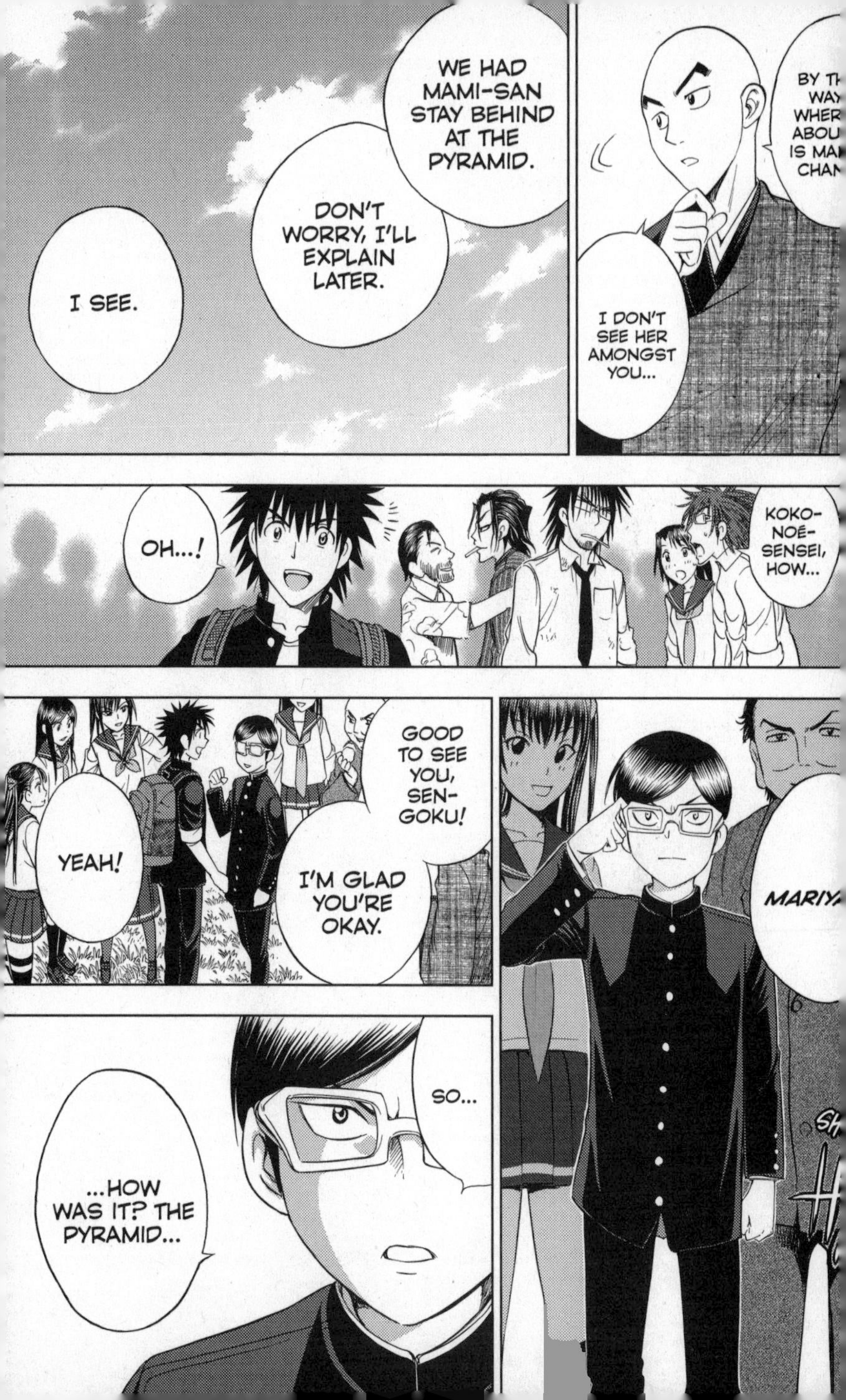
BY TH WAY WHER ABOU IS MA CHAN
I DON'T SEE HER AMONGST YOU...
WE HAD MAMI-SAN STAY BEHIND AT THE PYRAMID.
DON'T WORRY, I'LL EXPLAIN LATER.
I SEE.
KOKO-NOÉ-SENSEI, HOW...
OH...!
MARIYA
GOOD TO SEE YOU, SEN-GOKU!
I'M GLAD YOU'RE OKAY.
YEAH!
SO...
...HOW WAS IT? THE PYRAMID...

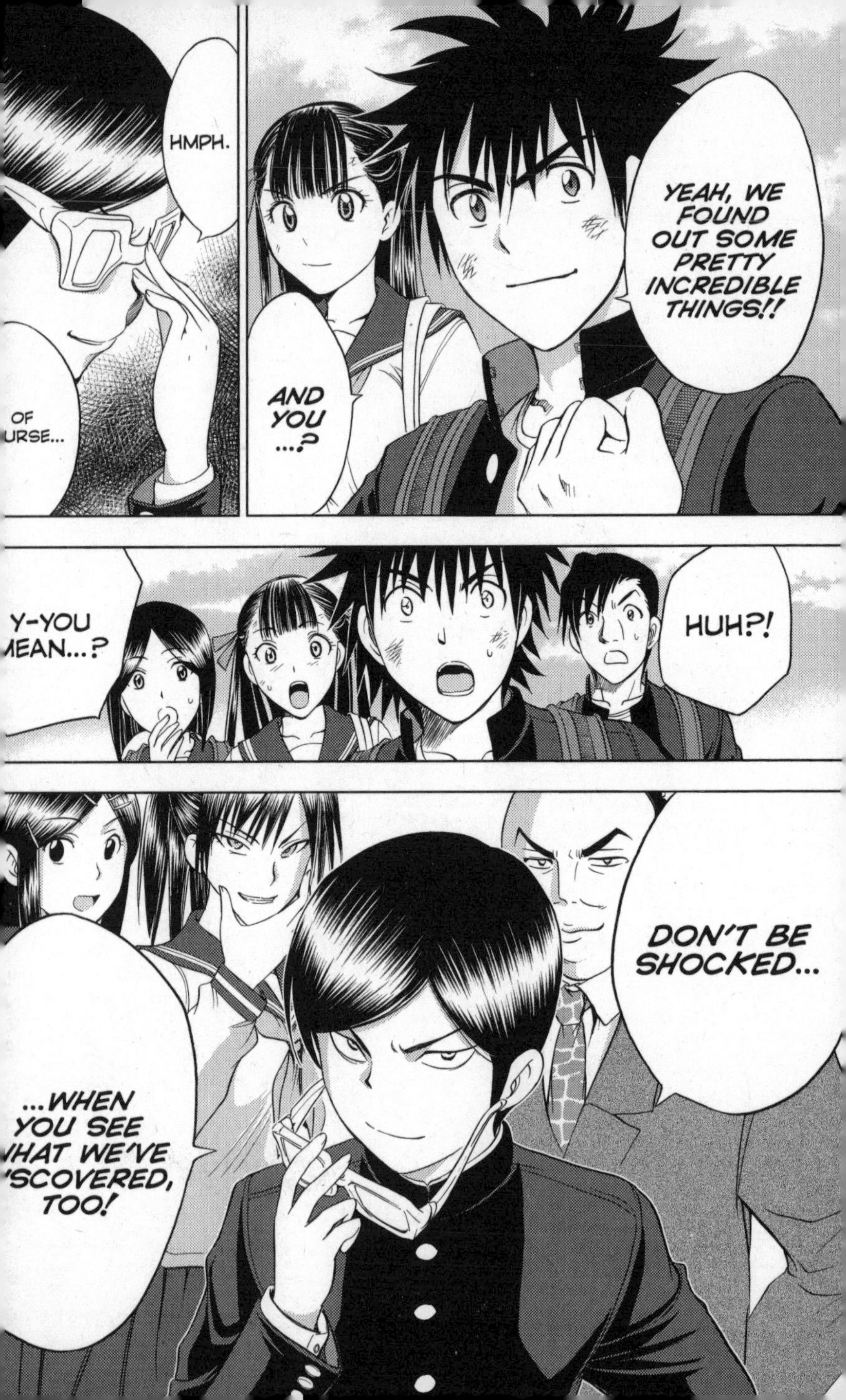
YEAH, WE FOUND OUT SOME PRETTY INCREDIBLE THINGS!!
AND YOU ...?
HMPH.
OF URSE...
HUH?!
Y-YOU MEAN...?
DON'T BE SHOCKED...
...WHEN YOU SEE HAT WE'VE SCOVERED, TOO!

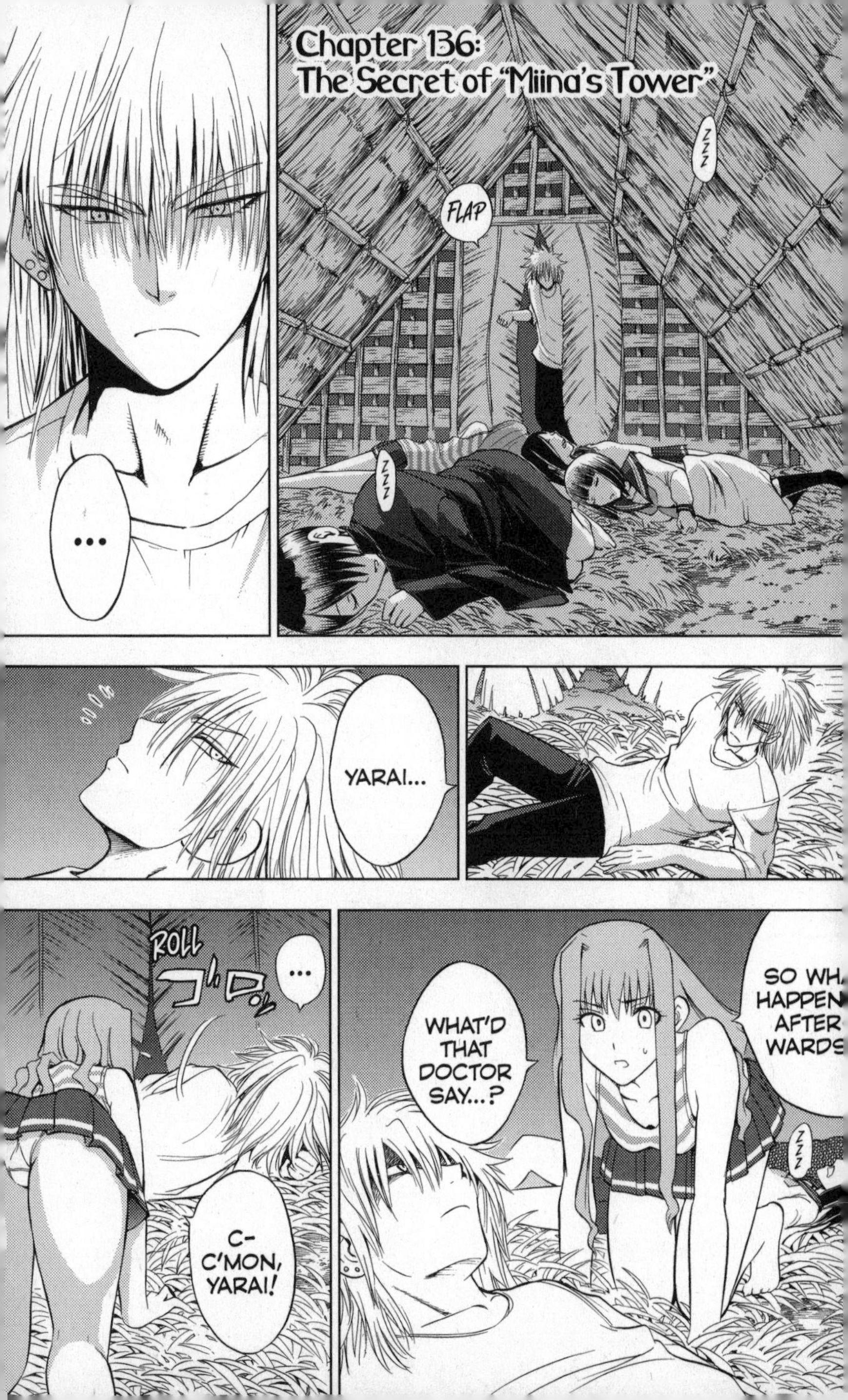

Chapter 136:
The Secret of "Miina's Tower"
ZZZ
FLAP
ZZZ
...
YARAI...
SO WHA HAPPEN AFTER WARDS
WHAT'D THAT DOCTOR SAY...?
ZZZ
ROLL
...
C-C'MON, YARAI!

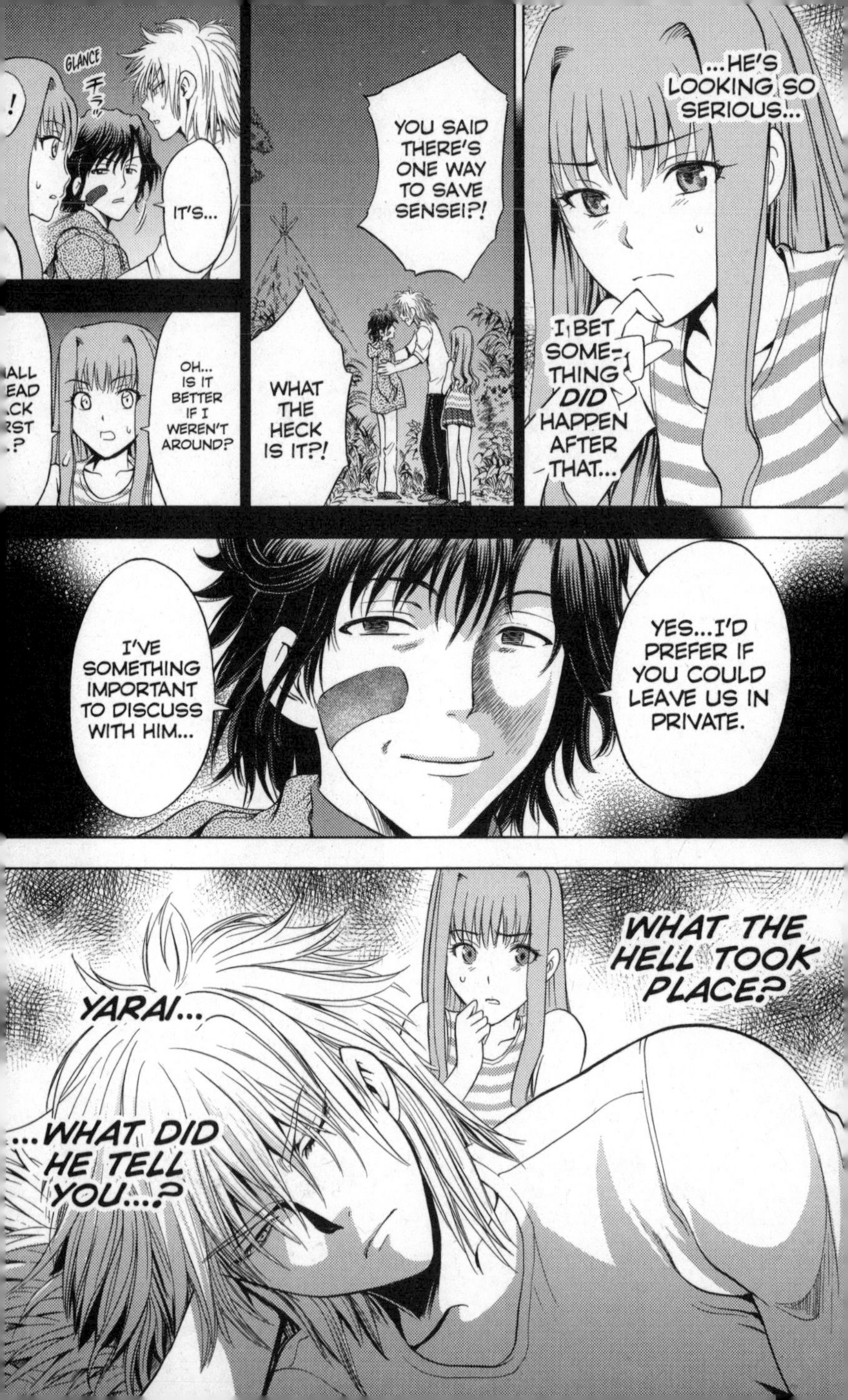
...HE'S LOOKING SO SERIOUS...
I BET SOMETHING *DID* HAPPEN AFTER THAT...
YOU SAID THERE'S ONE WAY TO SAVE SENSEI?!
WHAT THE HECK IS IT?!
GLANCE
!
IT'S...
OH... IS IT BETTER IF I WEREN'T AROUND?
YES...I'D PREFER IF YOU COULD LEAVE US IN PRIVATE.
I'VE SOMETHING IMPORTANT TO DISCUSS WITH HIM...
WHAT THE HELL TOOK PLACE?
YARAI...
...WHAT DID HE TELL YOU...?

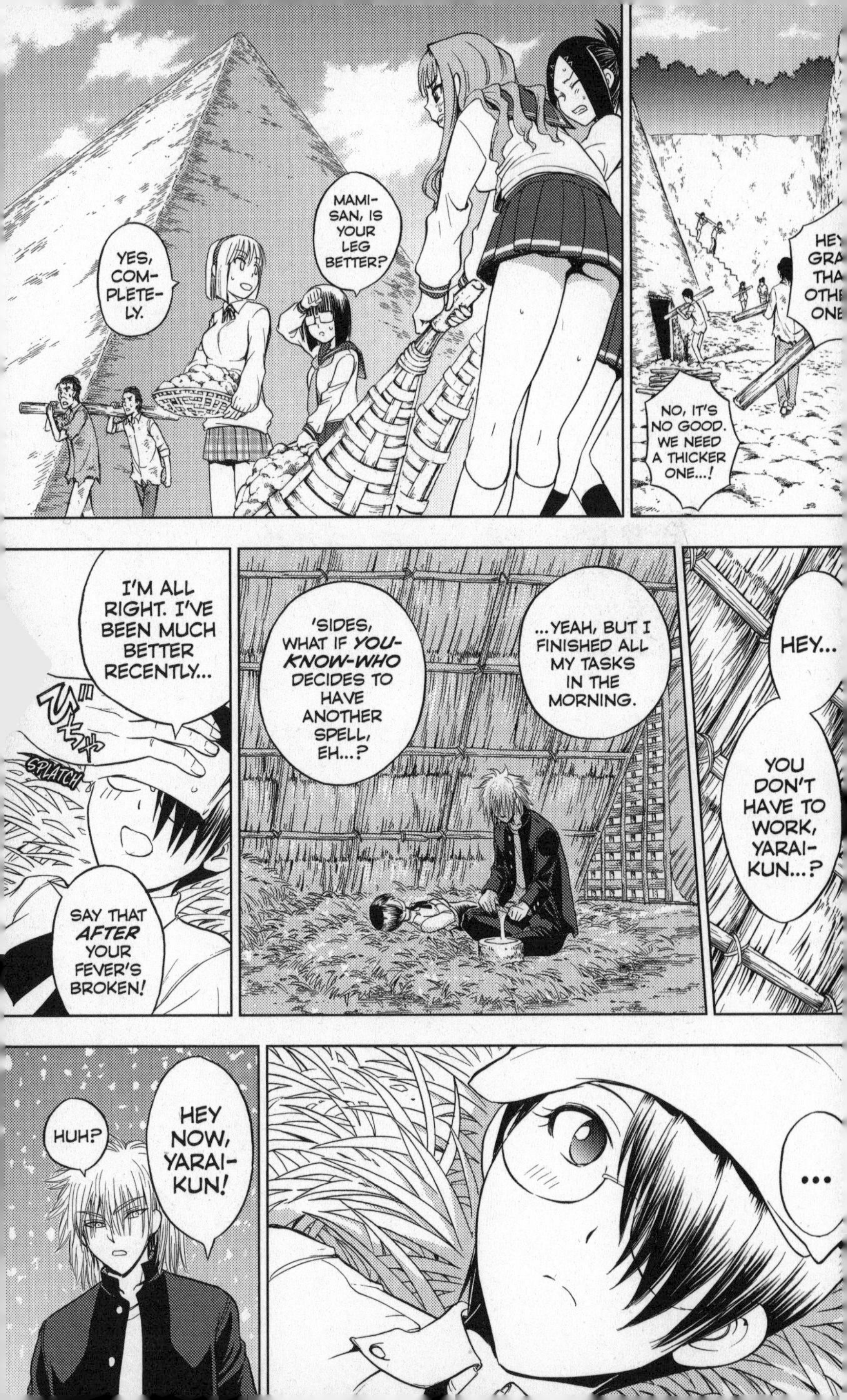
HEY GRA THA OTHE ONE
NO, IT'S NO GOOD. WE NEED A THICKER ONE...!
MAMI-SAN, IS YOUR LEG BETTER?
YES, COMPLETELY.
HEY...
YOU DON'T HAVE TO WORK, YARAI-KUN...?
...YEAH, BUT I FINISHED ALL MY TASKS IN THE MORNING.
'SIDES, WHAT IF *YOU-KNOW-WHO* DECIDES TO HAVE ANOTHER SPELL, EH...?
I'M ALL RIGHT. I'VE BEEN MUCH BETTER RECENTLY...
SPLATCH
SAY THAT *AFTER* YOUR FEVER'S BROKEN!
...
HEY NOW, YARAI-KUN!
HUH?

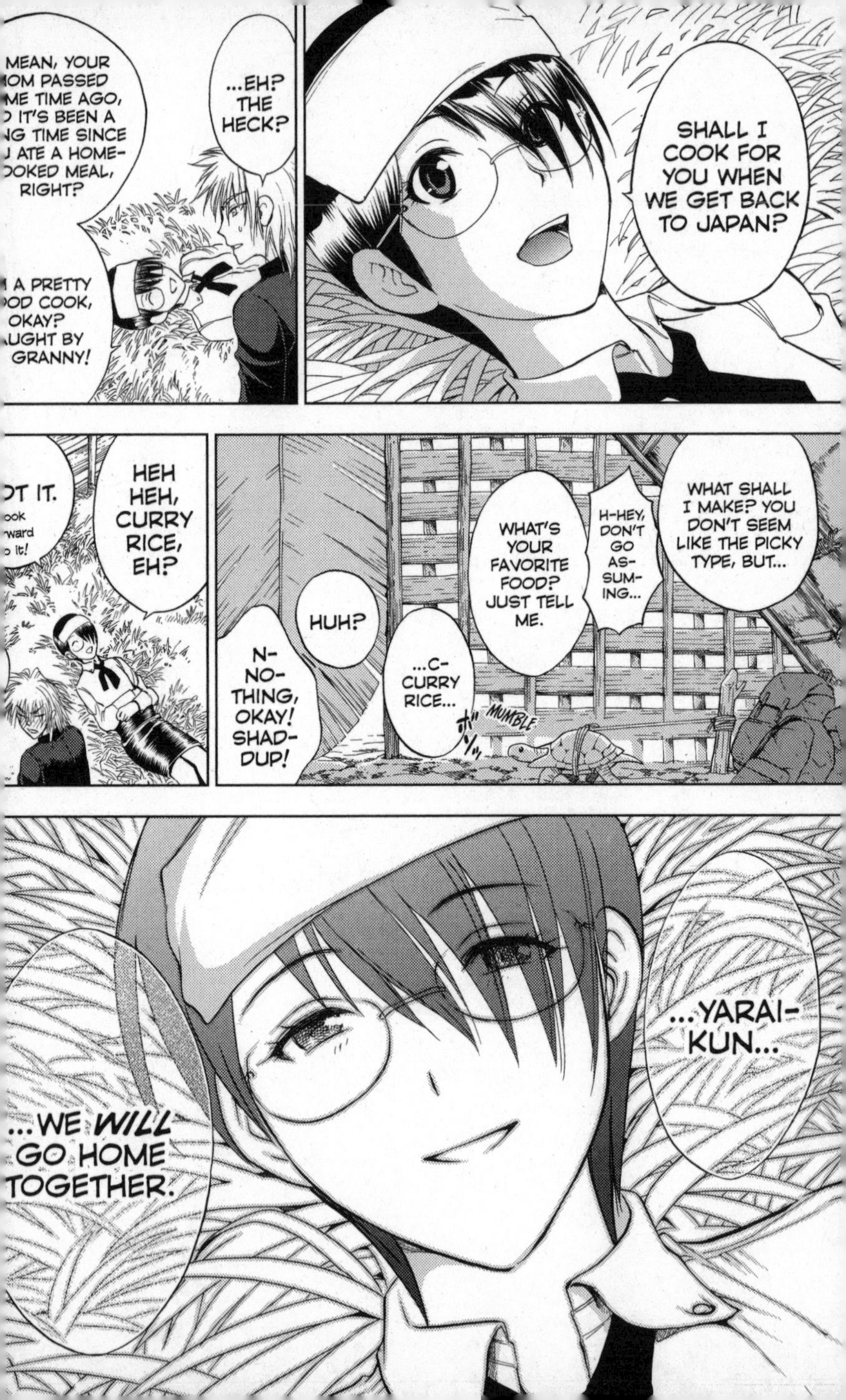
SHALL I COOK FOR YOU WHEN WE GET BACK TO JAPAN?
...EH? THE HECK?
MEAN, YOUR IOM PASSED ME TIME AGO, D IT'S BEEN A NG TIME SINCE U ATE A HOME-OOKED MEAL, RIGHT?
A PRETTY OD COOK, OKAY? UGHT BY GRANNY!
WHAT SHALL I MAKE? YOU DON'T SEEM LIKE THE PICKY TYPE, BUT...
H-HEY, DON'T GO AS-SUMING...
WHAT'S YOUR FAVORITE FOOD? JUST TELL ME.
...C-CURRY RICE...
MUMBLE
HUH?
N-NO-THING, OKAY! SHAD-DUP!
HEH HEH, CURRY RICE, EH?
OT IT.
ook ward o it!
...YARAI-KUN...
...WE *WILL* GO HOME TOGETHER.

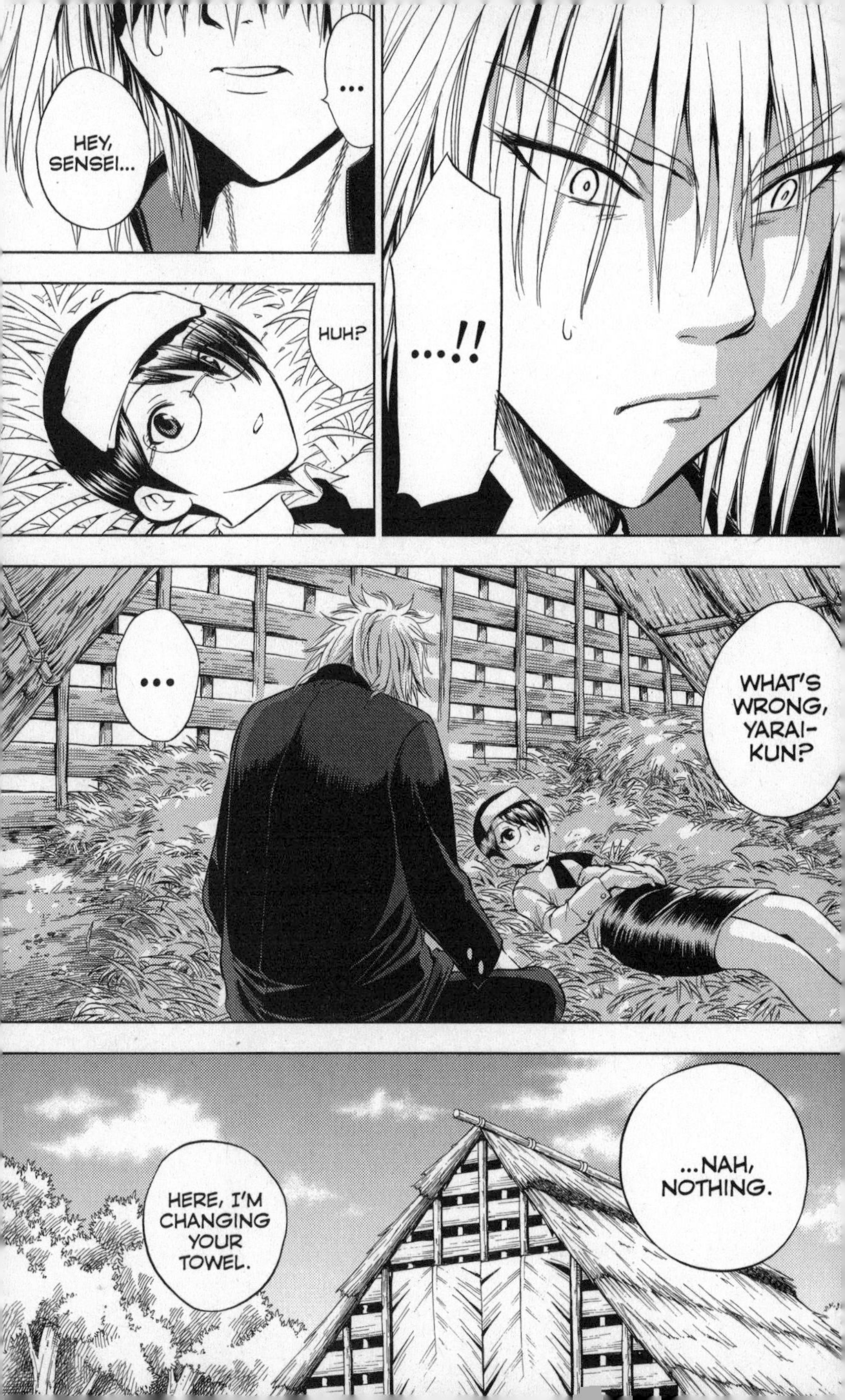
...!!
...
HEY, SENSEI...
HUH?
WHAT'S WRONG, YARAI-KUN?
...
...NAH, NOTHING.
HERE, I'M CHANGING YOUR TOWEL.

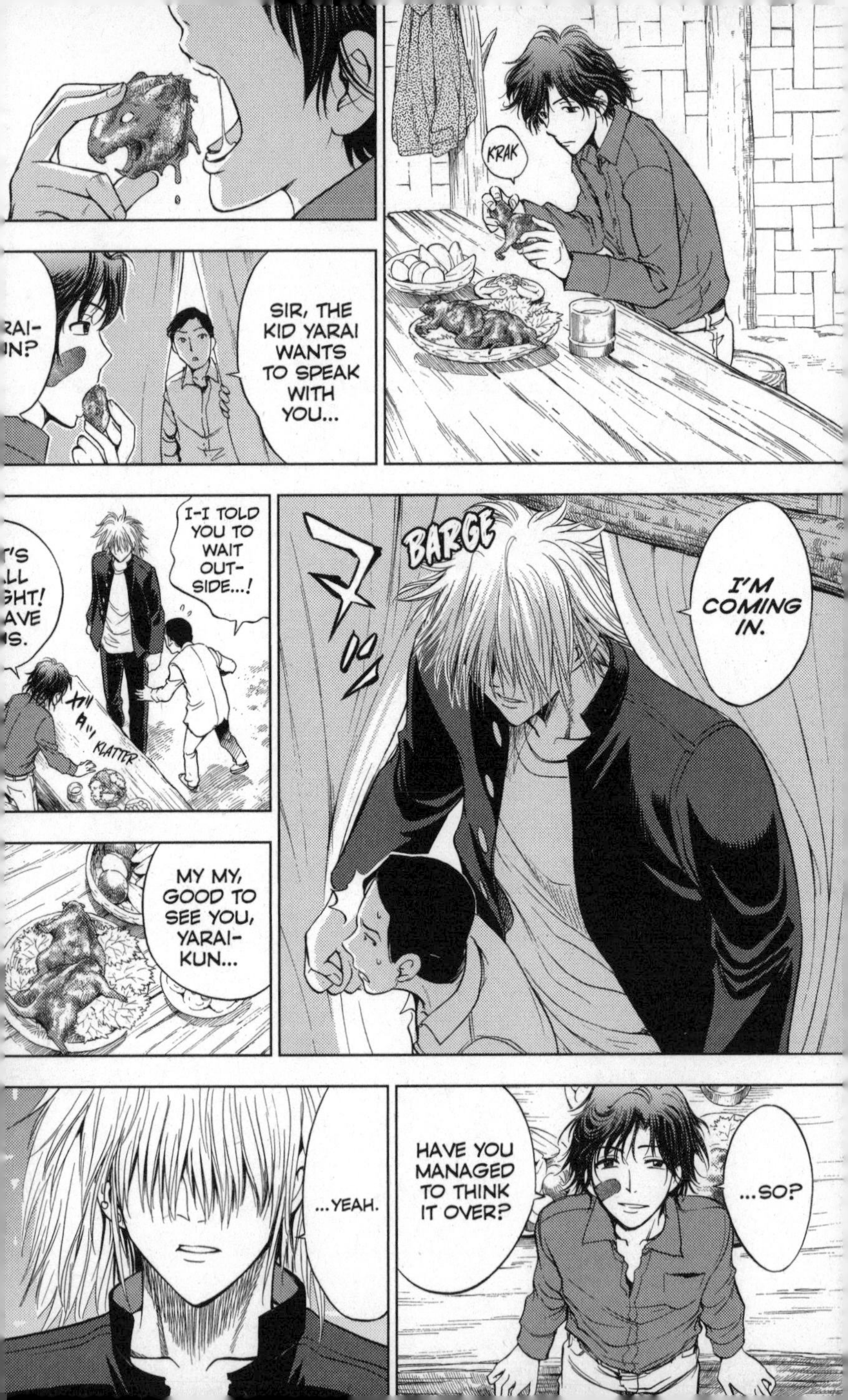
KRAK
SIR, THE KID YARAI WANTS TO SPEAK WITH YOU...
RAI- N?
BARGE
I'M COMING IN.
I-I TOLD YOU TO WAIT OUT-SIDE...!
T'S LL GHT! AVE S.
KLATTER
MY MY, GOOD TO SEE YOU, YARAI-KUN...
...SO?
HAVE YOU MANAGED TO THINK IT OVER?
...YEAH.

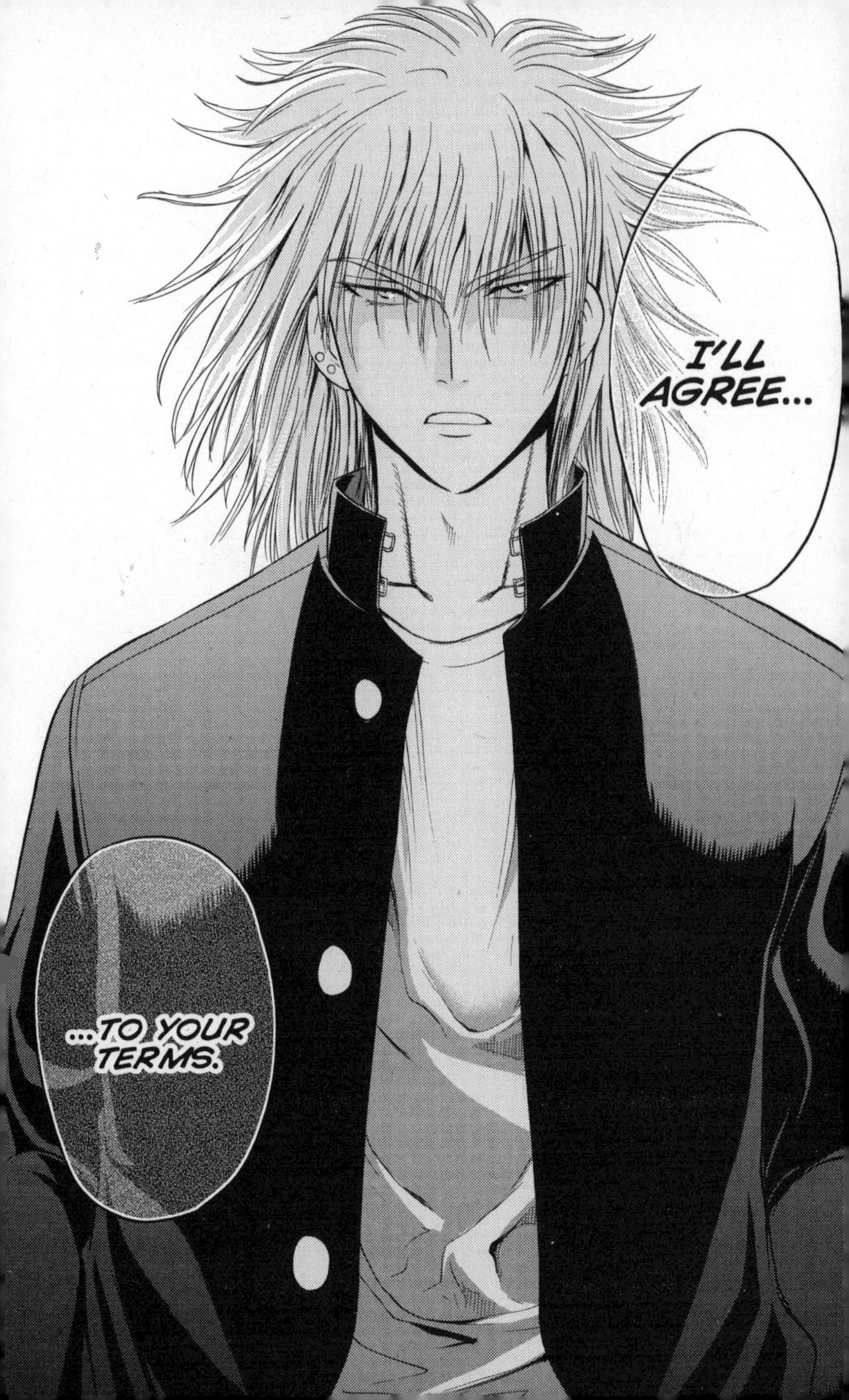
I'LL AGREE...
...TO YOUR TERMS.

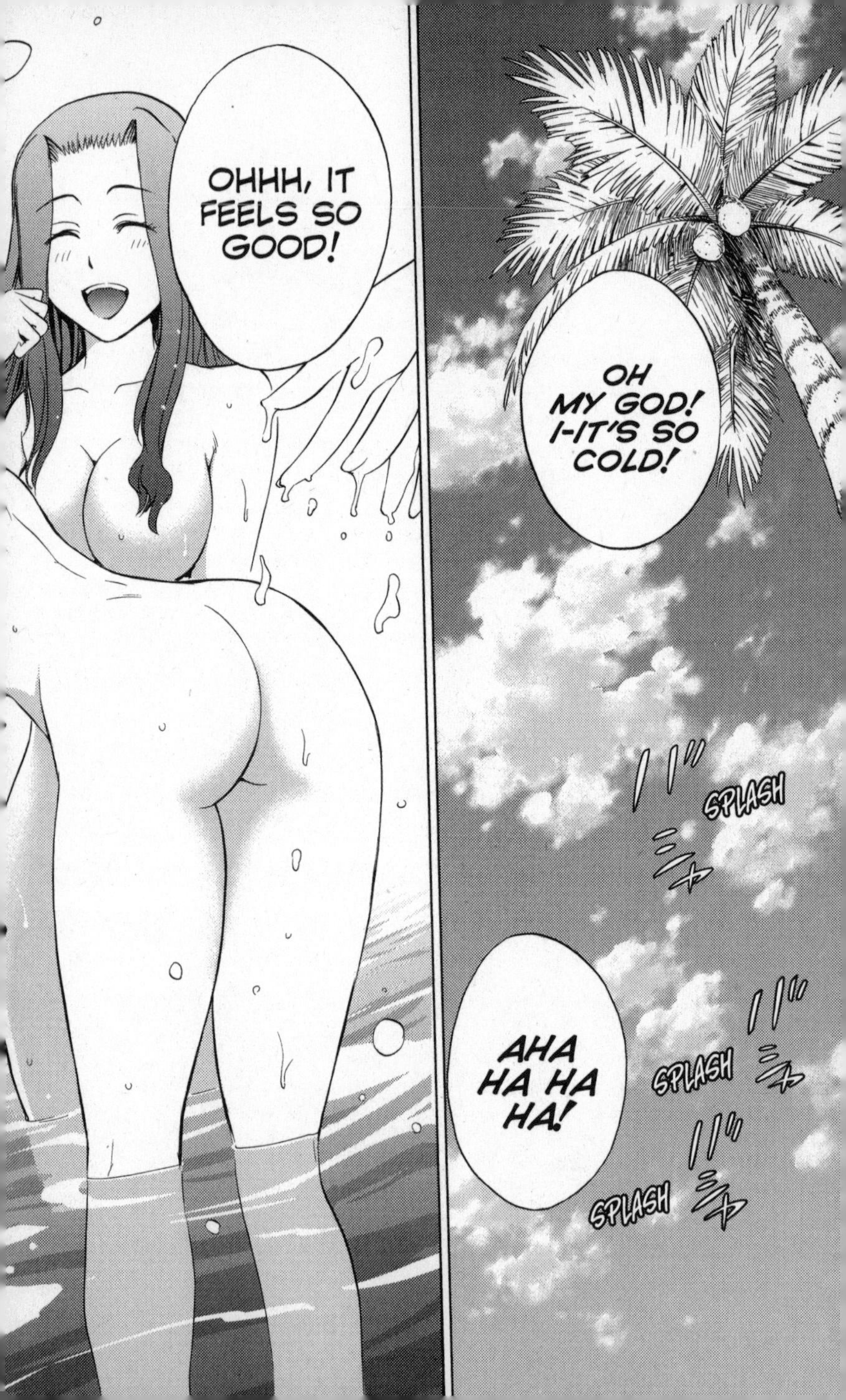
OH MY GOD! I-IT'S SO COLD!
SPLASH
AHA HA HA HA!
SPLASH
SPLASH
OHHH, IT FEELS SO GOOD!

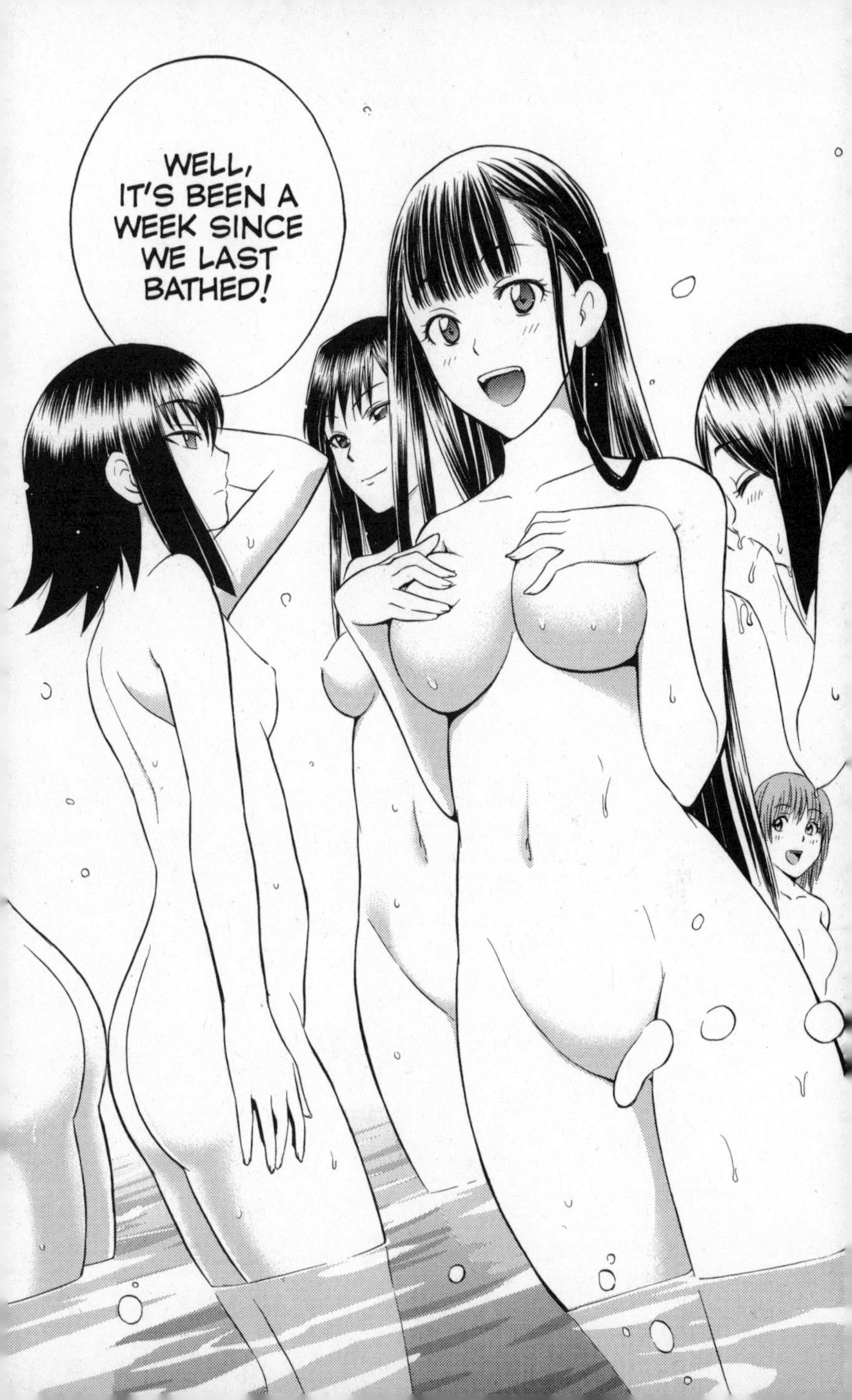
WELL, IT'S BEEN A WEEK SINCE WE LAST BATHED!

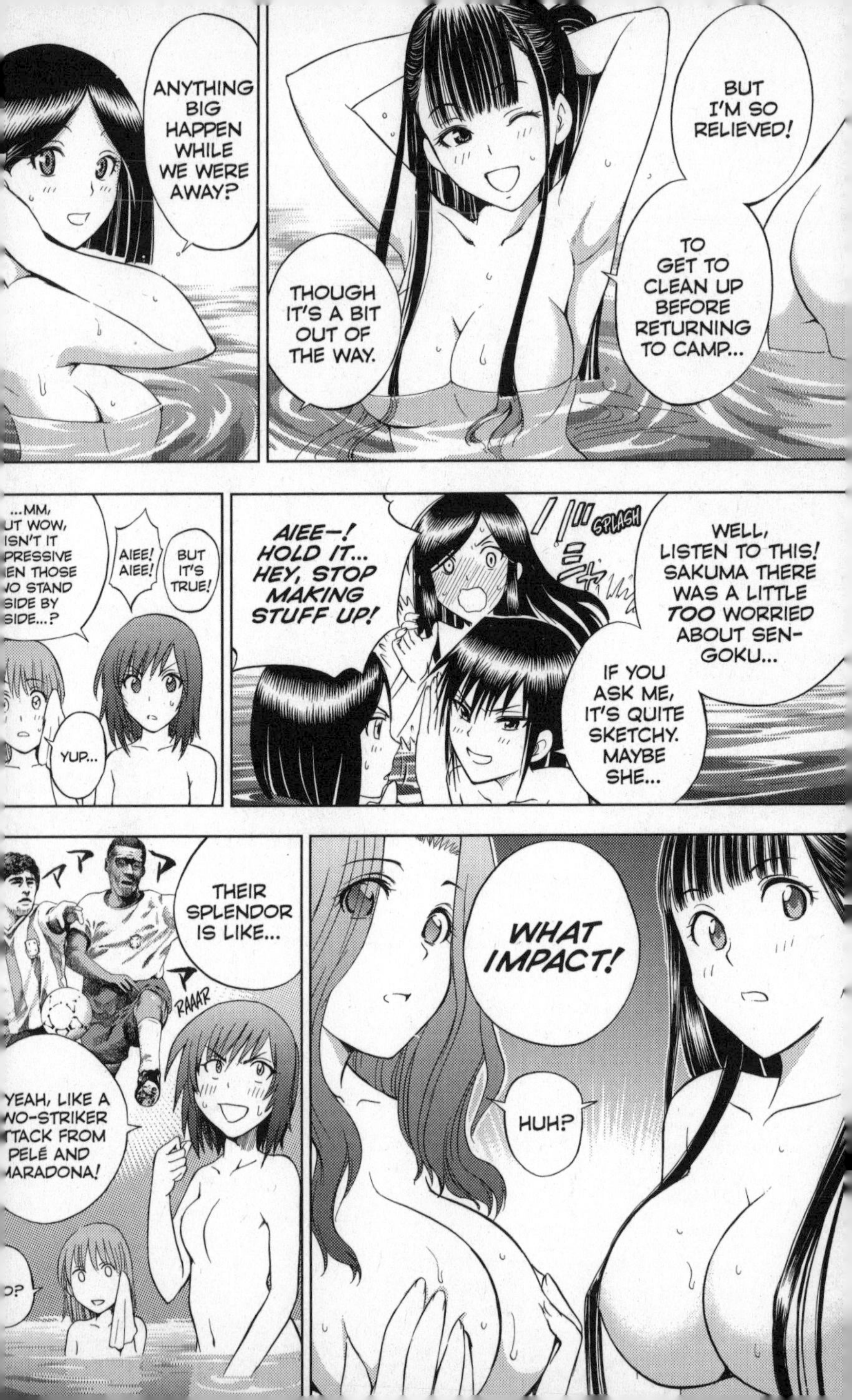
BUT I'M SO RELIEVED!
TO GET TO CLEAN UP BEFORE RETURNING TO CAMP...
THOUGH IT'S A BIT OUT OF THE WAY.
ANYTHING BIG HAPPEN WHILE WE WERE AWAY?
WELL, LISTEN TO THIS! SAKUMA THERE WAS A LITTLE *TOO* WORRIED ABOUT SEN-GOKU...
SPLASH
IF YOU ASK ME, IT'S QUITE SKETCHY. MAYBE SHE...
AIEE—! HOLD IT... HEY, STOP MAKING STUFF UP!
BUT IT'S TRUE!
AIEE! AIEE!
...MM, UT WOW, ISN'T IT PRESSIVE EN THOSE VO STAND SIDE BY SIDE...?
YUP...
WHAT IMPACT!
HUH?
THEIR SPLENDOR IS LIKE...
RAAAR
YEAH, LIKE A VO-STRIKER TTACK FROM PELÉ AND MARADONA!
O?

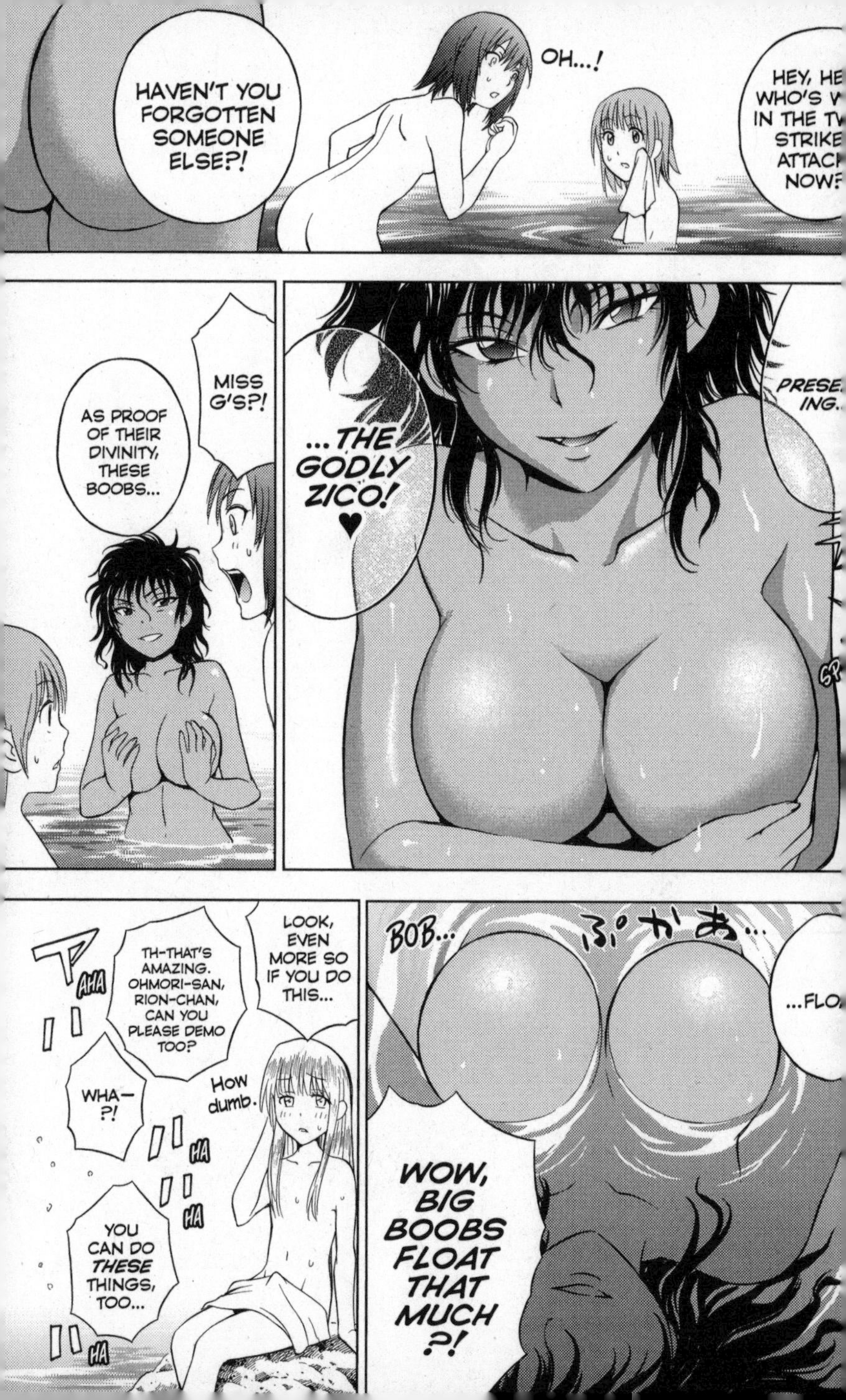
HEY, HE WHO'S W IN THE TW STRIKE ATTAC NOW?
OH...!
HAVEN'T YOU FORGOTTEN SOMEONE ELSE?!
PRESE ING..
...THE GODLY ZICO! ♥
MISS G'S?!
AS PROOF OF THEIR DIVINITY, THESE BOOBS...
BOB...
ぷかあ…
...FLO
WOW, BIG BOOBS FLOAT THAT MUCH?!
LOOK, EVEN MORE SO IF YOU DO THIS...
TH-THAT'S AMAZING. OHMORI-SAN, RION-CHAN, CAN YOU PLEASE DEMO TOO?
AHA
How dumb.
WHA—?!
HA
HA
YOU CAN DO THESE THINGS, TOO...
HA

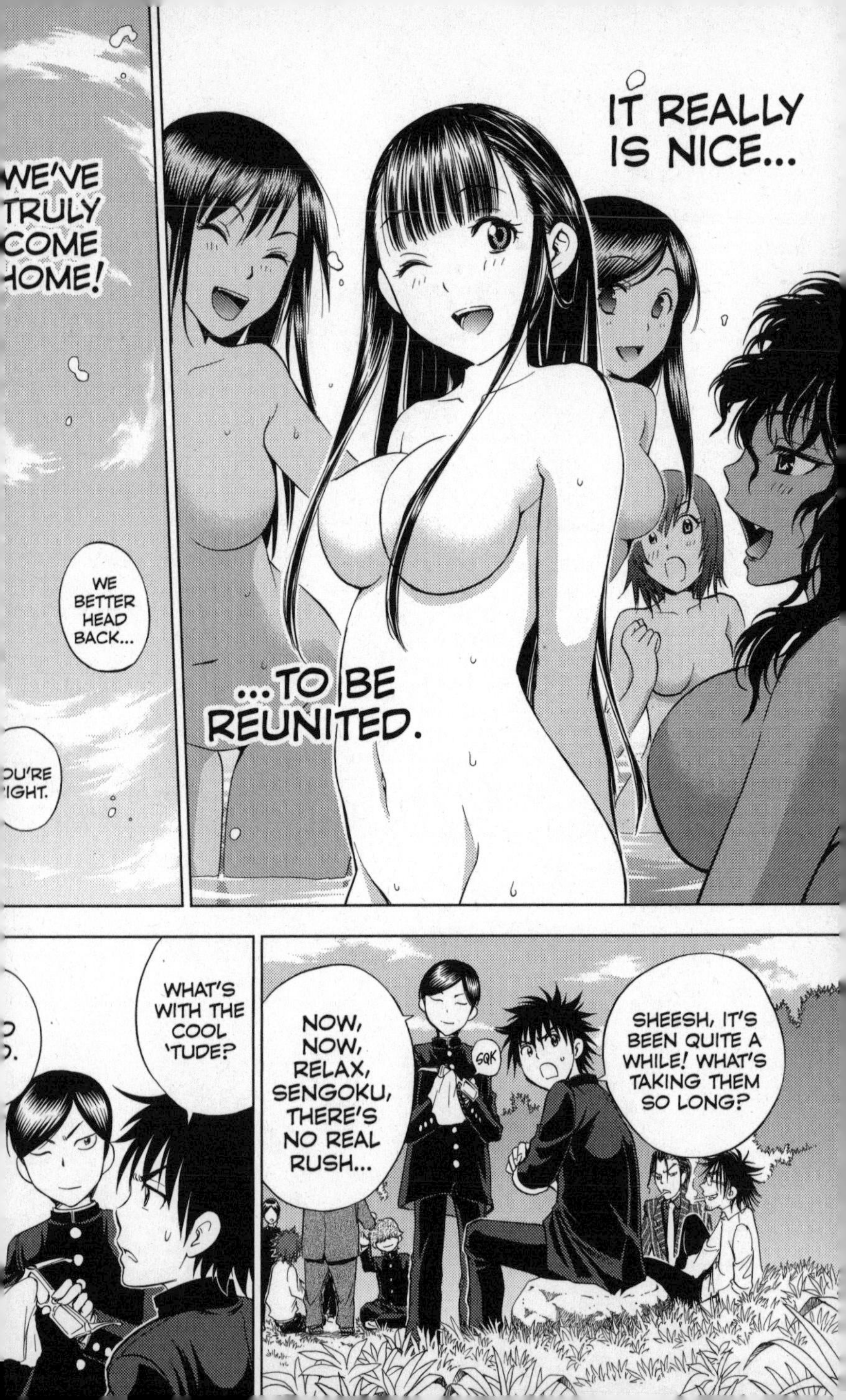
IT REALLY IS NICE...
...TO BE REUNITED.
WE'VE TRULY COME HOME!
WE BETTER HEAD BACK...
OU'RE IGHT.
SHEESH, IT'S BEEN QUITE A WHILE! WHAT'S TAKING THEM SO LONG?
SQK
NOW, NOW, RELAX, SENGOKU, THERE'S NO REAL RUSH...
WHAT'S WITH THE COOL 'TUDE?

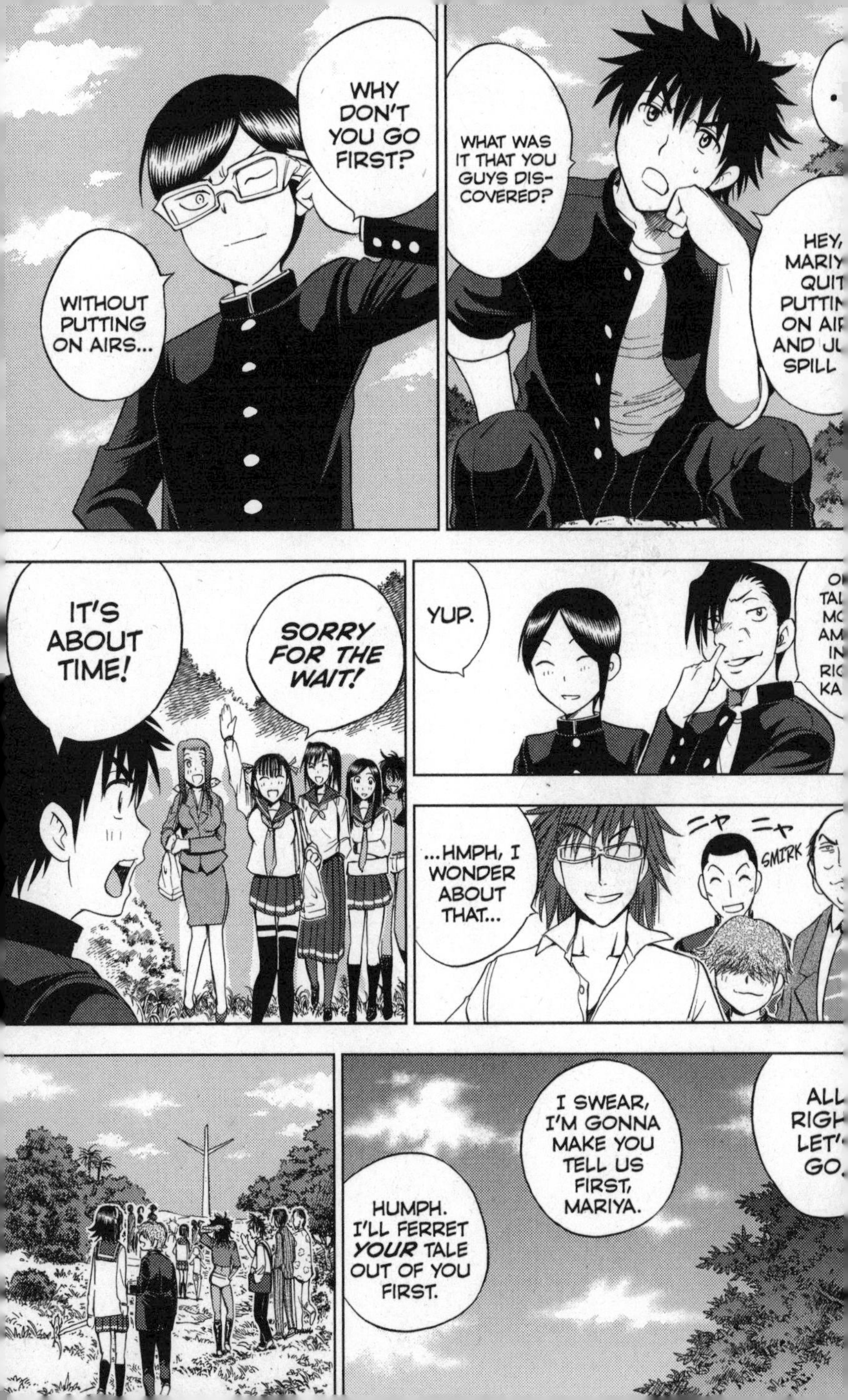
HEY, MARIY QUIT PUTTIN ON AI AND JU SPILL
WHAT WAS IT THAT YOU GUYS DIS-COVERED?
WHY DON'T YOU GO FIRST?
WITHOUT PUTTING ON AIRS...
YUP.
ニャ ニャ
SMIRK
...HMPH, I WONDER ABOUT THAT...
SORRY FOR THE WAIT!
IT'S ABOUT TIME!
ALL RIGH LET'S GO.
I SWEAR, I'M GONNA MAKE YOU TELL US FIRST, MARIYA.
HUMPH. I'LL FERRET *YOUR* TALE OUT OF YOU FIRST.

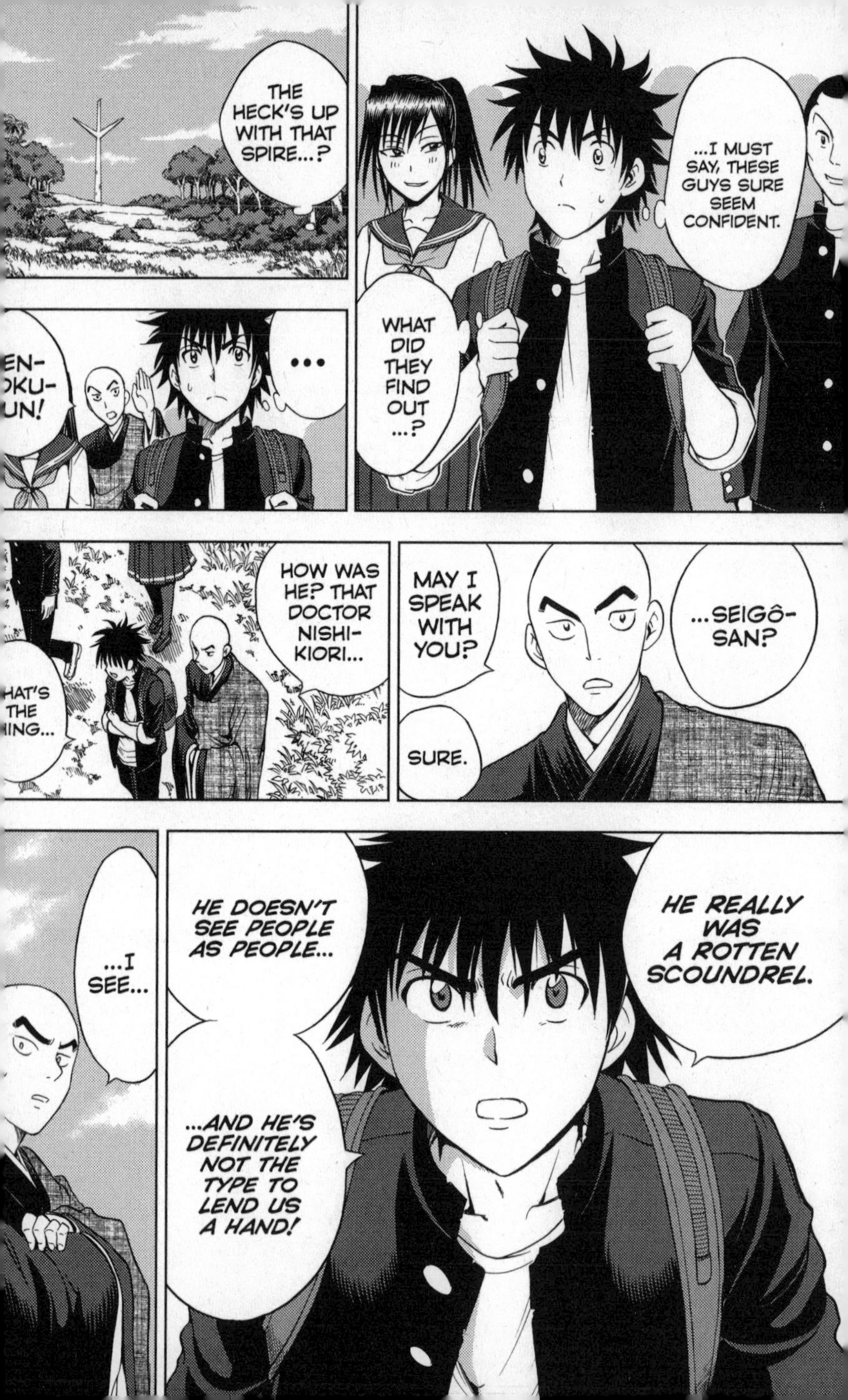
...I MUST SAY, THESE GUYS SURE SEEM CONFIDENT.
WHAT DID THEY FIND OUT...?
THE HECK'S UP WITH THAT SPIRE...?
...
EN-OKU-UN!
...SEIGÔ-SAN?
MAY I SPEAK WITH YOU?
SURE.
HOW WAS HE? THAT DOCTOR NISHIKIORI...
HAT'S THE HING...
HE REALLY WAS A ROTTEN SCOUNDREL.
HE DOESN'T SEE PEOPLE AS PEOPLE...
...AND HE'S DEFINITELY NOT THE TYPE TO LEND US A HAND!
...I SEE...

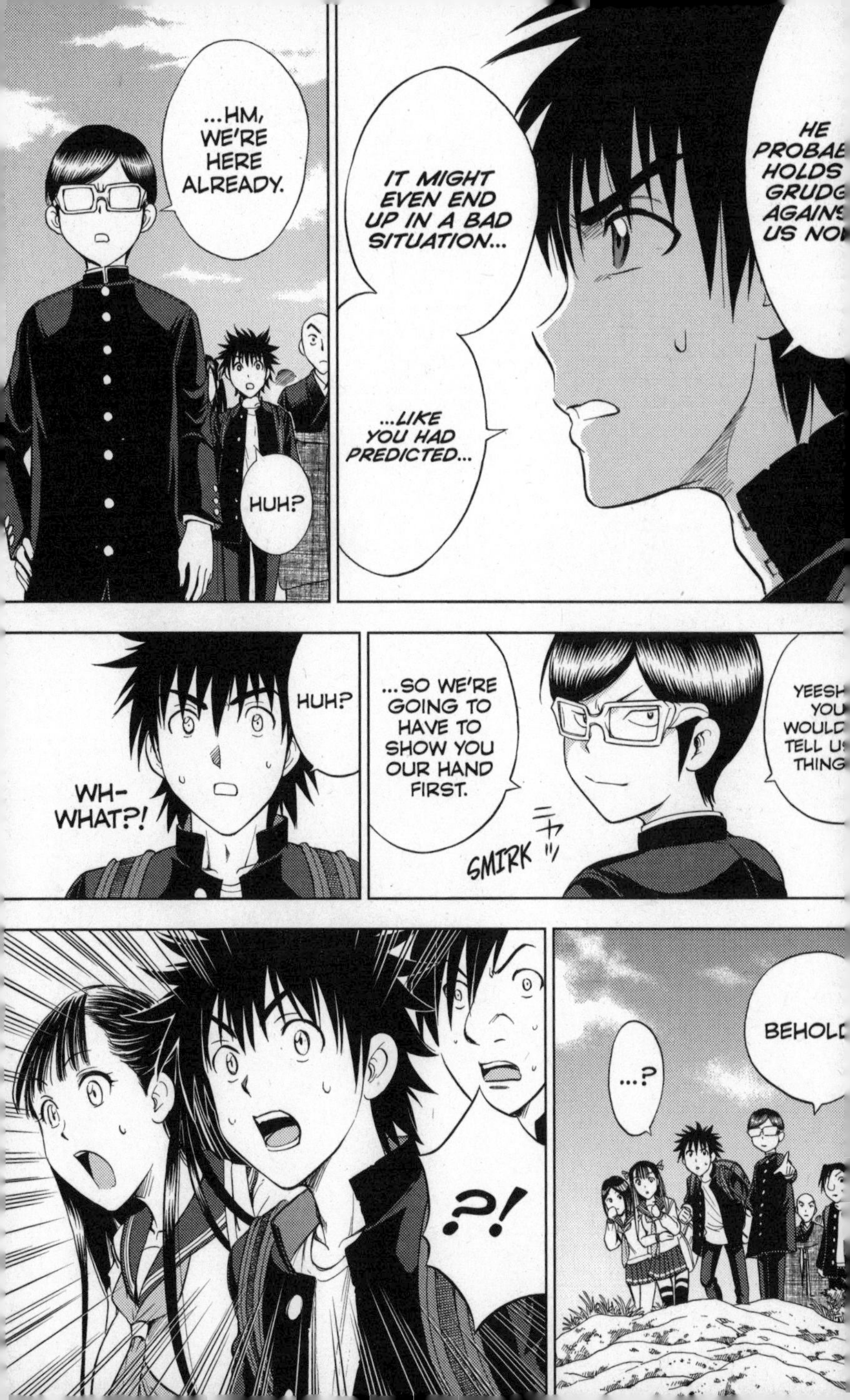
HE PROBAB HOLDS GRUDG AGAINS US NO
IT MIGHT EVEN END UP IN A BAD SITUATION...
...LIKE YOU HAD PREDICTED...
...HM, WE'RE HERE ALREADY.
HUH?
YEESH YOU WOULD TELL US THING
...SO WE'RE GOING TO HAVE TO SHOW YOU OUR HAND FIRST.
SMIRK
HUH?
WH- WHAT?!
BEHOLD
...?
?!

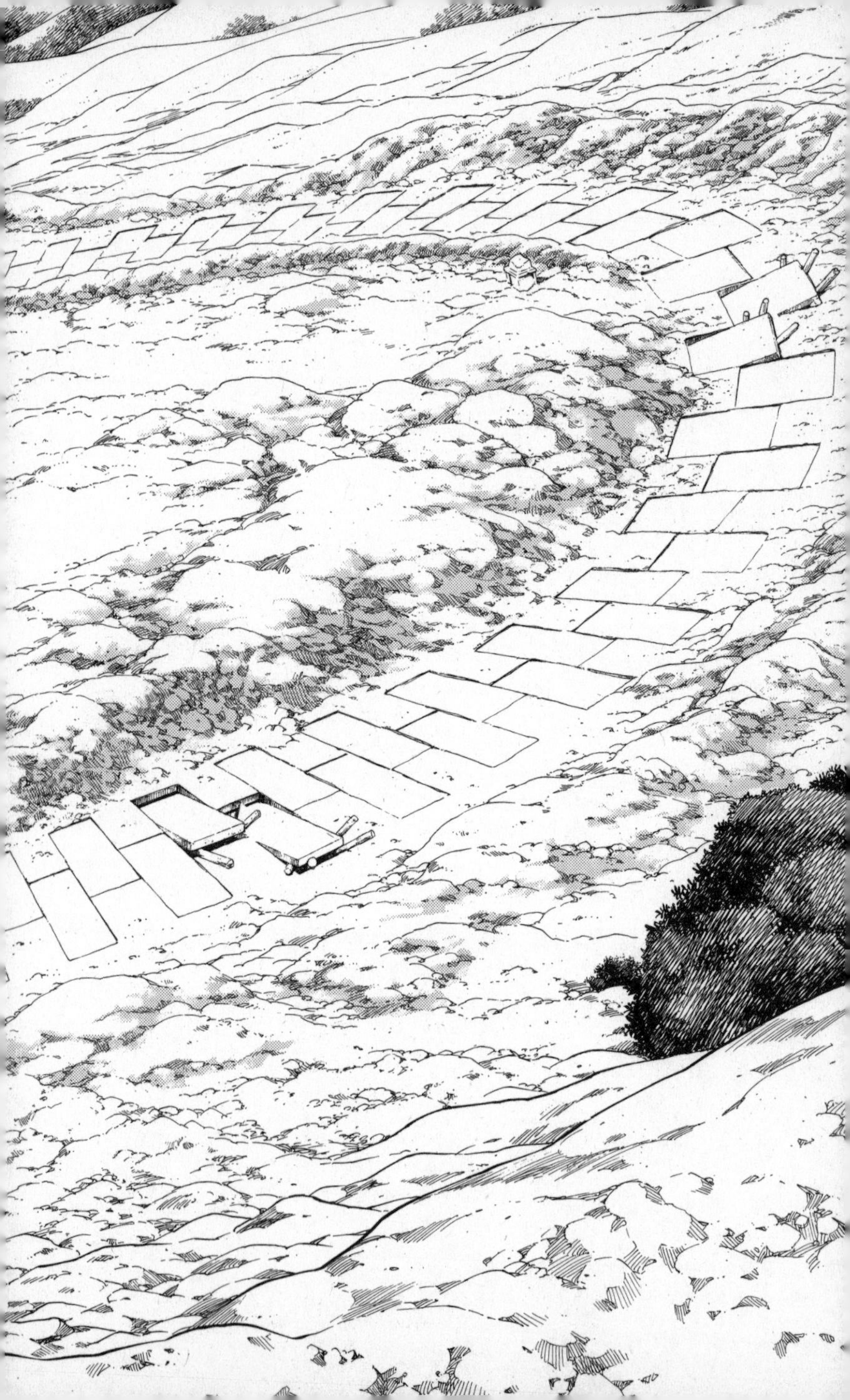

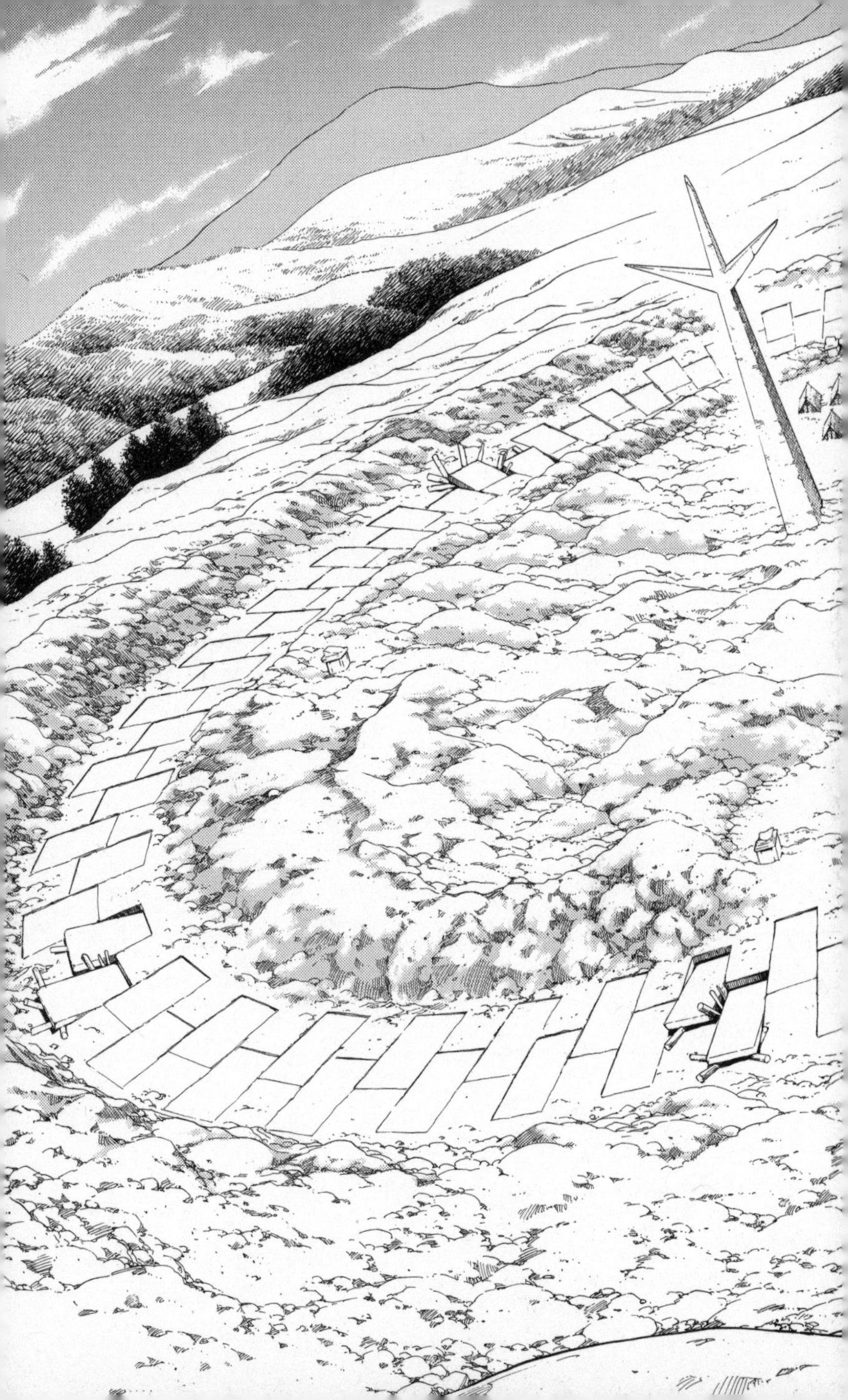

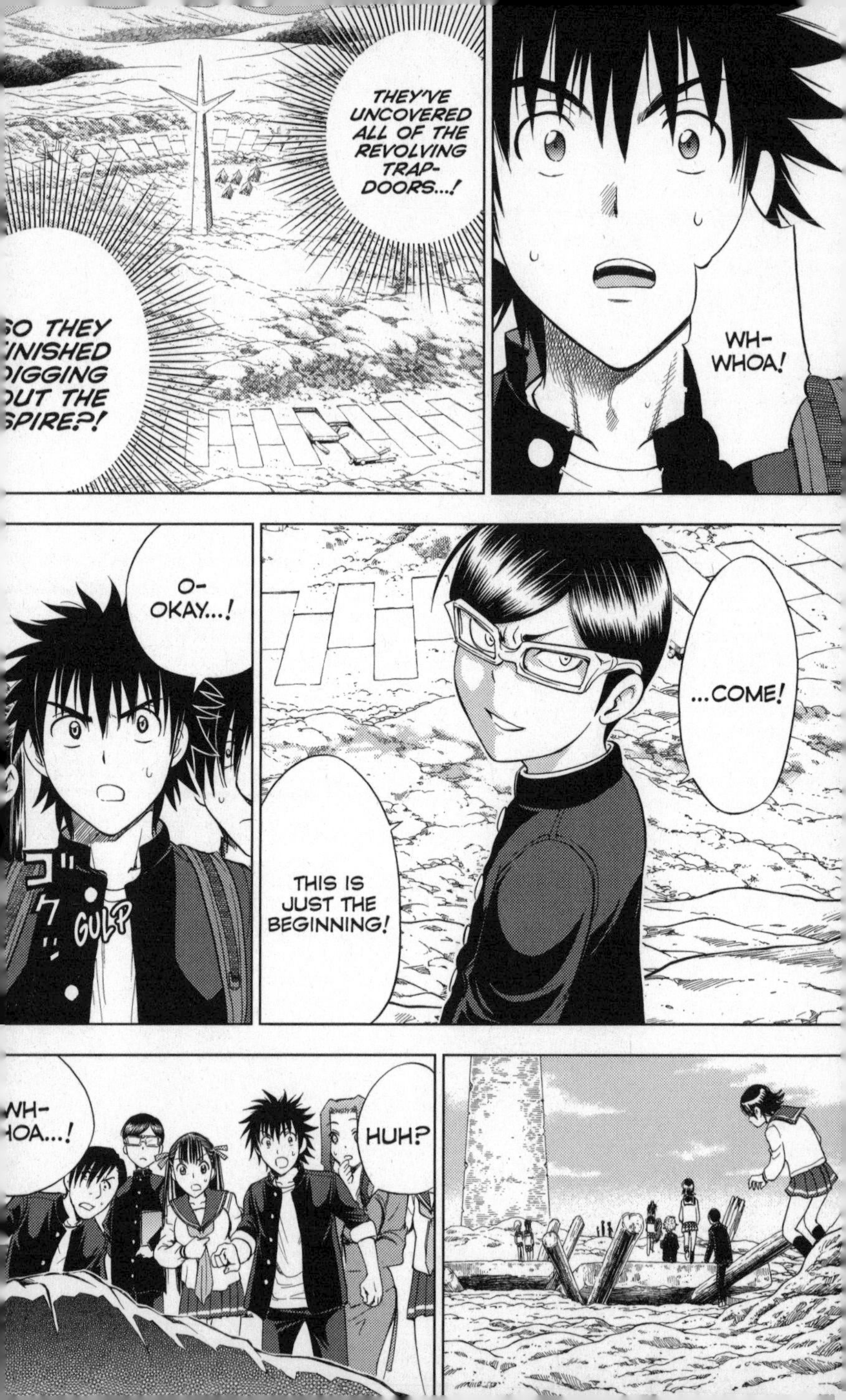
WH- WHOA!
THEY'VE UNCOVERED ALL OF THE REVOLVING TRAP-DOORS...!
SO THEY FINISHED DIGGING OUT THE SPIRE?!
...COME!
THIS IS JUST THE BEGINNING!
O- OKAY...!
GULP
HUH?
WH- WHOA...!

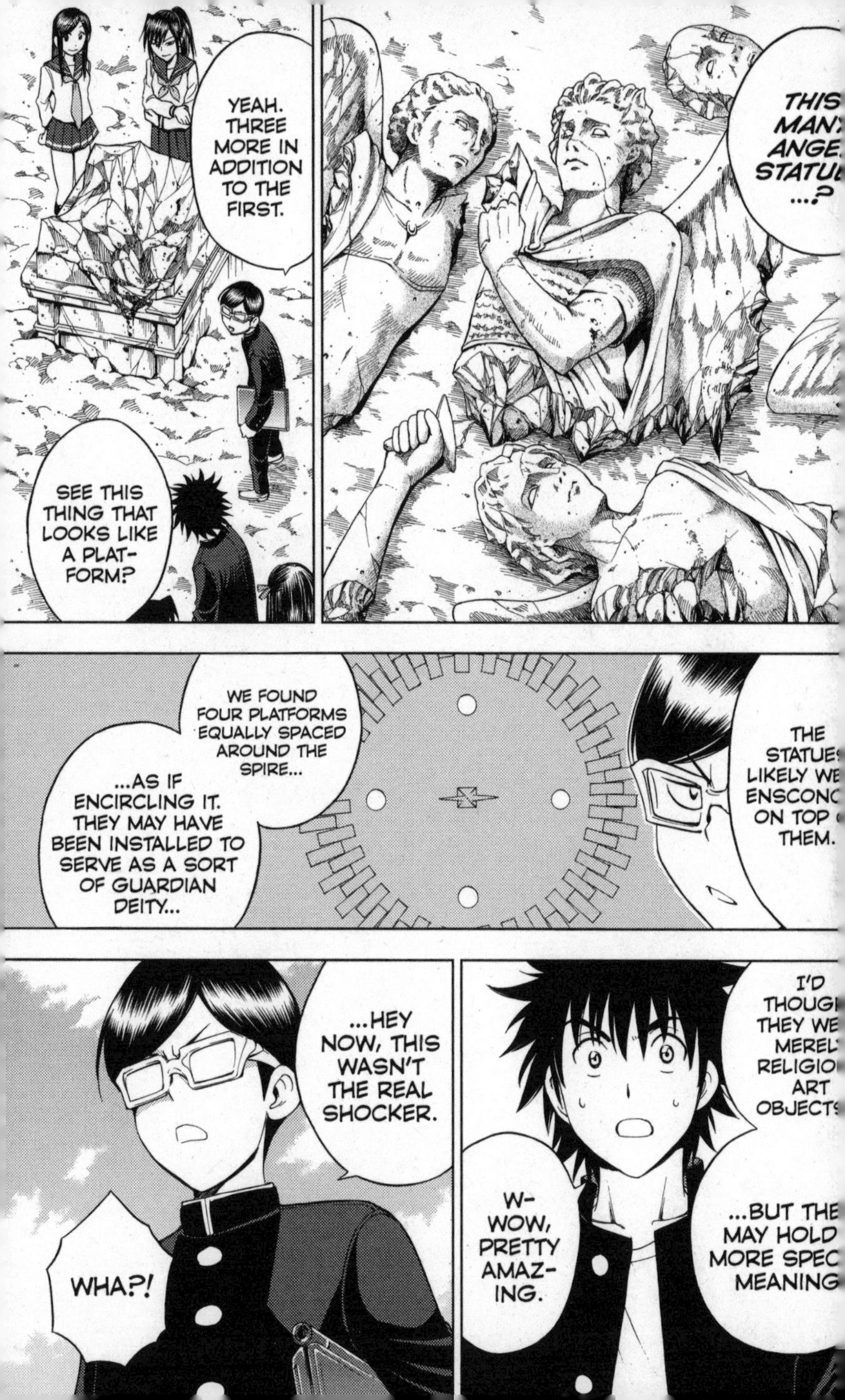
THIS MAN ANGE STATU ...?
YEAH. THREE MORE IN ADDITION TO THE FIRST.
SEE THIS THING THAT LOOKS LIKE A PLAT-FORM?
WE FOUND FOUR PLATFORMS EQUALLY SPACED AROUND THE SPIRE...
...AS IF ENCIRCLING IT. THEY MAY HAVE BEEN INSTALLED TO SERVE AS A SORT OF GUARDIAN DEITY...
THE STATUE LIKELY WE ENSCONC ON TOP THEM.
I'D THOUG THEY WE MEREL RELIGIO ART OBJECTS
...BUT THE MAY HOLD MORE SPEC MEANING
W-WOW, PRETTY AMAZ-ING.
...HEY NOW, THIS WASN'T THE REAL SHOCKER.
WHA?!

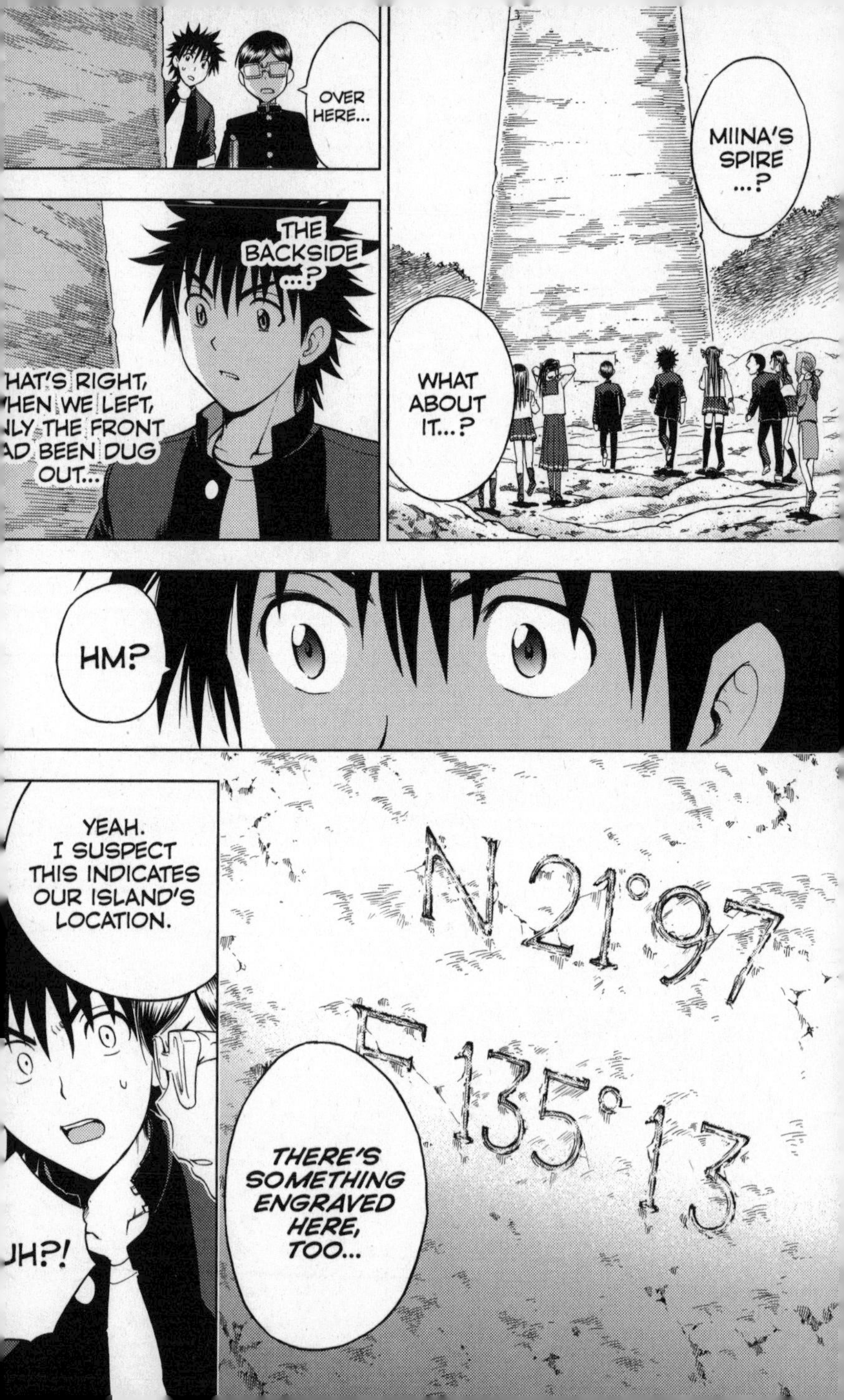
MIINA'S SPIRE ...?
WHAT ABOUT IT...?
OVER HERE...
THE BACKSIDE ...?
HAT'S RIGHT, HEN WE LEFT, NLY THE FRONT AD BEEN DUG OUT...
HM?
N21°97
E135°13
THERE'S SOMETHING ENGRAVED HERE, TOO...
YEAH. I SUSPECT THIS INDICATES OUR ISLAND'S LOCATION.
JH?!

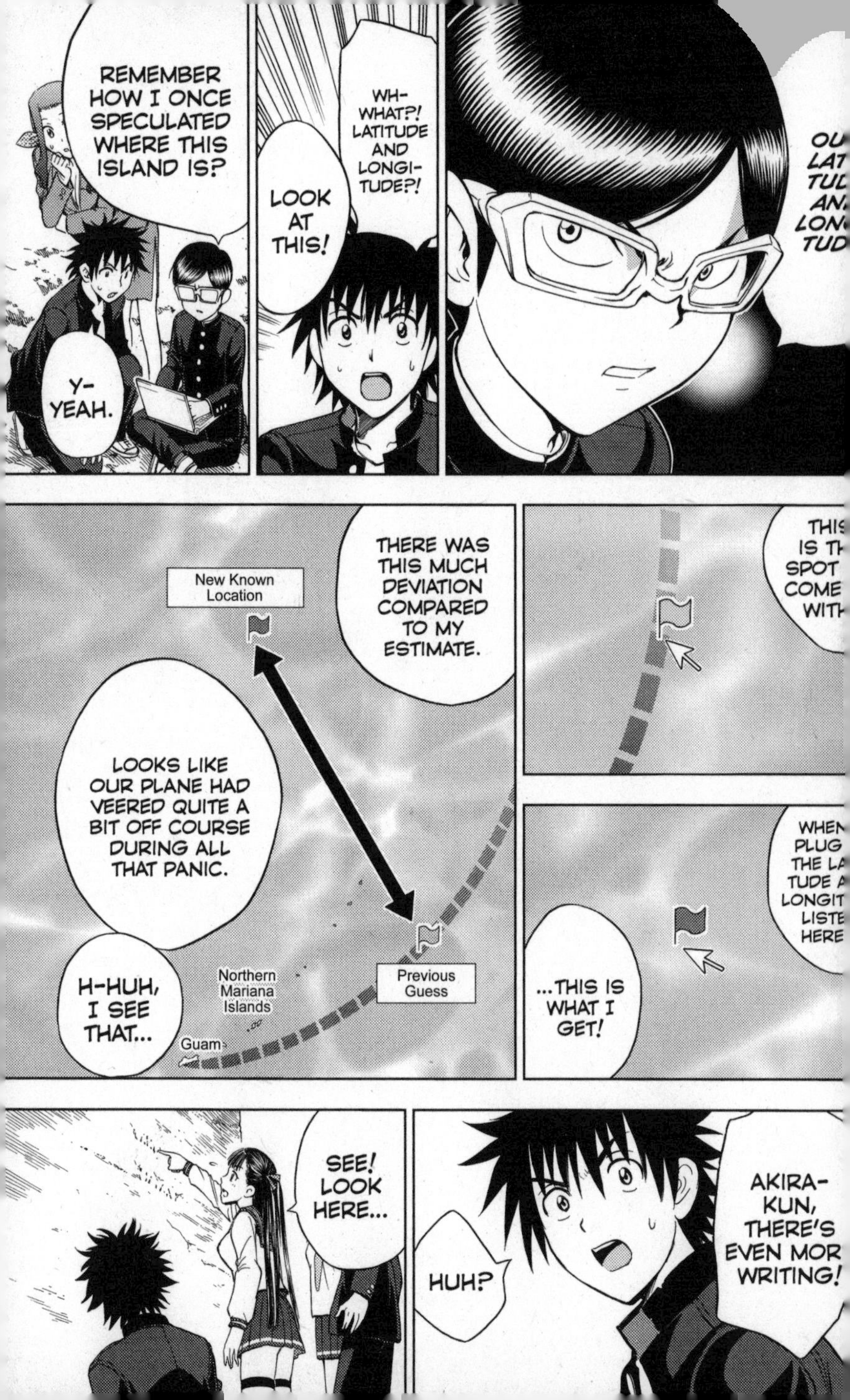
OU LAT TUL AN LONG TUD
WH- WHAT?! LATITUDE AND LONGI- TUDE?!
LOOK AT THIS!
REMEMBER HOW I ONCE SPECULATED WHERE THIS ISLAND IS?
Y- YEAH.
THIS IS TH SPOT COME WITH
WHEN PLUG THE LA TUDE A LONGIT LISTE HERE
...THIS IS WHAT I GET!
THERE WAS THIS MUCH DEVIATION COMPARED TO MY ESTIMATE.
New Known Location
LOOKS LIKE OUR PLANE HAD VEERED QUITE A BIT OFF COURSE DURING ALL THAT PANIC.
Previous Guess
Northern Mariana Islands
Guam
H-HUH, I SEE THAT...
AKIRA- KUN, THERE'S EVEN MOR WRITING!
HUH?
SEE! LOOK HERE...

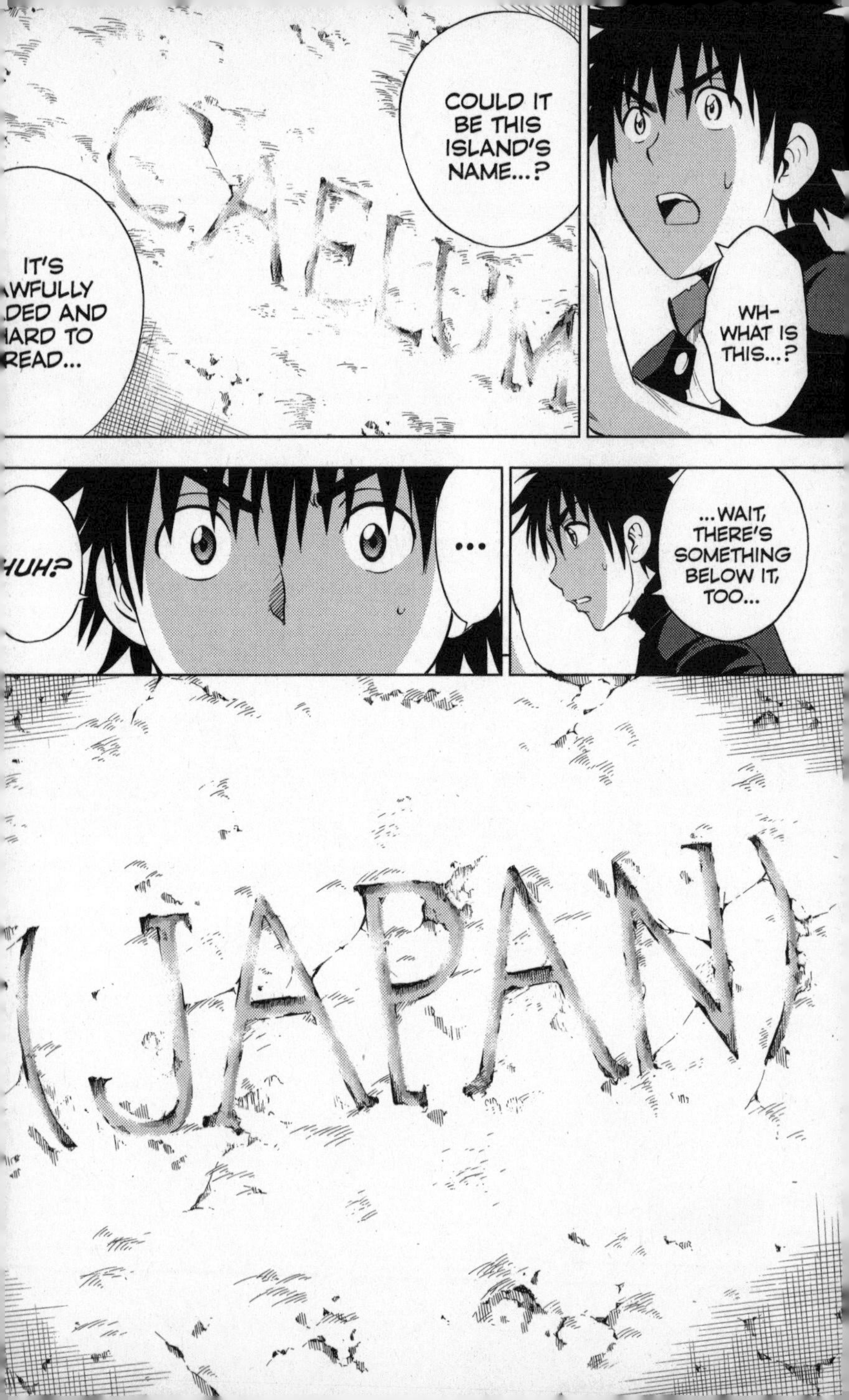
WH- WHAT IS THIS...?
COULD IT BE THIS ISLAND'S NAME...?
IT'S AWFULLY DED AND HARD TO READ...
...WAIT, THERE'S SOMETHING BELOW IT, TOO...
...
HUH?
JAPAN

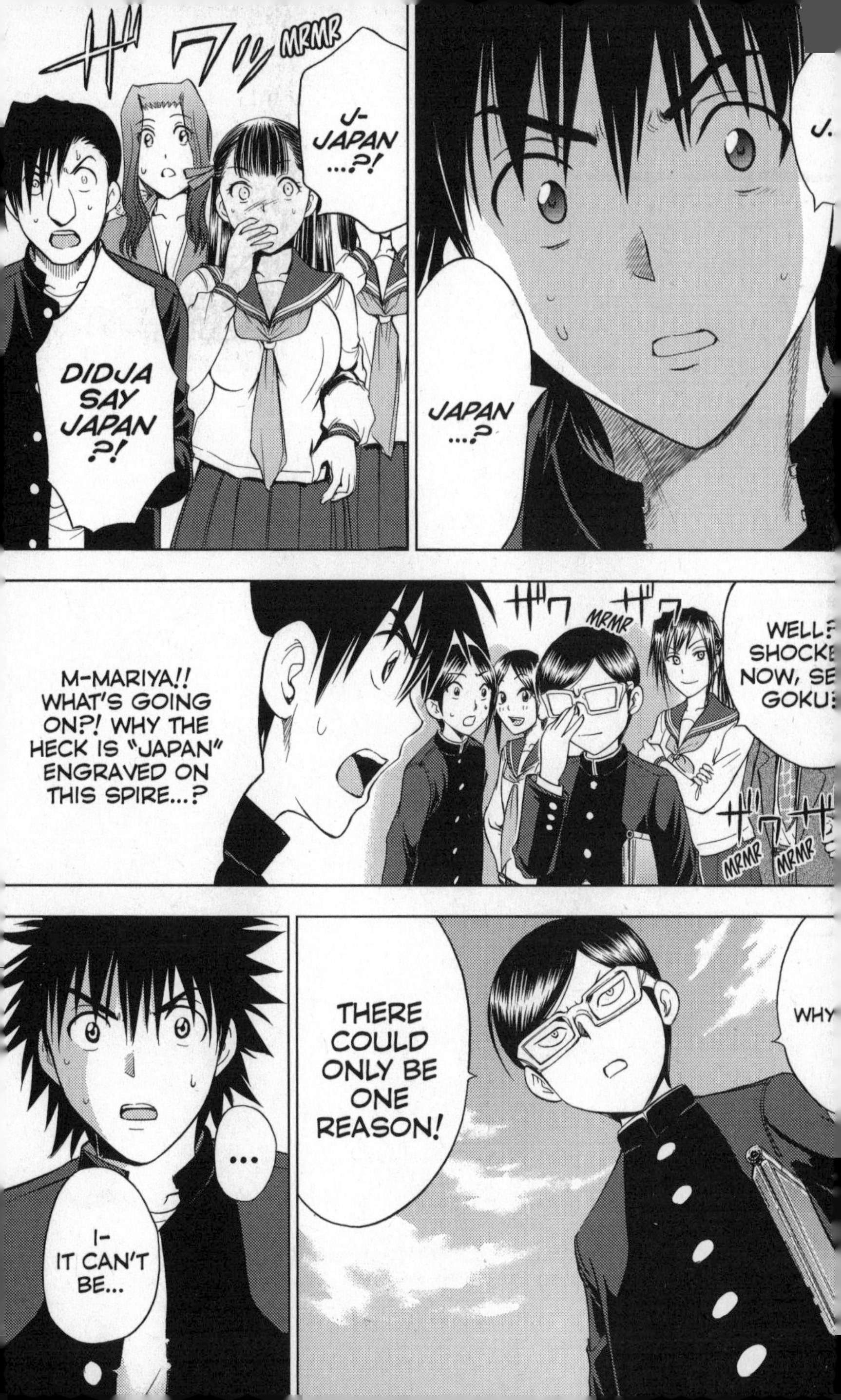
J..
JAPAN ...?
MRMR
J- JAPAN ...?!
DIDJA SAY JAPAN ?!
WELL?! SHOCKE NOW, SE GOKU!
MRMR
MRMR
MRMR
M-MARIYA!! WHAT'S GOING ON?! WHY THE HECK IS "JAPAN" ENGRAVED ON THIS SPIRE...?
WHY
THERE COULD ONLY BE ONE REASON!
...
I- IT CAN'T BE...

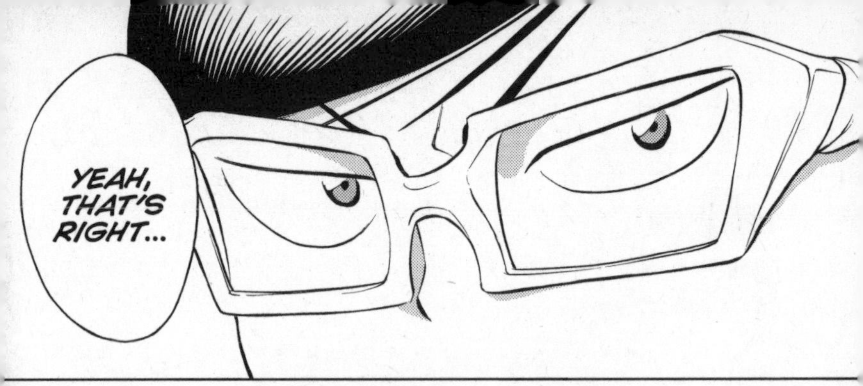
YEAH, THAT'S RIGHT...
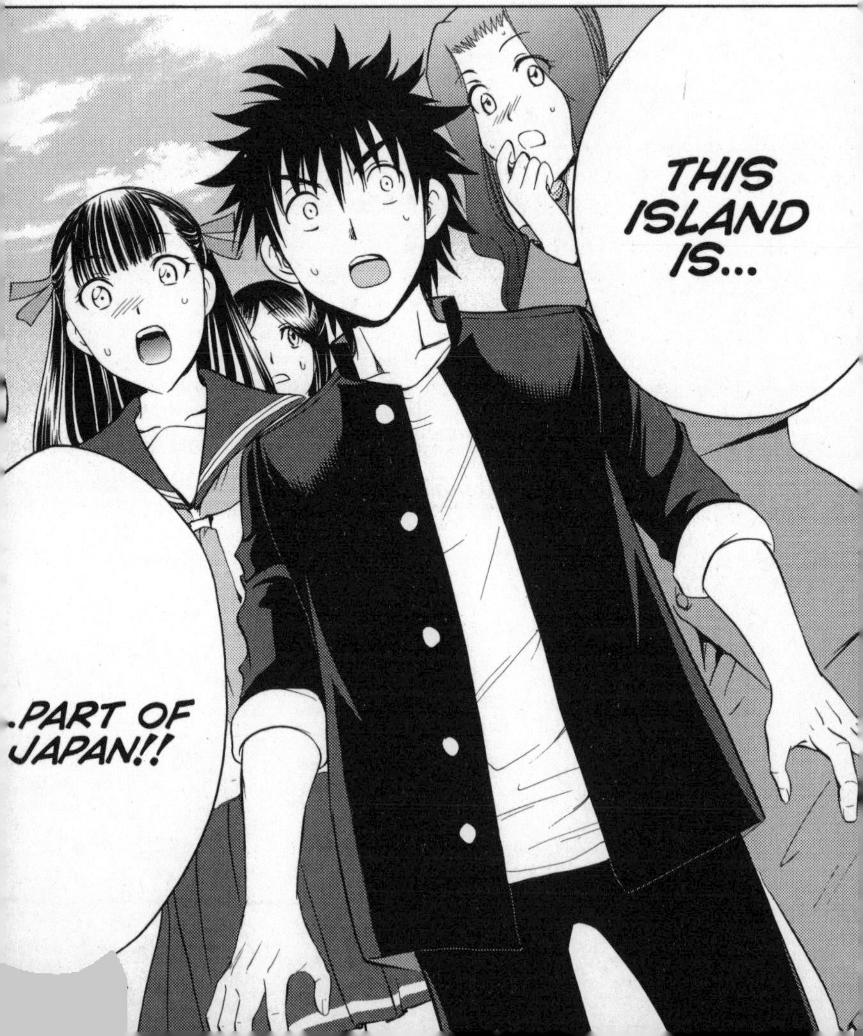
THIS ISLAND IS...
...PART OF JAPAN!!

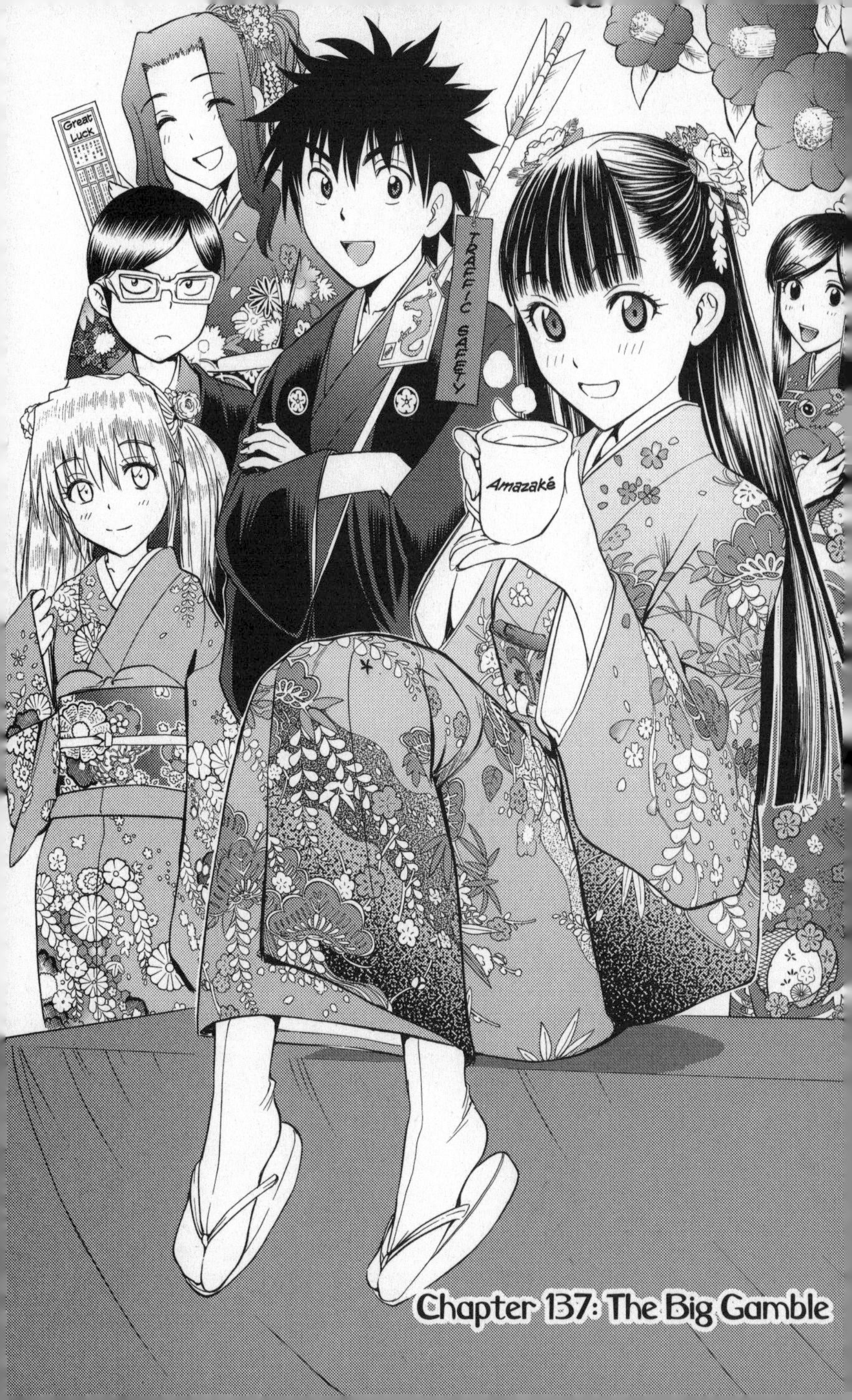
Great Luck
Traffic Safety
Amazaké

Chapter 137: The Big Gamble

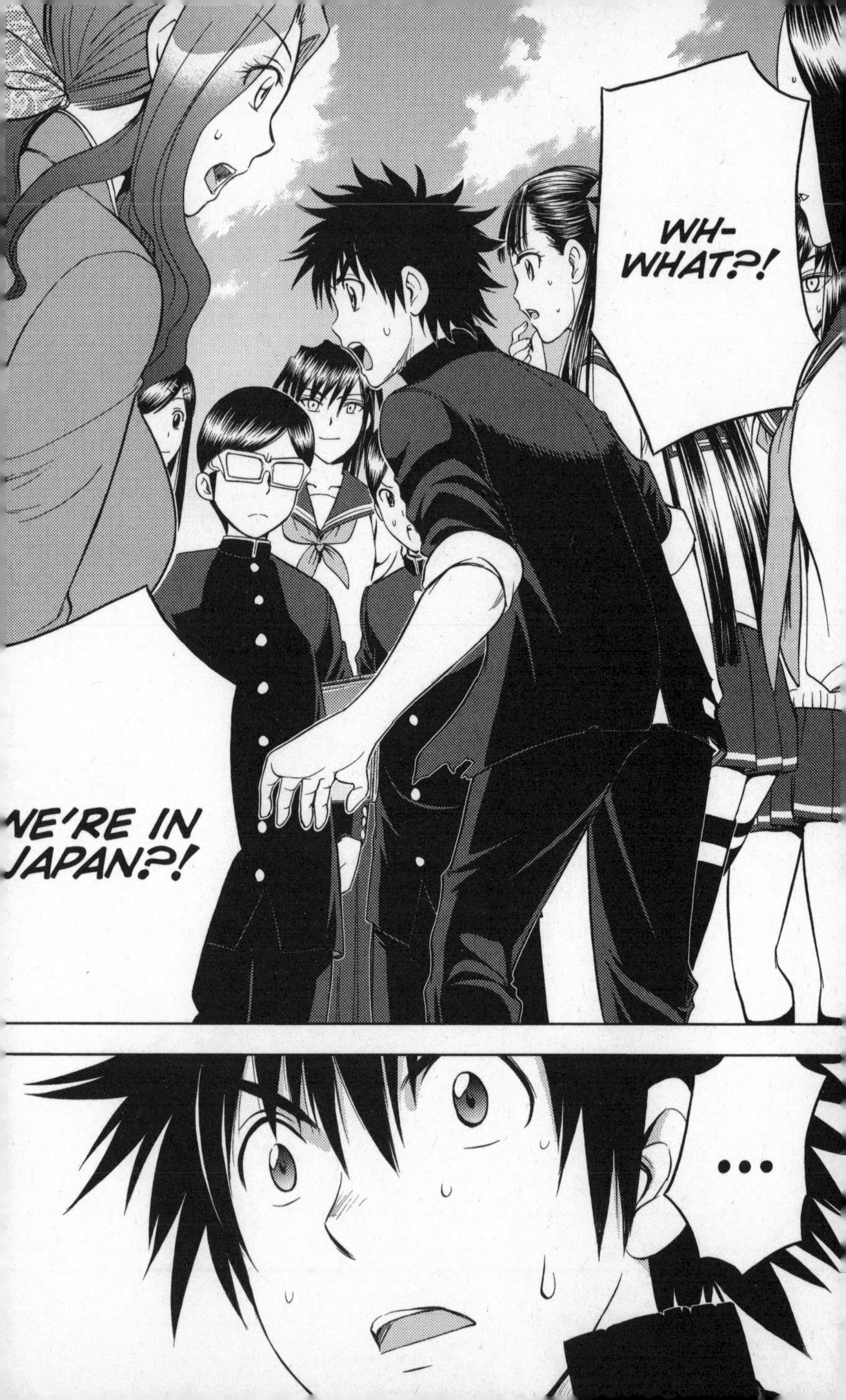
WH-WHAT?!
WE'RE IN JAPAN?!
...

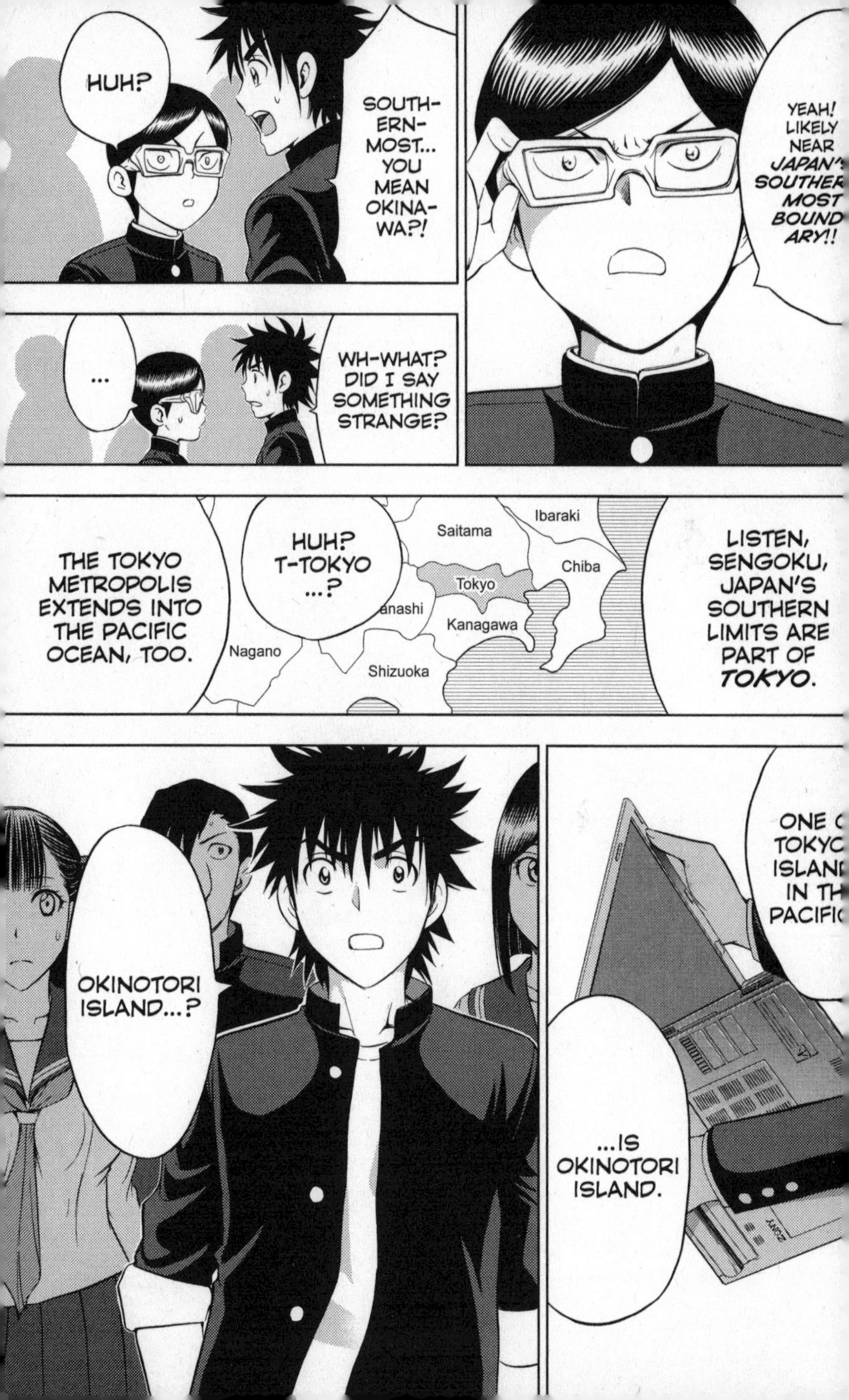
YEAH! LIKELY NEAR JAPAN'S SOUTHER MOST BOUND ARY!!
HUH?
SOUTH-ERN-MOST... YOU MEAN OKINA-WA?!
WH-WHAT? DID I SAY SOMETHING STRANGE?
...
LISTEN, SENGOKU, JAPAN'S SOUTHERN LIMITS ARE PART OF TOKYO.
Ibaraki
Saitama
Chiba
Tokyo
Kanagawa
anashi
Nagano
Shizuoka
HUH? T-TOKYO ...?
THE TOKYO METROPOLIS EXTENDS INTO THE PACIFIC OCEAN, TOO.
ONE O TOKYO ISLAND IN TH PACIFIC
...IS OKINOTORI ISLAND.
OKINOTORI ISLAND...?

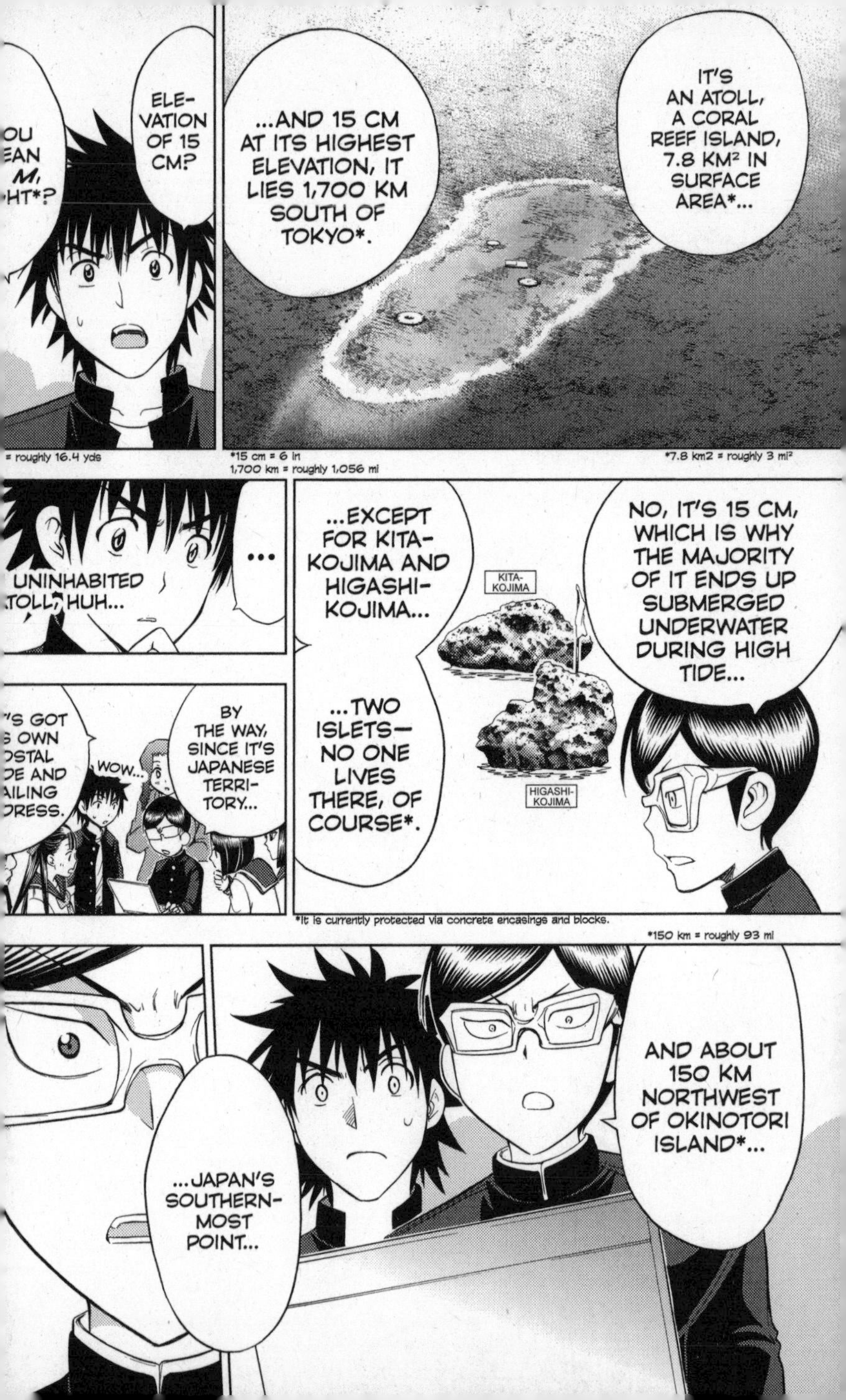
IT'S AN ATOLL, A CORAL REEF ISLAND, 7.8 KM² IN SURFACE AREA*...
...AND 15 CM AT ITS HIGHEST ELEVATION, IT LIES 1,700 KM SOUTH OF TOKYO*.
ELEVATION OF 15 CM?
OU EAN M, HT*?
NO, IT'S 15 CM, WHICH IS WHY THE MAJORITY OF IT ENDS UP SUBMERGED UNDERWATER DURING HIGH TIDE...
KITA-KOJIMA
HIGASHI-KOJIMA
...EXCEPT FOR KITA-KOJIMA AND HIGASHI-KOJIMA...
...TWO ISLETS—NO ONE LIVES THERE, OF COURSE*.
...
UNINHABITED TOLL, HUH...
BY THE WAY, SINCE IT'S JAPANESE TERRITORY...
WOW...
'S GOT OWN OSTAL DE AND AILING DRESS.
AND ABOUT 150 KM NORTHWEST OF OKINOTORI ISLAND*...
...JAPAN'S SOUTHERN-MOST POINT...

= roughly 16.4 yds

*15 cm = 6 in
1,700 km = roughly 1,056 mi

*7.8 km2 = roughly 3 mi²

*It is currently protected via concrete encasings and blocks.

*150 km = roughly 93 mi

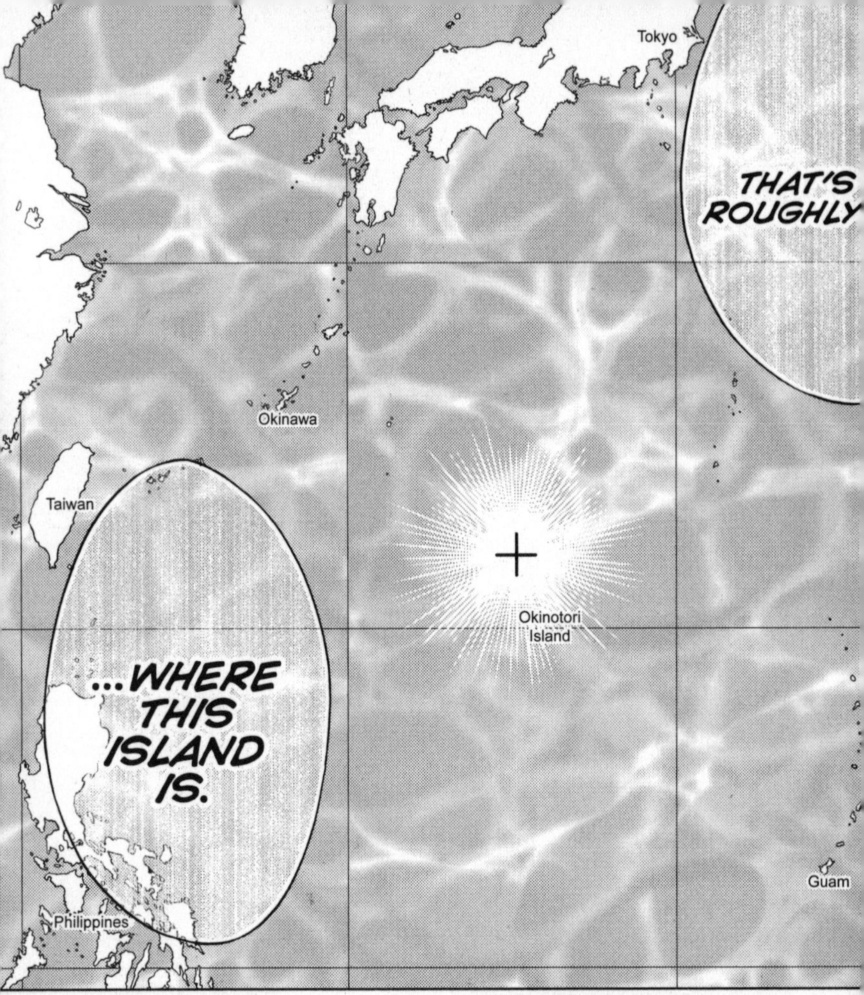
Tokyo
THAT'S ROUGHLY
...WHERE THIS ISLAND IS.
Okinawa
Taiwan
Okinotori Island
Guam
Philippines
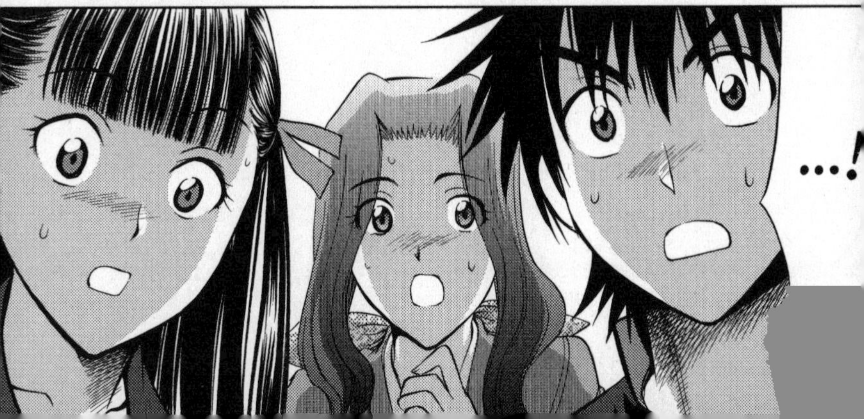
...!

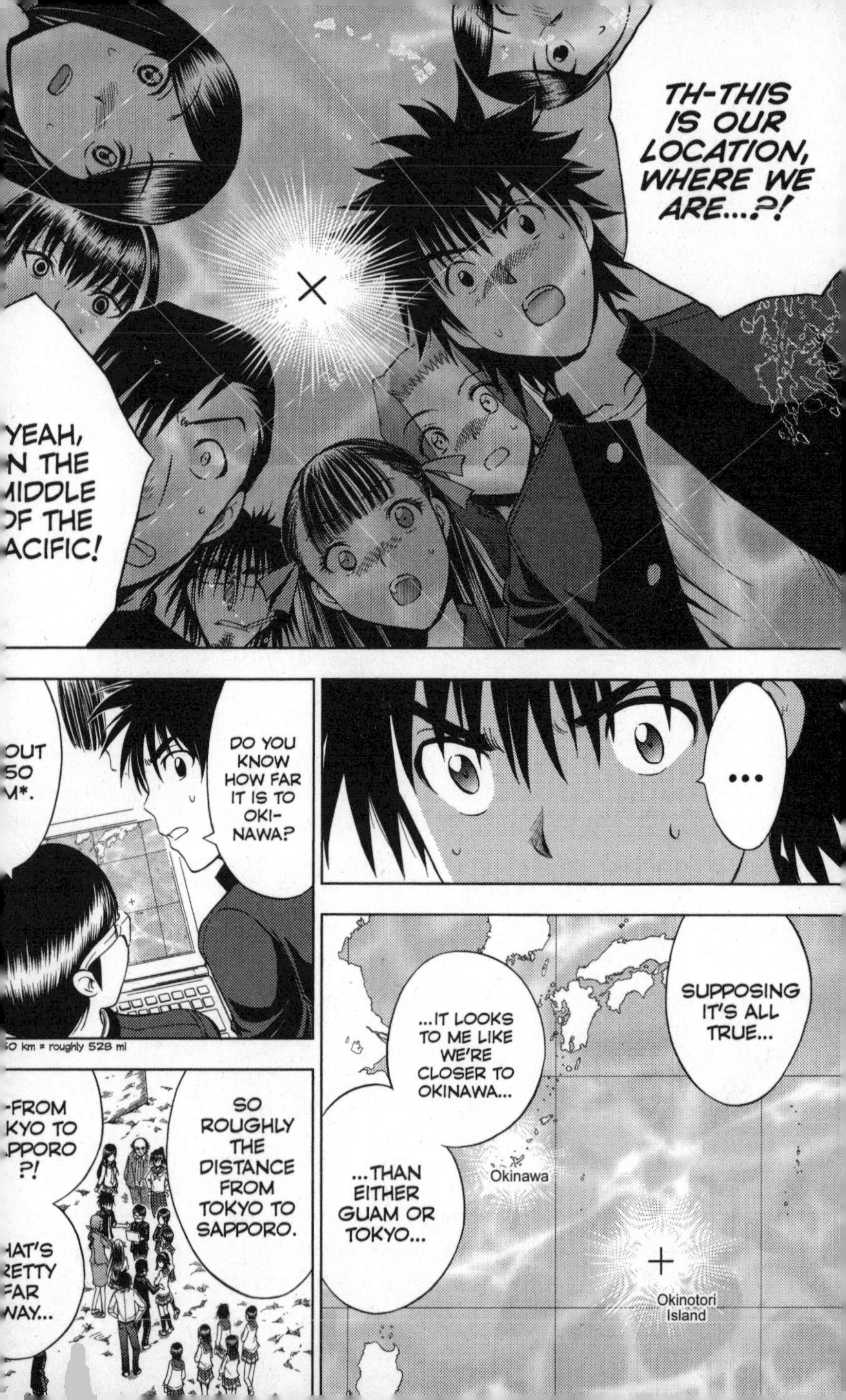
TH-THIS IS OUR LOCATION, WHERE WE ARE...?!
YEAH, N THE IDDLE OF THE ACIFIC!
...
DO YOU KNOW HOW FAR IT IS TO OKI-NAWA?
OUT 50 M*.
0 km = roughly 528 mi
SUPPOSING IT'S ALL TRUE...
...IT LOOKS TO ME LIKE WE'RE CLOSER TO OKINAWA...
...THAN EITHER GUAM OR TOKYO...
Okinawa
Okinotori Island
SO ROUGHLY THE DISTANCE FROM TOKYO TO SAPPORO.
-FROM KYO TO PPORO ?!
HAT'S RETTY FAR WAY...

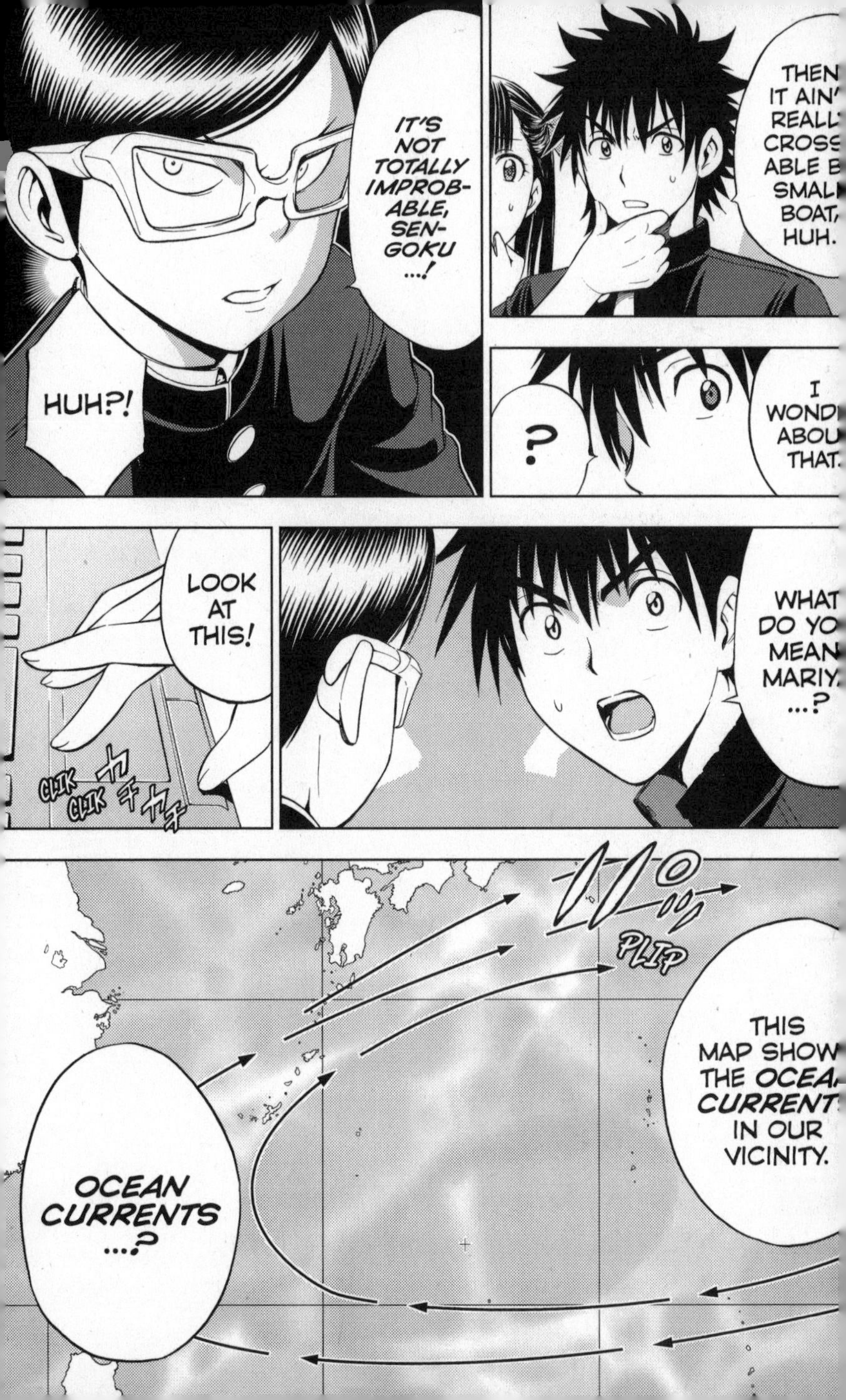
THEN IT AIN' REALL CROSS ABLE B SMAL BOAT, HUH.
I WOND ABOU THAT.
?
IT'S NOT TOTALLY IMPROB-ABLE, SEN-GOKU ...!
HUH?!
WHAT DO YO MEAN MARIY ...?
LOOK AT THIS!
CLIK CLIK
THIS MAP SHOW THE OCEA CURRENT IN OUR VICINITY.
PLIP
OCEAN CURRENTS ...?

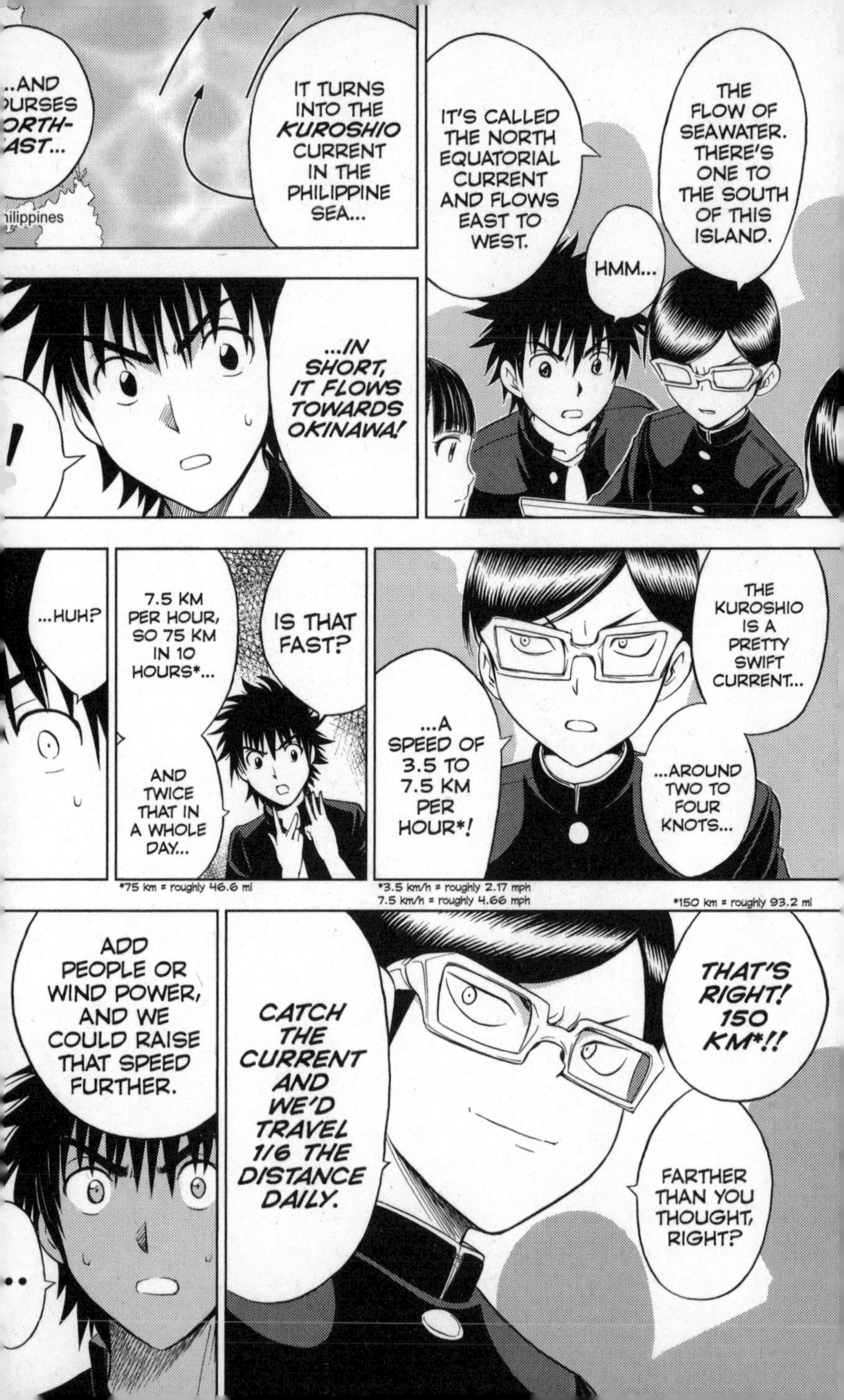
THE FLOW OF SEAWATER. THERE'S ONE TO THE SOUTH OF THIS ISLAND.
HMM...
IT'S CALLED THE NORTH EQUATORIAL CURRENT AND FLOWS EAST TO WEST.
IT TURNS INTO THE KUROSHIO CURRENT IN THE PHILIPPINE SEA...
..AND URSES ORTH- AST...
ilippines
...IN SHORT, IT FLOWS TOWARDS OKINAWA!
THE KUROSHIO IS A PRETTY SWIFT CURRENT...
...AROUND TWO TO FOUR KNOTS...
...A SPEED OF 3.5 TO 7.5 KM PER HOUR*!
IS THAT FAST?
7.5 KM PER HOUR, SO 75 KM IN 10 HOURS*...
AND TWICE THAT IN A WHOLE DAY...
...HUH?
*75 km = roughly 46.6 mi
*3.5 km/h = roughly 2.17 mph
7.5 km/h = roughly 4.66 mph
*150 km = roughly 93.2 mi
THAT'S RIGHT! 150 KM*!!
FARTHER THAN YOU THOUGHT, RIGHT?
CATCH THE CURRENT AND WE'D TRAVEL 1/6 THE DISTANCE DAILY.
ADD PEOPLE OR WIND POWER, AND WE COULD RAISE THAT SPEED FURTHER.

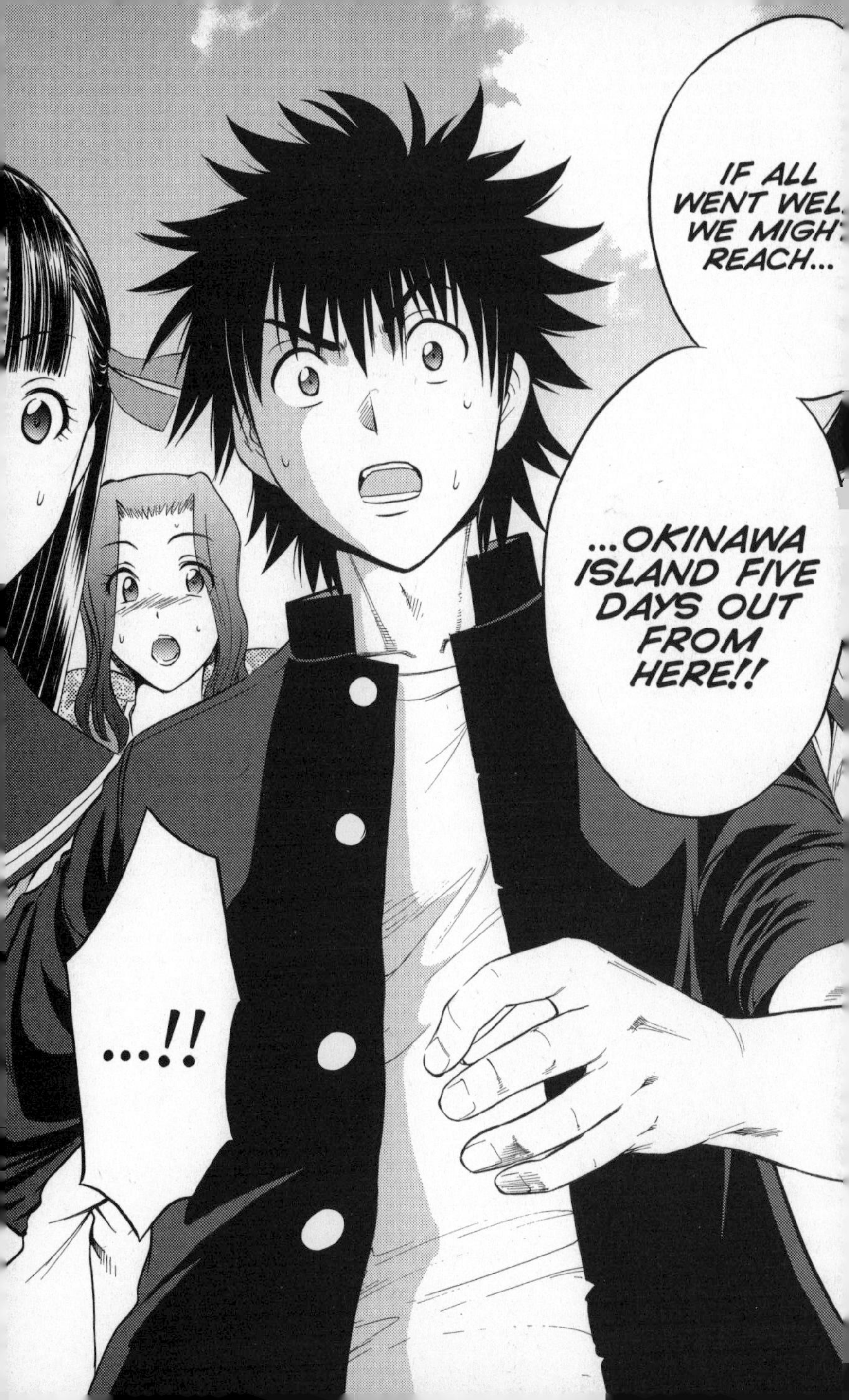
IF ALL WENT WEL WE MIGH REACH...
...OKINAWA ISLAND FIVE DAYS OUT FROM HERE!!
...!!

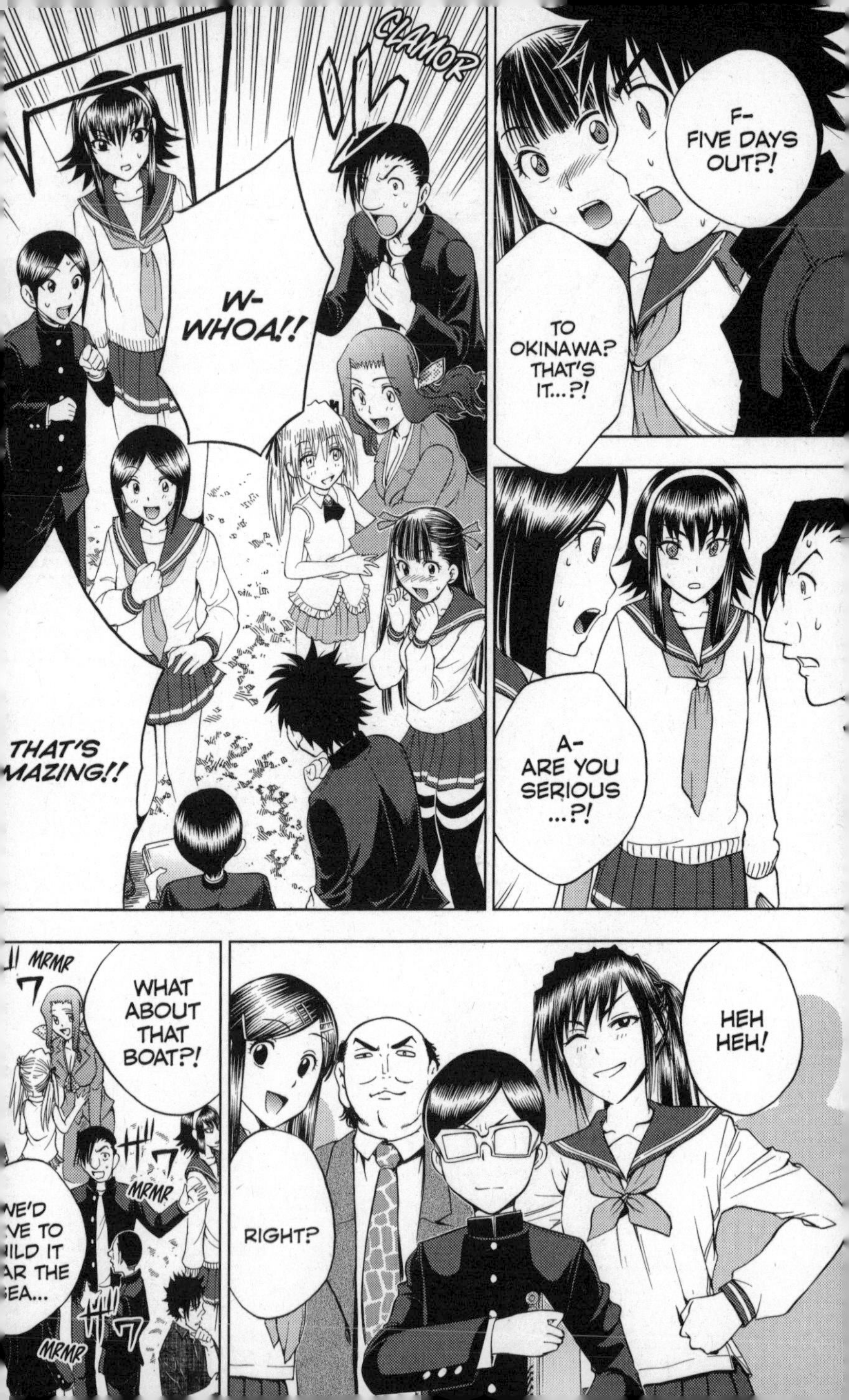
F- FIVE DAYS OUT?!
TO OKINAWA? THAT'S IT...?!
A- ARE YOU SERIOUS ...?!
CLAMOR
W- WHOA!!
THAT'S MAZING!!
HEH HEH!
RIGHT?
WHAT ABOUT THAT BOAT?!
MRMR
MRMR
E'D VE TO ILD IT AR THE EA...
MRMR

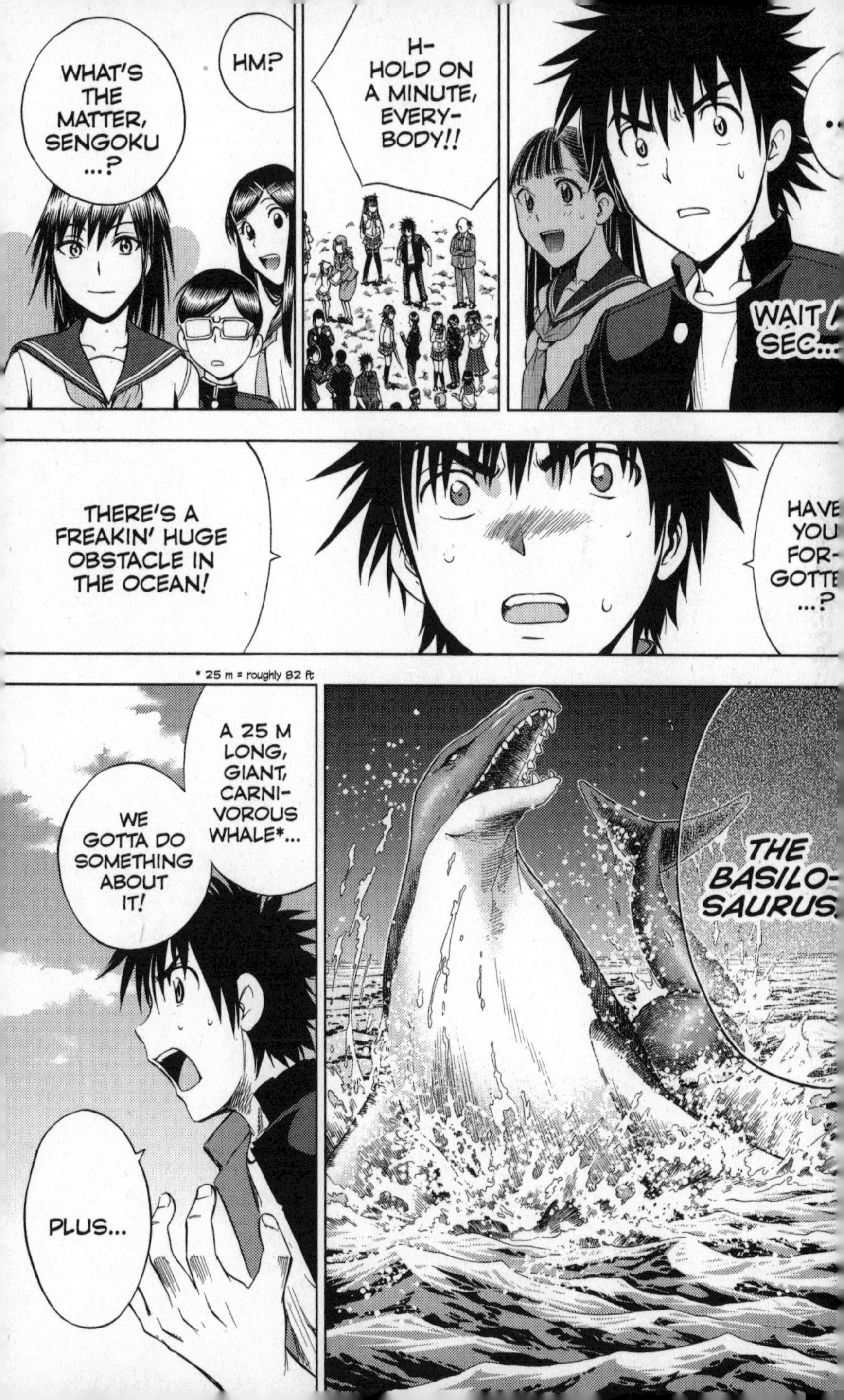
..
WAIT
SEC...
H- HOLD ON A MINUTE, EVERY-BODY!!
HM?
WHAT'S THE MATTER, SENGOKU ...?
HAVE YOU FOR-GOTTE ...?
THERE'S A FREAKIN' HUGE OBSTACLE IN THE OCEAN!
* 25 m = roughly 82 ft
THE BASILO-SAURUS.
A 25 M LONG, GIANT, CARNI-VOROUS WHALE*...
WE GOTTA DO SOMETHING ABOUT IT!
PLUS...

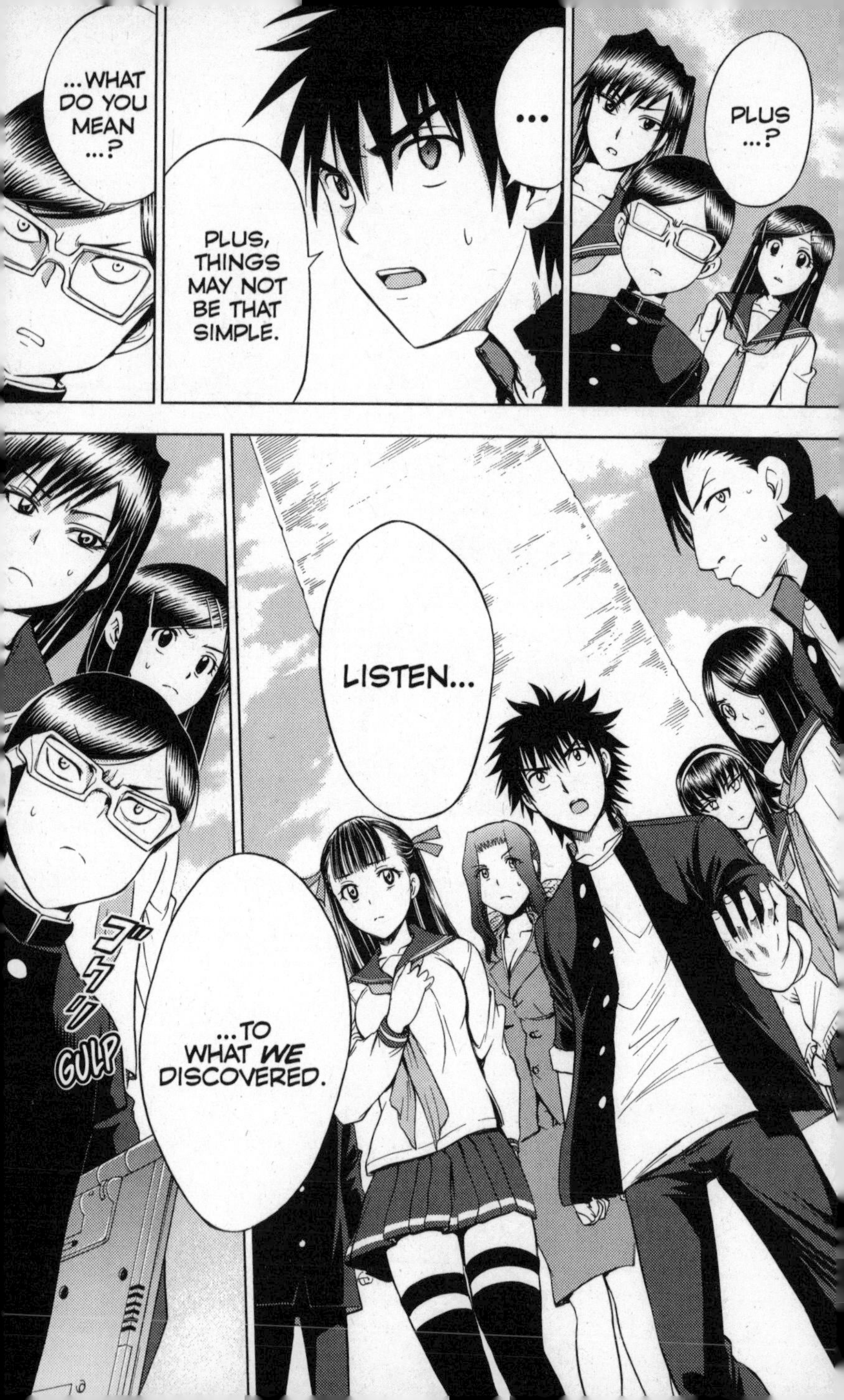
PLUS ...?
...
PLUS, THINGS MAY NOT BE THAT SIMPLE.
...WHAT DO YOU MEAN ...?
LISTEN...
...TO WHAT *WE* DISCOVERED.
GULP

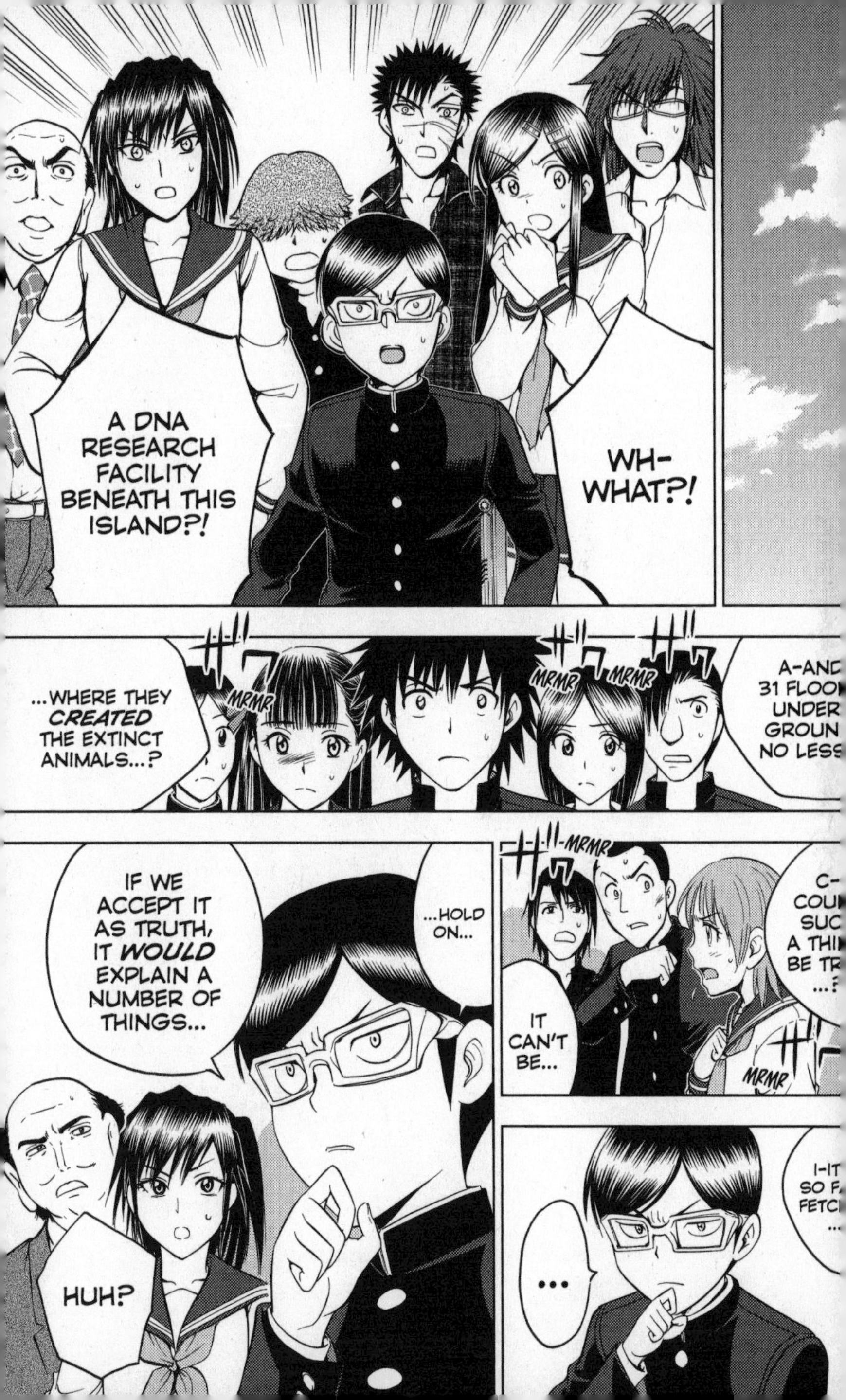
WH-WHAT?!
A DNA RESEARCH FACILITY BENEATH THIS ISLAND?!
A-AND 31 FLOO UNDER GROUN NO LESS
MRMR MRMR
MRMR
...WHERE THEY *CREATED* THE EXTINCT ANIMALS...?
MRMR
C-COU SUC A THI BE TR ...?
IT CAN'T BE...
MRMR
I-IT SO F FETC ...
...
...HOLD ON...
IF WE ACCEPT IT AS TRUTH, IT ***WOULD*** EXPLAIN A NUMBER OF THINGS...
HUH?

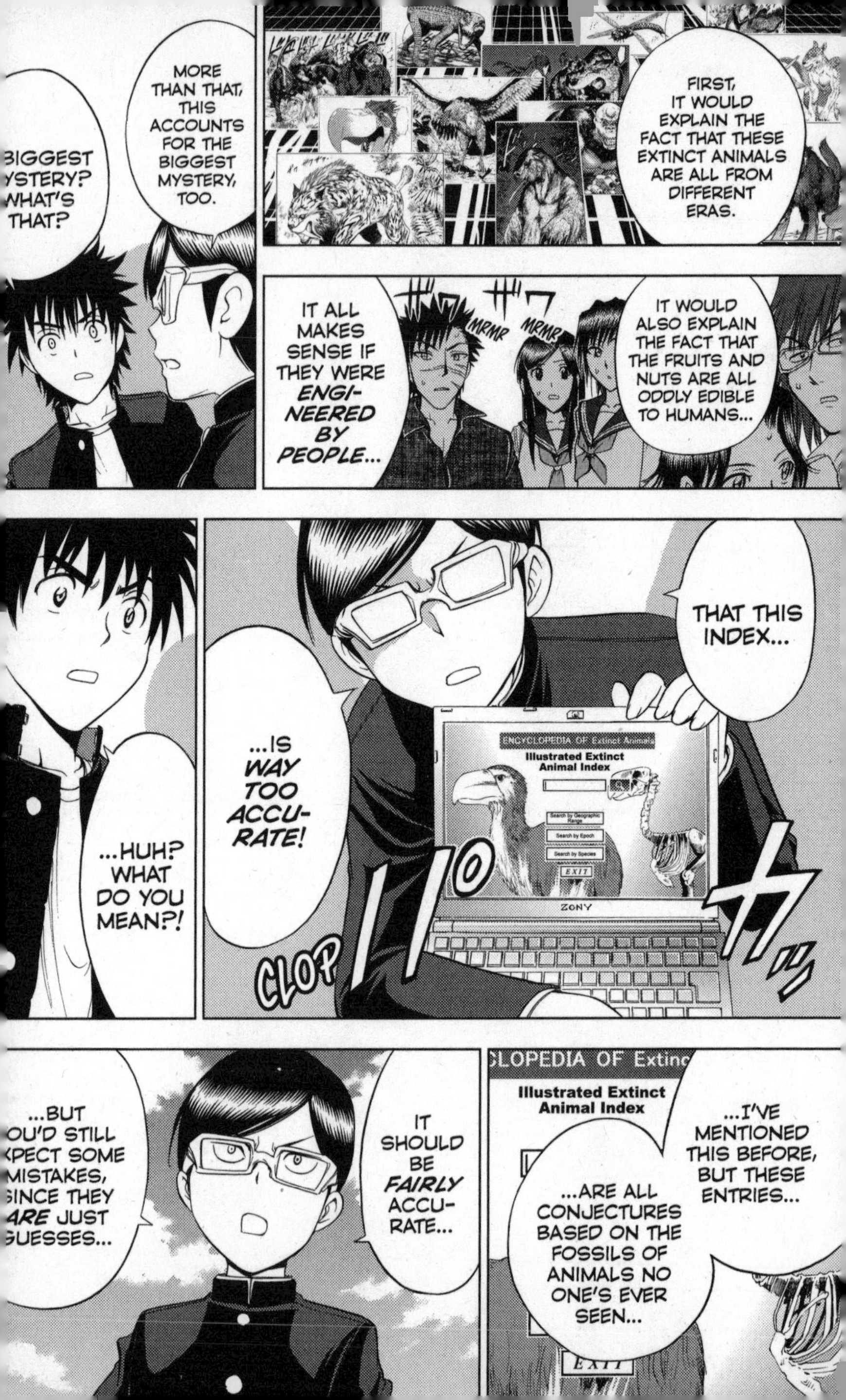
FIRST, IT WOULD EXPLAIN THE FACT THAT THESE EXTINCT ANIMALS ARE ALL FROM DIFFERENT ERAS.
IT WOULD ALSO EXPLAIN THE FACT THAT THE FRUITS AND NUTS ARE ALL ODDLY EDIBLE TO HUMANS...
MRMR
MRMR
IT ALL MAKES SENSE IF THEY WERE *ENGI-NEERED BY PEOPLE*...
MORE THAN THAT, THIS ACCOUNTS FOR THE BIGGEST MYSTERY, TOO.
BIGGEST YSTERY? WHAT'S THAT?
THAT THIS INDEX...
...IS *WAY TOO ACCU-RATE!*
ENCYCLOPEDIA OF Extinct Animals
Illustrated Extinct Animal Index
Search by Geographic Range
Search by Epoch
Search by Species
EXIT
ZONY
CLOP
...HUH? WHAT DO YOU MEAN?!
...I'VE MENTIONED THIS BEFORE, BUT THESE ENTRIES...
...ARE ALL CONJECTURES BASED ON THE FOSSILS OF ANIMALS NO ONE'S EVER SEEN...
CLOPEDIA OF Extinc
Illustrated Extinct Animal Index
EXIT
IT SHOULD BE *FAIRLY* ACCU-RATE...
...BUT OU'D STILL XPECT SOME MISTAKES, SINCE THEY *ARE* JUST GUESSES...

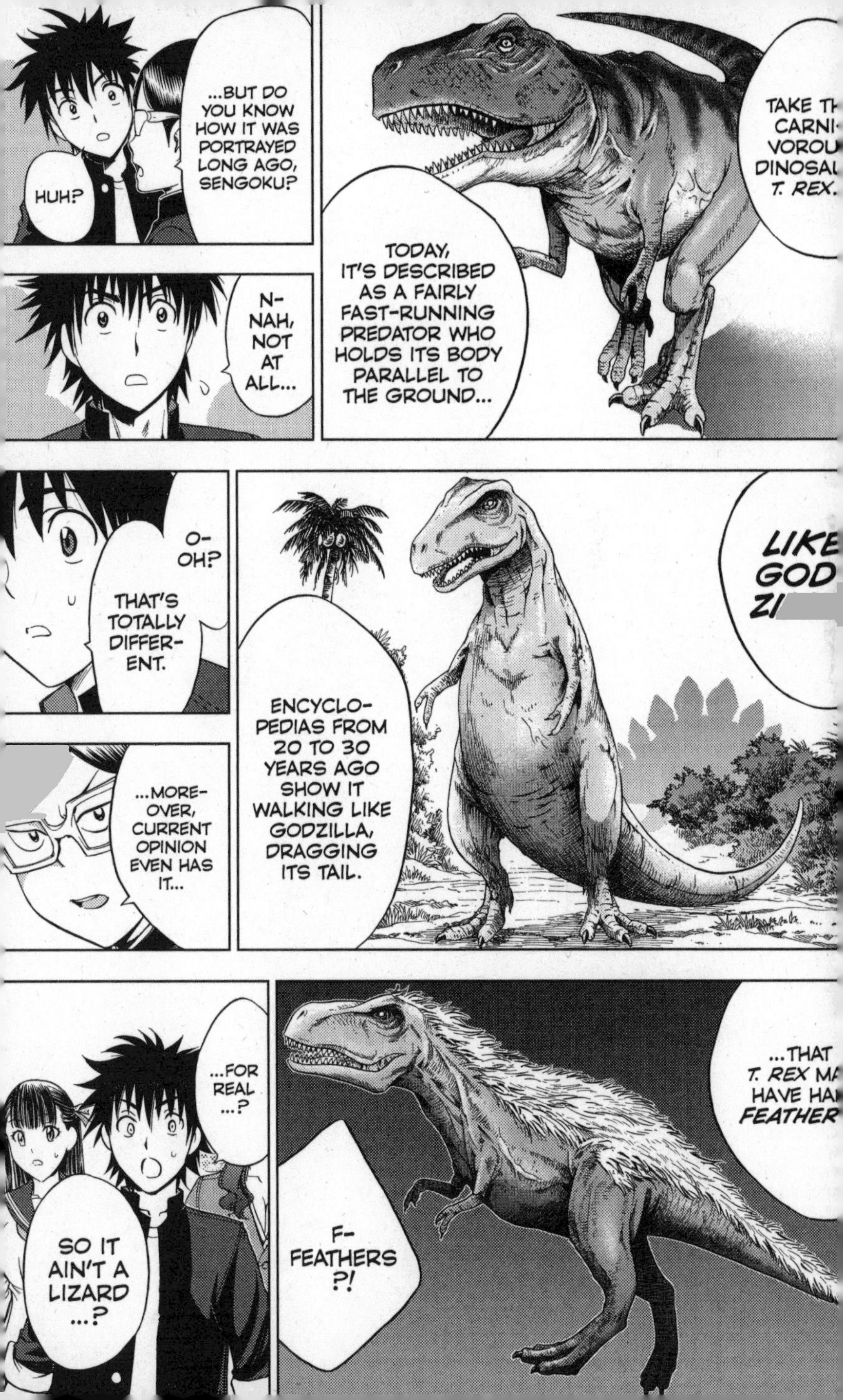
TAKE TH CARNI- VOROU DINOSAU T. REX.
TODAY, IT'S DESCRIBED AS A FAIRLY FAST-RUNNING PREDATOR WHO HOLDS ITS BODY PARALLEL TO THE GROUND...
...BUT DO YOU KNOW HOW IT WAS PORTRAYED LONG AGO, SENGOKU?
HUH?
N- NAH, NOT AT ALL...
LIKE GOD ZI
ENCYCLO- PEDIAS FROM 20 TO 30 YEARS AGO SHOW IT WALKING LIKE GODZILLA, DRAGGING ITS TAIL.
O- OH?
THAT'S TOTALLY DIFFER- ENT.
...MORE- OVER, CURRENT OPINION EVEN HAS IT...
...THAT T. REX MA HAVE HA FEATHER
F- FEATHERS ?!
...FOR REAL ...?
SO IT AIN'T A LIZARD ...?

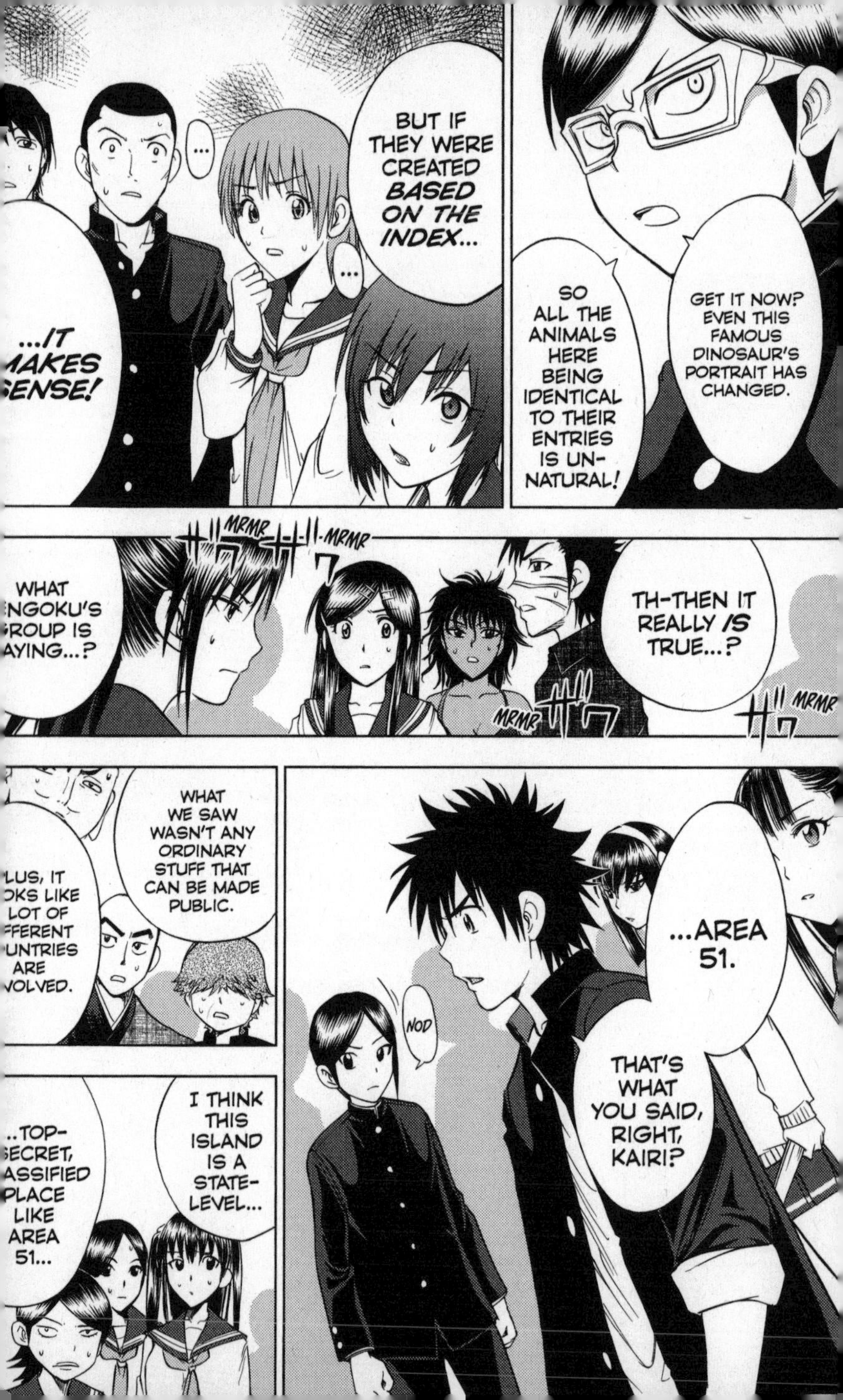
GET IT NOW? EVEN THIS FAMOUS DINOSAUR'S PORTRAIT HAS CHANGED.
SO ALL THE ANIMALS HERE BEING IDENTICAL TO THEIR ENTRIES IS UN-NATURAL!
BUT IF THEY WERE CREATED *BASED ON THE INDEX*...
...
...
...*IT AKES ENSE!*
MRMR
MRMR
TH-THEN IT REALLY *IS* TRUE...?
MRMR
WHAT NGOKU'S ROUP IS AYING...?
MRMR
...AREA 51.
THAT'S WHAT YOU SAID, RIGHT, KAIRI?
NOD
WHAT WE SAW WASN'T ANY ORDINARY STUFF THAT CAN BE MADE PUBLIC.
LUS, IT OKS LIKE LOT OF FFERENT UNTRIES ARE VOLVED.
I THINK THIS ISLAND IS A STATE-LEVEL...
..TOP-ECRET, ASSIFIED PLACE LIKE AREA 51...

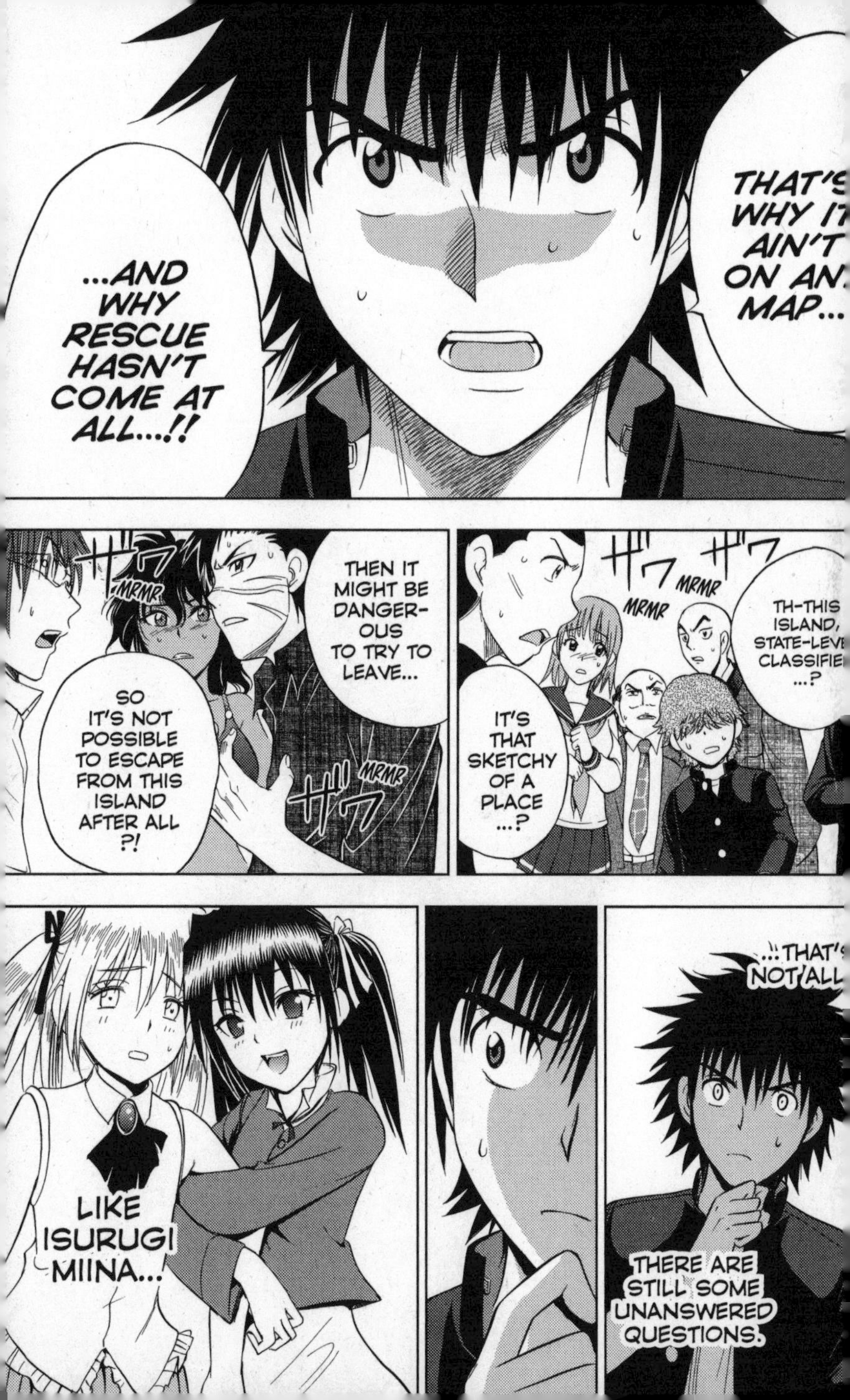
THAT'S WHY IT AIN'T ON AN MAP...
...AND WHY RESCUE HASN'T COME AT ALL...!!
ザワ ザワ
MRMR
MRMR
TH-THIS ISLAND, STATE-LEVE CLASSIFIE ...?
IT'S THAT SKETCHY OF A PLACE ...?
ザワ
MRMR
THEN IT MIGHT BE DANGER-OUS TO TRY TO LEAVE...
SO IT'S NOT POSSIBLE TO ESCAPE FROM THIS ISLAND AFTER ALL ?!
ザワ
MRMR
...THAT'S NOT ALL
THERE ARE STILL SOME UNANSWERED QUESTIONS.
LIKE ISURUGI MIINA...

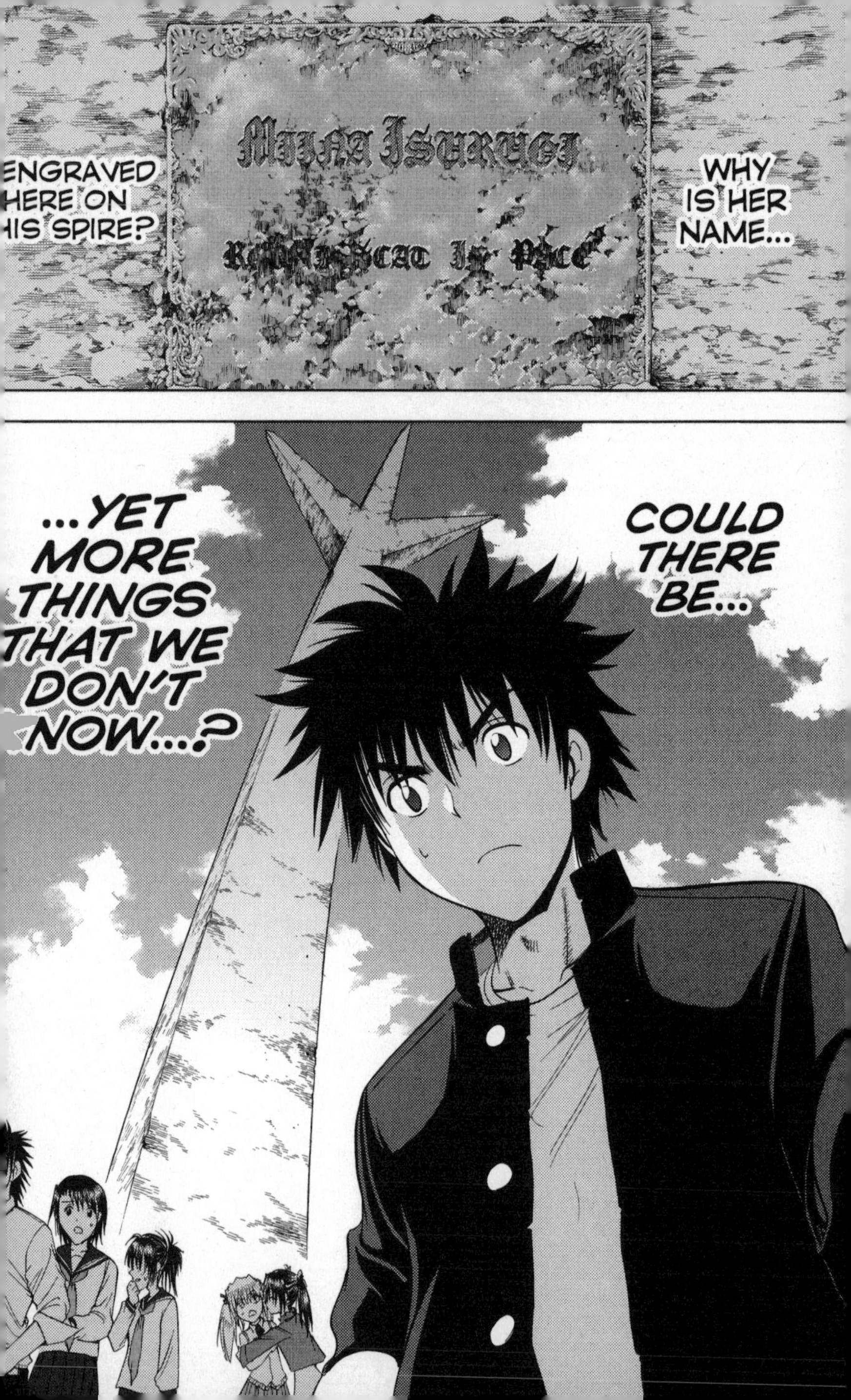
WHY IS HER NAME...
ENGRAVED HERE ON HIS SPIRE?
COULD THERE BE...
...YET MORE THINGS THAT WE DON'T NOW...?

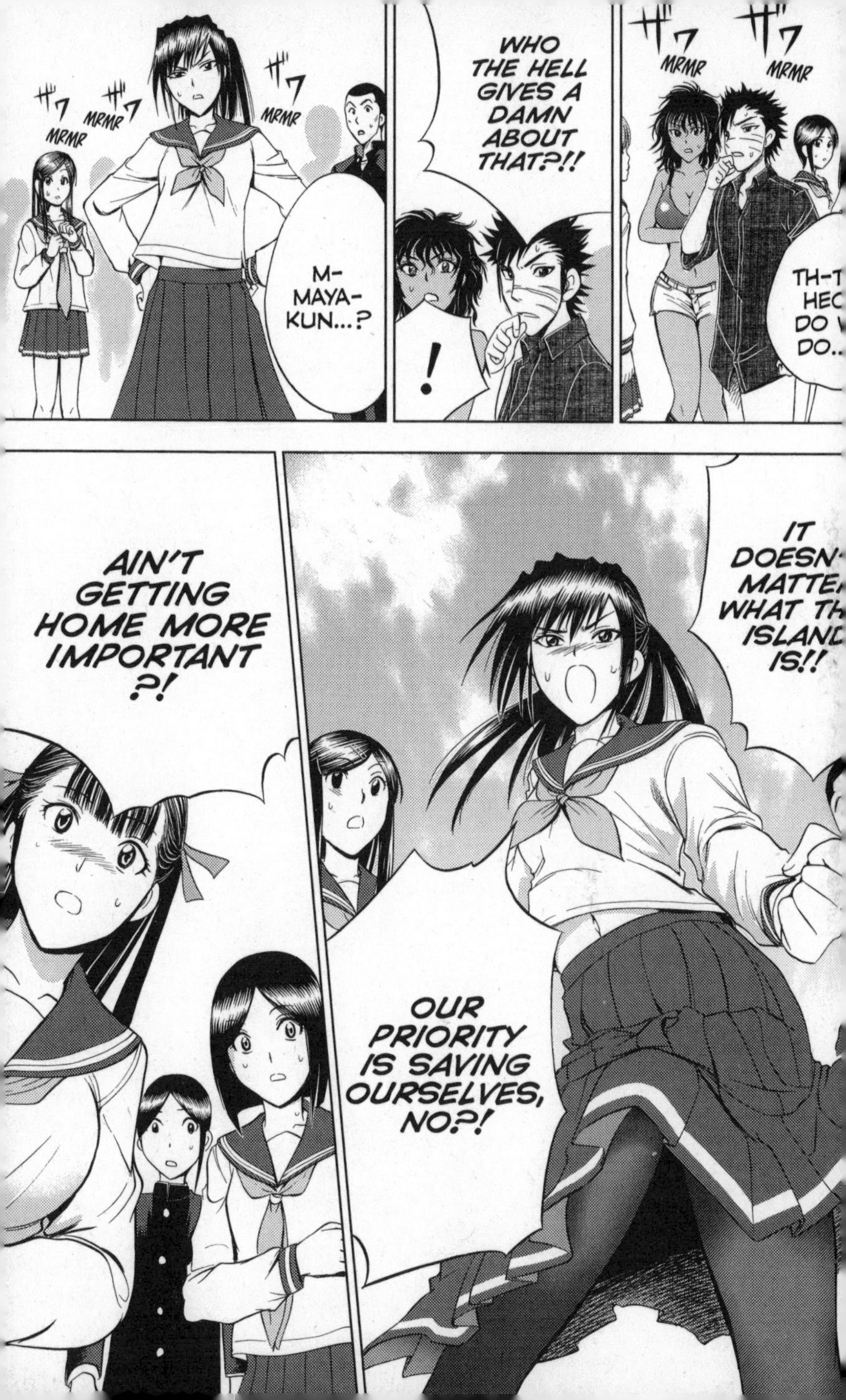
ザワ MRMR
ザワ MRMR
TH-T HEC DO DO...
WHO THE HELL GIVES A DAMN ABOUT THAT?!!
!
ザワ MRMR
ザワ MRMR
ザワ MRMR
M-MAYA-KUN...?
IT DOESN- MATTE WHAT TH ISLAN IS!!
OUR PRIORITY IS SAVING OURSELVES, NO?!
AIN'T GETTING HOME MORE IMPORTANT?!

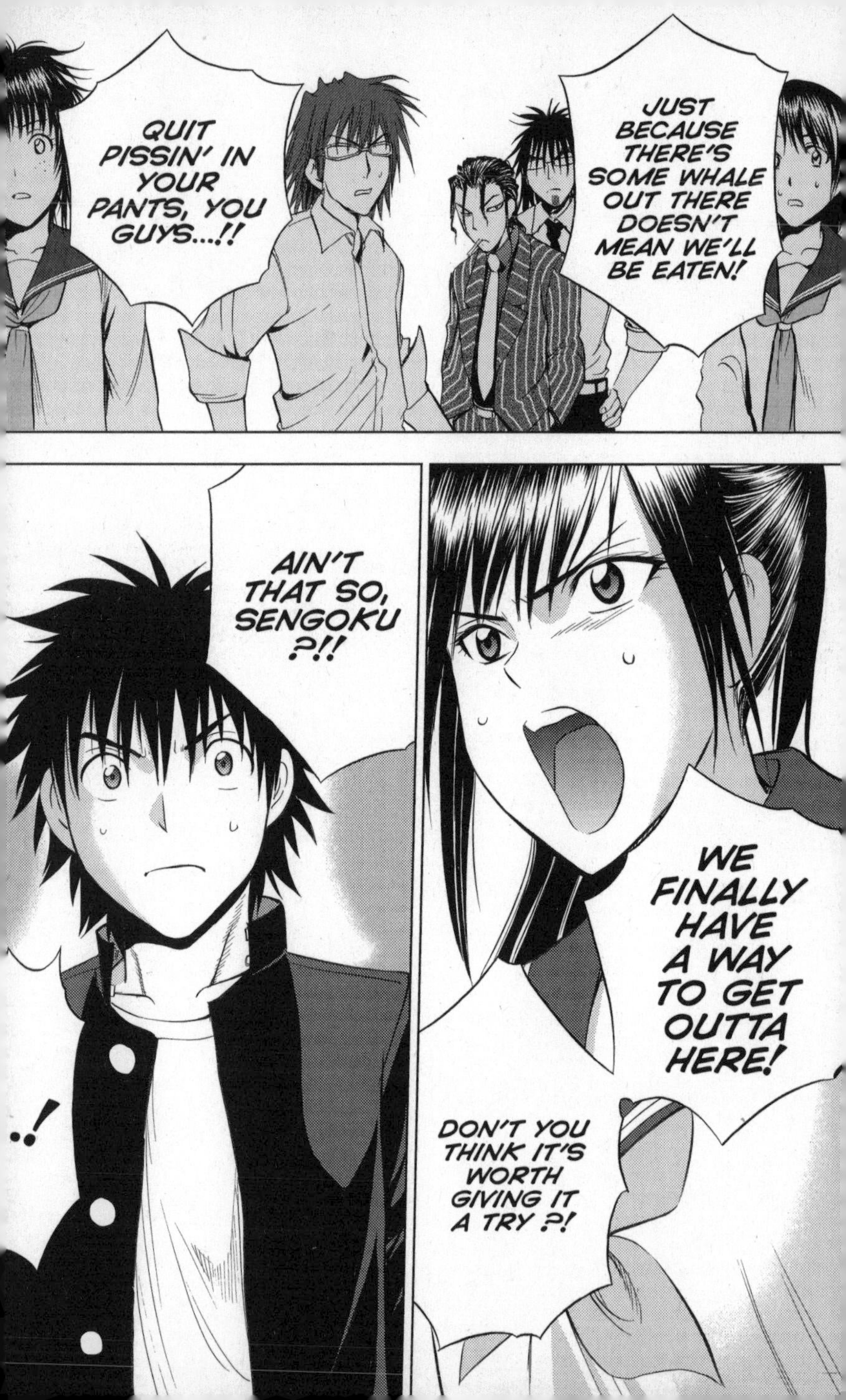
JUST BECAUSE THERE'S SOME WHALE OUT THERE DOESN'T MEAN WE'LL BE EATEN!
QUIT PISSIN' IN YOUR PANTS, YOU GUYS...!!
WE FINALLY HAVE A WAY TO GET OUTTA HERE!
DON'T YOU THINK IT'S WORTH GIVING IT A TRY ?!
AIN'T THAT SO, SENGOKU ?!!
..!

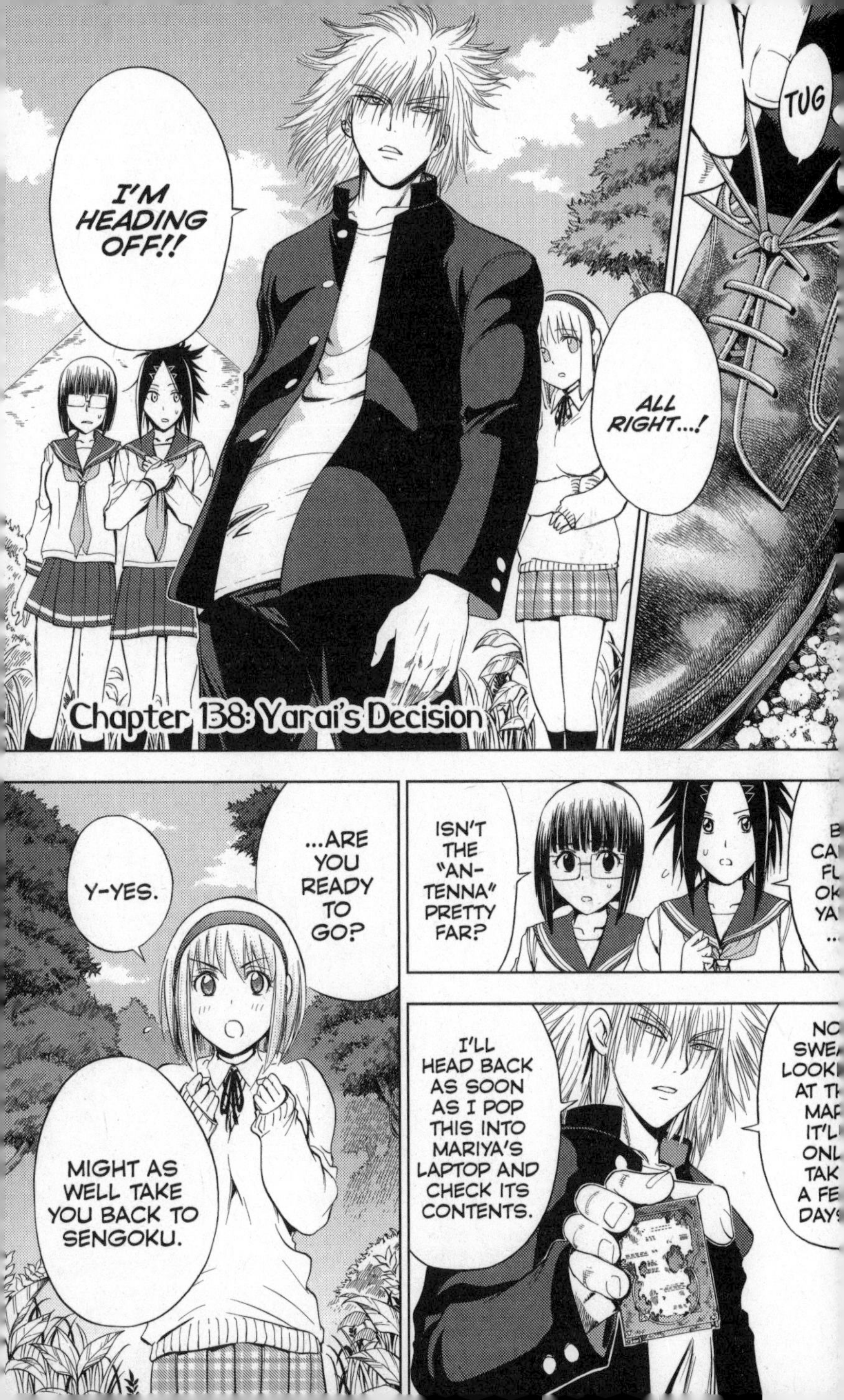
TUG
ALL RIGHT...!
I'M HEADING OFF!!
Chapter 138: Yarai's Decision
ISN'T THE "AN-TENNA" PRETTY FAR?
I'LL HEAD BACK AS SOON AS I POP THIS INTO MARIYA'S LAPTOP AND CHECK ITS CONTENTS.
...ARE YOU READY TO GO?
Y-YES.
MIGHT AS WELL TAKE YOU BACK TO SENGOKU.

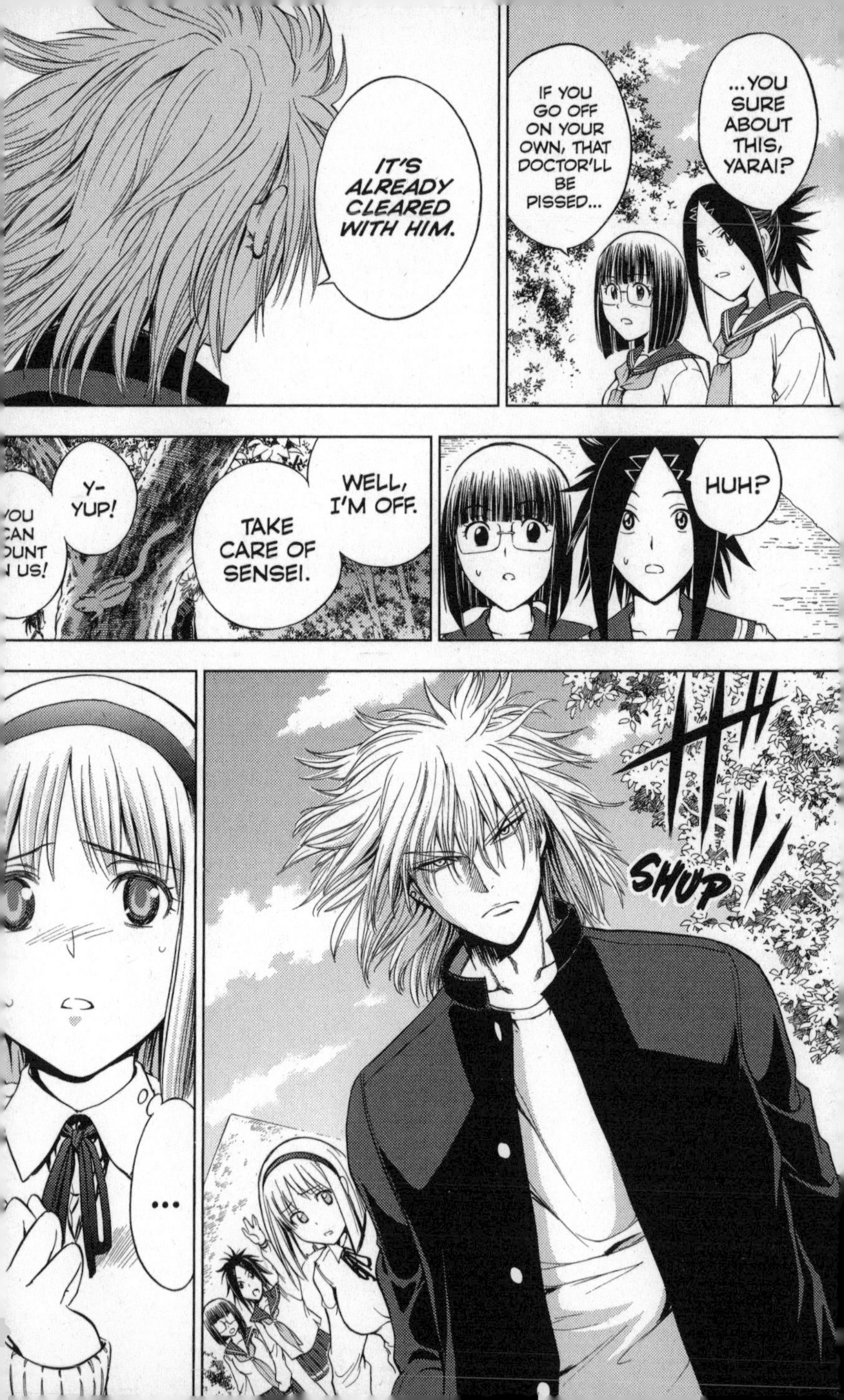
...YOU SURE ABOUT THIS, YARAI?
IF YOU GO OFF ON YOUR OWN, THAT DOCTOR'LL BE PISSED...
IT'S ALREADY CLEARED WITH HIM.
HUH?
WELL, I'M OFF.
TAKE CARE OF SENSEI.
Y-YUP!
OU CAN OUNT N US!
SHUP
...

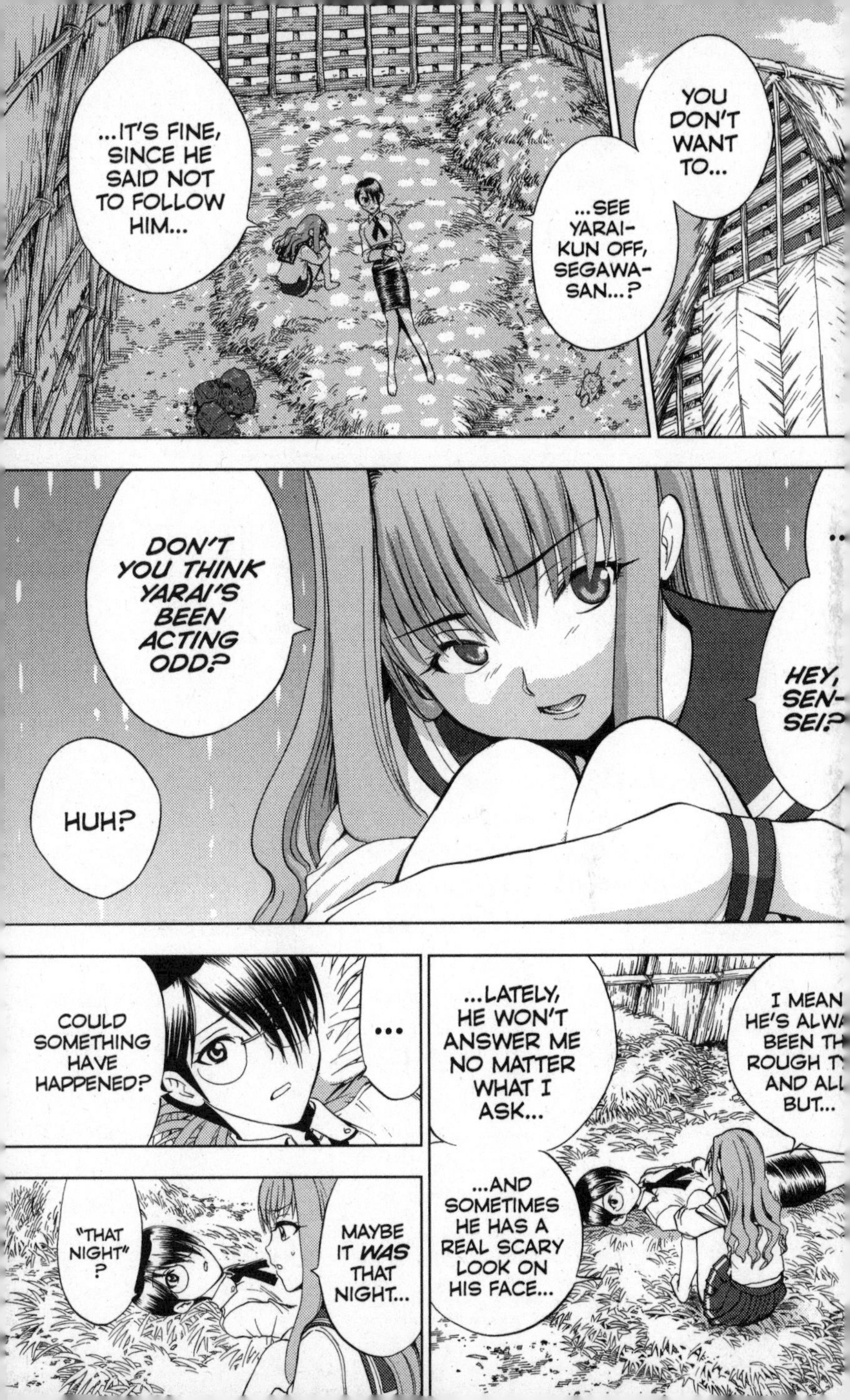
YOU DON'T WANT TO...
...SEE YARAI-KUN OFF, SEGAWA-SAN...?
...IT'S FINE, SINCE HE SAID NOT TO FOLLOW HIM...
...
HEY, SEN-SEI?
DON'T YOU THINK YARAI'S BEEN ACTING ODD?
HUH?
I MEAN HE'S ALWA BEEN TH ROUGH TY AND ALL BUT...
...LATELY, HE WON'T ANSWER ME NO MATTER WHAT I ASK...
...AND SOMETIMES HE HAS A REAL SCARY LOOK ON HIS FACE...
...
COULD SOMETHING HAVE HAPPENED?
MAYBE IT *WAS* THAT NIGHT...
"THAT NIGHT"?

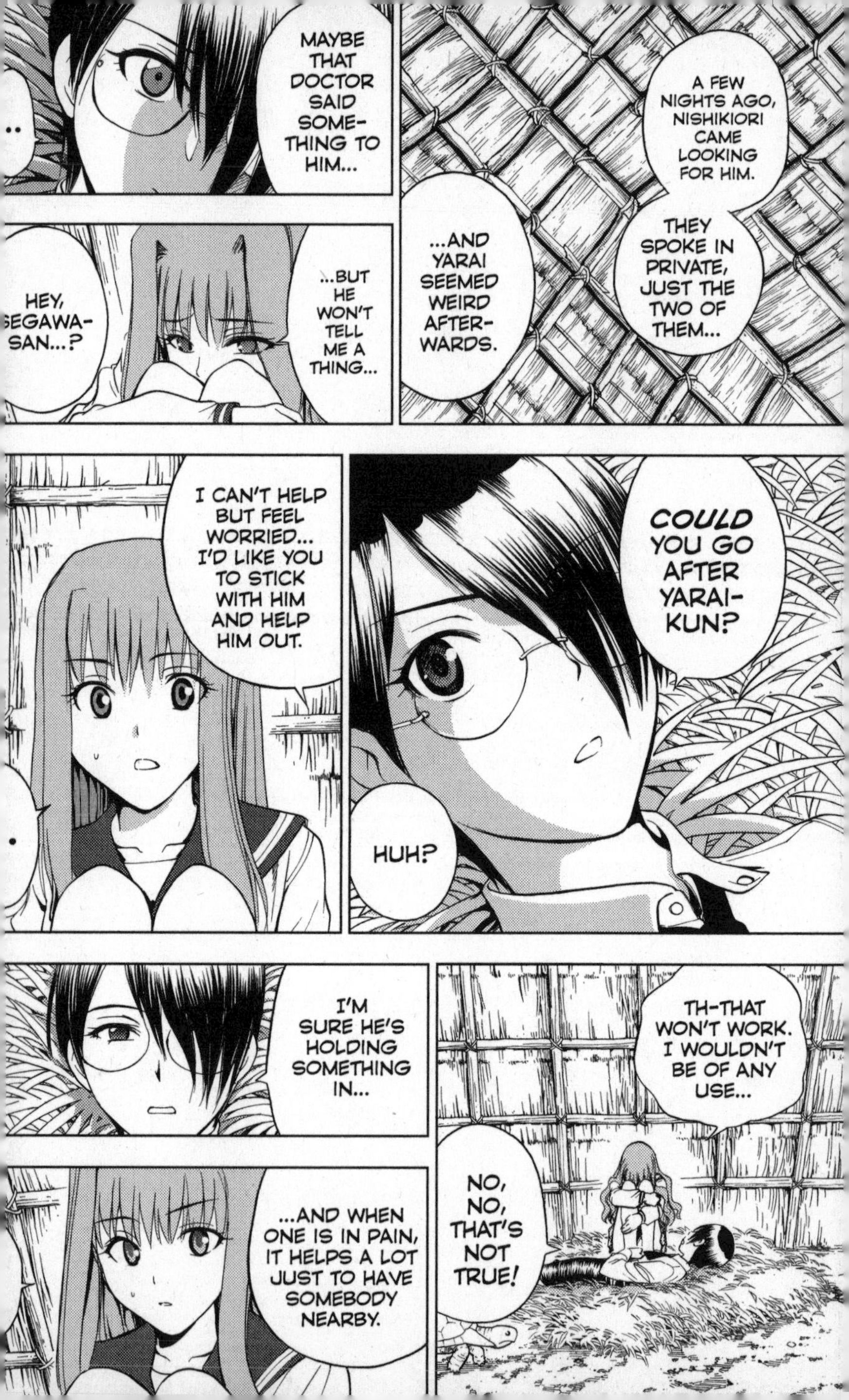
A FEW NIGHTS AGO, NISHIKIORI CAME LOOKING FOR HIM.
THEY SPOKE IN PRIVATE, JUST THE TWO OF THEM...
...AND YARAI SEEMED WEIRD AFTER-WARDS.
MAYBE THAT DOCTOR SAID SOME-THING TO HIM...
...BUT HE WON'T TELL ME A THING...
HEY, SEGAWA-SAN...?
COULD YOU GO AFTER YARAI-KUN?
HUH?
I CAN'T HELP BUT FEEL WORRIED... I'D LIKE YOU TO STICK WITH HIM AND HELP HIM OUT.
TH-THAT WON'T WORK. I WOULDN'T BE OF ANY USE...
NO, NO, THAT'S NOT TRUE!
I'M SURE HE'S HOLDING SOMETHING IN...
...AND WHEN ONE IS IN PAIN, IT HELPS A LOT JUST TO HAVE SOMEBODY NEARBY.

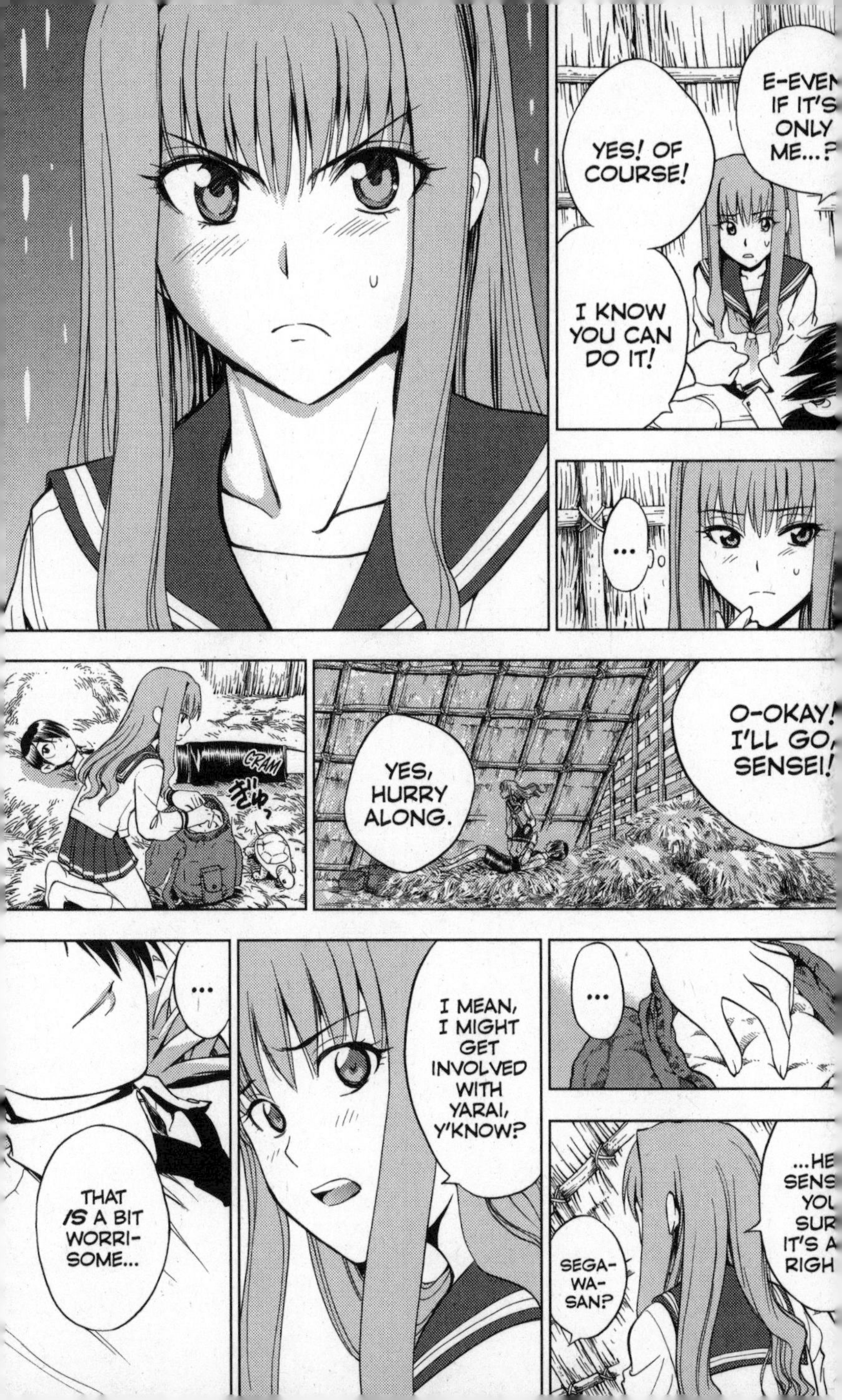
E-EVEN IF IT'S ONLY ME...?
YES! OF COURSE!
I KNOW YOU CAN DO IT!
...
O-OKAY! I'LL GO, SENSEI!
YES, HURRY ALONG.
GRAM
...
...HE SENS YOU SUR IT'S A RIGH
SEGA-WA-SAN?
I MEAN, I MIGHT GET INVOLVED WITH YARAI, Y'KNOW?
...
THAT *IS* A BIT WORRI-SOME...

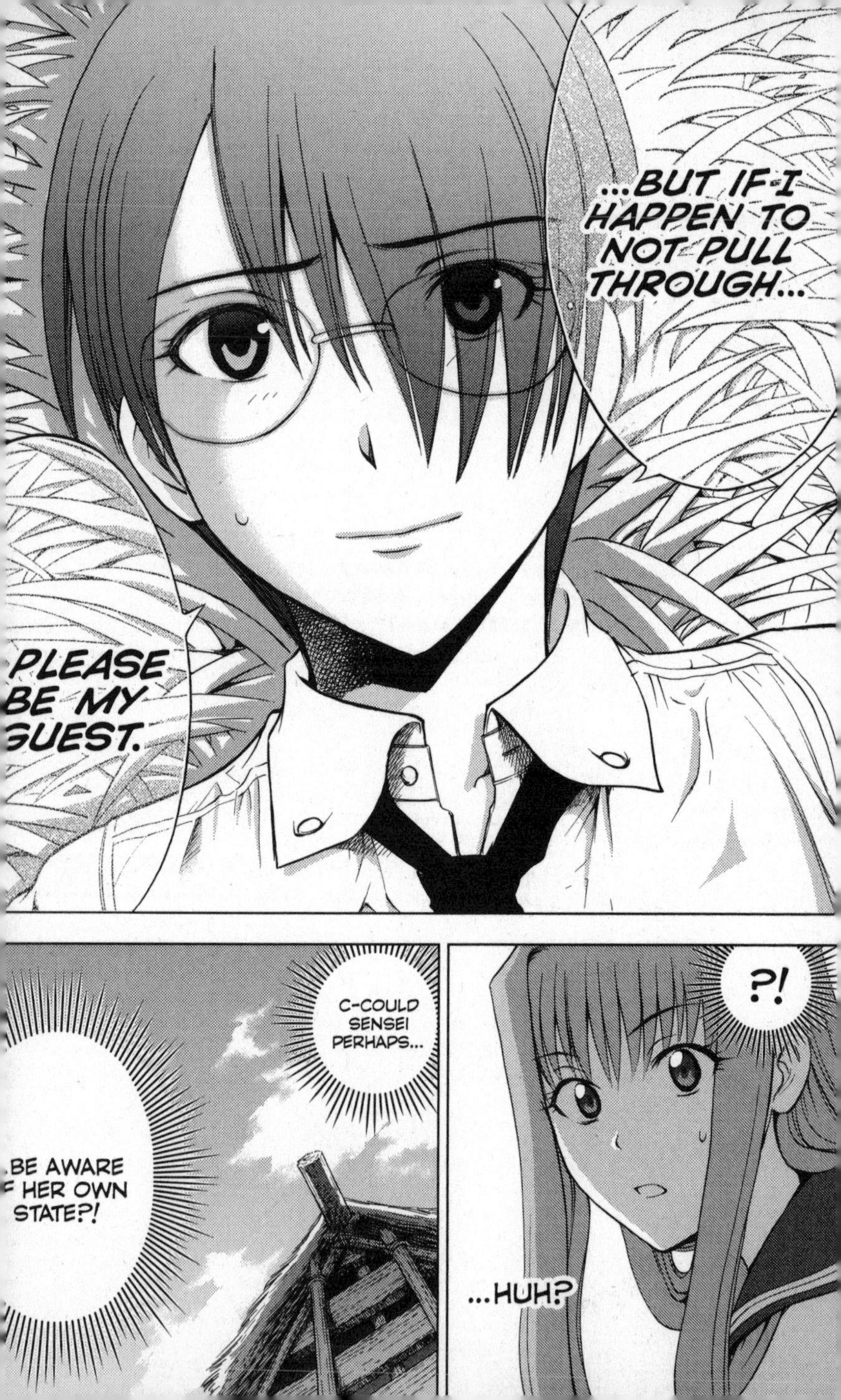
...BUT IF I HAPPEN TO NOT PULL THROUGH...
PLEASE BE MY GUEST.
?!
...HUH?
C-COULD SENSEI PERHAPS...
.BE AWARE F HER OWN STATE?!

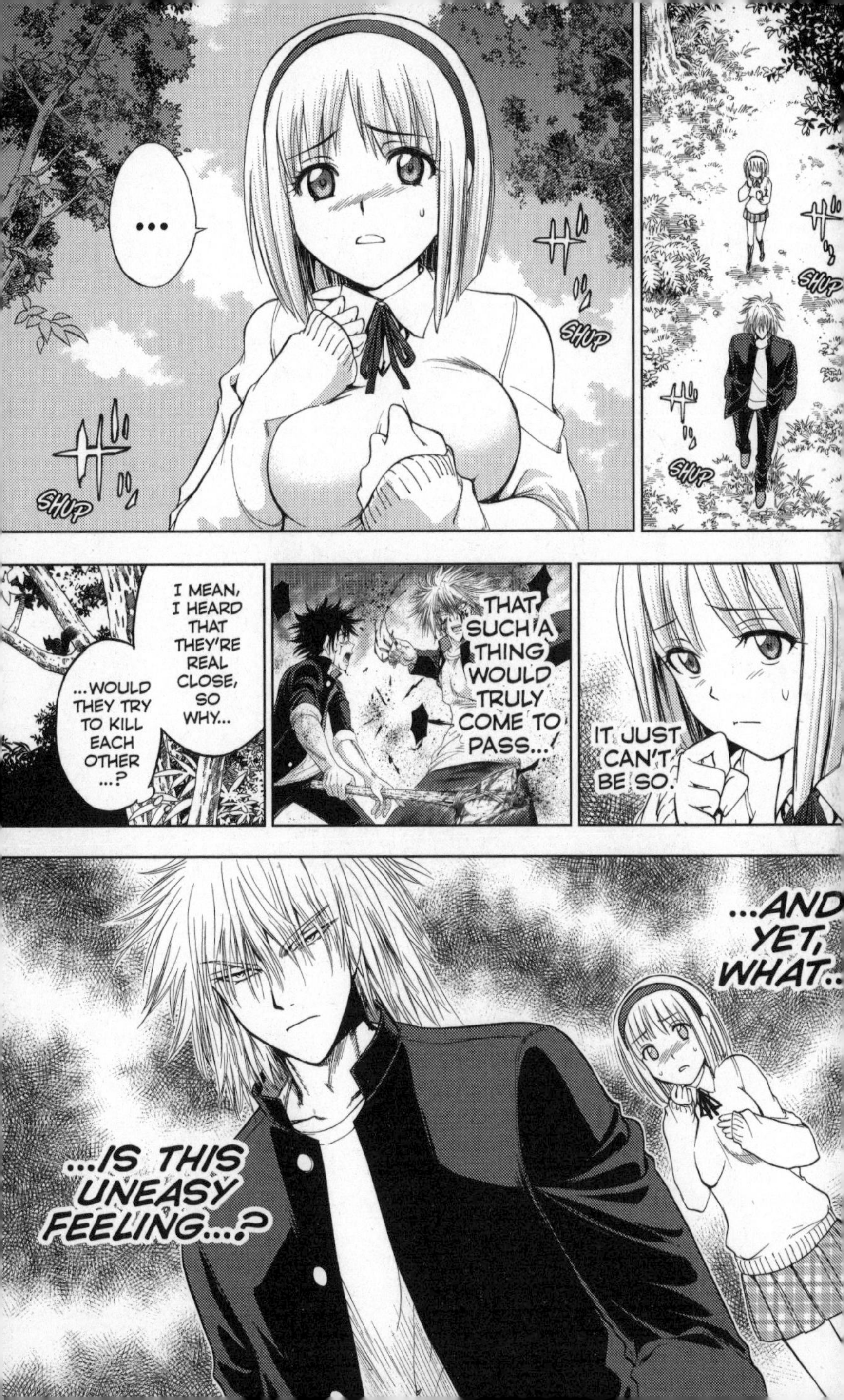
SHUP
SHUP
...
SHUP
SHUP
IT JUST CAN'T BE SO.
THAT SUCH A THING WOULD TRULY COME TO PASS...
I MEAN, I HEARD THAT THEY'RE REAL CLOSE, SO WHY...
...WOULD THEY TRY TO KILL EACH OTHER ...?
...AND YET, WHAT...
...IS THIS UNEASY FEELING...?

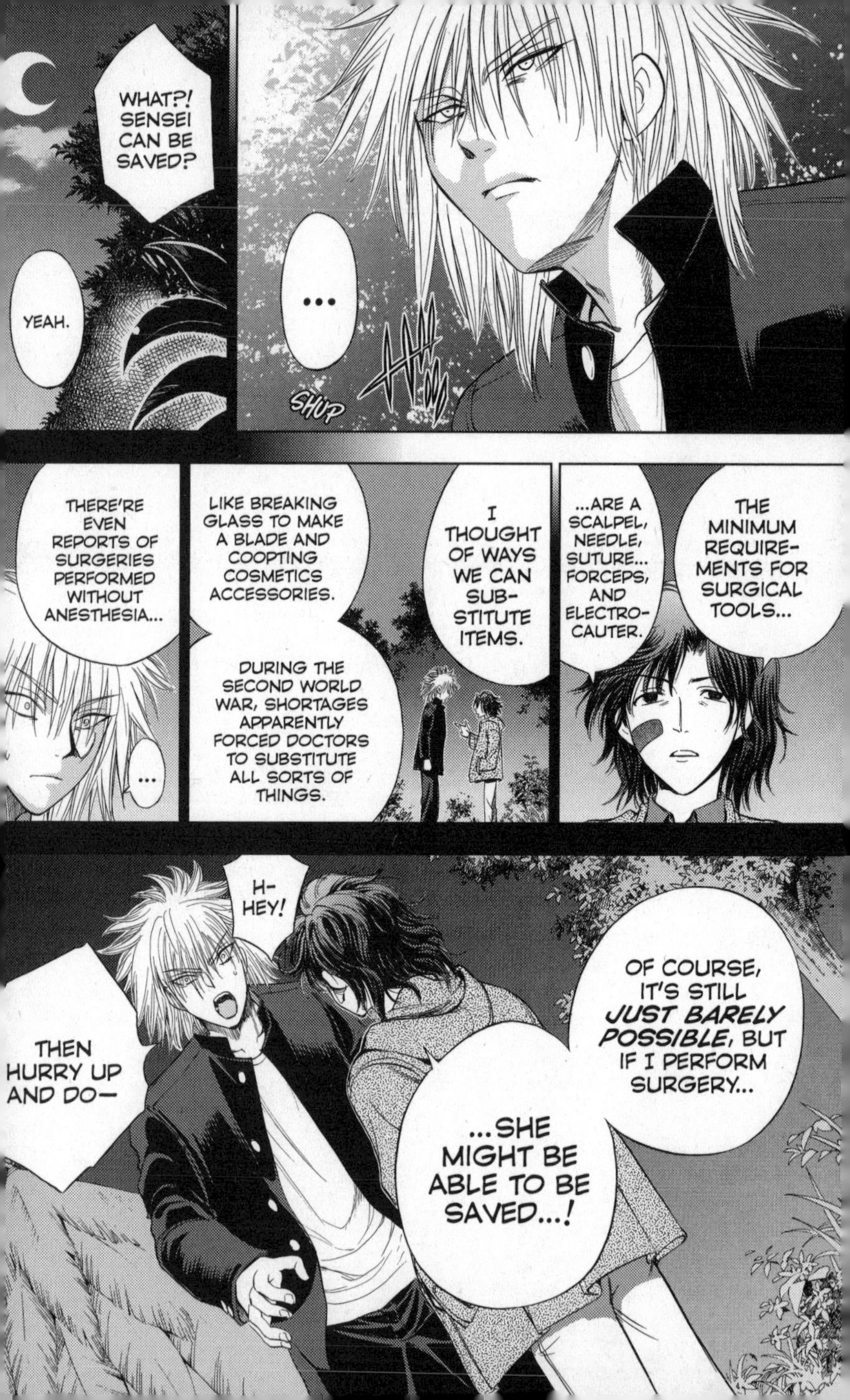
...
SHUP
WHAT?! SENSEI CAN BE SAVED?
YEAH.
THE MINIMUM REQUIRE-MENTS FOR SURGICAL TOOLS...
...ARE A SCALPEL, NEEDLE, SUTURE... FORCEPS, AND ELECTRO-CAUTER.
I THOUGHT OF WAYS WE CAN SUB-STITUTE ITEMS.
LIKE BREAKING GLASS TO MAKE A BLADE AND COOPTING COSMETICS ACCESSORIES.
DURING THE SECOND WORLD WAR, SHORTAGES APPARENTLY FORCED DOCTORS TO SUBSTITUTE ALL SORTS OF THINGS.
THERE'RE EVEN REPORTS OF SURGERIES PERFORMED WITHOUT ANESTHESIA...
...
OF COURSE, IT'S STILL *JUST BARELY POSSIBLE*, BUT IF I PERFORM SURGERY...
...SHE MIGHT BE ABLE TO BE SAVED...!
H-HEY!
THEN HURRY UP AND DO—

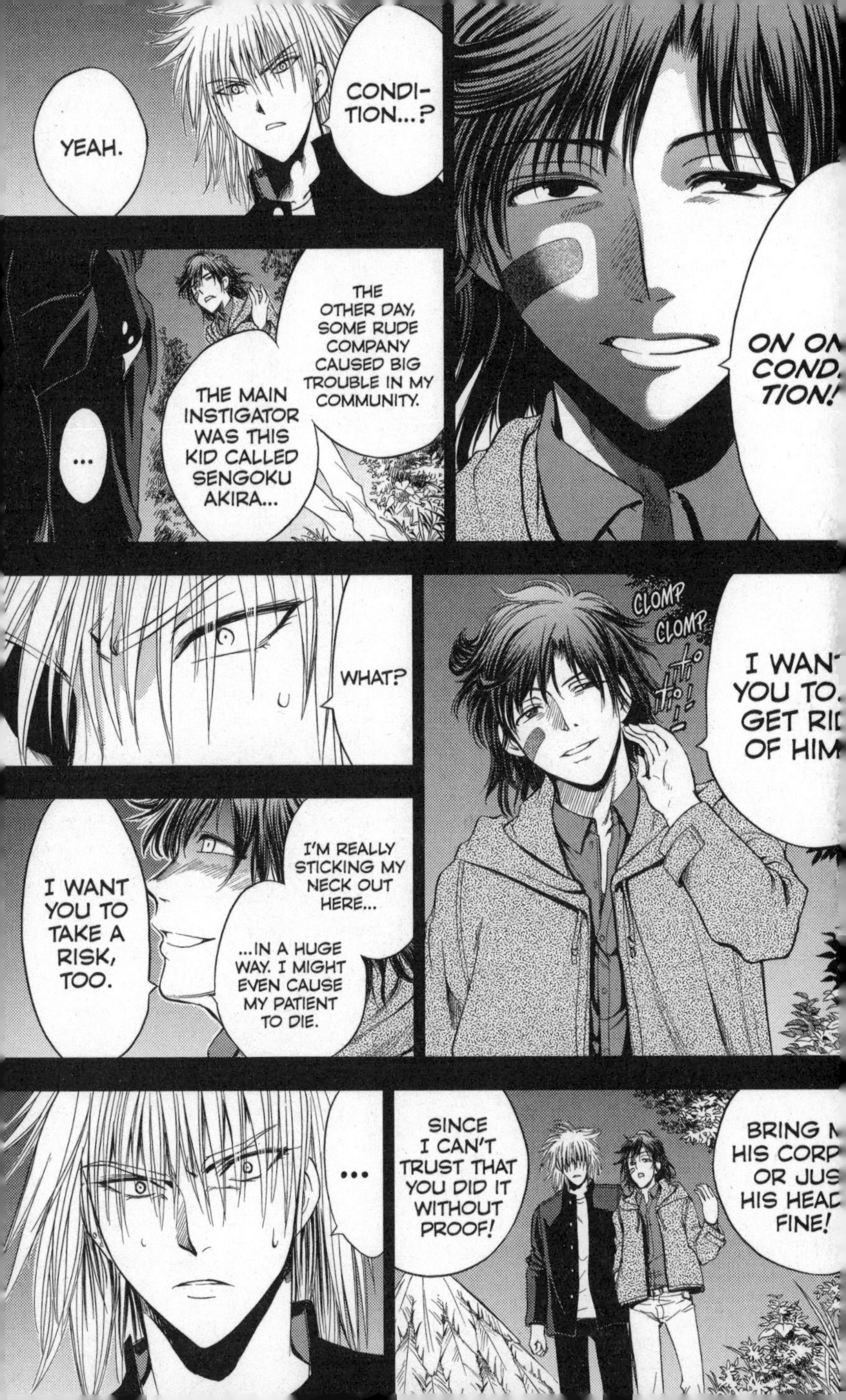

ON ON COND. TION!
CONDI- TION...?
YEAH.
THE OTHER DAY, SOME RUDE COMPANY CAUSED BIG TROUBLE IN MY COMMUNITY.
THE MAIN INSTIGATOR WAS THIS KID CALLED SENGOKU AKIRA...
...
CLOMP
CLOMP
I WAN YOU TO. GET RI OF HIM
WHAT?
I'M REALLY STICKING MY NECK OUT HERE...
...IN A HUGE WAY. I MIGHT EVEN CAUSE MY PATIENT TO DIE.
I WANT YOU TO TAKE A RISK, TOO.
BRING M HIS CORP OR JUS HIS HEAD FINE!
SINCE I CAN'T TRUST THAT YOU DID IT WITHOUT PROOF!
...

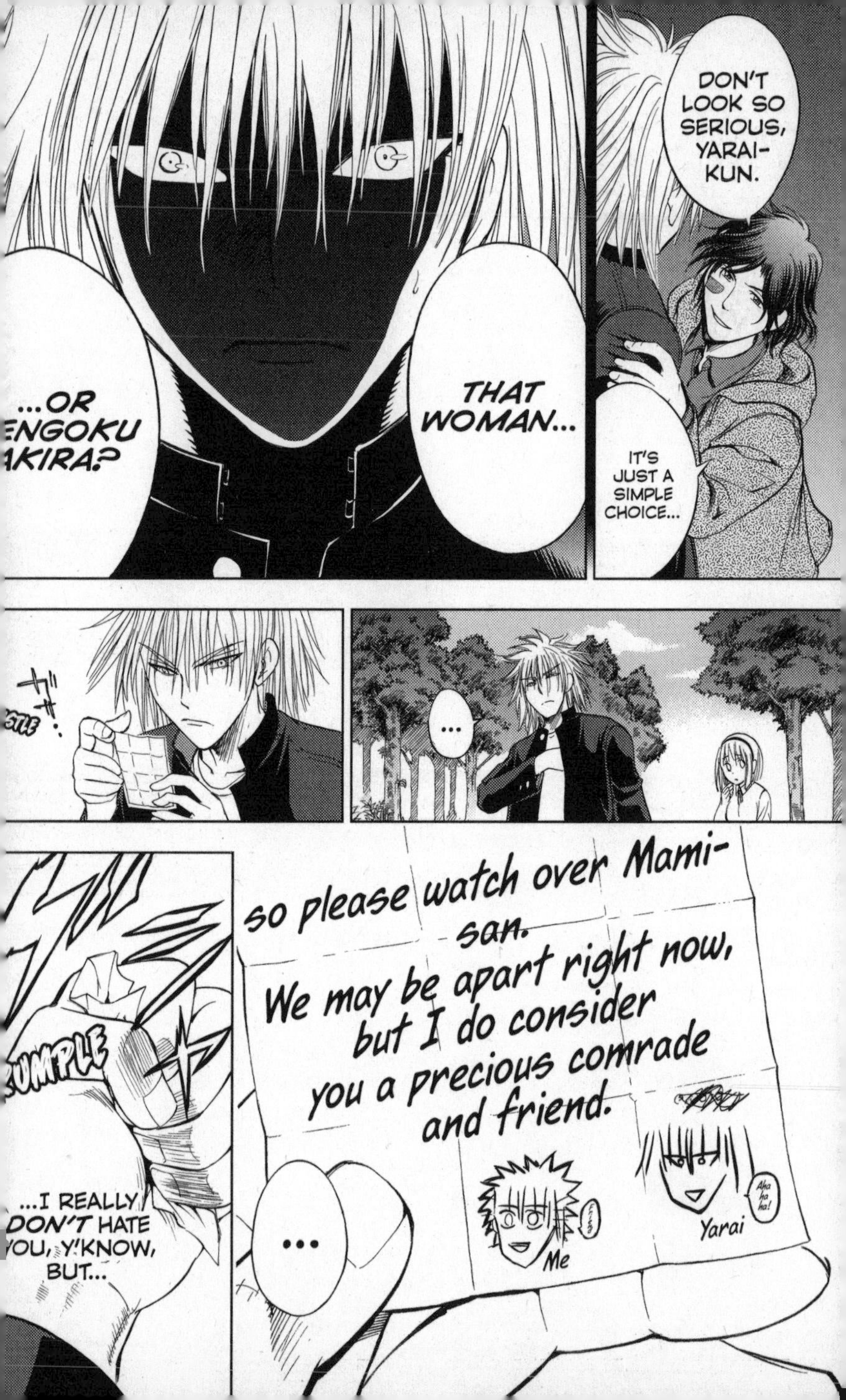
DON'T LOOK SO SERIOUS, YARAI-KUN.
IT'S JUST A SIMPLE CHOICE...
THAT WOMAN...
...OR ENGOKU AKIRA?
...
so please watch over Mami-san.
We may be apart right now, but I do consider you a precious comrade and friend.
Aha ha ha!
Yarai
Me
...
UMPLE
...I REALLY DON'T HATE YOU, Y'KNOW, BUT...

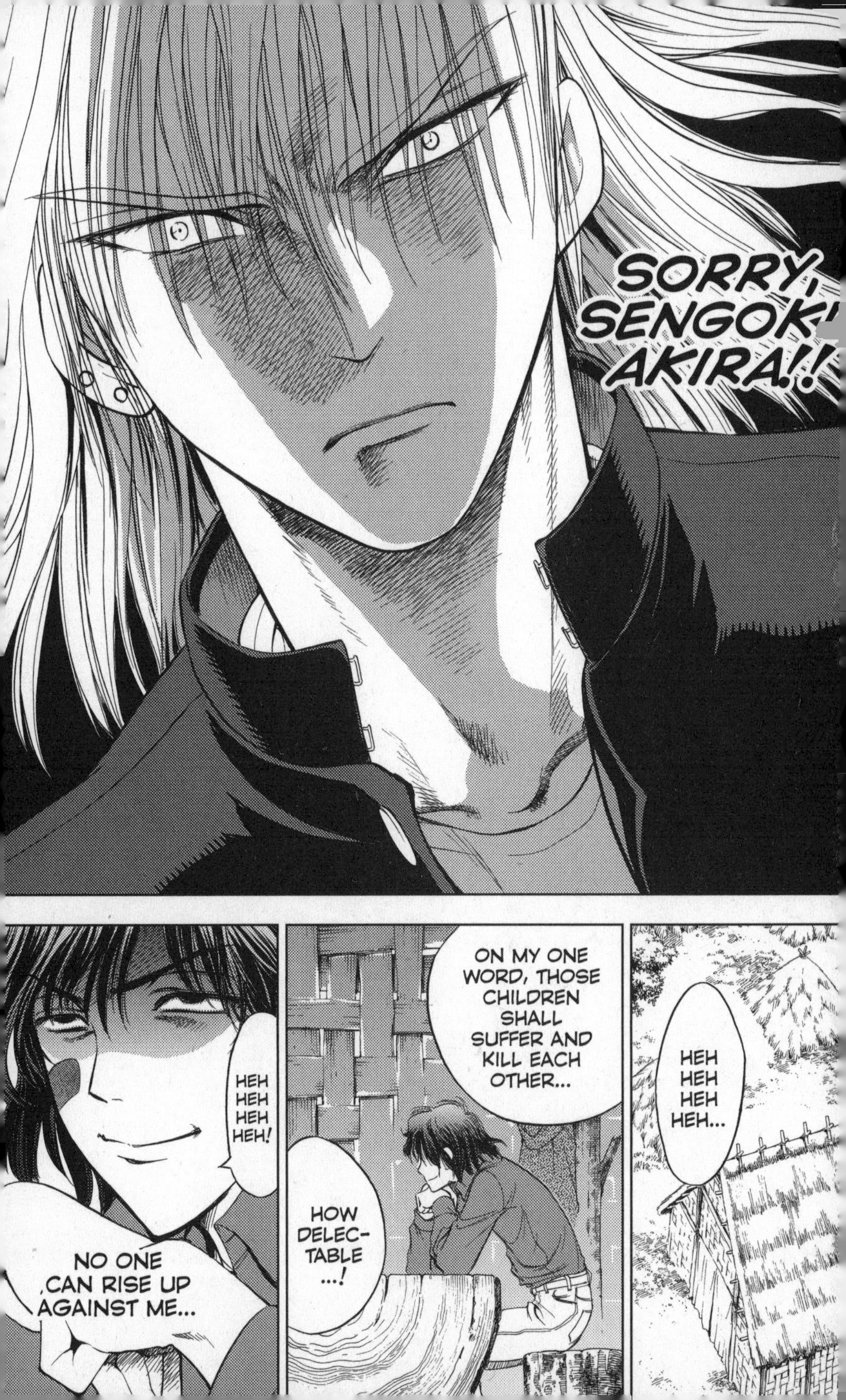
SORRY, SENGOK AKIRA!!
HEH HEH HEH HEH...
ON MY ONE WORD, THOSE CHILDREN SHALL SUFFER AND KILL EACH OTHER...
HOW DELEC-TABLE ...!
HEH HEH HEH HEH!
NO ONE CAN RISE UP AGAINST ME...

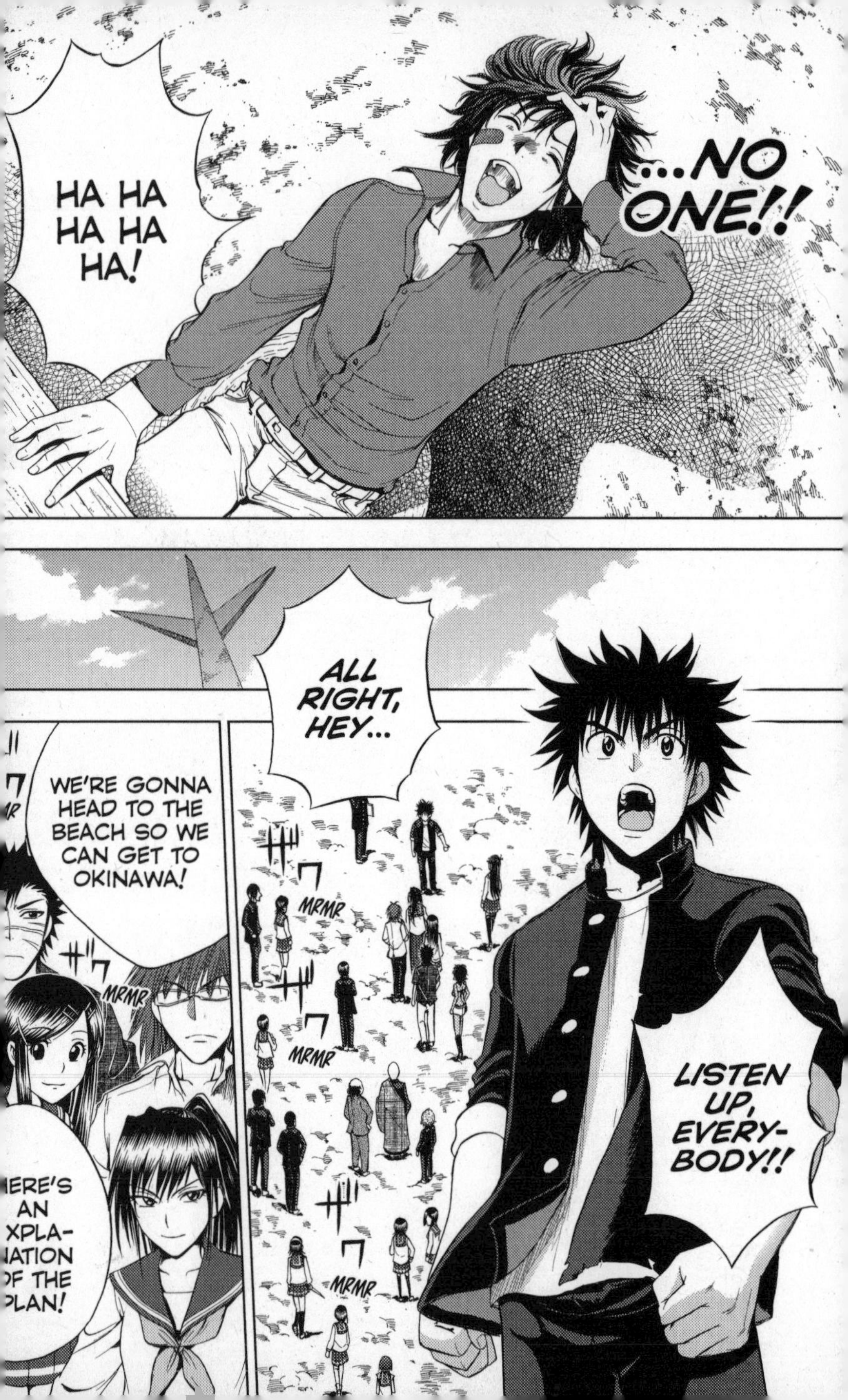
...NO ONE!!
HA HA HA HA HA!
ALL RIGHT, HEY...
LISTEN UP, EVERY-BODY!!
MRMR
MRMR
MRMR
WE'RE GONNA HEAD TO THE BEACH SO WE CAN GET TO OKINAWA!
MRMR
ERE'S AN XPLA-NATION OF THE PLAN!

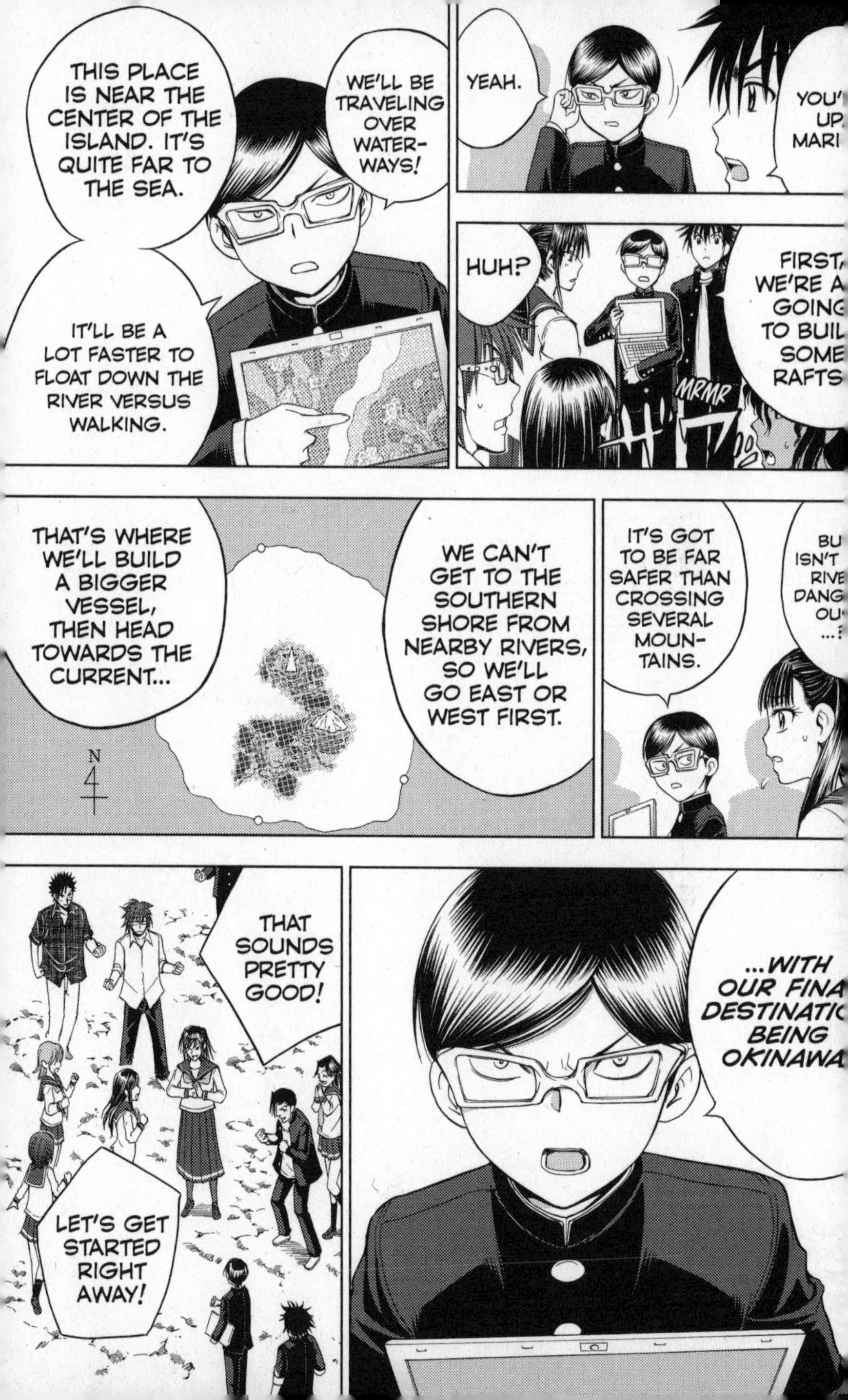

YOU' UP. MARI
YEAH.
FIRST, WE'RE A GOING TO BUIL SOME RAFTS
HUH?
MRMR
WE'LL BE TRAVELING OVER WATER-WAYS!
THIS PLACE IS NEAR THE CENTER OF THE ISLAND. IT'S QUITE FAR TO THE SEA.
IT'LL BE A LOT FASTER TO FLOAT DOWN THE RIVER VERSUS WALKING.
BU ISN'T RIVE DANG OU ...?
IT'S GOT TO BE FAR SAFER THAN CROSSING SEVERAL MOUN-TAINS.
WE CAN'T GET TO THE SOUTHERN SHORE FROM NEARBY RIVERS, SO WE'LL GO EAST OR WEST FIRST.
THAT'S WHERE WE'LL BUILD A BIGGER VESSEL, THEN HEAD TOWARDS THE CURRENT...
N
...WITH OUR FINA DESTINATI BEING OKINAWA
THAT SOUNDS PRETTY GOOD!
LET'S GET STARTED RIGHT AWAY!

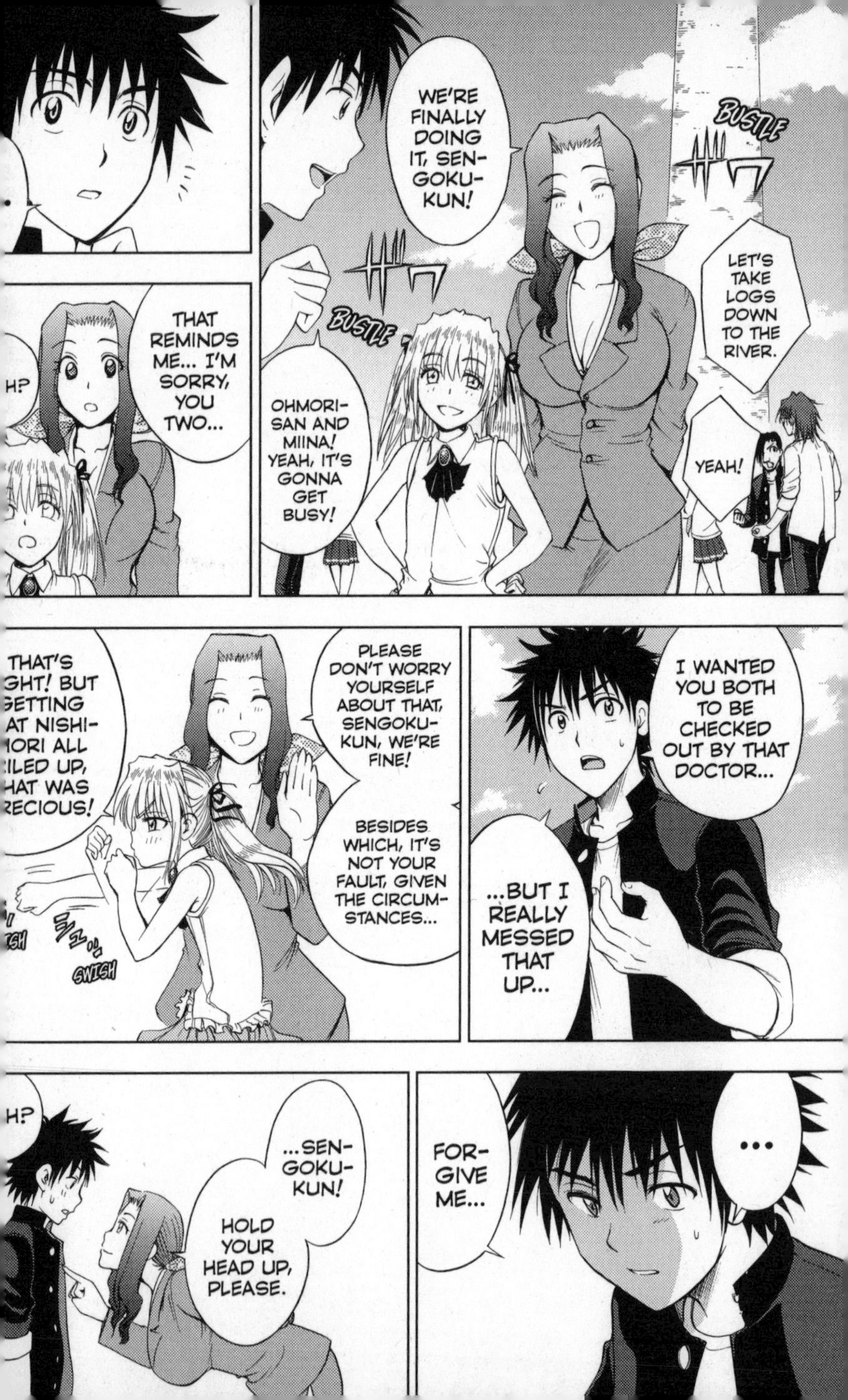
BUSTLE
WE'RE FINALLY DOING IT, SENGOKU-KUN!
LET'S TAKE LOGS DOWN TO THE RIVER.
YEAH!
BUSTLE
OHMORI-SAN AND MIINA! YEAH, IT'S GONNA GET BUSY!
THAT REMINDS ME... I'M SORRY, YOU TWO...
H?
I WANTED YOU BOTH TO BE CHECKED OUT BY THAT DOCTOR...
...BUT I REALLY MESSED THAT UP...
PLEASE DON'T WORRY YOURSELF ABOUT THAT, SENGOKU-KUN, WE'RE FINE!
BESIDES WHICH, IT'S NOT YOUR FAULT, GIVEN THE CIRCUMSTANCES...
THAT'S GHT! BUT GETTING AT NISHI-MORI ALL ILED UP, HAT WAS RECIOUS!
SWISH
...
FOR-GIVE ME...
...SEN-GOKU-KUN!
HOLD YOUR HEAD UP, PLEASE.
H?

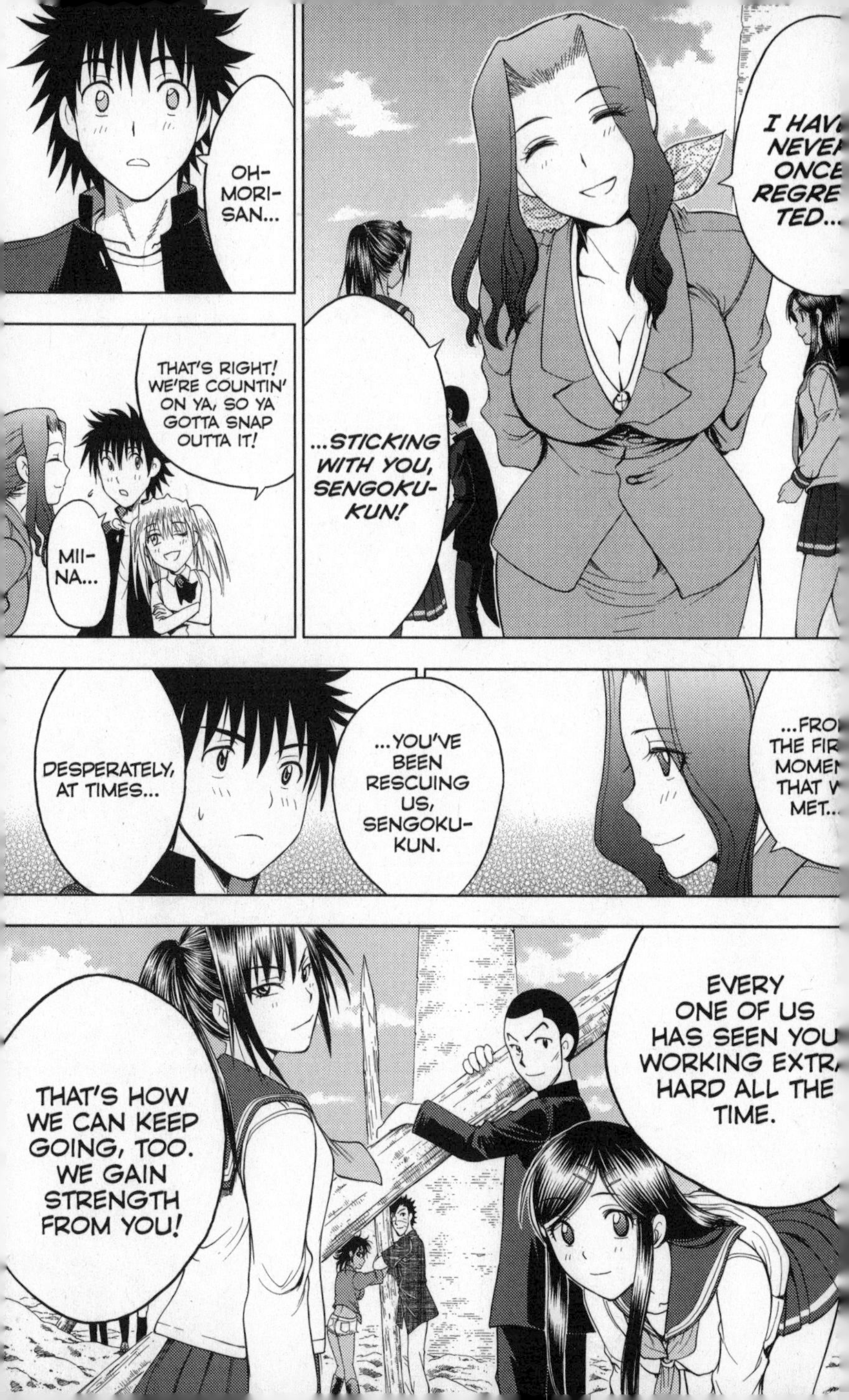
I HAVE NEVER ONCE REGRE- TED...
...STICKING WITH YOU, SENGOKU-KUN!
OH-MORI-SAN...
THAT'S RIGHT! WE'RE COUNTIN' ON YA, SO YA GOTTA SNAP OUTTA IT!
MII-NA...
...FROM THE FIRST MOMENT THAT WE MET...
...YOU'VE BEEN RESCUING US, SENGOKU-KUN.
DESPERATELY, AT TIMES...
EVERY ONE OF US HAS SEEN YOU WORKING EXTRA HARD ALL THE TIME.
THAT'S HOW WE CAN KEEP GOING, TOO. WE GAIN STRENGTH FROM YOU!

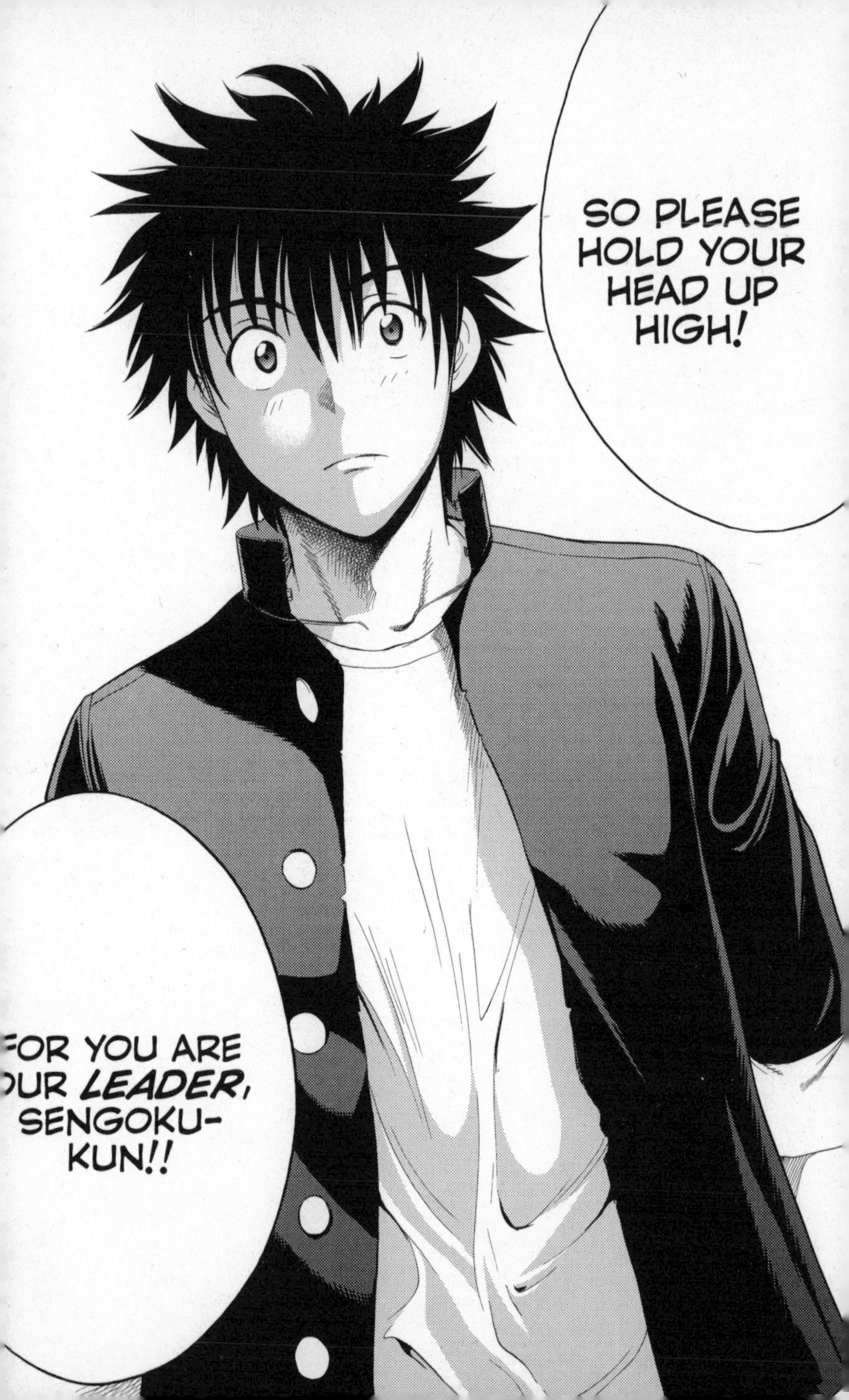
SO PLEASE HOLD YOUR HEAD UP HIGH!
FOR YOU ARE OUR *LEADER*, SENGOKU-KUN!!

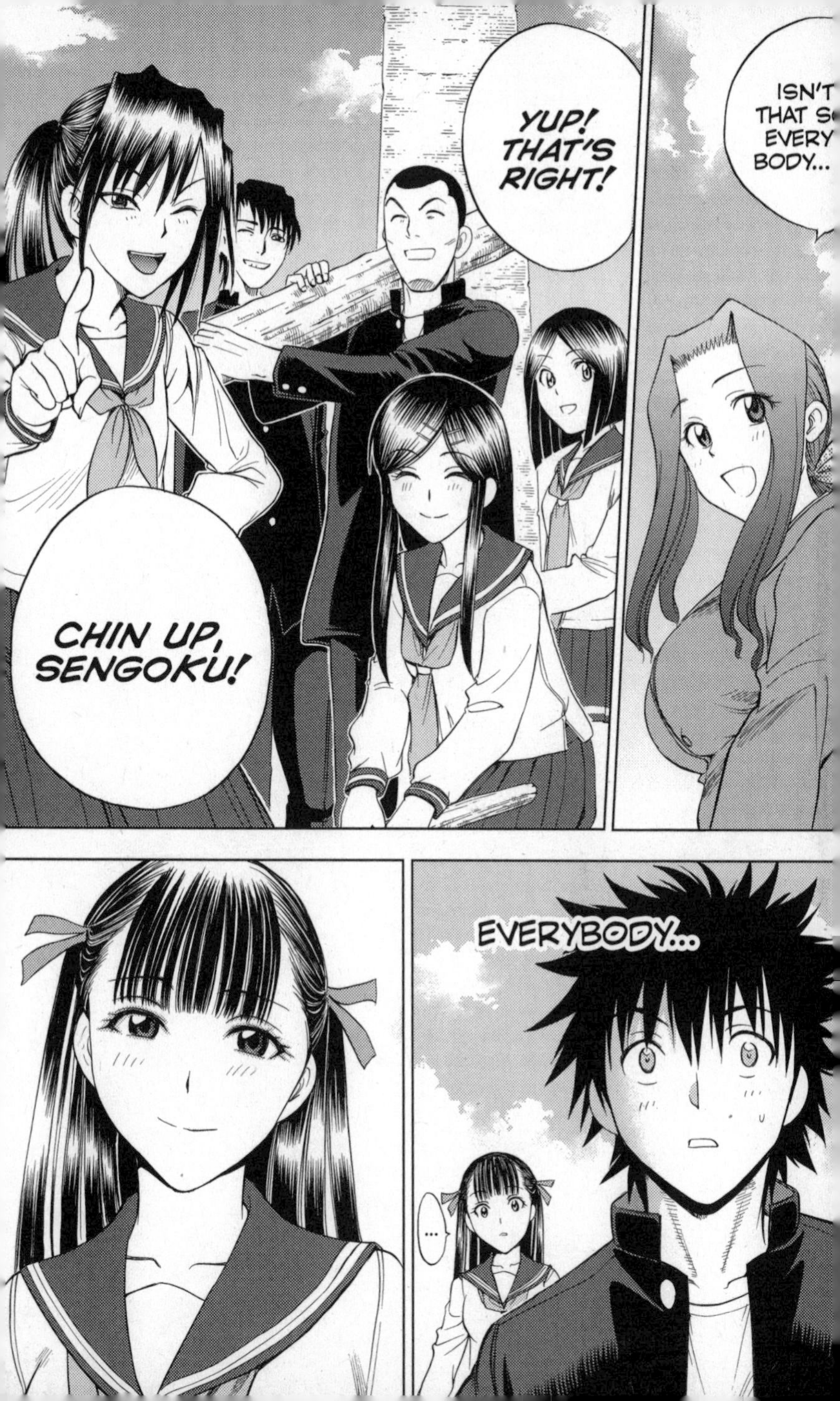

ISN'T THAT S EVERY BODY...
YUP! THAT'S RIGHT!
CHIN UP, SENGOKU!
EVERYBODY...
...

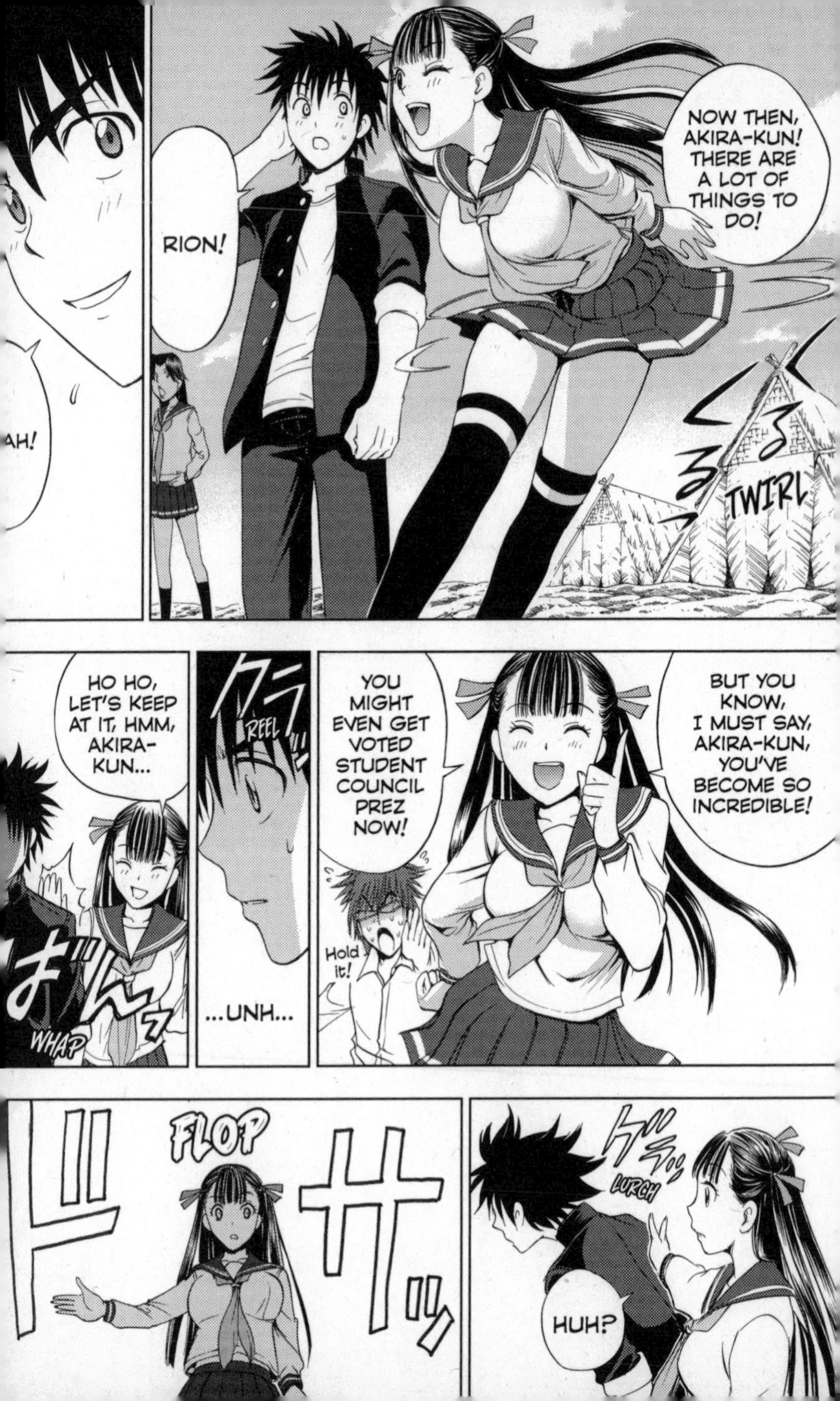

NOW THEN, AKIRA-KUN! THERE ARE A LOT OF THINGS TO DO!
RION!
TWIRL
AH!
BUT YOU KNOW, I MUST SAY, AKIRA-KUN, YOU'VE BECOME SO INCREDIBLE!
YOU MIGHT EVEN GET VOTED STUDENT COUNCIL PREZ NOW!
Hold it!
REEL
...UNH...
HO HO, LET'S KEEP AT IT, HMM, AKIRA-KUN...
WHAP
LURCH
HUH?
FLOP

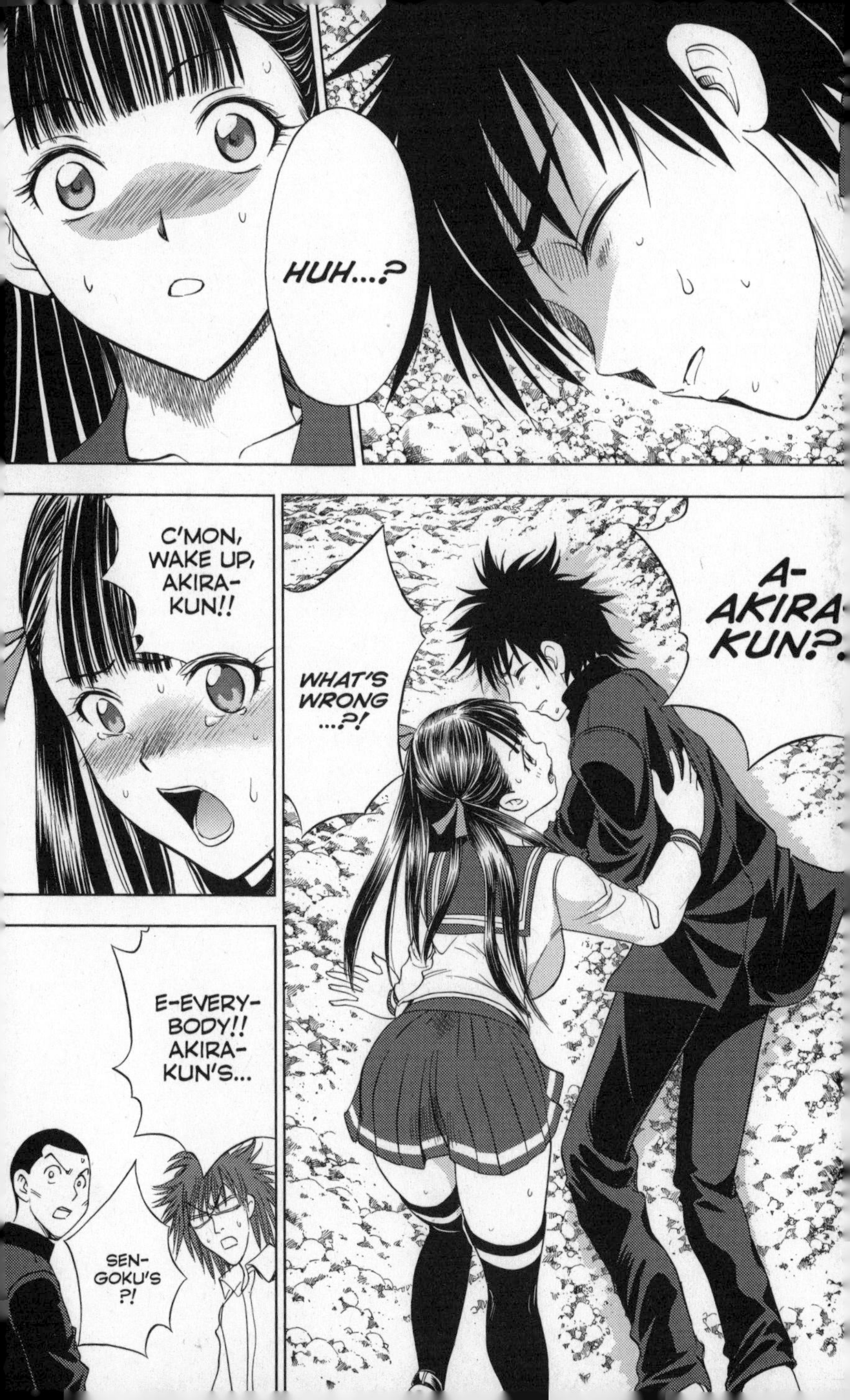
HUH...?
A-AKIRA-KUN?.
WHAT'S WRONG...?!
C'MON, WAKE UP, AKIRA-KUN!!
E-EVERYBODY!! AKIRA-KUN'S...
SEN-GOKU'S?!

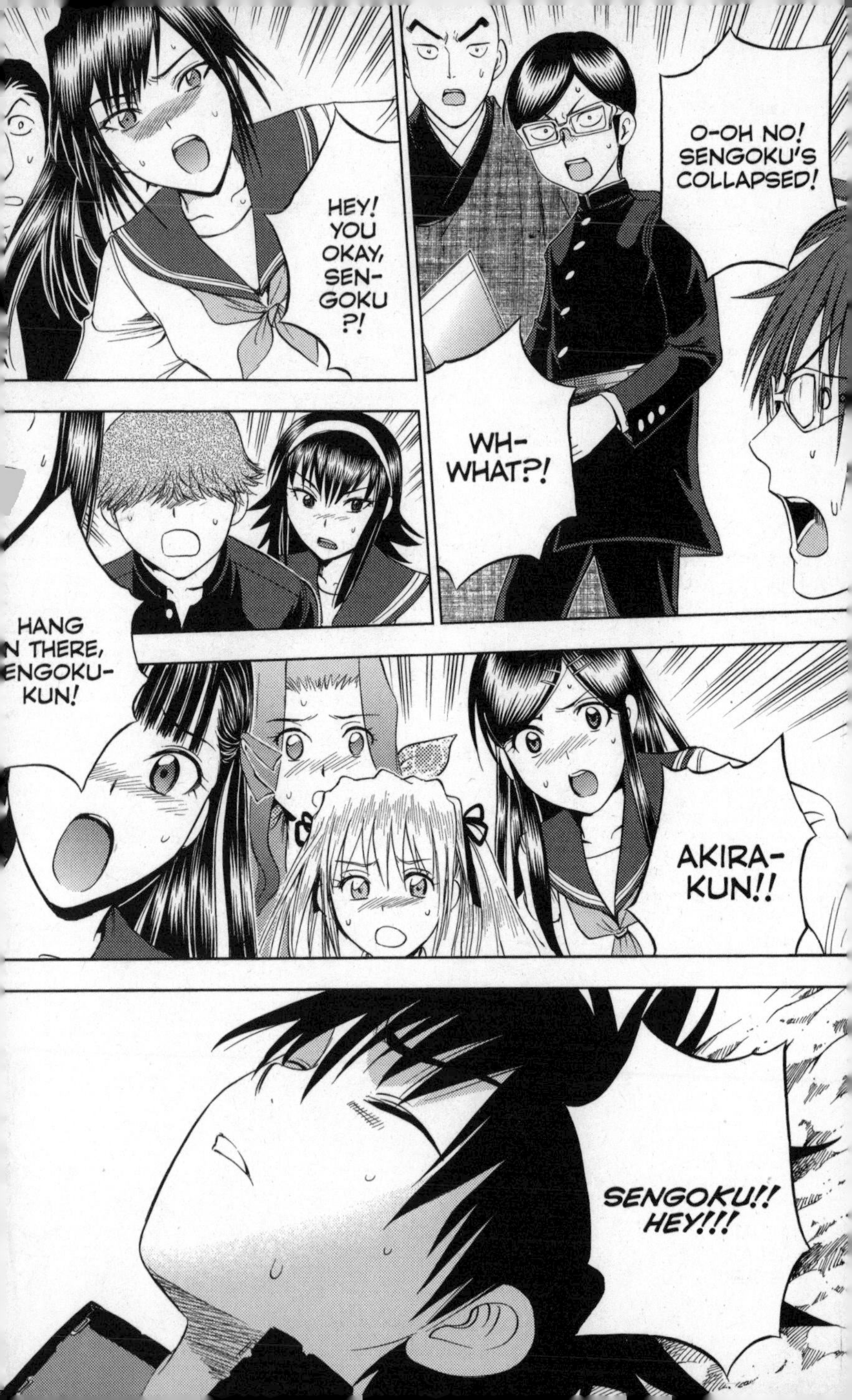
O-OH NO! SENGOKU'S COLLAPSED!
WH-WHAT?!
HEY! YOU OKAY, SEN-GOKU?!
AKIRA-KUN!!
HANG N THERE, ENGOKU-KUN!
SENGOKU!! HEY!!!

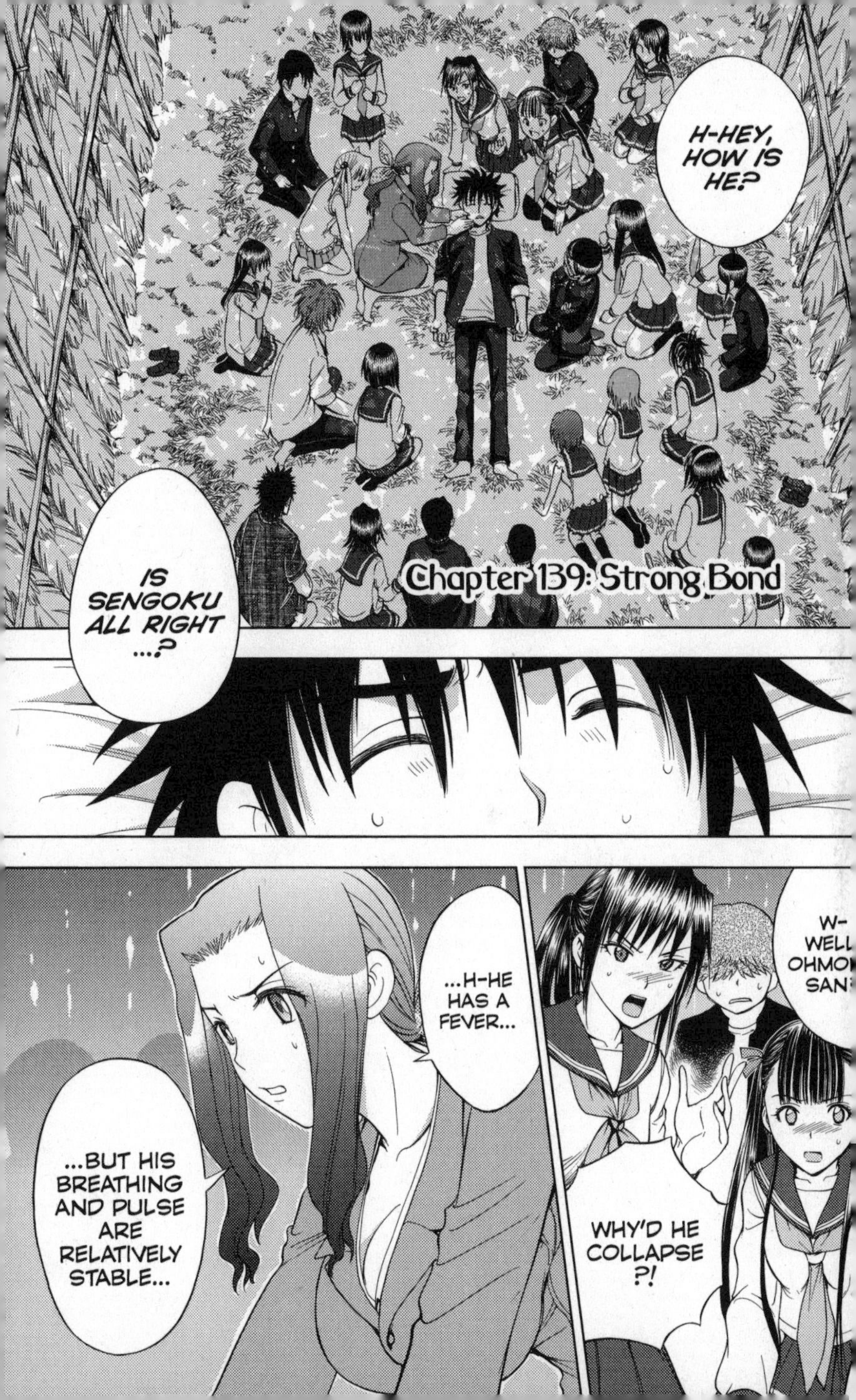
H-HEY, HOW IS HE?
IS SENGOKU ALL RIGHT ...?
Chapter 139: Strong Bond
W- WELL OHMO SAN
WHY'D HE COLLAPSE ?!
...H-HE HAS A FEVER...
...BUT HIS BREATHING AND PULSE ARE RELATIVELY STABLE...

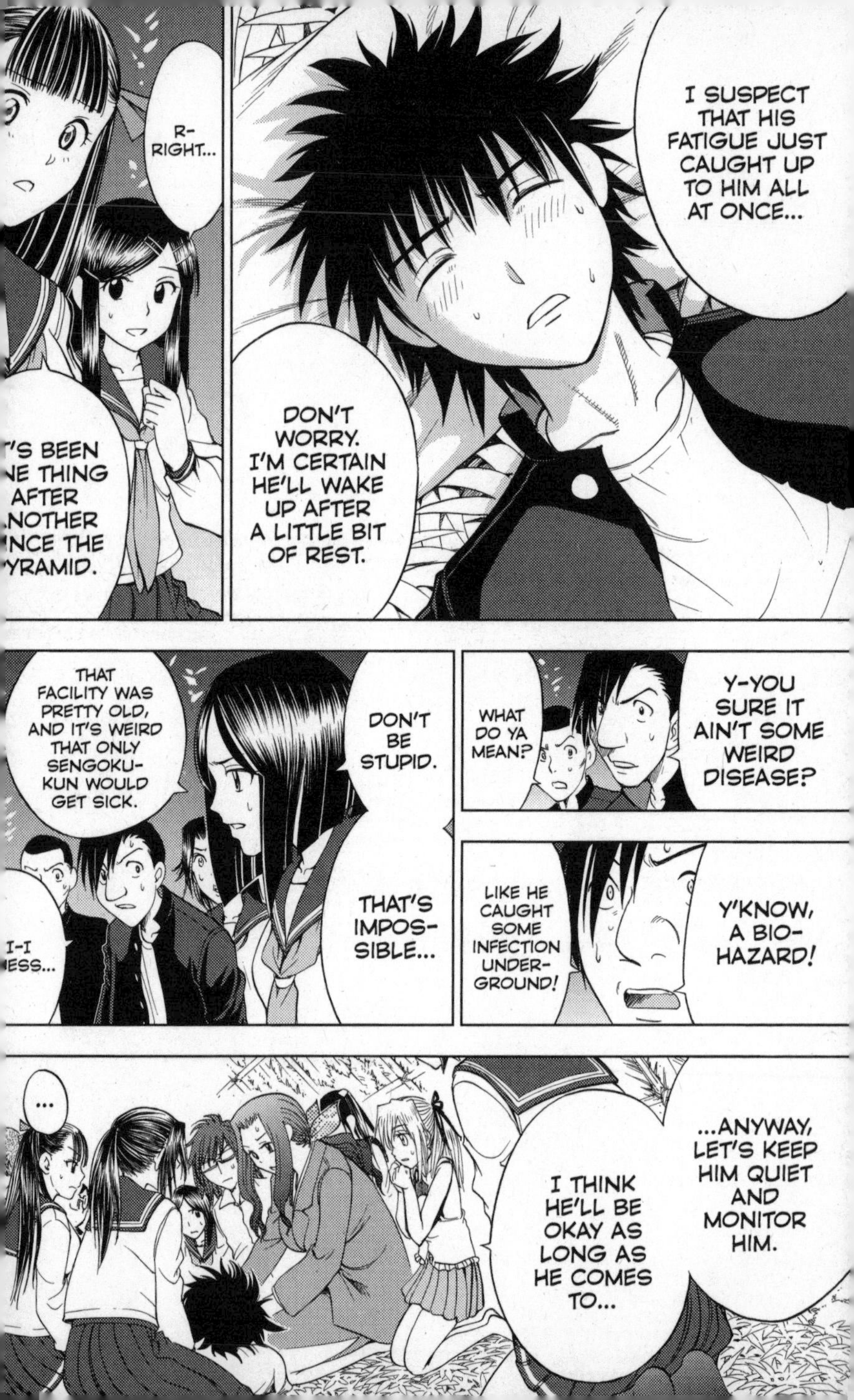
I SUSPECT THAT HIS FATIGUE JUST CAUGHT UP TO HIM ALL AT ONCE...
DON'T WORRY. I'M CERTAIN HE'LL WAKE UP AFTER A LITTLE BIT OF REST.
R-RIGHT...
'S BEEN NE THING AFTER NOTHER NCE THE YRAMID.
Y-YOU SURE IT AIN'T SOME WEIRD DISEASE?
WHAT DO YA MEAN?
Y'KNOW, A BIO-HAZARD!
LIKE HE CAUGHT SOME INFECTION UNDER-GROUND!
DON'T BE STUPID.
THAT'S IMPOS-SIBLE...
THAT FACILITY WAS PRETTY OLD, AND IT'S WEIRD THAT ONLY SENGOKU-KUN WOULD GET SICK.
I-I ESS...
...ANYWAY, LET'S KEEP HIM QUIET AND MONITOR HIM.
I THINK HE'LL BE OKAY AS LONG AS HE COMES TO...
...

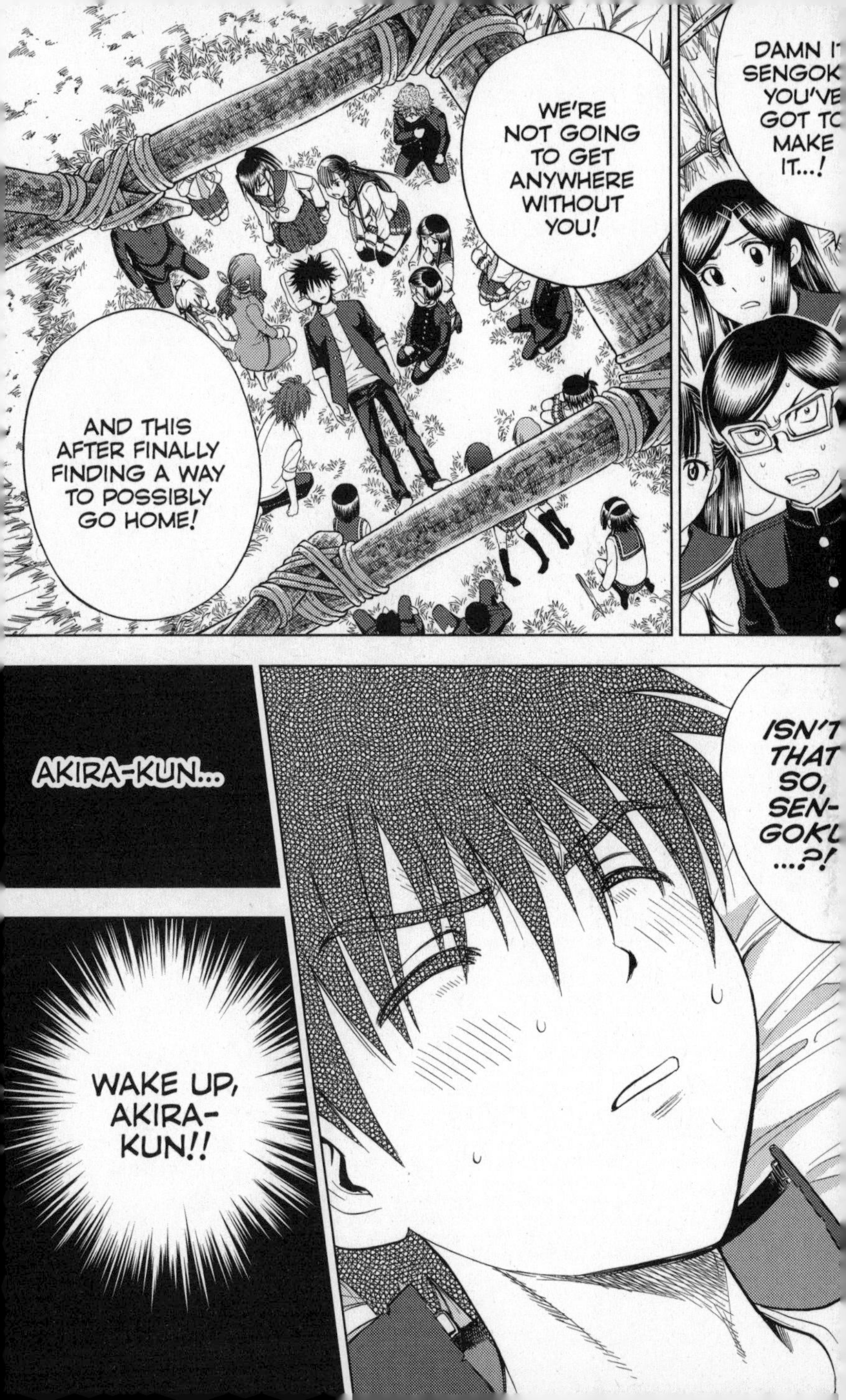
DAMN IT SENGOK YOU'VE GOT TO MAKE IT...!
WE'RE NOT GOING TO GET ANYWHERE WITHOUT YOU!
AND THIS AFTER FINALLY FINDING A WAY TO POSSIBLY GO HOME!
ISN'T THAT SO, SEN-GOKU ...?!
AKIRA-KUN...
WAKE UP, AKIRA-KUN!!

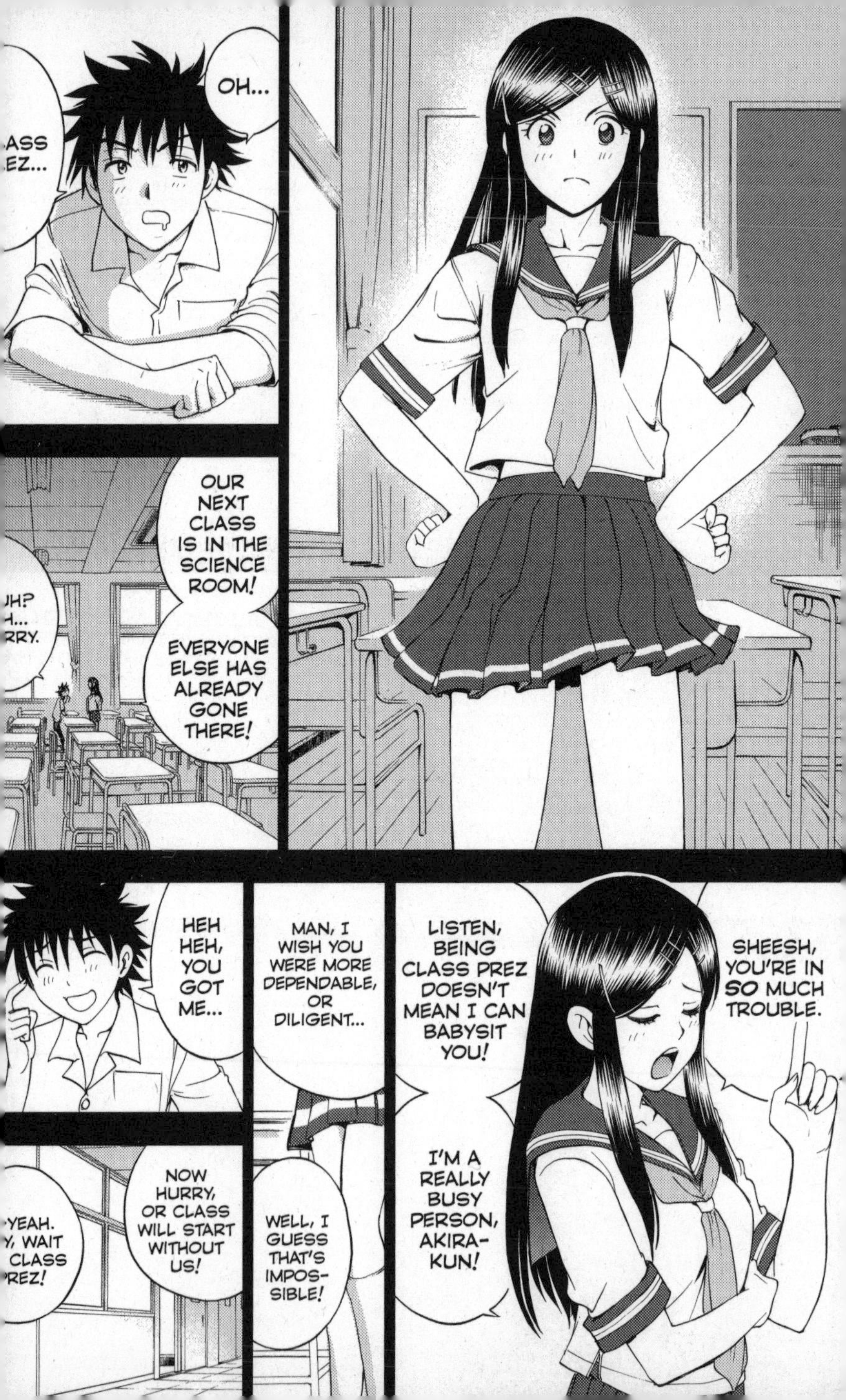
OH...
ASS
EZ...
OUR NEXT CLASS IS IN THE SCIENCE ROOM!
EVERYONE ELSE HAS ALREADY GONE THERE!
UH?
H...
RRY.
SHEESH, YOU'RE IN SO MUCH TROUBLE.
LISTEN, BEING CLASS PREZ DOESN'T MEAN I CAN BABYSIT YOU!
I'M A REALLY BUSY PERSON, AKIRA-KUN!
MAN, I WISH YOU WERE MORE DEPENDABLE, OR DILIGENT...
WELL, I GUESS THAT'S IMPOS-SIBLE!
HEH HEH, YOU GOT ME...
NOW HURRY, OR CLASS WILL START WITHOUT US!
YEAH.
Y, WAIT
CLASS
PREZ!

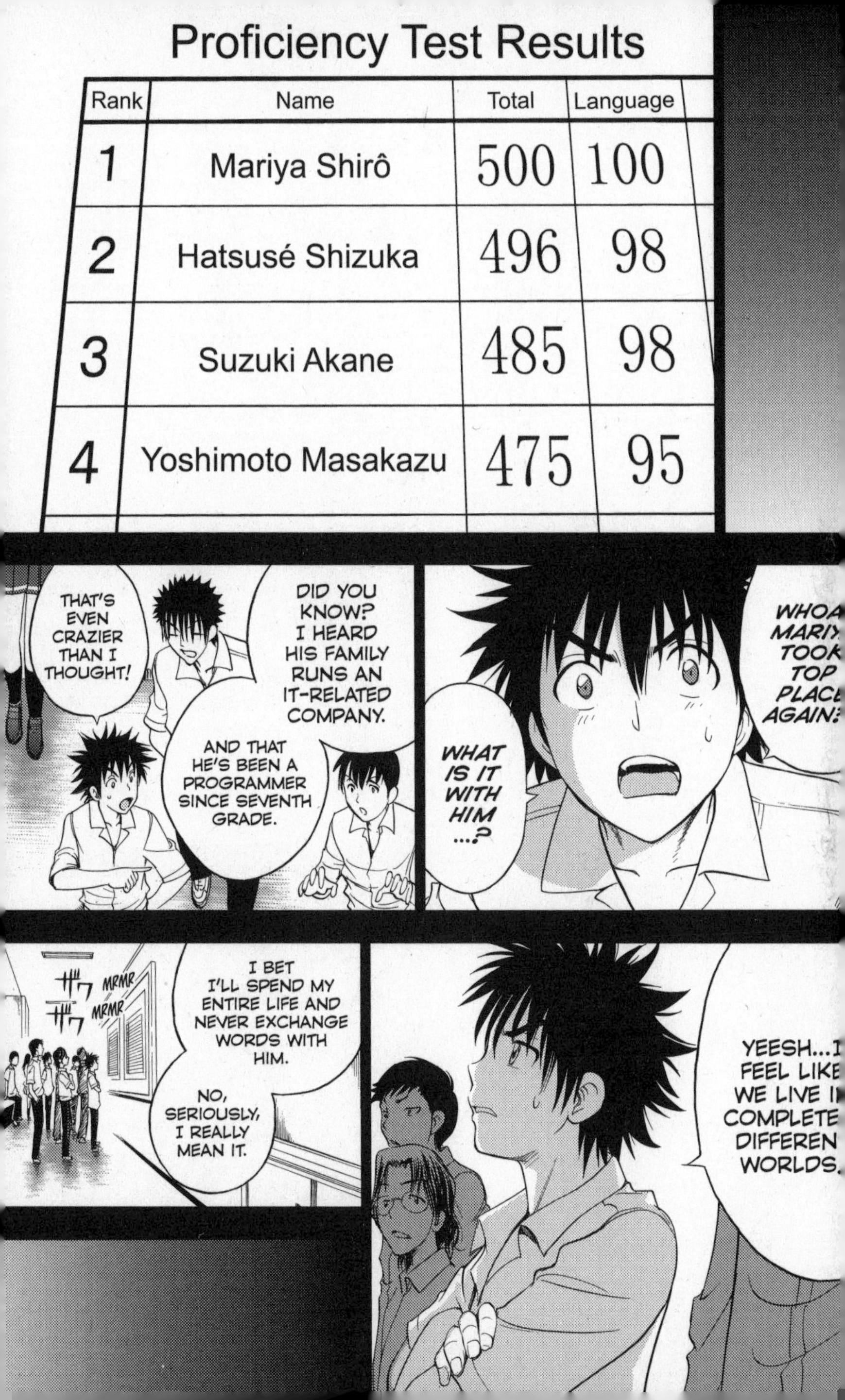
Proficiency Test Results
Rank | Name | Total | Language
1 | Mariya Shirô | 500 | 100
2 | Hatsusé Shizuka | 496 | 98
3 | Suzuki Akane | 485 | 98
4 | Yoshimoto Masakazu | 475 | 95
WHOA MARIY TOOK TOP PLACE AGAIN?
WHAT IS IT WITH HIM ...?
DID YOU KNOW? I HEARD HIS FAMILY RUNS AN IT-RELATED COMPANY.
AND THAT HE'S BEEN A PROGRAMMER SINCE SEVENTH GRADE.
THAT'S EVEN CRAZIER THAN I THOUGHT!
YEESH...I FEEL LIKE WE LIVE I COMPLETE DIFFEREN WORLDS.
ザワ MRMR
ザワ MRMR
I BET I'LL SPEND MY ENTIRE LIFE AND NEVER EXCHANGE WORDS WITH HIM.
NO, SERIOUSLY, I REALLY MEAN IT.

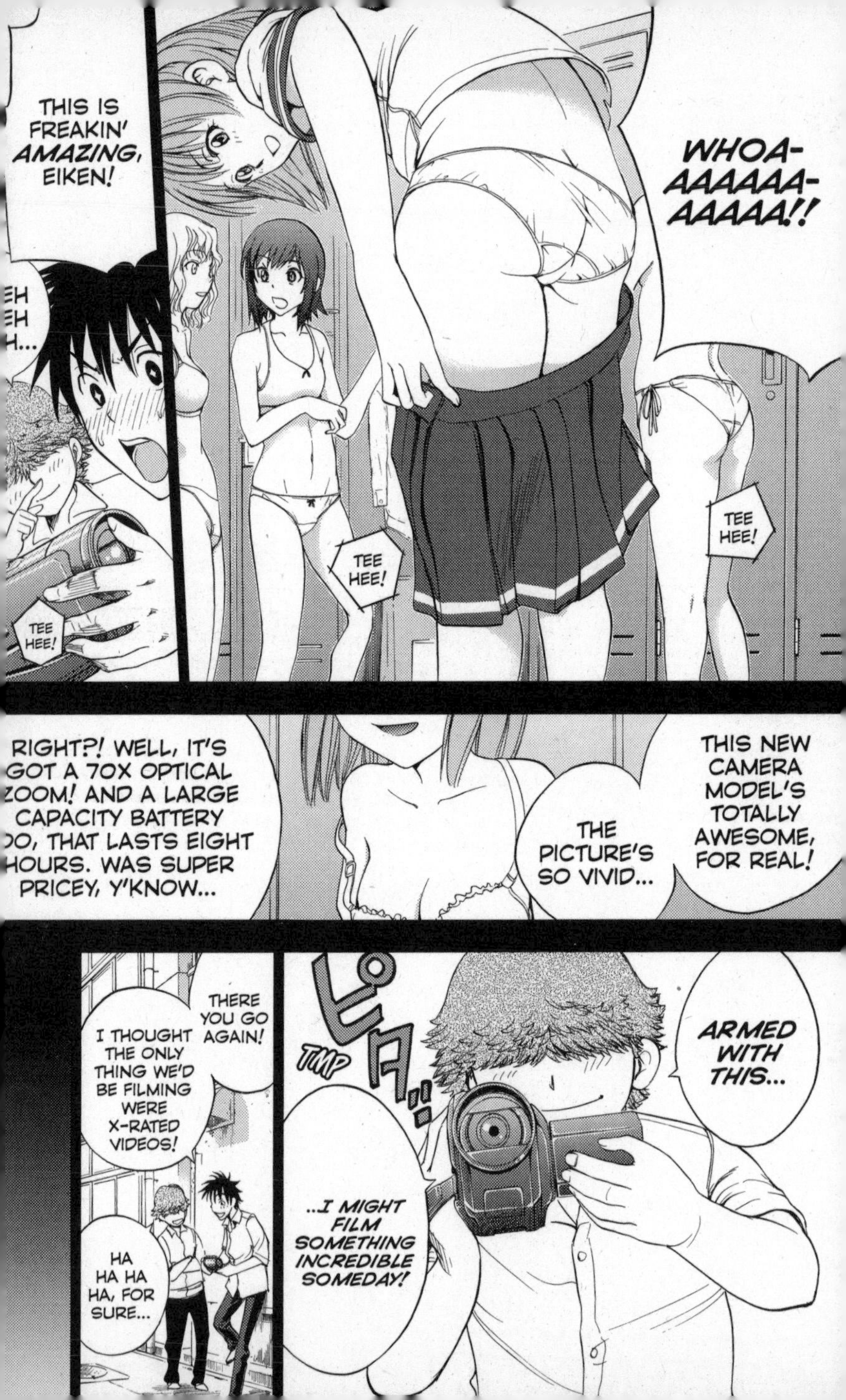
WHOA-AAAAAA-AAAAA!!
TEE HEE!
TEE HEE!
THIS IS FREAKIN' AMAZING, EIKEN!
EH EH H...
TEE HEE!
THIS NEW CAMERA MODEL'S TOTALLY AWESOME, FOR REAL!
THE PICTURE'S SO VIVID...
RIGHT?! WELL, IT'S GOT A 70X OPTICAL ZOOM! AND A LARGE CAPACITY BATTERY TOO, THAT LASTS EIGHT HOURS. WAS SUPER PRICEY, Y'KNOW...
ARMED WITH THIS...
ピタ
TMP
...I MIGHT FILM SOMETHING INCREDIBLE SOMEDAY!
THERE YOU GO AGAIN!
I THOUGHT THE ONLY THING WE'D BE FILMING WERE X-RATED VIDEOS!
HA HA HA HA, FOR SURE...

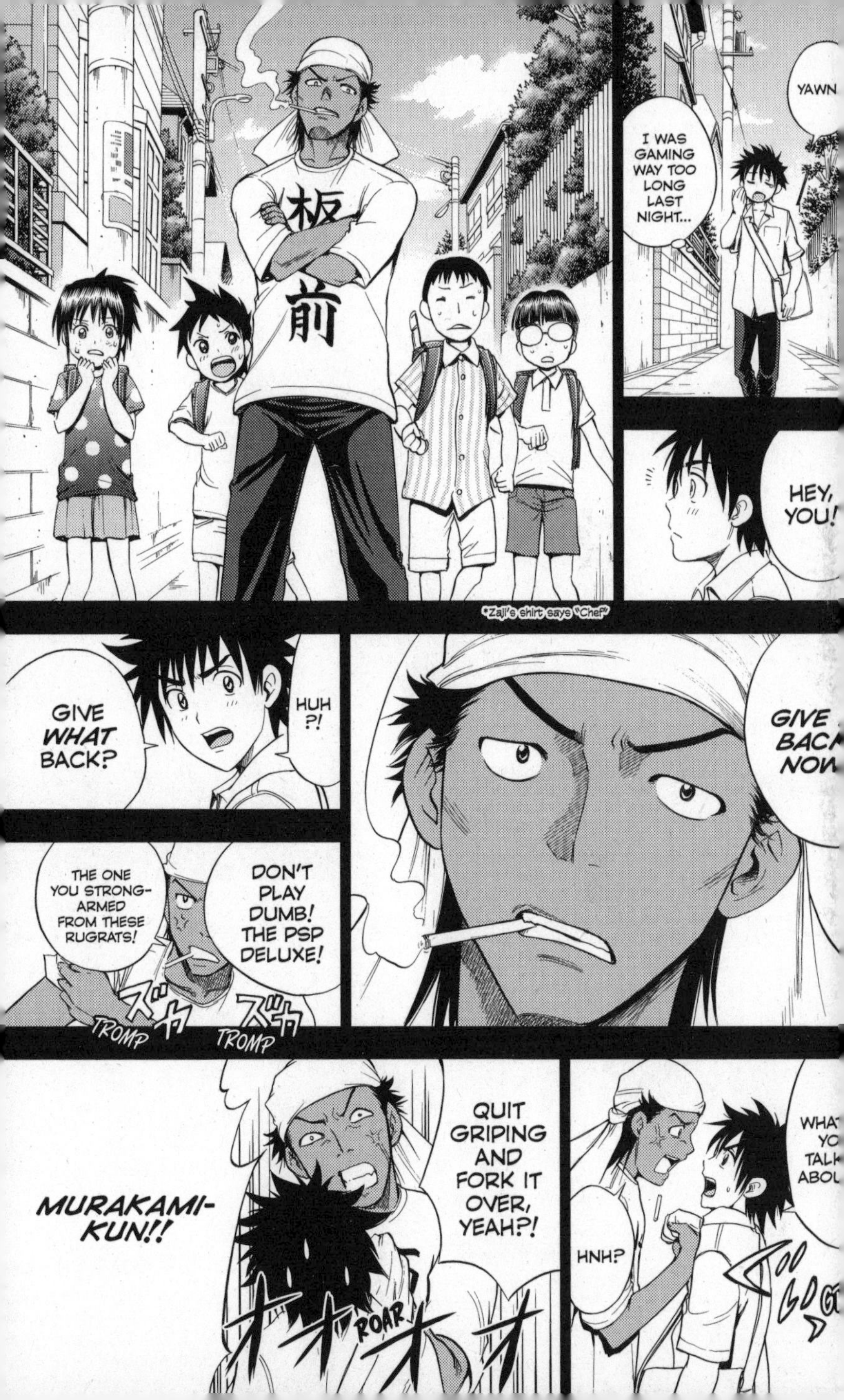
YAWN
I WAS GAMING WAY TOO LONG LAST NIGHT...
HEY, YOU!
*Zaji's shirt says "Chef"
GIVE BAC NOW
HUH ?!
GIVE WHAT BACK?
DON'T PLAY DUMB! THE PSP DELUXE!
THE ONE YOU STRONG-ARMED FROM THESE RUGRATS!
TROMP
TROMP
WHAT YO TALK ABOU
HNH?
QUIT GRIPING AND FORK IT OVER, YEAH?!
MURAKAMI-KUN!!
ROAR

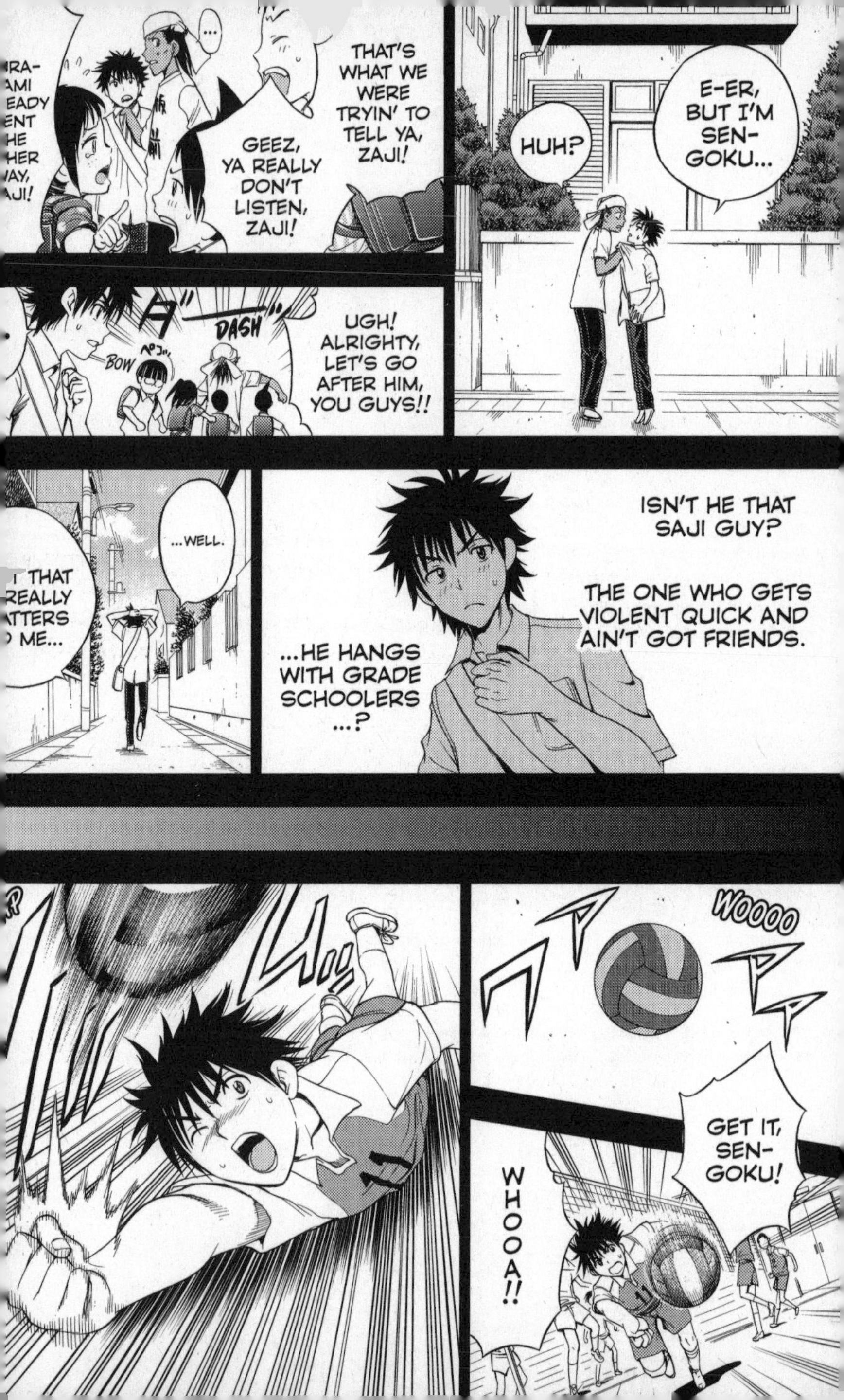

E-ER, BUT I'M SEN-GOKU...
HUH?
THAT'S WHAT WE WERE TRYIN' TO TELL YA, ZAJI!
GEEZ, YA REALLY DON'T LISTEN, ZAJI!
...
UGH! ALRIGHTY, LET'S GO AFTER HIM, YOU GUYS!!
DASH
BOW
ISN'T HE THAT SAJI GUY?
THE ONE WHO GETS VIOLENT QUICK AND AIN'T GOT FRIENDS.
...HE HANGS WITH GRADE SCHOOLERS ...?
...WELL.
WOOOO
GET IT, SEN-GOKU!
WHOOOA!!

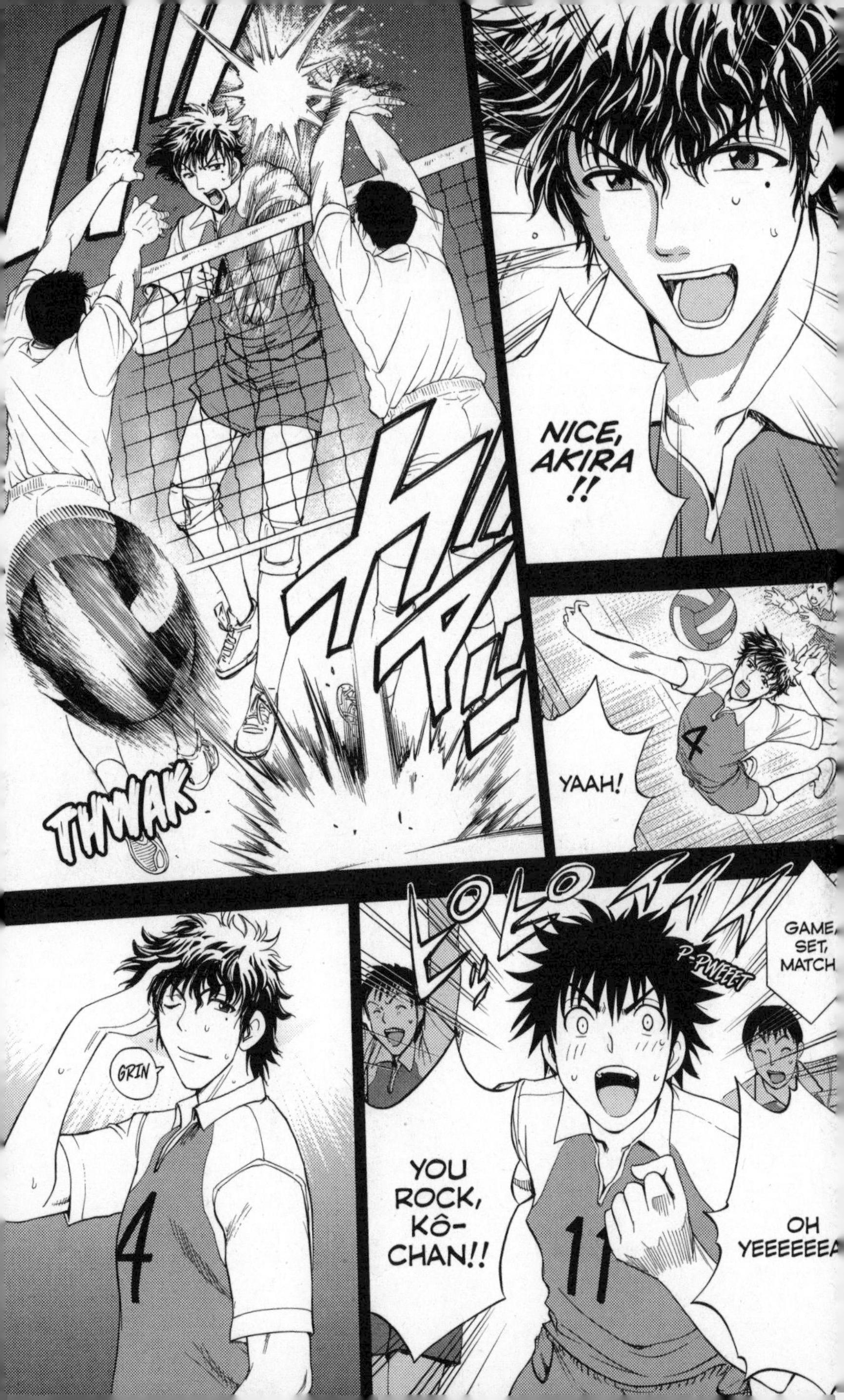
NICE, AKIRA!!
YAAH!
THWAK
GAME, SET, MATCH
P-PWEEET
OH YEEEEEEA
YOU ROCK, KÔ-CHAN!!
GRIN

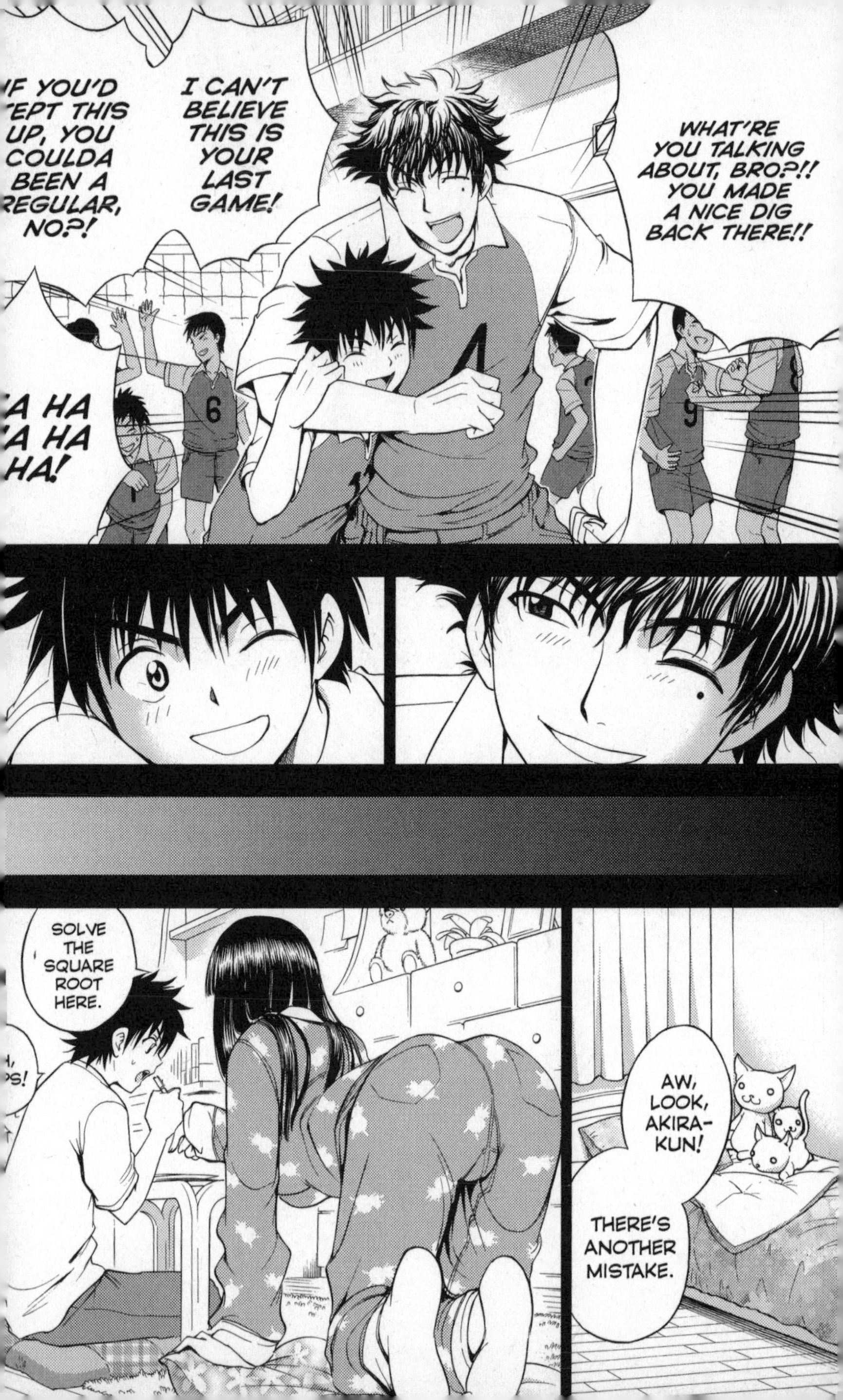
WHAT'RE YOU TALKING ABOUT, BRO?!! YOU MADE A NICE DIG BACK THERE!!
I CAN'T BELIEVE THIS IS YOUR LAST GAME!
F YOU'D EPT THIS UP, YOU COULDA BEEN A EGULAR, NO?!
A HA A HA HA!
AW, LOOK, AKIRA-KUN!
THERE'S ANOTHER MISTAKE.
SOLVE THE SQUARE ROOT HERE.
H, PS!

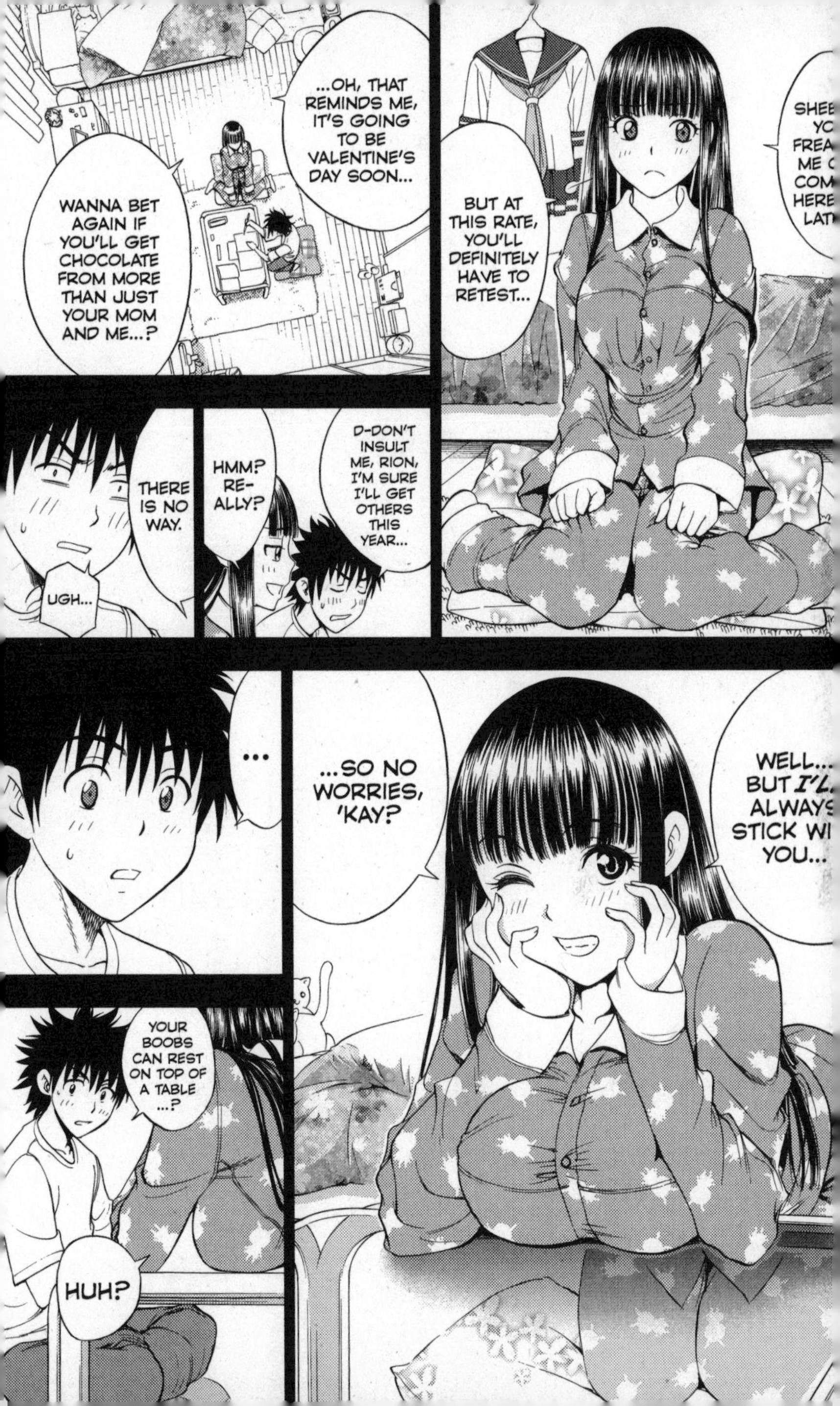
SHEE YO FREA ME C COM HERE LAT
BUT AT THIS RATE, YOU'LL DEFINITELY HAVE TO RETEST...
...OH, THAT REMINDS ME, IT'S GOING TO BE VALENTINE'S DAY SOON...
WANNA BET AGAIN IF YOU'LL GET CHOCOLATE FROM MORE THAN JUST YOUR MOM AND ME...?
D-DON'T INSULT ME, RION, I'M SURE I'LL GET OTHERS THIS YEAR...
HMM? RE-ALLY?
THERE IS NO WAY.
UGH...
WELL... BUT I'L ALWAYS STICK WI YOU...
...SO NO WORRIES, 'KAY?
...
YOUR BOOBS CAN REST ON TOP OF A TABLE ...?
HUH?

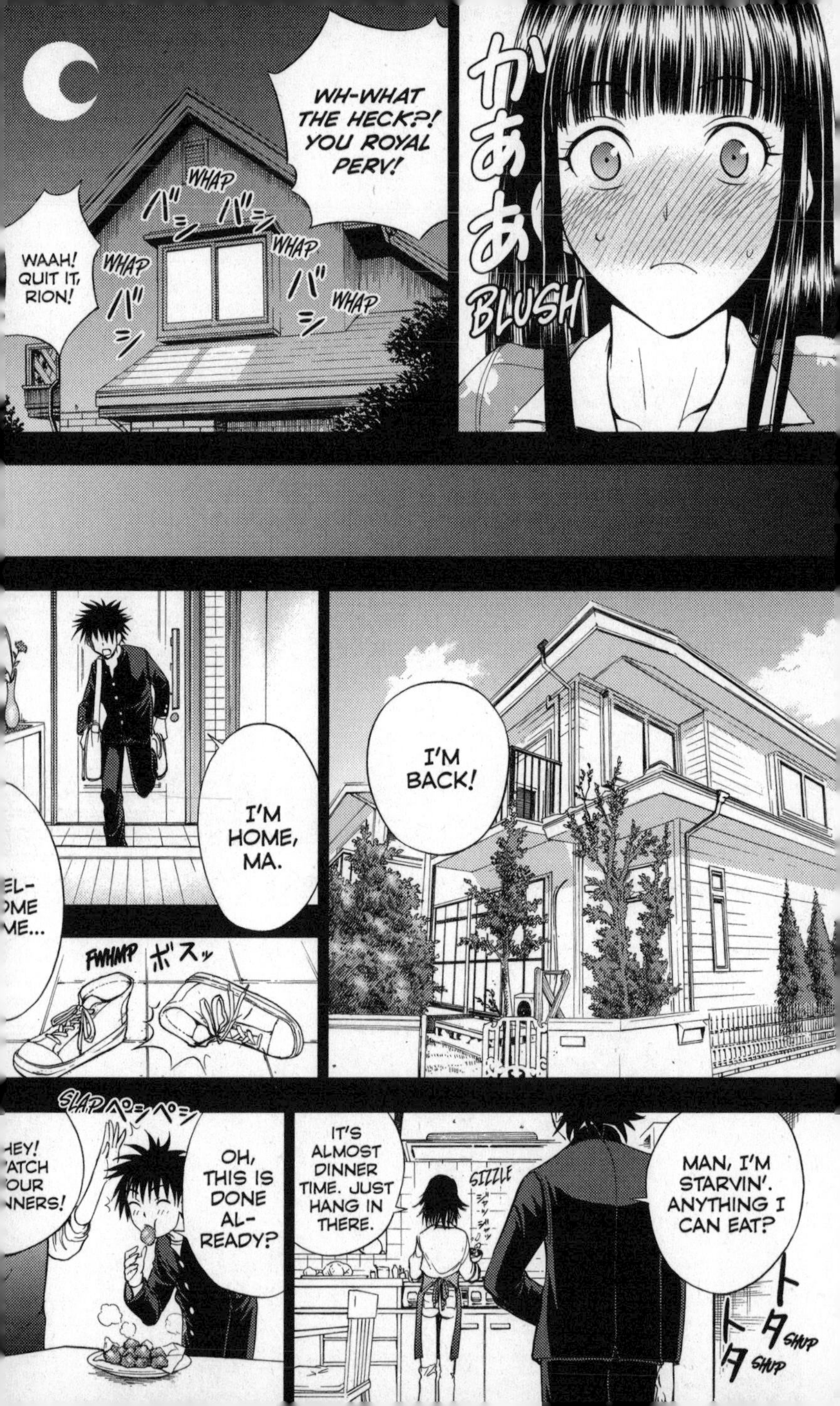
かあぁ
BLUSH
WH-WHAT THE HECK?! YOU ROYAL PERV!
WHAP バシ
WHAP バシ
WHAP バシ
WHAP バシ
WAAH! QUIT IT, RION!
I'M BACK!
I'M HOME, MA.
EL- OME ME...
FWHMP ボスッ
MAN, I'M STARVIN'. ANYTHING I CAN EAT?
トタトタ SHUP SHUP
IT'S ALMOST DINNER TIME. JUST HANG IN THERE.
SIZZLE ジャッジャッ
OH, THIS IS DONE AL-READY?
HEY! ATCH OUR NNERS!
SLAP ペシペシ

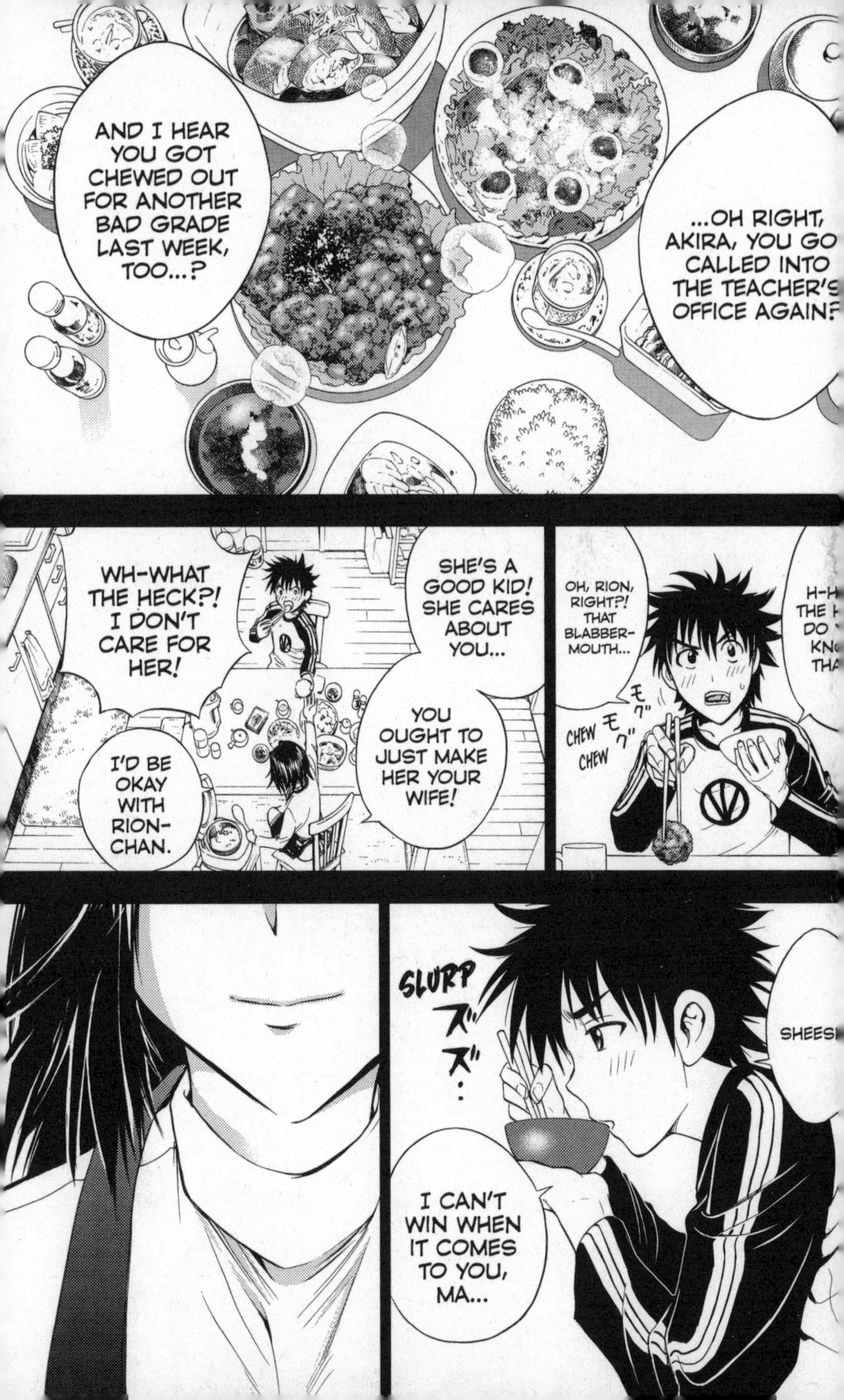
...OH RIGHT, AKIRA, YOU GO CALLED INTO THE TEACHER'S OFFICE AGAIN?
AND I HEAR YOU GOT CHEWED OUT FOR ANOTHER BAD GRADE LAST WEEK, TOO...?
OH, RION, RIGHT?! THAT BLABBER-MOUTH...
モグモグ
CHEW CHEW
SHE'S A GOOD KID! SHE CARES ABOUT YOU...
YOU OUGHT TO JUST MAKE HER YOUR WIFE!
WH-WHAT THE HECK?! I DON'T CARE FOR HER!
I'D BE OKAY WITH RION-CHAN.
SLURP ズズ…
I CAN'T WIN WHEN IT COMES TO YOU, MA...

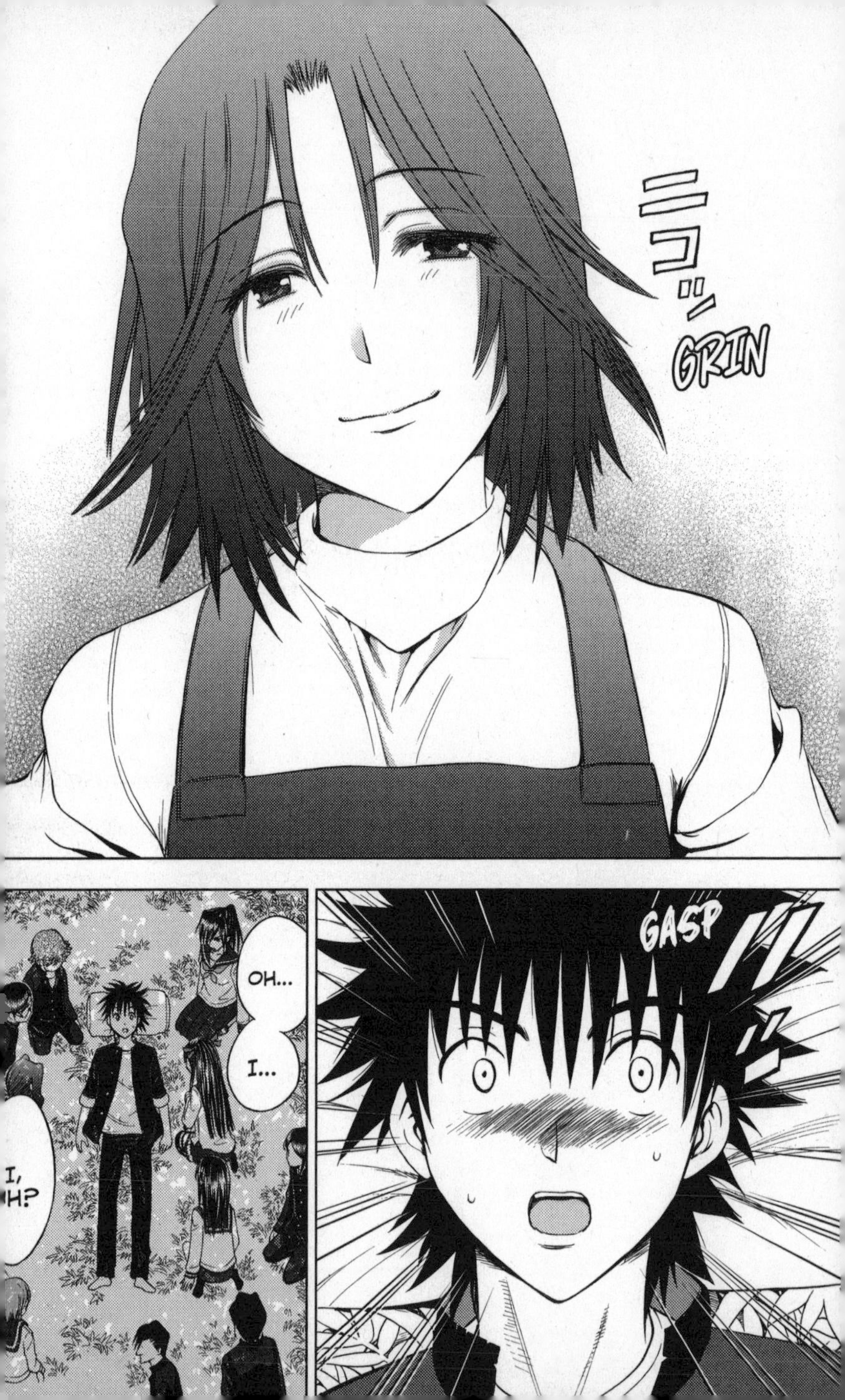
ニコッ
GRIN
GASP
OH...
I...
I,
H?

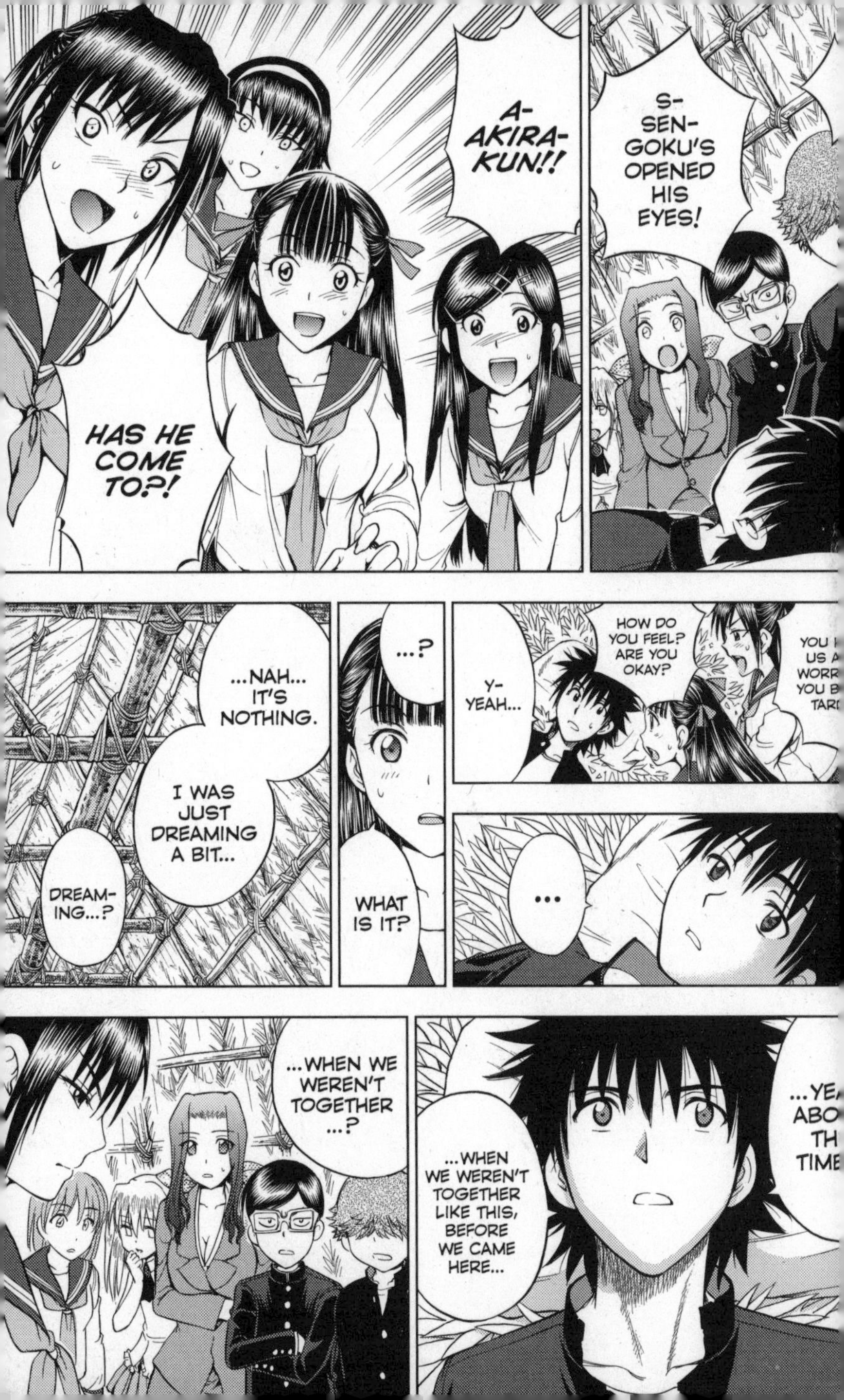
S-SEN-GOKU'S OPENED HIS EYES!
A-AKIRA-KUN!!
HAS HE COME TO?!
YOU I US A WORR YOU B TARD
HOW DO YOU FEEL? ARE YOU OKAY?
Y-YEAH...
...
...?
WHAT IS IT?
...NAH... IT'S NOTHING.
I WAS JUST DREAMING A BIT...
DREAM-ING...?
...YEA ABO TH TIME
...WHEN WE WEREN'T TOGETHER LIKE THIS, BEFORE WE CAME HERE...
...WHEN WE WEREN'T TOGETHER ...?

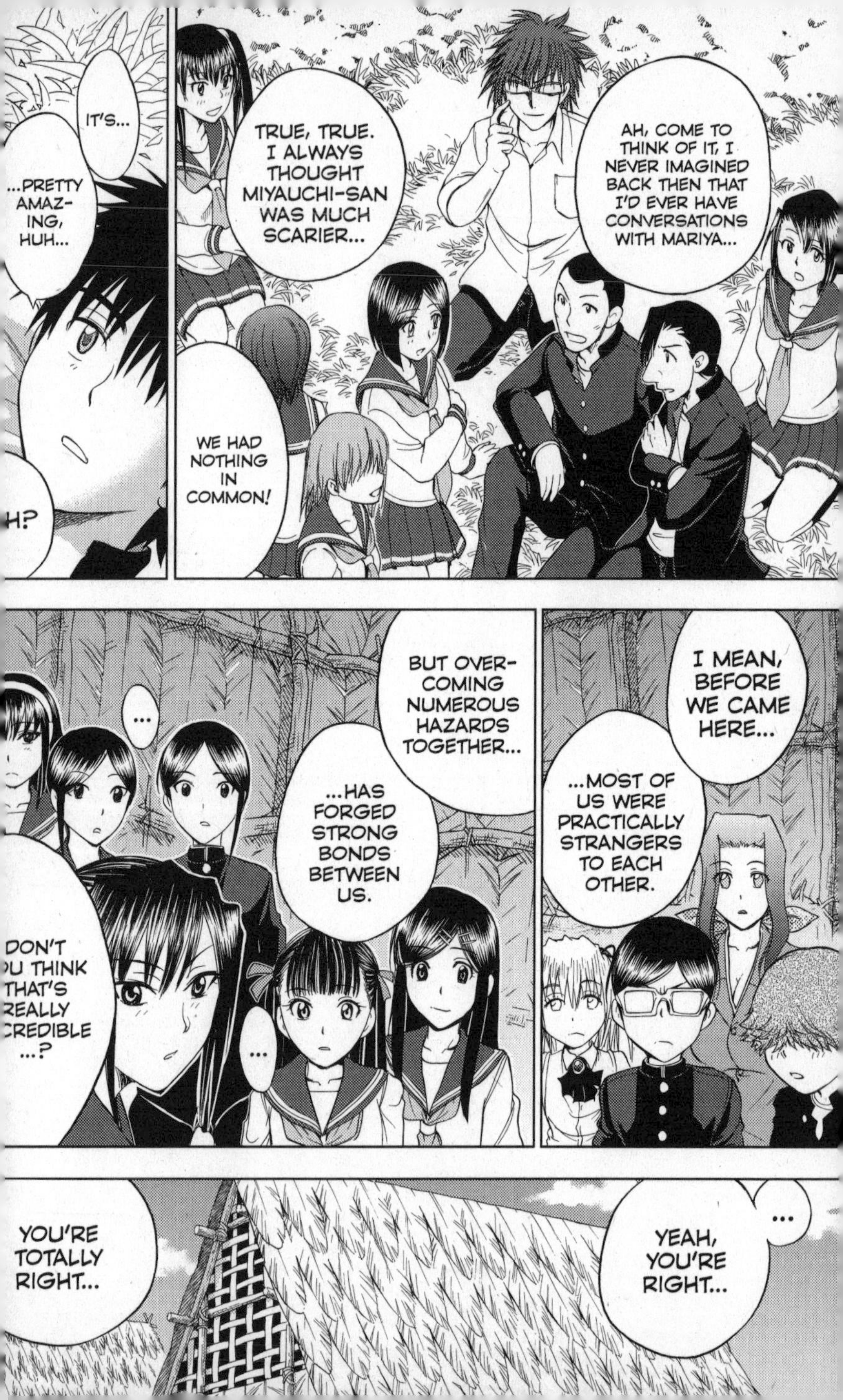
AH, COME TO THINK OF IT, I NEVER IMAGINED BACK THEN THAT I'D EVER HAVE CONVERSATIONS WITH MARIYA...
TRUE, TRUE. I ALWAYS THOUGHT MIYAUCHI-SAN WAS MUCH SCARIER...
WE HAD NOTHING IN COMMON!
IT'S...
...PRETTY AMAZ-ING, HUH...
H?
I MEAN, BEFORE WE CAME HERE...
...MOST OF US WERE PRACTICALLY STRANGERS TO EACH OTHER.
BUT OVER-COMING NUMEROUS HAZARDS TOGETHER...
...HAS FORGED STRONG BONDS BETWEEN US.
...
...
DON'T U THINK THAT'S REALLY CREDIBLE ...?
...
YEAH, YOU'RE RIGHT...
YOU'RE TOTALLY RIGHT...

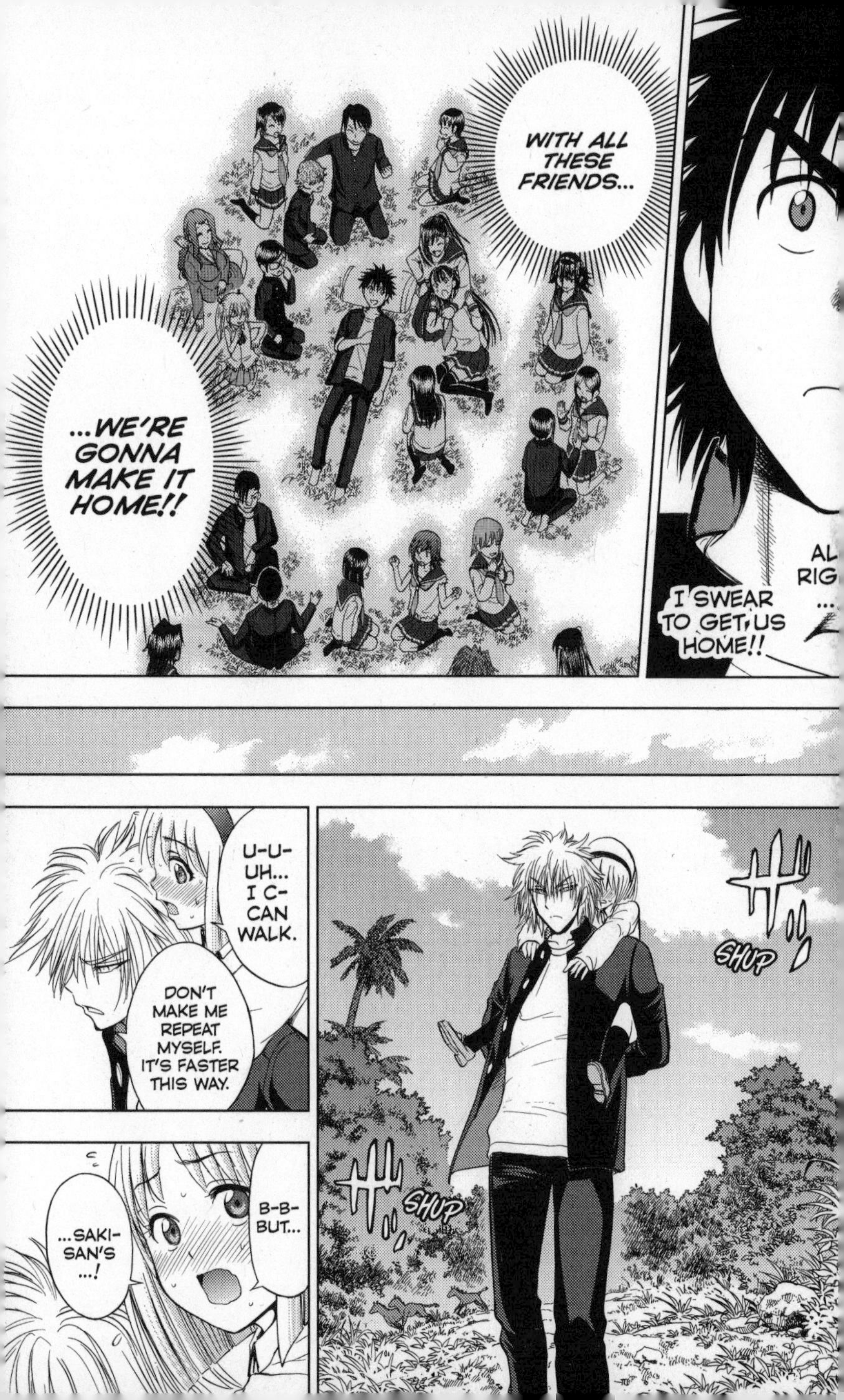

AL RIG ...
I SWEAR TO GET US HOME!!
WITH ALL THESE FRIENDS...
...WE'RE GONNA MAKE IT HOME!!
SHUP
SHUP
U-U-UH... I C-CAN WALK.
DON'T MAKE ME REPEAT MYSELF. IT'S FASTER THIS WAY.
B-B-BUT...
...SAKI-SAN'S ...!

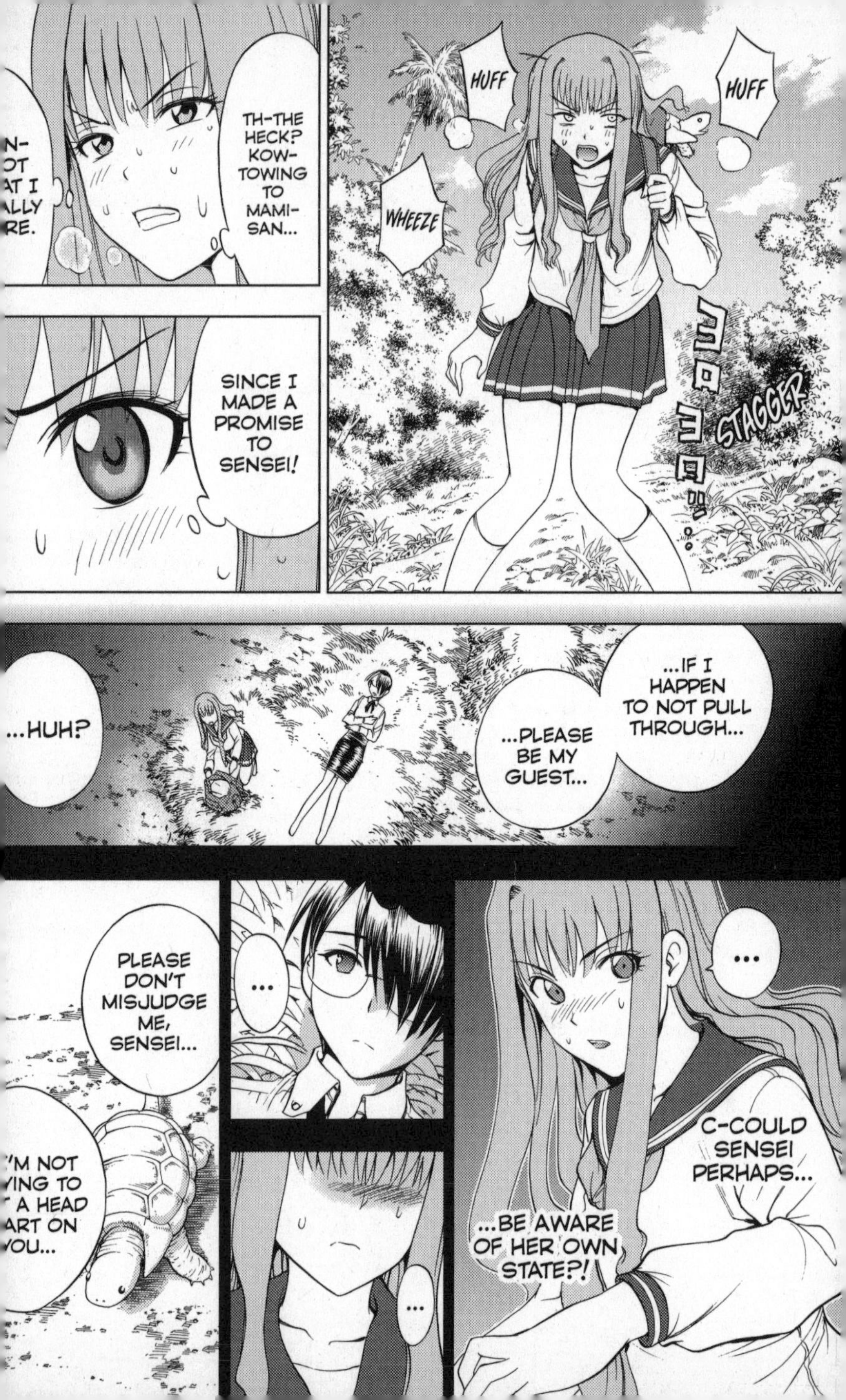
HUFF
HUFF
WHEEZE
STAGGER
TH-THE HECK? KOW-TOWING TO MAMI-SAN...
N-OT AT I ALLY RE.
SINCE I MADE A PROMISE TO SENSEI!
...IF I HAPPEN TO NOT PULL THROUGH...
...PLEASE BE MY GUEST...
...HUH?
...
C-COULD SENSEI PERHAPS...
...BE AWARE OF HER OWN STATE?!
...
...
PLEASE DON'T MISJUDGE ME, SENSEI...
'M NOT YING TO A HEAD ART ON YOU...

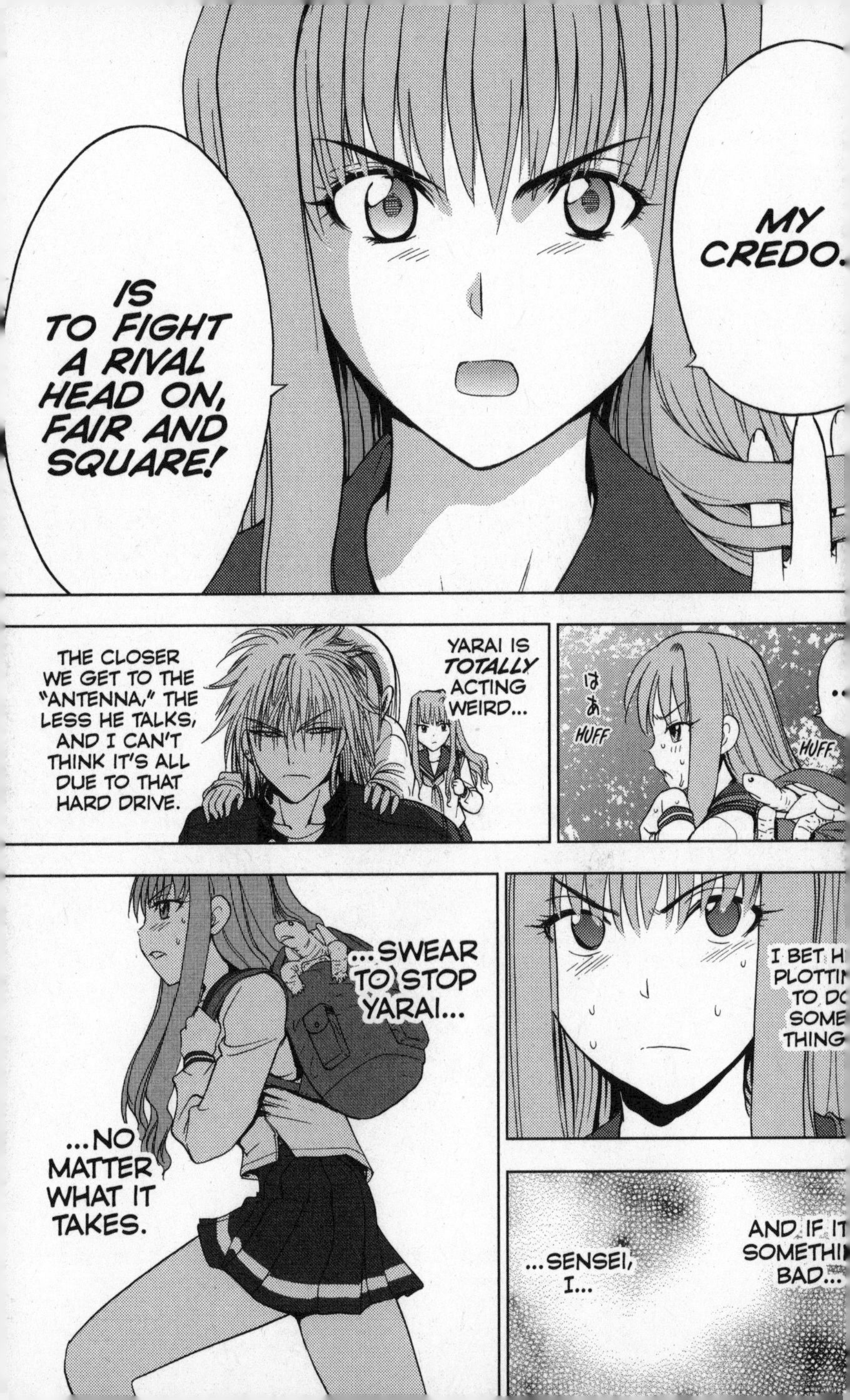
MY CREDO.
IS TO FIGHT A RIVAL HEAD ON, FAIR AND SQUARE!
...
はあ HUFF
HUFF
YARAI IS TOTALLY ACTING WEIRD...
THE CLOSER WE GET TO THE "ANTENNA," THE LESS HE TALKS, AND I CAN'T THINK IT'S ALL DUE TO THAT HARD DRIVE.
I BET H PLOTTIN TO DO SOME THING
AND IF IT SOMETHIN BAD...
...SENSEI, I...
...SWEAR TO STOP YARAI...
...NO MATTER WHAT IT TAKES.

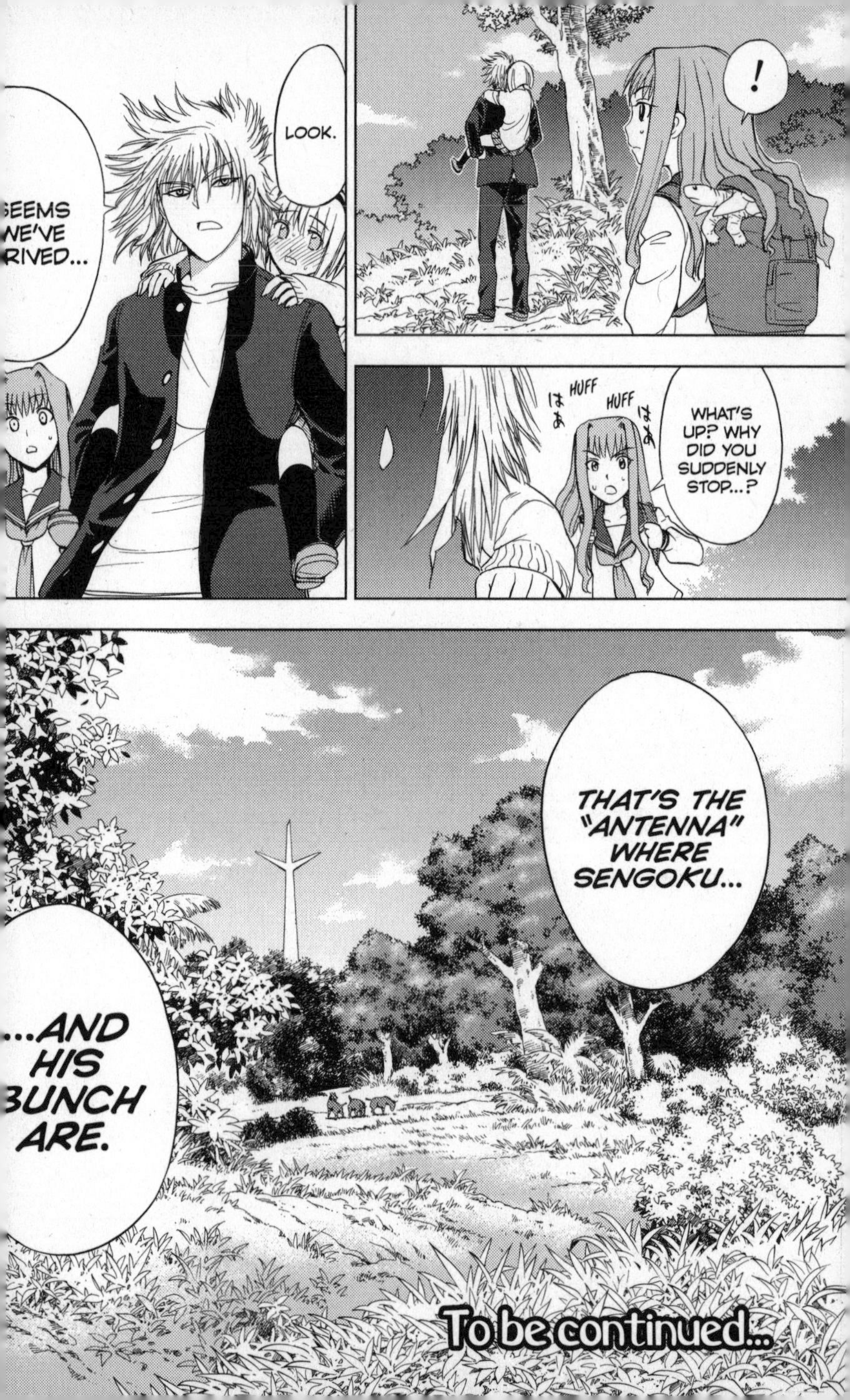
!
HUFF はあ HUFF はあ
WHAT'S UP? WHY DID YOU SUDDENLY STOP...?
LOOK.
SEEMS WE'VE RIVED...
THAT'S THE "ANTENNA" WHERE SENGOKU...
...AND HIS BUNCH ARE.
To be continued...

Character profile

Miyauchi Maya

Born November 21
Scorpio
14 years old
160 cm tall*
Blood type A
BWH: 80•58•84**

*160 cm = 5'4"
**BWH: 80•58•84 = BWH: 32•23•34

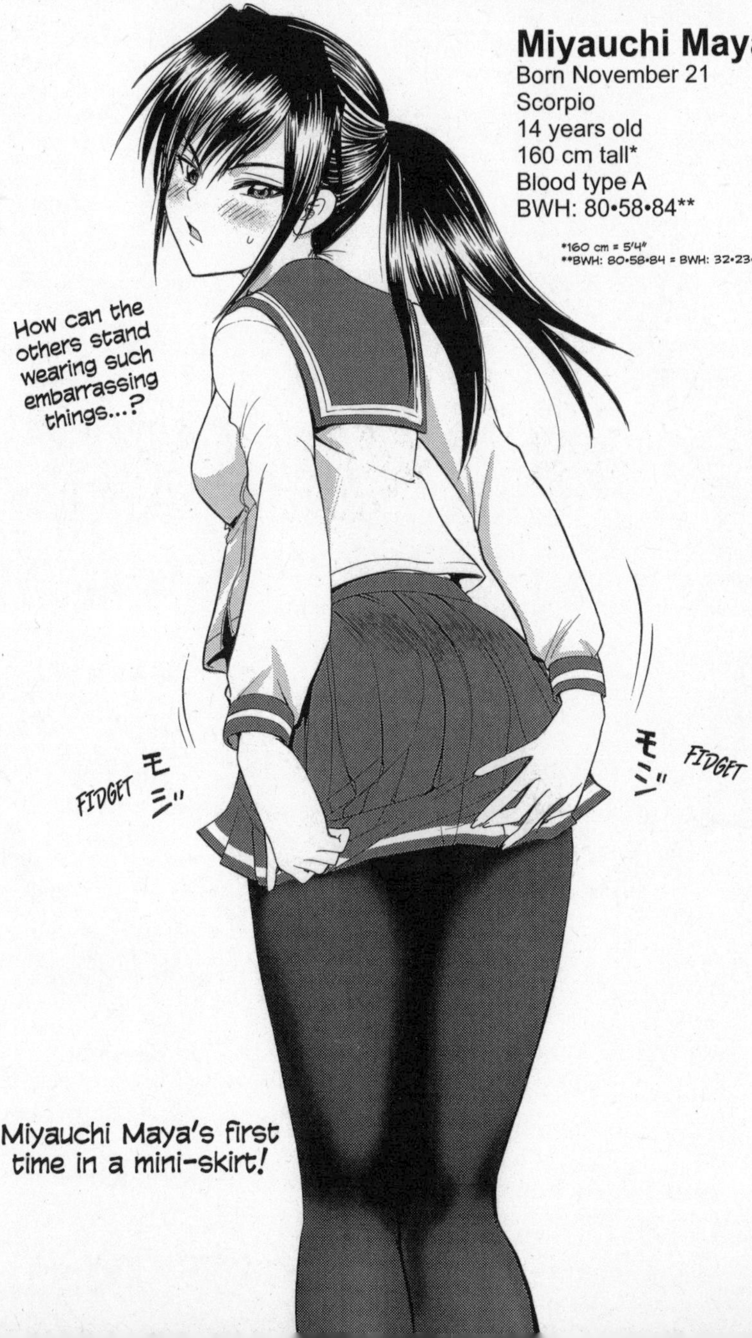
How can the others stand wearing such embarrassing things...?
モジ
FIDGET
モジ
FIDGET
Miyauchi Maya's first time in a mini-skirt!

Cage of Eden volume 16 is a work of fiction. Names, characters, places, and incidents are the products of the author's imagination or are used fictitiously. Any resemblance to actual events, locales, or persons, living or dead, is entirely coincidental.

A Kodansha Comics Trade Paperback Original.

Published in the United States by Kodansha Comics, an imprint of Kodansha USA Publishing, LLC, New York.

Publication rights for this English edition arranged through Kodansha Ltd., Tokyo.

First published in Japan in 2012 by Kodansha Ltd., Tokyo, as *Eden no Ori* 16

ISBN 978-1-61262-560-7

Printed in the United States of America.

www.kodanshacomics.com

9 8 7 6 5 4 3 2 1

Translator: Mari Morimoto
Lettering: Morgan Hart
Kodansha Comics edition cover design: Phil Balsman